SOCIAL LIFE
IN OLD VIRGINIA

From the "Institutional History of Virginia
in the Seventeenth Century"

by
PHILIP ALEXANDER BRUCE

with an Introduction by
HARVEY WISH
Western Reserve University

D1103761

CAPRICORN BOOKS
NEW YORK

CONTENTS

PAGE

INTRODUCTION, BY HARVEY WISH vii

PART I
RELIGION AND MORALS

CHAPTER

I. EARLY RELIGIOUS SPIRIT . . . 3

II. PROOFS OF POPULAR RELIGIOUS FEELING . 15

III. PUBLIC MORALS—SABBATH OBSERVANCE . 28

IV. PUBLIC MORALS—DRUNKENNESS AND PROFANITY 38

V. PUBLIC MORALS—BASTARDY AND SLANDER 45

VI. THE PARISH—HOW FORMED . . . 55

VII. PARISH GOVERNMENT—THE VESTRY . 62

VIII. PARISH GOVERNMENT—DUTIES OF VESTRY 73

IX. PARISH GOVERNMENT—CHURCH WARDENS 79

X. PARISH CHURCH—HOW BUILT . . 94

XI. PARISH CHURCH—PLATE AND ORNAMENTS 109

XII. THE CLERGY—HOW PROCURED . . 116

XIII. THE CLERGY—THEIR TENURE . . 131

XIV. THE CLERGY—THEIR REMUNERATION . 145

XV. THE CLERGY—THEIR GLEBES AND PARSONAGES 163

iii

Contents

CHAPTER   PAGE

XVI. THE CLERGY—THEIR ESTATES . . 177

XVII. THE CLERGY—THEIR DUTIES . . 186

XVIII. THE CLERGY—THEIR GENERAL CHARACTER 194

XIX. THE CLERGY—INDIVIDUAL OFFENDERS . 208

XX. STRUGGLE TO ENFORCE CONFORMITY . 215

XXI. DISSENT—THE QUAKERS . . . 222

XXII. DISSENT—THE QUAKERS . . . 238

XXIII. DISSENT—THE PURITANS . . . 252

XXIV. DISSENT—PRESBYTERIANS AND PAPISTS . 262

XXV. ATHEISM AND WITCHCRAFT . . . 276

PART II

EDUCATION

I. SENTIMENT IN FAVOUR OF EDUCATION . 293

II. SENTIMENT IN FAVOUR OF EDUCATION . 308

III. HOW THE VIRGINIANS WERE EDUCATED—
ENGLISH SCHOOLS 316

IV. PRIVATE TUTORS 323

V. THE OLD FIELD SCHOOL . . . 331

VI. FREE SCHOOLS—THOSE PROJECTED IN TIME
OF COMPANY 343

VII. FREE SCHOOLS—THE SYMMES AND EATON 350

VIII. OTHER FREE SCHOOLS 357

IX. HIGHER INSTITUTIONS—THE INDIAN COL-
LEGE 362

Contents

CHAPTER		PAGE
X.	HIGHER INSTITUTIONS—PROJECTED COLLEGE OF 1660–1	374
XI.	HIGHER INSTITUTIONS—WILLIAM AND MARY COLLEGE	380
XII.	HIGHER INSTITUTIONS—WILLIAM AND MARY COLLEGE	390
XIII.	LIBRARIES—VALUE ATTACHED TO BOOKS	402
XIV.	LIBRARIES—SIZE OF COLLECTIONS	410
XV.	LIBRARIES—SIZE OF COLLECTIONS	421
XVI.	LIBRARIES—SIZE OF COLLECTIONS	430
XVII.	GENERAL CULTURE	442
XVIII.	DEGREE OF ILLITERACY	450

PHILIP A. BRUCE, INTERPRETER
OF THE PLANTER CLASS

EVEN a half century of productive Southern scholarship has failed to render obsolete the colonial histories of Virginia written by Philip Alexander Bruce (1856–1933). While enlightened younger historians of colonial Virginia can no longer subscribe to the outdated race and class prejudices of the turn of the century reflected in some of Bruce's writings, they cannot escape the necessity of revealing their continuing indebtedness to the meticulous historian who explored many British and American archives for his detailed picture of social life, economic and legal institutions, and the semifeudal class distinctions of Old Virginia. Of his prolific writings, the most indispensable work was a two-volume *Institutional History of Virginia in the Seventeenth Century* (1910), that deserves a reintroduction to modern readers.

Bruce was an architect of the now familiar historical image of the Plantation South, although he must have been aware of the romantic literary creation of the planter's world described in John P. Kennedy's *Swallow Barn* or

William A. Caruther's *The Cavaliers of Virginia*. This grand theme also absorbed his nostalgic Virginia contemporary, Thomas Nelson Page, and the influential historian Ulrich B. Phillips of Georgia, who dedicated one of his major histories of the South to the planters "who in the piping ante-bellum times schooled multitudes white and black to the acceptance of higher standards, who in the wartime proved staunch and who in the troublous upheaval and readjustment wrought more sanely and more wisely than the world yet knows." [1]

Bruce shared these sentiments and knew plantation life at first hand even more intimately than the Georgian; and both specialized in economic history. He was proud of the fact that his seventeenth-century Scottish ancestors had migrated to Virginia as members of the London Company and as planters. They belonged to that powerful colonial ruling class that he studied so intensively. Born on March 7, 1856, in "Staunton Hill," Charlotte County, Virginia, the son of a wealthy tobacco planter, he spent an aristocratic youth in a distinguished Victorian mansion, read voraciously especially in literature and history, enjoyed the opportunities of his class for horseback riding, fishing, and other recreations, and attended the traditional Old Field School run by a clergyman and patronized by planter families. (The school is fully discussed in the *Institutional History*.)

---

1. See the editor's chapter, "Ulrich B. Phillips and the Image of the Old South," *The American Historian* (Oxford, 1960).

Although he was only nine when the Civil War ended, he retained a lasting impression of the artillery rumbling in the distance and of his father, a captain in the Confederate army. He was to write nostalgically of this era in *Brave Deeds of Confederate Soldiers* and in a biography of Robert E. Lee. Not less important as a social conditioner of this historian of the planter class was the fact that his mother was Sarah A. Seddon, daughter of another wealthy Virginia planter and sister of the reactionary but cultivated James A. Seddon, Secretary of War under the Confederacy.

The calamities of war apparently did not seriously curtail the Bruce fortunes nor the boy's opportunity to acquire a good classical education at an academy and at the University of Virginia. He left for the Harvard Law School to earn an LL.B. in 1878 and returned to the University of Virginia for advanced study in legal subjects and the liberal arts. For some years he practiced law in Baltimore, wrote editorials for the *Richmond Times,* and did other free-lance writing, until he decided to make a career as a gentleman-historian untroubled by the discomforts of earning a living as a history teacher.[2]

It seemed logical for his alma mater to commission him to write his five-volume *History of the University of Virginia* (1920–22). This monumental work, the most informative and generally enlightening university history up

2. John C. Metcalf, "Philip A. Bruce," *Library of Southern Literature,* Supp. #1 (Atlanta, 1923), 91–114; Thomas Abernethy, "Philip A. Bruce," *Dictionary of American Biography,* Supp. I, 128–129.

to that day, drew upon extensive private as well as official manuscript sources and dealt broadly with every phase of undergraduate, graduate, and professional education. Student life and professorial achievements furnished readable material; and most interesting was his sympathetic account of the relationship between Thomas Jefferson and the founding of the University of Virginia. Among the enthusiastic reviewers of the history was Professor William P. Trent, a liberal who had rebelled against the reactionary trend in some of the Southern colleges and had left the University of the South at Sewanee to accept a professorship in English at Columbia.[3]

During the years that he was still practicing law, Bruce published his first book, *The Plantation Negro as a Freeman* (1889). Like most Southern conservatives, he believed that emancipation had broken off all points of contact between the Negro cabin and the planter's mansion, resulting in the deterioration of the Negro's lot. Whites, in response to Negro hostility, had ceased to attend the affairs of blacks and a dangerous social chasm had developed. Out of Reconstruction, he believed, had come the incendiary force of Negro suffrage, thus undermining the white's chief instrument of self-defense. Like U. B. Phillips, he asserted that the key to racial antagonism was the white's fear of the numerical strength of the Negro.

He painted a gloomy picture of the starving Negro unable to compete with the white, immersed in superstitions, and resorting to violence. Bruce offered various proposals for educating a Negro elite, especially normal schools for teachers and preachers; but he also favored the idea of deporting Negroes if this could be done without bankrupting the South. (In his editorials for the *Richmond Times* and in a letter of 1901 to *The Independent,* he charged that educators had failed with the Negro because they assumed that he was "simply an ignorant white man with a black skin." He now urged the simplest subjects for Negroes under a state system and a second Peabody or Slater Fund to educate Negro preachers in religious seminaries.[4])

The Plantation Negro as a Freeman called for a Solid South to maintain racial order. It was written at a time when the Ben Tillman and Vardaman extremists wished to go much further than Bruce toward some racist solution. In a long letter to *The Nation* of July 30, 1911, Bruce endorsed the new wave of municipal segregation laws in the South that were intended to supplement the older state Jim Crow laws. Optimistically, he forecast the partial solution of the race problem through the rise of an all-Negro city within hitherto mixed neighborhoods in which Negro leaders would run their own schools, police departments, health services, transportation system, and other segregated services within a federation of a biracial city run by the whites.

4. See Bruce's letter in W. T. Harris, "Education of the Negro," *Atlantic Monthly,* 69 (1892), 721–736.

This "domiciliary segregation" seemed to him a kind of democratic self-government.[5]

Such ideas were further reflected in his book of 1905, *The Rise of the New South,* which appeared in a historical series edited by Guy Carleton Lee of Johns Hopkins University. The author began with a bleak estimate of the situation at the end of Reconstruction: "During sixteen years [the South] had been beset by enemies, either as invading armies striving to conquer it, or as robbers seated in its places of authority and contending like so many foul birds in the division of the small remaining spoil." That the South had surmounted these disasters by the end of the century he attributed to its complete racial homogeneity in the midst of racial pressures, a rapidly growing economic diversification, rich resources, and the elimination of Negro power through disfranchisement. For the future he saw a South completely assimilated to the prosperous pattern of the Northern and Western states.

These racist beliefs insured the ephemeral quality of those books and articles dealing with the freedmen and the New South. Like the conservative Bourbons, he stressed the romantic image of the feudal antebellum tie between the large planter and the slaves who depended upon him and now he mourned the glory that had departed. Fortunately for the lasting reputation of his solid historical books, he chose to immerse himself in the seventeenth-century plantation where elitist conditions were actually as aristocratic as he liked them to be.

5. *The Nation,* 93 (1911), 119.

2

Bruce finished an intensive apprenticeship for his *Institutional History of Virginia* in 1896 when he completed a two-volume *Economic History of Virginia in the Seventeenth Century*. At first he planned to cover the period between the Revolution and the Civil War, but he decided that this was impossible without knowing the basic colonial era upon which too little research had been done. Before many years it became clear that he would never leave the seventeenth century, considering the huge task of assimilating mountains of local land office records, county and parish records, and private letters. No thorough history of Virginia existed.

His book described the reasons for colonization, the Indian economy, the acquisition of land, the use of indentured servants and slaves, the plantation economy, the rise of towns and trade. Like other "institutional" historians of that day—including Herbert Baxter Adams of the new graduate school at the Johns Hopkins University and his very influential disciple Frederick Jackson Turner—he stressed the impact of material forces, the decisive role of soil exhaustion, and the wasteful one-crop system as clues to Southern life. He anticipated another leading economic historian of the South, U. B. Phillips, in making the plantation (as Turner did the frontier) the main determinant in shaping society.

He argued that the management of large tobacco plantations and the direction of numerous slaves created in the ruling class an aristocratic psychology made up of habits of self-reliance and an intense love of liberty. This idea came from Edmund Burke, who had said in his famous address on conciliation with America, "In such a people the haughtiness of domination combines with the spirit of freedom, fortifies it and renders it invincible." Bruce concluded that the plantation system created a rural gentry "as proud as that of England."

The reviewers were generally quite favorable, save for an occasional complaint of prejudice in minimizing the evils of slavery. They agreed that tobacco and the feudal land system were the mainspring of Virginia history. Bruce had indeed traced the influence of tobacco upon economics, politics, diplomacy, and church organization. All joined in praising the meticulous research, but some complained of the wearisome detail. One or two criticized the acceptance of John Smith as a trustworthy witness, considering his promotional motives. Such was the observation in *The American Historical Review* of Bruce's chief historical rival among Virginia's historians, Alexander Brown, who regarded Smith as a jaundiced critic of the Virginia Company. But he too conceded that Bruce had handled the subject quite fairly considering the paucity of sources for the early years. Among the enthusiastic reviewers was another historian who asserted that Bruce had rescued Virginia's history from a haze of tradition and a halo of romance to construct the best account of agricultural growth for any state of the Union.[6]

6. *The Nation*, 62 (1896), 399–400; Stephen B. Weeks, *Yale Review*, 5 (1897), 94–98; William B. Weeden, *Journal of Political Economy*, 4 (1896), 537–541; *The American Historical Review*, 1 (1896), 538–541.

Still another related volume that was issued before the magnum opus of the *Institutional History* was the highly readable *Social Life of Virginia in the Seventeenth Century* (1907). To fill a gap in state history due to a scarcity of sources on the purely social aspects of Virginia life, Bruce spent years in London achives, examined the parish records, collected scattered pamphlets, and read hitherto unpublished personal memoirs buried in the letter books of the great planters William Byrd and William Fitzhugh.

More confidently than ever, he stressed the aristocratic plantation theme: "The whole power of Virginia society even in the times when universal [male] suffrage prevailed was directed by the landowners." He came close to indorsing the myth of John Fiske and others that Virginia was populated by the romantic Cavaliers, and noted that in 1649 alone seven ships of Cavaliers came to Virginia. "Virginia was the only city of refuge left in his Majesty's dominions in those times for distressed cavaliers." He pictured the aristocratic ramifications of the power of the Church of England and cited genealogical evidence for the high lineage of many old Virginia families. Much of the *Social Life of Virginia* dealt with the hearty colonial recreations that contrasted greatly with the "gloomy influence of the austere fanaticism of the Puritan." Out of this society, marked by the unusually strong class distinctions of planters, "gentlemen," "misters," and "yeomen," had come the Virginia elite of Washington, Jefferson, Henry, Madison, Monroe, and Marshall.

Once more the critics praised his patient scholarship, interesting style, breadth of treatment, and reliability. By this time, only a few questioned Bruce's aristocratic interpretation of the era of John Smith and William Fitzhugh.[7]

With the publication in 1910 of the two-volume *Institutional History of Virginia in the Seventeenth Century,* Bruce fully justified his apprenticeship of a quarter of a century in this field. The subtitle is informative: "An Inquiry into the Religious, Moral, Educational, Legal, Military, and Political Condition of the People"—which was intended to supplement rather than to supplant his earlier volumes. Actually, the bulk of the first volume, consisting of 459 pages dealing with Religion, Morals, and Education, which has been selected for reproduction in the present edition, represents the best treatment of social history yet written by Bruce and was far superior to the presentation of this type of informal history by the contemporary John Bach McMaster, who frequently resorted to trivia and superficial analysis to attain readability. McMaster too had his bias which favored the middle class and looked askance at the newer immigration and trade unions.

Bruce's own racial bias is scarcely evident in this work, although his pride of class remains. Much as he admired Virginia, he pointed out to his readers how puritanical the colony actually was in many respects, especially in enforcing Sabbath-day observance and in severely punishing those who did not conform to the compulsory church at-

7. *William and Mary College Quarterly,* 16 (1908), 145–147.

tendance laws or violated the prohibitions against various games and even light tasks on Sunday. While the community encouraged traditional amusements and pleasures, woe befell those who turned to drunkenness, bastardy, slander, and fornication. As in both Old and New England, magistrates and the clergy ordered public humiliations for those guilty of such crimes.

The emphasis upon "institutional" history is significant, for this method was then widely adopted by social scientists of that era, from H. B. Adams, the historian, to Veblen and Wesley Mitchell, the economists. While some "institutionalists" drew their interpretive framework from the Darwinian stages of social evolutionism, as F. J. Turner did, others like Philip Bruce were content with the institutionalist's detailed historical search for the growth of social attitudes and organizations arising from environmental and especially economic influences. But while most institutionalists were critics of the social status quo, Bruce remained a staunch admirer of the conservative social order into which he was born. He shared the beliefs of certain institutionalists in the possibility of achieving a high level of scientific history comparable to the accuracy of the sciences. Quite a few Southerners, including Virginians, had been trained in the new German-inspired scientific technique of Leopold von Ranke through the Johns Hopkins University seminar of H. B. Adams or the rigid (though pro-Southern) seminars of Dunning and Burgess at Columbia. In 1892 some admirers of this scientific school of historiography helped to found the *Virginia Magazine of History and Biography* with which Bruce was associated.

Modern historians like William E. Dodd, author of *The Old South* (1937) and *The Cotton Kingdom* (1921), have leaned heavily upon the Bruce framework of colonial aristocracy despite their own social liberalism. Bruce traced the influence of the planter upon such institutions as the Vestry, which was much of the time self-perpetuating. These planter members of the parish enforced morals, gave poor relief, hired the clergy, and administered other local affairs. The planters who dominated the courts attained, according to Bruce, a high level of justice. (Some may question whether this objectivity was always reflected in master-servant disputes.) When he described the Field Schools—as he does in this edition—there is little doubt that he thoroughly understood the educational system of which he was once a part. While he favored Virginia over New England on such issues as education for the elite and attitudes toward witchcraft, he was not far from the truth. Above all, he pictured Virginia as an extension of all parts of Old England; here were typical Englishmen devoted to monarchy, Anglicanism, and generous social traditions. Tidewater Virginians were homogeneous conservatives unchanged by immigration.

However, Bruce admitted that slavery was "incongruous" amid free English institutions, but argued that the slave was happy and identified himself with the feudal baronial ideal even if he was at the bottom of the scale. His treatment of the Negro did reflect a certain prejudice, for he dwelt upon their crimes and acts of violence. He recognized other determinants besides tobacco and slaves and noted that land abundance checked the transmission of feudal primogeniture. Limited wealth, not baronial preference, checked the growth of free grammar schools and Old World legal procedures; the planters in the Vestry and county courts sought to educate the children of the poor.

The various appreciative reviews of the *Institutional History of Virginia* praised Bruce's craftsmanship, though some complained of Virginian chauvinism and class prejudices. Dr. Lyon G. Tyler, president of the College of William and Mary and editor of the college *Quarterly,* found the work luminous, correct, erudite, and outstanding among all histories of Virginia, though he complained, "Probably Dr. Bruce is inclined to give a little too aristocratic a turn to society in Virginia, which the records of the seventeenth century do not bear him out in." [8]

Even the major revisionist of Virginia's colonial history, Thomas J. Wertenbaker of the University of Virginia, quotes Bruce so frequently in his *Patrician and Plebeian in Virginia* (1910) that his indebtedness is obvious. But he complained, "Colonial Virginia has often been pictured as the land of the aristocratic planter, the owner of thousands of acres and hundreds of slaves." He demonstrated that the

8. See also *The Nation,* 91 (1910), 262–264; *North American Review,* 192 (1910), 708; *The American Historical Review,* 16 (1910), 139–143. This essay omits the relatively minor book of patriotic biographies, notable for its original treatment and defense of the reputation of Edgar Allan Poe, *The Virginia Plutarch* (2 vols., University of North Carolina, 1929). It is pleasantly reviewed by Professor Dumas Malone of the University of Virginia in *The American Historical Review,* 35 (1929–30), 885–887, but quite critically treated by Professor David S. Muzzey in *Current History,* 32 (1929), 216.

numerous yeomanry were the real backbone of Virginia. "It is true that most of the leaders came from the aristocracy, but it was the small farmer who owned the bulk of the land, produced the larger part of the tobacco crop, could outvote the aristocrat fifty to one, and made up the rank and file of the army in the colonial wars." Furthermore, he felt that Bruce avoided generalizations in favor of details. Wertenbaker did destroy the last shreds of the Cavalier myth which Bruce had been reluctant to discard altogether. But the younger scholar could not prove that the colony was necessarily democratic because of its small-farmer majority.

A still younger scholar, Louis B. Wright of the Huntington Library, drew extensively from Bruce among others to prove that the upper 5 percent dominated. His book, *The First Gentleman of Virginia* (1940), elaborates upon the main thesis of the *Institutional History,* noting the planter's similarity to his counterpart in English society, his impressive libraries, and pervasive power. He felt that while Wertenbaker had corrected many romantic notions of the elite, he tended to attach greater importance to the freeman than was the case.

Thus Bruce, for all his shortcomings on race and class, had written a work that was still largely definitive by mid-century. His central thesis still stood: The seventeenth-century Virginia was ruled by an elite of large planters, unusually enlightened by the standards of their day, who dominated paternalistically almost every major phase of life, culture, and social organization.

HARVEY WISH
Western Reserve University

Part I
Religion and Morals

CHAPTER I

Early Religious Spirit

ALTHOUGH the first settlement of Virginia had its principal motive in the practical commercial objects always so powerfully influencing the English mind, yet there is no reason to think that the laymen who set that memorable enterprise on foot, as well as the clergymen who encouraged it,[1] were not deeply sensible of the religious aspect of so great an action. The burning ambition of Columbus was to find a western waterway to the East, but, as is so well known, he never lost sight of the glory that would fall to his lot should he carry the Faith further than it had ever before gone. No such religious ardor as this colored the hopes of the intrepid adventurers who founded Jamestown; but back of all their thirst of gold and trade calculations, there existed a spirit that was eager to extend to the savage inhabitants of the new land all the blessings of the Christian Belief. In the royal instructions for the government of Virginia accompanying the letters of 1606, the President and Council were strictly enjoined to see to it that the ''word and service

[1] There was one clergyman among the small number of persons obtaining the grant of the charter of 1606, whilst in the list of those receiving the charter of 1609, the names of one bishop and seven clergymen appear. Among those subscribing to the company's stock under the charter of 1612, were seven clergymen and one dean.

of God were preached, planted, and used" among the Indians residing within the limits of the Colony; and in the same remarkable document, an order was given to the English settlers to treat the heathen people in those parts "with unfailing kindness, and to draw them to the true service and knowledge of God" by all proper and available means.[1] One of the principal reasons assigned for the grant of the first Virginia charter was that the great enterprise which it authorized to be undertaken would enhance the glory of the Divine Majesty by "propagating the Christian religion to such people as yet live in darkness and miserable ignorance of the true knowledge and worship of God."[2] The *True and Sincere Declaration*, published in 1609, went so far as to say that the first object of the plantation was "to preach and baptize into the Christian religion, to recover out of the armes of the Devill, a number of poore and miserable soules wrapt up unto death in almost invincible ignorance."[3]

There were among the early settlers many persons who had a most vivid and fervid conception of the religious duty the English owed to the savage people found in possession of the country. "What a crown of glory," exclaimed John Rolfe, "shall be set upon their heads who shall faithfully labour herein!"[4] "What is more excellent, more precious, more glorious," exclaims Ralph Hamor, with even greater enthusiasm, "than to convert a heathen nation from worshipping the devill to the saving knowledge and

[1] Instructions for the Government of the North and South Virginia Colonies, 1606; see Brown's *Genesis of the United States*, vol. i., p. 67.

[2] See Virginia Charter of 1606.

[3] Brown's *Genesis of the United States*, vol. i., p. 339.

[4] Rolfe's *Relation of Virginia*, *Va. Hist. Register*, vol. i., No. iii.

true worship·of God in Jesus Christ?" Robert Johnson, a leading member of the London Company, made an eloquent appeal to every English subject to take part "in this high and acceptable work tending to advance and spread the Kingdom of God and the knowledge of the Truth; so many millions of men and women, savage and blind, that never saw the true light before their eyes, to enlighten their minds and comfort their souls."[1] The same religious and philanthropic note was struck by the distinguished clergymen who delivered sermons for the advancement of the plantation.[2] But perhaps the noblest of all the men who, in these early times, were interested in the Indians' spiritual welfare was George Thorpe, justly described as a "worthy, pious, and religious gentleman"; he came out to Virginia to serve as the manager of the college projected for the conversion and education of Indian youths; but his only reward for his untiring zeal was to perish miserably by a blow of the tomahawk in the massacre of 1622, when so many fell in the same treacherous attack.

In 1619, the first General Assembly convening in Virginia, in order to lay a sure foundation for turning the Indian tribes to Christianity commanded the authorities of each town, city, borough, and plantation in the Colony to secure by peaceful means a certain number of Indian children with the view of bringing them up in "a religious and civil course of life." The most promising of these native youths were to be grounded in the rudiments of English learning

[1] These words are from *Nova Britannia* written by Johnson.

[2] For instance, the sermon of the Rev. Wm. Symonds, April 15, 1609; of Rev. Daniel Price, May 28, 1609; of Rev. Mr. Crashaw, Febry. 21, 1609; and of Rev. Richard Crackenthorpe, March 24, 1608.

in order to fit them to enter the college which it was proposed to set up; and when they had been graduated from this institution, they were expected to go out as missionaries among their Indian kindred.[1]   The project of a school and college for the education of young Indians was one in which, not only the London Company, but also the King himself showed a deep interest; in 1620, James I gave orders that a letter should be dispatched to the Archbishops of Canterbury and York commanding them to send out, through the bishops of the different dioceses, an appeal to all the members of the Anglican Church to assist, by their contributions, in establishing these institutions, as well as in promoting other pious works in the Colony. It was stated in this letter that the Company had already begun to build churches and found schools for the savages' conversion and training, but as the expense was heavy, aid was needed.   This appeal did not prove in vain, for fifteen hundred pounds sterling was collected.[2]   In the course of the same year, fifty agricultural servants were transported to Virginia for the purpose of meeting, by the returns from their labor, the charge of educating thirty Indian children in "true religion and civility." [3]

Numerous instances of private gifts and bequests for the advancement of the same general object are recorded in the history of this early period.   For example, in 1602, the elder Nicholas Ferrer left three hundred pounds sterling by will for the conversion of infidel

[1] Assembly Minutes, 1619, *Colonial Records of Virginia*, State Senate Doct., Extra, 1874.

[2] The King's letter will be found in Campbell's *History of Virginia*, p. 146.

[3] Abstracts of Proceedings of Va. Co. of London, vol. i., p. 67.

children; this sum was to be paid by his executors to Sir Edwin Sandys and John Ferrer, officers of the Company, as soon as ten Indian pupils had been enrolled in the projected college; but in the meanwhile, the interest derived from the fund was to be expended in compensating three citizens of Virginia who, on their own account, should undertake to bring up, each in his own house, a young Indian in the Christian religion.[1] A few years subsequent to Ferrer's bequest, Rev. George Ruggle left one hundred pounds sterling to be devoted to the same general purpose.[2]

During the early months following the first settlement,—the English not yet having had an opportunity of obtaining an insight into the natives' unalterable ferocity,—the opinion prevailed that their character might be softened by the occult influence of the English prayer book, though not one word in it was really intelligible to the aboriginal brain. In the course of 1608, a band of eighteen savages were captured, and, with the exception of one who was soon released, they were, for some time, brought every morning and evening to the divine service held at those hours in the church at Jamestown.[3] But the chronicler fails to record whether their hearts were touched. How different from the lovely Indian heroine, Pocahontas! "I was moved," exclaims Gov. Dale, with fervent admiration, "by her desire to be taught and instructed in the knowledge of God, her capableness of understanding, her aptness and willingness to receive any good impression, also the spiritual"; and his success in converting this beautiful "unregen-

[1] Abstracts of Proceedings of Va. Co. of London, vol. i., p. 55.
[2] Ibid. p. 108.
[3] Works of Captain John Smith, p. 36, Arber's edition.

erate to regeneration" afforded him extraordinary satisfaction.[1]   There is hardly a more interesting or inspiring fact in the history of these early years than the solicitude shown by this stern English soldier (who pitilessly enforced discipline with the wheel, musket, and noose) for the Indian girl's conversion to the Christian Belief. "I caused her," he informs us, "to be carefully instructed in the Christian religion, who, after she had made some good progress therein, renounced publicly her Country's idolatry; openly confessed her Christian faith; and was, as she desired, baptized."

Pocahontas stood a person apart among the members of her own race; but it was not until the frightful massacre of 1622 took place that the colonists clearly perceived this to be so. The revulsion of feeling caused by that sanguinary event dissipated the kindness which was prepared to make so many sacrifices for christianizing and civilizing the Indian tribes. Rev. Jonas Stockton gave expression to the general opinion when he declared that it would be impossible to change the hearts of the savages "until their priests and ancients" were put to the sword.[2]   This was the earliest utterance of the belief formulated by a later observation into the more precise saying: "the only good Indian is a dead Indian."   The massacre of 1644, the final effort of the grim and treacherous Opechancanough to destroy the English population, smothered for a very long time what remained of the missionary spirit among the whites; after this, no active step seems to have been taken to spread the Christian religion among the surviving tribes, although the special

[1] *Works of Captain John Smith*, p. 512, Arber's edition.
[2] See Campbell's *History of Virginia*, p. 165.

orders given to each succeeding Governor inculcated the work of conversion as one of the most urgent of the executive duties. When, at the close of the century Nicholson was appointed to the highest office in the Colony, he was directed by the English authorities to recommend to the General Assembly the passage of laws which would ensure the education of the Indians and negroes in the Christian Faith. Nor did he fail to carry out an instruction so congenial to his own wishes. The House of Burgesses, however, when their attention was called to the subject by him, returned a discouraging reply: "The negroes born in this country," so its answer ran, "are generally baptized and brought up in the Christian religion, but for negroes imported hither, the gross bestiality and rudeness of their manners, the variety and strangeness of their languages, and the weakness and shallowness of their minds, render it in a manner impossible to make any progress in their conversion." On the other hand, the House pronounced the proposed conversion of the Indians to be more promising in the light of the recent endowment by the executors of that "pious and noble benefactor," Robert Boyle, of a department in William and Mary College for the special purpose of spreading Christianity among them.[1] Whatever religious zeal might have accomplished among them in the closing years of the century would, no matter how resolute and untiring that zeal was, have been certainly diminished by the steady decline in the size of the aboriginal population; by 1669, the number of bowmen residing in the vicinity of the English settlements had fallen off to seven hundred and twenty-five[2]; while the entire body of

[1] Minutes of Council, June 2, 1699, *B. T. Va.*, vol. lii.
[2] Hening's *Statutes*, vol. ii., p. 275.

Indian inhabitants residing within the Colony's boundaries probably did not exceed three thousand individuals.

The surviving records of the Seventeenth century contain numerous proofs of the strong religious feeling which shaped the opinions and influenced the conduct of the Virginians from the time of the earliest settlement of the country. The first adventurers, as we have seen, came over with many noble, but, as later events proved, extravagant plans for spreading the Christian doctrines among the Indian tribes. Apart from this lofty missionary spirit, which animated so many high-minded men among them, we find the whole body of these first pioneers showing on every proper occasion their loyalty to the religious observances familiar to them from childhood. Daily, the founders of Jamestown attended morning and evening prayers, and joined in singing a psalm[1]; on each recurring Sunday, two sermons were preached before them; and once every three months, they received the Holy Communion. "Surely God did most mercifully hear us," piously exclaims one of these early chroniclers.[2] The Colony's preservation from complete destruction in these years was again and again attributed by Captain Smith to the direct intervention of the Almighty, whose providence, however dark the hour, never failed them. Daily, during his adventurous and tempestuous voyage up the Chesapeake Bay, Smith read the morning and evening prayers to his companions; and together, under

[1] Newes from Virginia, *Works of Capt. John Smith*, p. 36, Arber's edition.

[2] *Works of Captain John Smith*, pp. 956–8, Arber's edition. After the death of Rev. Robert Hunt, a homily was delivered on Sunday until his successor arrived.

the open sky, and in the midst of those wild and hitherto unexplored waters, they sang a hymn.[1] De la Warr (who was described as being both a pious and a valiant man), on landing at Jamestown, fell on his knees, and, in the presence of the awed and reverent people, made a long and silent prayer; then rising to his feet, headed the procession, which moved slowly and solemnly to the church, where a sermon was heard. One of the first orders given by him was for the repair of this edifice. Daily, during his administration, prayers were read at ten o'clock in the morning and at four in the afternoon; on Sunday, two sermons were preached; and on Thursday, one. The Governor was accompanied to church by the entire body of gentlemen and officials, and was attended by a guard of fifty halberdiers dressed in red cloaks, the livery of the West family. His chair, placed in the choir, was lined with green velvet, whilst the cushion on which he knelt during prayers was made of the same rich stuff.[2]

On Sir Thomas Dale's arrival at Jamestown in May, 1611, he first repaired to the church, and there heard a sermon preached by Rev. Mr. Pooley. Rev. Alexander Whitaker eulogized him as a "religious and valiant man," and also as one "of a great knowledge of divinity, and of a good conscience in all his doings," however stern and exacting he may have appeared to be at times. During his administration, a sermon was delivered in the church every Sunday morning; and in the afternoon of the same day, there was also an examination there in the catechism; whilst every Saturday night, religious services were held in the governor's

---

[1] *Works of Capt. John Smith*, p. 118, Arber's edition.

[2] Purchas, vol. iv., p. 1754.

house under the direction of Whitaker, who, with four other citizens, chosen for their religious life, had charge of the affairs of the Church. The communion service was celebrated once every month; and once every year a day was set apart for a general fast.[1]

Dale writing to a friend, a clergyman in London, refers with pious humility to his own great work in laying a sure foundation for the Colony's prosperity; "what recompense or what reward for which," he said, "by whom or where, I know not where to expect but from Him in whose vineyard I labour, whose Church with greedy appetite I desire to erect."[2] Of all those terrible *Divine and Martial Laws*, which he thought necessary for the complete repression of every form of disorder and wrong doing, he enforced with most strictness the numerous provisions adopted to compel respect for religion and the different ecclesiastical ordinances. The duty was imposed upon every officer to see that "God was served"; and each was commanded to set the example to all persons under him by a regular attendance at morning and evening prayers. Whoever omitted going to church was punished for the first offence by the loss of his day's allowance; for the second, by a severe whipping; and for the third, by his condemnation to the galleys for a period of six months. Profanation of God's name by an unlawful oath was, for the second offence, to be punished with a bodkin's thrust through the tongue; and for the third, with death; and the penalty of death also was

[1] Letter of Whitaker to M. G., June 18, 1614, Hamor's *Discourse*. A sermon was required by the "Divine and Martiall Lawes" to be delivered also on every Wednesday. By the same laws, the clergyman and his four assistants were directed "to find out the neglects of the people in their duties and service to God."

[2] See Dale's letter in Hamor's *Discourse*.

to be paid by whoever stole one of the sacred articles belonging to the church building.[1]

The colonists' religious punctuality in these early times is illustrated in the action of "one Fairfax," whose home was situated about a mile from Jamestown. It happened that, only a few days before, a settler residing not far from him had been treacherously killed by a band of Chickahominies. When Sunday arrived, Fairfax did not allow this fact to deter him from attending the services at Jamestown. His wife left their house and went along the path to meet him on his return, and while they were both thus absent the Indians, creeping in, slew their three young children and a boy; and also butchered a second youth who had stolen away from church while prayers were going on.[2]

Among the most important acts passed by the Assembly of 1619, the first to convene in the Colony, were those designed to advance the religious and moral welfare of the people. Perhaps, not the least remarkable of these laws was the one requiring all the clergymen residing in Virginia to come together at Jamestown at least once every three months, and after consulting with each other, to "determine whom it was fit to excommunicate"; but the names of such persons were to be submitted to the Governor before the act of excommunication could be legally promulgated.[3] A similar spirit is shown to have animated the highest authorities of the Colony in these early times by the numerous proclamations which they issued against

---

[1] See Divine and Martial Lawes, 1611, in Force's *Historical Tracts*.

[2] *Works of Capt. John Smith*, p. 558, Arber's edition.

[3] Minutes of Assembly, 1619, p. 27, *Colonial Records of Va.*, State Senate Doct., Extra, 1874.

the vices of drunkenness and profanity.[1] This spirit was again and again inculcated by the instructions delivered to every Governor on his appointment. In the far seeing orders drawn up for the guidance of the persons placed at the head of the expedition of 1607, they were urged to obey and fear God, "the giver of all goodness, for every plantation which our Heavenly Father hath not planted shall be rooted out."[2] This pious invocation was in substance repeated from decade to decade; for instance, in 1626, Sir George Yeardley was strictly enjoined to see that both he and the people of the Colony "served Almighty God duly and daily with a view of drawing a blessing on all their endeavours"[3]; and the like invocation to later Governors was not less earnest and imperative.

[1] For an example, see British Colonial Papers, vol. iii., No. 9.
[2] *Works of Capt. John Smith*, p. xxxvii., Arber's edition.
[3] Robinson Transcripts, p. 44.

CHAPTER II

Proofs of Popular Religious Feeling

A S we have seen, one of the regulations enforced by
Governor Dale was the observance of an annual
fast day. Throughout the Seventeenth century,
the reverent feeling of the people found expression in
setting apart certain days of the year for humiliation
or thanksgiving. The twenty-second of March, rendered forever memorable in the community's history
by the first great massacre of the unsuspecting whites
by the Indians, was commemorated by a solemn fast;
and as late as 1643, the General Assembly required
every clergyman in Virginia to give notice from his
pulpit in ample time for this pious duty to be performed
by each member of his congregation.[1] The following
year, a second great massacre occurred; and so deep
was the impression made on the popular mind by this
catastrophe, that at first the last Wednesday in every
month was set apart as a day of humiliation, to be
wholly dedicated to prayers and sermons, in order that
"God might avert his heavy judgments" from the unfortunate Colonists.[2] The General Assembly, having
in 1668, adopted a resolution declaring that the numerous sins of the people were such as to provoke the
anger of God and draw down his punishment unless

[1] MS. Laws of Va., 1643, Clerk's office, Portsmouth, Va.
[2] Hening's *Statutes*, vol. i., p. 289.

they repented in time, appointed the twenty-seventh of August of that year a day of fasting; and all persons were warned to cease working, gambling, and drinking on that day, under the penalty of a heavy fine for disobedience.[1]   When the Insurrection of 1676 came to an end, Bacon being dead, the fourth of May and the twenty-second of August were selected by those who had triumphed as days of general thanksgiving.[2] Twelve years afterwards, the House of Burgesses, deeply moved by the heavy mortality which at that time prevailed throughout Virginia, and publicly deploring this terrible condition as the result of the crying sins of the people, appealed to the Governor to appoint a day of fasting for the General Assembly alone, and a second day for a public fast in all parts of the Colony.[3]

In 1692, Governor Andros issued his proclamation for a day of thanksgiving to be celebrated at Jamestown, where the General Assembly was about to convene; and for a second day, of a later date, in which the entire Colony was to participate; at this time, Virginia was declared to have been "signally blessed by a gracious Providence"; and there was a universal desire for a public expression of the popular gratitude.[4]

[1] Hening's *Statutes*, vol. ii., p. 265.

[2] *Ibid.*, p. 399.

[3] Colonial Entry Book, 1682–95, p. 523.

[4] The Proclamation will be found in Henrico County Records, vol. 1688–97, p. 415, Va. St. Libr.   It ran as follows:

"By his Excellency, A Proclamation.

"Almighty God of his infinite Goodness and Mercy has in many ways been graciously pleased to bestow his great blessings on this, their Majestys' Colony and Dominion of Virginia, And a General Assembly being called and soon to sit to consider and advise of such things as may be for the glory of God, the Honr. of their Majestys and the Peace and Welfare of this Colony and the in-

In the course of the same year, Andros directed that the twenty-fifth of September, which happened to fall on Sunday, should be observed as a day of public thanksgiving on account of the great victory the English fleet had recently won over the French [1]; whilst in the following year, he appointed the seventeenth of May for the holding of services in all the churches and chapels-of-ease in order to implore Providence to mitigate an epidemic of measles, a malady then rapidly spreading. [2] Again, in 1696, the Governor issued his proclamation calling upon the people to offer up, on a day set apart, special prayers of thanksgiving [3]; and in

---

habitants thereof, I, Sir Edward Andros, Knt. their Majestys' Lt. and Govr. General of Virginia, with the advice and consent of the Council, do, therefore, hereby appoint that, on Sunday, the fifth day of this instant March, prayers and supplications be made to Almighty God at James city for the continuance of His blessings, and that He will be graciously pleased to give His Divine assistance to the proceedings of the said Genl. Assembly, And that on Sunday the 19th of this Instant, the same be solemnized in the respective churches and chapels throughout this whole Colony and Dominion, And do desire and require all ministers and readers to be diligent in the due performance of their duties accordingly at the times and places appointed that all persons may join in their prayers and supplications to Almighty God in imploring his Blessings and Assistance upon this extraordinary occasion—Given under my hand, and the Seal of the Colony and Dominion this first day of March, in the 5th year of the Reign of our Sovereign Lord and Lady, King William and Queen Mary, Anno Dom. 1692.

"To Sheriff of Henrico County or his Deputy,

"E. ANDROS.

"God save the King and Queen. Vera Copia." We find the following entry in the Minutes of the General Assembly for 1692: "Ordered that Mr. Speaker give the thanks of the House to Mr. Stephen Fouace for his sermon preached before ye General Assembly on the Public Thanksgiving Day." Minutes of Genl. Ass., April 16, 1692, Co. Entry Book, 1682-95.

[1] Essex County Records, vol. 1692-5, p. 201, Va. St. Libr.
[2] Henrico County Records, Orders June 1, 1696.
[3] Essex County Records, vol. 1692-5, p. 254, Va. St. Libr.

1698, when there was an extraordinary mortality prevailing in some parts of the Colony, in consequence of a disorder which it was feared would further widen its ravages, the same official designated a day of fasting for observance by the inhabitants of Jamestown where the disease was most violent; and a later day by the remaining population of Virginia, whether as yet attacked or not.[1]

There are many proofs that these appointments by the Governor of days for general humiliation or thanksgiving had the sympathetic approval of the great body of the people; and that they were celebrated throughout the Colony with feelings of unaffected heartiness and reverence.

Perhaps, under no circumstances did the religious spirit of the Virginians in the Seventeenth century find more remarkable expression than when they came to write their last wills. Some examples of this testamentary piety may be given. In 1656, Robert Dunster bequeathed "his soul to God and his sin to the Devil."[2] Thomas Hunt, of Northampton county, was not content with such summary brevity: in his will, he asserted his great sorrow for his iniquities; his belief in their remission and forgiveness through the merits and sacrifices of Christ; his faith in the Resurrection and Final Judgment; and his absolute assurance of inheritance of eternal happiness in the life hereafter.[3] John Godfrey, of Rappahannock, was even more

[1] British Colonial Papers, B. T. Va., 1698, vol. vi., p. 357. In 1692, Walter Clotworthy and his housekeeper were indicted in Henrico County for working on a fast day; see Records, vol. 1688–97, pp. 321–2, Va. St. Libr.

[2] Isle of Wight County, Wills for 1656. Dunster was a clergyman.

[3] Northampton County Records, vol. 1654–5, folio p. 90.

elaborate in his testamentary confessions:—he began by declaring that he was in his senses only by "leave of Almighty God"; and that God alone knew how soon it would be before a mortal sickness would fall on him. Divine justice required that, for the "sins and wickedness daily enacted among us," all the people should be cut off without mercy; not, it appears, indirectly by the divine sword, as it were, but directly by the Indian tomahawk. "May the Lord, however," he writes, "not suffer us to come to such an untimely end as to be destroyed by the heathen, but we can expect no other, for without sound repentance from ye bottom of ye heart, there is small hope of grace." "This is to certify to all persons whom it may concern," he concludes, "that I bequeathe my soule to Almighty God that gave it to me unto ye meritorious death and passion of my blessed Saviour and Redeemer, Jesus Christ, that was crucified for my sins." [1] Col. John Stringer, the presiding justice of the Northampton county court, decided that he could not advance the cause of religion better than by an explicit confession of faith in his will. "I bequeathe my soul," he wrote, "to God, who first gave it to me, Father, Son and Spirit in Unity and Trinity, and Trinity in Unity, who hath redeemed and preserved me by and through Jesus Christ, and also died for my sinns, and for the sinns of all peoples that truly believe in Him by unfeigned faith and repentance, for whose sake and loving kindness I hope to entertain everlasting life, wherefore, Dear Father, have mercy upon my soul." [2]

Innumerable other last testaments couched in language marked by equal religious devotion might

---

[1] Rappahannock County Records, vol. 1677–82, p. 48.
[2] Northampton County Records, vol. 1689–98, p. 8.

be quoted. In some, an anti-climax appears, which shows that the thought of death for the time being had dulled the makers' sense of humor; for instance, after a most fervent expression of repentance for sin and of hope of salvation, there will follow immediately the bequest of a "feather bed" or "female calf" to some near kinsman. John Emerson, having given directions in his will that his body should be "civilly and decently interred," and having prayed to God to "send us all a happy meetinge in his Kingdom," concluded as follows: "I desire that it may be remembered that my executors doe receive of Anne Sowerby my bolster belonging to this bed under me."[1] Another testator, after a moving expression of his religious hopes closes with these words: "I give to Thomas Parramore one serge suit, and to Francis Parramore one yearling heifer."[2]

George Jordan of Surry county, provided in his will for a pious observance which was to end only with the "destruction of the world"; he directed that, on the fifteenth day of every October, a sermon in his daughter's memory should be delivered in the house he had occupied in his lifetime; and when that day happened to fall on Sunday, the Holy communion was to be administered also. All the people residing in the neighbourhood were to be invited year after year, and entertained with an ample supply of meat and drink before they departed for their homes. Anticipating that the day's celebration in the manner thus laid down might fall into disuse as time went on, he prescribed in his will that whoever should come into possession of the land, "although it be a thousand

[1] Surry County Records, Wills for 1676.
[2] Northampton County Records, vol. 1655–58, p. 64.

generations hence," should forfeit it, should he fail to "perform this sermon and prayer."[1]

One of the most ordinary provisions of wills at this period was that the testators' children should be taught how to read the Bible.[2]

Some of the Virginians were not content to confine their final expression of faith, or their last wishes to their wills; there is at least one very remarkable instance in which the tombstone was made to complement the last testament in this respect. Colonel Richard Cole, of Westmoreland county, who, there is reason to think, had led a somewhat wayward and rollicking life, ordered the following verse to be cut into the slab which was to cover his grave:

> "Here lies Dick Cole, a grievous sinner,
> That died a little before dinner,
> Yet hoped in Heaven to find a place
> To satiate his soul with grace." [3]

The few letters belonging to private correspondence which have descended to us from the Seventeenth century breathe a spirit as full of reverence for religion as the spirit observable in such a large proportion of the wills recorded during the same period. It is especially conspicuous in the letters of William Fitzhugh, a man distinguished for pious feeling; and it is far from lacking in those of the elder William Byrd, although these show in many ways less sensibility. "I hope," he wrote to his son in London, "that (your master) will see you improve your time, and that you become

---

[1] Surry County Records, vol. 1671–84, p. 295, Va. St. Libr.

[2] An example will be found in a will preserved in the Northampton County Records, vol. 1666–72, folio p. 55.

[3] Westmoreland County Records, vol. 1665–77, p. 186.

careful to serve God as you ought, without which you cannot expect to do well here or hereafter."[1]

It frequently happened that religious books were so highly valued by their owners that they were by name bequeathed to children or friends; especially was it common to make gifts of Bibles by last will[2]; and other volumes were often included with them. For instance, in 1675, Devereux Godwin, of Northampton, who was apparently a blacksmith, left his son, not only his Bible, but also a copy of *Smith's Sermons*, both of which were, no doubt, endeared to him by long and familiar use.[3] Robert Hodge, of Lower Norfolk, in 1681, bequeathed to each of his godsons and god-daughters residing in Virginia, a Bible, and also two volumes of sermons, to be delivered to them before two years had passed after his death.[4] Sometimes, the bequest of a religious book is found in an odd association with other bequests of a less pacific character; for example, in 1640, John Holloway left by will to Peter Long "a muskett, and Raine on ye Ephesians," a combination of testamentary gifts that recalls the famous lines of Hudibras about the Puritans of his day, "who did build their faith upon the holy text of pike and gun."[5] At this time, however, the Indians were suspected of restlessness, which, in a few years, actually led to the second great massacre of the whites;

[1] Letters of William Byrd; see also p. xlii. of Introduction to Bassett's edition of the second William Byrd's *Works*.

[2] See Lower Norfolk County Records, vol. 1651-6, p. 47. Nathaniel Hill, of Henrico County, bequeathed his "big Bible" to his son: but should this son die first, then to John Worsham; see Records, vol. 1677-92, orig. p. 476.

[3] Northampton County Records, vol. 1674-9, p. 123.

[4] Lower Norfolk County Antiquary, vol. ii., p. 34; see also Lower Norfolk County Records, Orders Oct. 18, 1681.

[5] Northampton County Records, Orders Aug. 31, 1643.

the bequest of a musket was something to excite gratitude at an hour when, in numerous homes, the morning and evening prayers were always read with several guns placed close at hand and prepared for instant use.[1]

Religious books form one of the most ordinary entries in the inventories of personal estates appraised during the Seventeenth century.   There were few such estates of even moderate proportions that did not include either a couple of Bibles, or that almost equally popular and revered volume, *The Whole Duty of Man*.[2] Among the articles of value in Walter Broadhurst's possession were two Bibles one of which was ornamented with silver clasps and a silver chain.[3]   Mrs. Jane Hastry owned one Bible and two volumes of sermons,[4] and Francis Eppes, a Bible in quarto, containing both the service and the Apocrypha.[5]   Two Bibles formed a part of the personal estate of Chris-

[1] In 1643, a general law required that at least one member of every family in the Colony should bring with him to church on Sunday a fixed gun, with the necessary amount of powder and shot; Hening's *Statutes*, vol. i., p. 263.

[2] Bibles were for sale in all the colonial stores.   The following from the Northampton County Records for 1684 is of interest in this connection: "Elizabeth Daniell came into the store and called to ye merchant Jackson for one of his Bibles, and he handed her one, and she bid ye Jackson's assistant that was booking what goods he delivered to booke her ye s^d booke. And as she had ye sd. Bible in her hand, she said to Richard Sheppard 'Now if you will downe on your knees, I will give ye this Bible,' which he promised her to do, and on that she gave him ye Bible, and he had it in his pocket, and ye said Merchant afterwards said that was ye ninth Bible ye said Elizabeth had had of him."   Northampton County Records, vol. 1683–89, p. 105.

[3] Westmoreland County Records, Orders April 17, 1661.

[4] Northampton County Records for 1665.   This volume is improperly marked 1655–8; see last part, p. 13.

[5] Henrico County Records, vol. 1677–92, orig. p. 97.

topher Branch[1]; and the sermons of Robert Sanderson and the works of Josephus a part of the Farrar estate.[2] A citizen of Henrico, in 1685, owned a large illustrated Bible, appraised at one pound sterling and five shillings, or twenty-five dollars in our present American currency.[3] John Lewis, who also resided in Henrico, possessed a Cambridge print Bible in quarto.[4] The family Bible of Mrs. Elizabeth Digges was valued at one pound sterling after it had been long in use.[5] The personal estate of William Cocke included three Bibles, one testament, one *Practice of Piety*, one Common Prayer Book and one Psalter.[6]

The *Practice of Piety* seems to have been a favourite religious book in Virginian households at this time; among those who possessed it were John Lankfield and Captain Henry Woodhouse, of Lower Norfolk.[7] William Kennedy, of the same county, owned a copy of *Pilgrim's Progress*,[8] while John Panewell, of Northampton, owned a copy of the *Exposition of Paul to the Thessalonians*.[9] Among the numerous works composing the library of Charles Parkes, who was a citizen of the latter county, were fifteen books of divinity, representing about thirty volumes in all, some bound in

[1] Henrico County Records, vol. 1677–92, orig. p. 218.

[2] *Ibid.*, vol. 1677–92, orig. p. 267.

[3] *Ibid.*, vol. 1677–92, orig. p. 321.

[4] *Ibid.*, vol. 1688–97, p. 105, Va. St. Libr.

[5] York County Records, Inventory, Aug. 24, 1692; see also *William and Mary College Quart.*, vol. iii., p. 247.

[6] Henrico County Records, vol. 1688–97, p. 490, Va. St. Libr. This list might be almost indefinitely extended.

[7] Lower Norfolk County Records, Orders Nov. 30, 1640; also vol. 1686–95, year 1687.

[8] Lower Norfolk County Antiquary, vol. ii., p. 35.

[9] Northampton County Records, vol. 1680–92, p. 315. Panewell was no doubt the original form of the well known Virginia name Pannill.

quarto, but the majority in large octavo.   One of these works was Baxter's *Saints' Everlasting Rest*, which enjoyed an extraordinary degree of popularity in those times.[1]   Of the three hundred and ninety-one works composing Ralph Wormeley's library at Rosegill, one hundred and twenty-three bore upon religious or moral topics.[2]   The library of Arthur Spicer, a distinguished lawyer, who lived toward the end of the century, contained among numerous other works, four Bibles printed in English, and one in Latin; a large *Concordance of the Bible*, a *Practice of Piety*, and several volumes of sermons; it also contained Perkins on *Divinity*, Brown's *Errors*, Exon's *Contemplations*, and Sir Matthew Hale's work of the same name, Usher's *Answer to the Jesuits*, Prynne's *Prelacy*, and a *Defence of Constantine;* also treatises on church canons, church discipline, and the Christian policy; and discourses on the Principles of Natural Religion and the Doctrines of the Christian Faith. Standard volumes of a more general nature were the *Decay of Piety*, the *Vindication of Godliness*, the *Marrow of Divinity*, *Moral Gallantry*, and *Bowels of Tender Mercy*.[3]   Among the works treating of religious and moral subjects found in the library of Richard Watkins, of York county, in 1669, were Robotham's *Preciousness of Christ*, Roberts's *Evidences*, *Vanity of Worldly Pleasures*, Small's *Psalm Books*, and Matby's *Legacy*.[4] These religious works belonging to the Wormeley, Spicer, and Watkins collections reveal a rather wide field of moral studies; and they probably represent the ground covered by the religious reading of a majority

[1] See Northampton County Records for 1696, Parkes Inventory.
[2] William and Mary College Quart., vol. ii., p. 170.
[3] *Ibid.*, vol. ii., p. 170.
[4] York County Records, vol. 1664–72, p. 453, Va. St. Libr.

of cultivated Virginians of that day who were not ordained clergymen.

Additional light is thrown upon the religious spirit of the colonists in the Seventeenth century by the number of testamentary gifts during that period for the benefit of the destitute. I have, in a former work, referred to several among those made to the poor residing in England[1]; a few made to indigent persons in Virginia may be mentioned to show their general character. In 1655, Captain John Moon, a merchant and planter left by will four cows to serve as a stock for-ever for fatherless children without means of support or education, superannuated persons past their labour, and lame persons greatly improverished, whose homes were situated in the lower parish of Isle of Wight county.[2] Five years later, Samuel Fenn, of York, bequeathed five pounds sterling to the use of Middleton parish[3]; and a similar bequest was, about 1672, made to the parish of Martin's Brandon[4]; both of which gifts were, no doubt, primarily for the relief of the indigent. In 1667, Daniel Boucher, of Isle of Wight county, gave directions by will that his executors should furnish one loaf of bread to every destitute person to be found in his parish; and also an ox to the whole number of poor residing there. The testator's object was evidently to provide a feast at which every pauper might at least for once enjoy a hearty meal.[5] A few years later, Robert Griggs, of Lancaster, bequeathed twenty thousand pounds of tobacco to the poor; and he further

---

[1] See Bruce's *Social Life of Virginia in the Seventeenth Century*, chapt. ix.

[2] Isle of Wight County, Wills for 1655.

[3] York County Records, vol. 1657–62, p. 248, Va. St. Libr.

[4] Robinson Transcripts, p. 259.

[5] Isle of Wight County Records, vol. 1661–1719, p. 53.

revealed his benevolent disposition by ordering his slaves to be liberated as soon as each should reach a specified age.[1]   Ralph Langley, of York, in 1683, left by will one third of his residuary estate to the destitute belonging to his parish[2]; and Edward Deeley, following the example of Langley, who had also endowed his parish church, bequeathed twenty shillings to the use of the church in which he himself had been in the habit of worshipping.[3]   In 1690, George Spencer, of Lancaster, in his will gave directions that ten thousand pounds of tobacco, forming a part of his estate, should be distributed among the poor of Whitechapel parish[4]; and two years afterwards, Benjamin Read made a similar testamentary gift to the destitute of Mulberry Island parish, to be paid by the sale of land in England which he owned.[5]   Richard Trotter, in 1699, left one thousand pounds of tobacco to the destitute inhabitants of Charles parish, in York.[6]

[1] Lancaster County Will Books, vol. 1674–89, folio p. 90.

[2] York County Records, vol. 1675–84, orig. p. 485.

[3] Henrico County Records, vol. 1688–97, p. 63, Va. St. Libr.

[4] Lancaster County Records, vol. 1690–1709, p. 11.

[5] York County Records, vol. 1690–94, p. 257, Va. St. Libr.   The amount of Read's bequest was twenty pounds sterling, which had then the purchasing power of five hundred dollars at the present day.

[6] *Ibid.*, vol. 1694–1702, p. 194, Va. St. Libr.   This list might be greatly extended.

CHAPTER III

Public Morals: Sabbath Observance

THE religious spirit of the people was reflected in a more conspicuous way still in the strict regulations adopted to ensure a proper observance of the Sabbath. I have already dwelt upon the provisions for church attendance which formed a part of the "Divine and Martial Laws" enforced during the administrations of Gates and Dale. During Argoll's administration, the penalty for failing to be present at divine services on Sunday and on a holiday, was, throughout the following night, to lie neck and heels in the Corp de Guard. Should the delinquent be a servant, the imprisonment was to continue for a week; but if a freeman, and it was his second offence, the punishment was to be prolonged for a whole month; whilst a third offence was to subject him to the like punishment for a year and a day.[1]

The first General Assembly to meet in Virginia passed a law requiring of every citizen attendance at divine services on Sunday. The penalty imposed for a failure to be present was not at this time so severe as during the arbitrary rule of Argoll; if the delinquent was a freeman, he was to be compelled to pay three shillings for each offence, to be devoted to the church; and should

[1] Argoll's Edicts, May 28, 1618; see Brown's *First Republic*, p. 278, and Randolph MS., vol. iii., p. 144.

he be a slave, he was to be sentenced to be whipped.[1]
The penalty of three shillings had by 1632, been reduced
to one, but, in the course of that year, the General
Assembly strictly enjoined all commanders, captains,
and churchwardens to see to it that no person remained
away from church without lawful excuse; and they
were warned that, should they omit to perform their
duty in this respect, they must "answer before God for
such evils and plagues wherewith Almighty God may
justly punish his people for neglecting so good and
wholesome a law."[2]   That the statute was rigidly
enforced is shown by the number of cases in which
persons were summoned before the county courts to
answer for what was described as "a breach of the
Sabbath."[3]

A violation of the Sabbath, it seems, might, in these
early times, be committed in a great variety of ways,
a few of which may be mentioned as examples.   For
instance, it was not lawful to go on a journey unless
with the view of attending divine services, or performing some duty not to be deferred; nor was the use of
firearms allowed except to frighten marauding birds
from the cornfields, or to resist an Indian attack.[4]   In
1648, Oliver Segar, of new Poquoson parish, in York,
was presented by the grand jury for the offence of fishing on Sunday, which, in his case, was rendered more

[1] Minutes of Assembly, 1619, p. 28, *Colonial Records of Virginia,*
Senate Document, Extra 1874.   This law was re-enacted in substance
in 1629; see Randolph MS., vol. iii., p. 213.

[2] Hening's *Statutes*, vol. i., p. 155.

[3] See the case of Robert Martin in Lower Norfolk County Records,
Orders Febry. 15, 1642.

[4] Hening's *Statutes*, vol. i., pp. 261, 434.   An Act of Assembly
passed as late as 1696 forbade travelling on Sunday; see Colonial
Entry Book, vol. lxxxix., p. 182.   This was but one of repeated
enactments of the same law.

heinous by the fact that, on this particular day, the sacrament had been administered. As a punishment for his sacrilegious conduct, Segar was ordered by the county court to build a bridge across a swamp through which the road to the parish church had been laid off.[1] A less expensive punishment seems to have been inflicted on Henry Truit, found guilty in Accomac of the same offence.[2] A fine of one hundred pounds of tobacco was, about the middle of the century, imposed on Thomas Williams, of Lower Norfolk, for getting drunk on the Sabbath, and he was ordered to pay that amount into the county treasury.[3] In 1650, Henry Crowe, having found it impossible to resist the temptation of drawing his tobacco plants on Sunday, owing very probably to the first good season for doing so having fallen on this day, was summoned for that offence before the county court, and only escaped a heavy fine by an humble promise to amend.[4] This incident throws into a strong light the authorities' determination to enforce a strict observance of the Sabbath; in a community given over, practically to the exclusion of all other interests, to the cultivation of tobacco, it must have appeared to many an excusable act to take advantage of what was perhaps the first moist day, and perhaps might be the last, for weeks, to transfer their plants to the field.

About the middle of the century, the grand jury of Lower Norfolk made a sharp complaint as to the general indifference to the observance of Sunday at that time prevailing in all parts of the county; and they

[1] York County Records, vol. 1638–48, p. 386, Va. St. Libr.

[2] Accomac County Records, vol. 1673–6, p. 262.

[3] Lower Norfolk County Records, vol. 1646–51, p. 12.

[4] *Ibid.*, vol. 1646–51, p. 152.

proceeded to charge the entire population with a breach of the day, but at the same time softened the character of the offense by stating that they considered it was largely due to the lack of a godly and competent minister; and they urged that the vacancy should be at once supplied in order to bring about a change in so deplorable a condition. They indicted Thomas Wright for breaking the Sabbath himself, and causing his laborers to do so; and also Mrs. Elizabeth Lloyd for requiring her servants, on the same day, to follow all their customary employments. George Hankings was presented because he was in the habit of leaving his house on Sunday with his tools in his hands; and Thomas Goodrich, for having gone on two long journeys at times when he should have been in attendance at divine service.[1]

An Act, passed in 1658, declared that, under no circumstances, should it be legal to transport goods by boat on Sunday. This was designed to prevent the loading and unloading of sea-going vessels on that day, the penalty for which offence was either a fine of one hundred pounds of tobacco, or confinement in the stocks.[2] The same year, it was strictly forbidden to deliver any writ on the Sabbath; it seems to have been the sheriffs' habit up to this time to serve all such documents at the church door, first, because they were able to find there any person they were seeking, and secondly, because they thus avoided the fatigue and loss of time that would have been entailed by a ride to this person's home, which perhaps was situated

[1] Lower Norfolk County Antiquary, vol. iii., p. 29; see also Lower Norfolk County Records, vol. 1651–6, p. 113. Some of these offenders were of the Quaker faith.

[2] Hening's *Statutes*, vol. i., p. 434.

on a remote plantation. These officers' intrusion at the church meetings in their character of sheriffs was justly regarded as repugnant to the religious aspects of such an occasion.[1]

If possible, the determination to enforce the strict observance of the Sabbath was, during the last quarter of the century even stronger than it had been previous to that period. Not infrequently, however, as formerly, the person indicted for being absent from church was able to offer a good excuse; for instance, in Accomac, in 1663, one person evaded the fine by proving that, on the Sunday when he was declared to be delinquent, he was not present in the county at all; and another, that he had transferred his membership from Nandua church to Occahannock.[2] In 1665, eleven persons were indicted in Northampton for violating the Sabbath by remaining away from the parish church[3]; ten years later, the grand jury of Surry presented twenty-nine for the like offense, and among them were citizens of such prominence as Bartholomew Owen, John Hunnicutt, and Thomas Busby. It is quite probable that the larger number of these delinquents were persons belonging to the Quaker sect, which had now begun to cause some disturbance in the Colony.[4] A few years later, eleven persons were presented in Surry for the same offense; and a majority of these were perhaps of the same faith.[5]

It was, however, not always the dictates of conscience that kept the delinquent away from the regular religious

[1] Hening's *Statutes*, vol. i., p. 457.
[2] Accomac County Records, vol. 1663–6, folio p. 54.
[3] Northampton County Records, vol. 1664–74, folio p. 10.
[4] Surry County Records, vol. 1671–84, p. 120, Va. St. Libr.
[5] *Ibid.*, vol. 1671–84, p. 299, Va. St. Libr.

services; it was observed one Sunday, in 1678, that there were very few persons present in the principal church of Accomac, and, at the same time, there were "above twenty" drinking at John Cole's house at the hour "of ye sermon." Cole, it seems, owned the most popular tavern situated in the county,[1] and it was here that a part of the congregation were passing the interval of divine service, while the benches in the sacred edifice near by were almost empty of worshippers. This happened only a few years after the close of the Insurrection of 1676, and it is quite probable that that turbulent event had left the body of the people in a somewhat demoralized state. This view is confirmed by the grand jury's action in Lower Norfolk in the same year in which these citizens of Northampton showed so openly their disregard of the consecrated character of Sunday,—that body deliberately presented every clergyman in the county as well as all other persons there possessing ecclesiastical authority, because they had failed to enforce attendance on divine service as celebrated "according to ye canons of ye Church of England"; in consequence of which, the Sabbath had been profaned by evil disposed men and women "who made of the Lord's Day what their pleasures led to." [2]

In the course of 1681, thirty-two persons, most of whom, perhaps, belonged to the dissenting sects, were indicted in Surry for omitting to go to church; and in the following October, thirteen. It shows the peaceful demeanour of the people of this county that the only other offense, pronounced to be criminal by the law, committed by them during this year was

[1] Accomac County Records, vol. 1676–8, p. 127.
[2] Lower Norfolk County Records, vol. 1675–86, p. 40.

defamation.[1] It was provided in the bond of Samuel
Thompson, an innkeeper of Surry in 1681, that he
should suffer no persons except his servants to remain
in his tavern on holidays and Sundays during the hours
divine services were in progress in the parish church,[2]
—a far from unusual proof of the extraordinary care
taken by the county courts to preserve the sacred
character of these days from being violated by idle
dissipation. Six persons, who, in 1682, had been
indicted in York for their failure to attend church,
excused themselves on the ground that they were
Quakers; nevertheless each was fined fifty pounds for
his offense.[3] In the following year, several persons
were indicted in this county for absenting themselves
from divine worship, but as it was the first time they
had done so, they were dismissed without being mulcted.[4]
Two years later, nine persons were indicted; but it
is again probable that most of these were members of
a dissenting sect.[5]

After the passage of the Toleration Act by Parliament, which allowed all persons, of whatever religious
denomination, to attend their own church, the authorities of Virginia, in response to the general sentiment
of the people, continued to enforce respect for the sacred
character of Sunday. In 1699, petitions, proceeding

[1] Surry County Records, vol. 1671–84, pp. 441, 465, Va. St. Libr.

[2] *Ibid.*, vol. 1671–84, p. 576, Va. St. Libr.

[3] York County Records, vol. 1675–84, pp. 448, 462, Va. St. Libr.
Four of these Quakers bore the names respectively of Robert
Pritchard, Isaac Goddin, Edward and James Thomas. In 1684,
John Goode was indicted in Henrico county because, during sixteen
years' residence in the parish, he had not once attended church.
He also was probably a Quaker; see Henrico County Records, vol.
1677–92, orig. p. 274.

[4] York County Recods, vol. 1675–84, orig. p. 547.

[5] *Ibid.*, vol. 1684–7, p. 92, Va. St. Libr. .

simultaneously from Lancaster, Gloucester and Accomac counties, all lying widely apart, were laid before the House of Burgesses, in which it was prayed, as a means of saving the Sabbath from violation, that every citizen, to whatever sect he might belong, should be compelled on that day to attend "some congregation or place of worship."[1] It was, no doubt, under the influence of this proposition that, in the course of the same year, the General Assembly adopted a law which provided that any adult failing to be present at some form of religious services should be fined five shillings, or fifty pounds of tobacco.[2]

We have already seen of what a violation of the Sabbath was deemed to consist previous to the middle of the century. A few instances may be given to show the character of what was considered to be such after that date. In 1678, Edward Hastell, of Lower Norfolk, was indicted because he had been seen carrying a gun on Sunday. Another person, residing in the same county, was, a few years afterwards, presented because he had on that day, hired his horse out; a third, because he had sent one of his servants to a neighbouring tannery with a hide; and a fourth because he had trimmed and replanted his nursery.[3] Sarah Purdy was indicted, in 1682, in the same county, for shelling corn on Sunday[4]; John Fulford, in 1685, for fetching a pair of shoes from the maker's at his master's

---

[1] Minutes of House of Burgesses, May 10, 1699, B. T. Va., vol. lii.

[2] Hening's *Statutes*, vol. iii., p. 168. In 1690, Nicholson issued a proclamation calling upon the justices of the peace to enforce the laws passed to prevent a violation of Sunday; see York County Records, vol. 1687–91, p. 522, Va. St. Libr.

[3] Lower Norfolk County Records, Orders Oct. 16, 1678; vol. 1675–86, p. 202.

[4] *Ibid.*, Orders June 17, 1682.

command; John Carpenter and Thomas Cortney, for fishing; Walter Wilder, for killing a deer; John Fleetwood, for going on a journey; Thomas Gordon, for selling liquor; and Elizabeth Cook, for getting drunk.[1] John Wright, of York, was presented because he had, on Sunday, ordered his slaves to bring water as a preparation for planting tobacco.[2] In 1686, Henry Turner was indicted in Henrico for stripping tobacco on Sunday; and in Middlesex, in 1690, Alexander Smith, also indicted for the same offense, was tried by a jury and condemned to pay a large fine for the use of the parish.[3] Two years afterwards, Francis James, of Richmond county, was presented for selling cider on the same day[4]; whilst about the same time, William Cocke, of Henrico, was presented for "carrying a bag of wheate" on the Sabbath[5]; Robert Deputy, of Essex, for playing cards[6]; Thomas Smith, of Accomac, for fetching a runlet of cider; John Fenn, of the same county, for picking up tobacco[7]; and Henry Jackson, of Northampton, a mulatto, for driving a cart.[8]

Sometimes the violation of the Sabbath took a more turbulent form; for instance, in 1692, William Thorn-

[1] Lower Norfolk County Records, vol. 1675–86, p. 219².

[2] York County Records, vol. 1675–84, orig. p. 606.

[3] Henrico County Records, vol. 1677–92, orig. pp. 402, 431. "On going to Turner's house, the deponent met Turner at ye door with about half a dozen leaves of stripped tobacco in his hands, and going in, deponent see Turner's wife a stripping tobacco; ye deponent asked him saying: 'Harry what makes you stripp tobᵒ on Sunday?' and he replied he wanted one layer to fill up a hogshead." The reference to Smith will be found in Middlesex County Records, Orders Febry. 2, 1690.

[4] Richmond County Records, Orders Nov. 2, 1692.

[5] Henrico County Records, Orders June 2, 1690.

[6] Essex County Records, Orders April 10, 1693.

[7] Accomac County Records, vol. 1670–97, pp. 146, 176.

[8] Northampton County Records, 1689–98, p. 427.

bury, of Richmond county, was indicted because he had, on several occasions, at divine service, uttered extravagant words in an audible voice, which had greatly disturbed the congregation; and he had even gone so far as to lay violent hands upon persons who were present.[1] Sometimes, the violation took the form of profane swearing as well as of fighting[2]; sometimes, as we have already seen, of fiddling and dancing.[3]

It is evident from the preceding instances, which might be multiplied almost indefinitely, that, during the Seventeenth century, the supervision exercised by the authorities to ensure a proper observance of the Sabbath was, in some respects, quite as strict in Virginia as it was in New England, where the stern and austere code of the Puritans was so rigidly enforced in all the departments of life. Even the most trivial violations of the sacred character of the day were invariably punished; and this seems all the more remarkable in a community where all the amusements and pleasures within the people's reach were heartily encouraged provided that they were not carried to a point dangerous to the peace and moral health of society.

---

[1] Richmond County Records, Orders Nov. 2, 1692.

[2] See case of John Knox, Elizabeth City County Records, Orders Sept. 18, 1695.

[3] In addition to the cases already mentioned, see that of William Johnson in Accomac County Records, vol. 1697–1705, folio p. 43.

CHAPTER IV

Public Morals: Drunkenness and Profanity

WHILE there was a strong disposition among the members of all classes to drink rather freely, still there are many evidences that, when this disposition was pressed to the point of open intemperance, the law stepped in to check and repress it. There was no opposition to the enjoyment of liquor taken in moderation, but there was a determined hostility to its being taken in excess. The regulations to prevent this were among the strictest adopted during that period to root up vice in general; at the same time, they reveal that there was no intention to put an end to a reasonable degree of drinking.

As early as 1619, when the first General Assembly to meet in the Colony convened, a law was passed to punish drunkenness. If it happened to be the first offence of the person guilty, he was to be merely reproved in private by the minister of his parish; if his second, then he was to be rebuked in public; and if his third, was to be imprisoned during twelve hours in the house of the provost marshal. If the drunkenness was repeated, in spite of this last penalty, he was to receive such punishment as the Governor and Council should think his case should call for.[1] In 1623, the

[1] Minutes of Assembly, 1619, p. 20, *Colonial Records of Virginia*, Senate Doct., Extra, 1874.

General Assembly heartily confirmed a proclamation recently issued by those officers for the prevention of the same vice.[1] Under an Act passed in 1631, a person guilty of intoxication was required to pay five shillings in every instance in which he had been detected[2]; and again, in the following year, the same penalty was imposed.[3]

That the repression of drunkenness was strictly enforced in all parts of the Colony is revealed by numerous entries in the county records. For example, in 1638, John Vaughan, Samson Robins, and their wives, of Accomac, were condemned to sit in the stocks during the progress of divine service in the parish church because they had been found intoxicated; and twelve months afterwards, the same punishment was inflicted on David Wheatley for the like offence.[4] This sentence was perhaps passed on these persons owing to their inability to pay the fine prescribed. In 1648, the county court of Lower Norfolk required Rowland Morgan, as a penalty for his having been guilty of the "loathesome sinn of drunkenness," to build a pair of stocks, and set them up in front of the court-house door.[5] At this time, the common punishment for this form of vice seems to have been, at least for members of the very lowest class in the community, to place the culprit in this implement, where he would be exposed to the gaze, and perhaps to the missiles of the jeering onlookers.[6] If, however, the culprit was a

[1] British Colonial Papers, vol. iii., No. 9.

[2] Randolph MS., vol. iii., p. 217.

[3] Hening's *Statutes*, vol. i., p. 193. This provision was taken from the English Statute, 4 Jac. I., Cap. 5.

[4] Accomac County Records, vol. 1632–40, pp. 129, 145, Va. St. Libr.   [5] Lower Norfolk County Records, vol. 1646–51, p. 104.

[6] See a case in Lower Norfolk County Records, vol. 1656–66, p. 18.

servant, or a person not yet of age, his master or parents could obtain for him exemption from such disgrace by paying his fine; and, no doubt, this course was also open to any person found guilty of the same vice who had sufficient means at his disposal to meet the charge.[1] By an Act of Assembly passed in 1657–8 it was declared that no drunkard should be capable of holding public office; and three convictions were to be taken as proving such a character.[2]

Perhaps, there was no county in Virginia during the Seventeenth century in which there was more laxness in the smaller morals than in Henrico, a condition quite probably due to the fact that the county was both thickly settled and situated directly on the frontier. It will be interesting to investigate how far drunkenness prevailed in that community at this period as almost certainly reflecting the most extreme license in this form of self-indulgence then to be observed in Virginia. The reports of the grand juries, show, however, that nowhere was the vice more carefully watched or more promptly punished. In the presentments for 1678 seven citizens were named as having been "disguised with drink," two of whom were of the highest social rank.[3] In 1685, the number indicted at one session of

---

[1] Hening's *Statutes*, vol. i., p. 433. See case of Richard Wilson in Northampton County Records, vol. 1657–64, folio p. 34. If the offense was attended with aggravated circumstances, it is probable that a fine alone was not considered to be sufficient punishment. The following is from the York Records: "Whereas Nicholas Tailor was presented to this Court by the vestry of the Poquoson for coming out of the church drunk, and in full view of the congregation in tyme of divine service, there spewing, It is ordered that for his sd. offense, he be put in the stocks, and there remain until released by the Court." York County Records, vol. 1664–72, p. 36, Va. St. Libr.   [2] Hening's *Statutes*, vol. i., p. 433.

[3] Henrico County Records, vol. 1677–92, orig. p. 70.

court did not exceed six; and each of these, it seems, had of his own motion admitted his guilt. One of the grand jurymen making the report presented a fellow juryman, who promptly presented his accuser for the same offense. It is notable that, on this occasion, five of the grand jury had no charge of a like kind to advance against any person in the community.[1] At another session of the same court held in the course of this year, there were only two indictments for drunkenness[2]; while during the term held in June, 1686, three persons alone were presented for this vice; and in 1690, five. It shows the strict manner in which the grand jurymen interpreted their duty that, among those persons indicted in the course of 1690, was James More, who was presented on the ground that he had been overheard to say: "I am devilishly cold and fuddled."[3] In 1691, two cases were dismissed because the persons charged were able to swear that, although they had been drinking, yet they were in full possession of their senses, with memory perfect, and capable of performing any business assigned to them.[4] The court, however, declined to admit that the fact that a person was "deep in liquor" at the time was any palliation of violent conduct; when, in 1692, Captain Chamberlaine offered this as his excuse for breaking out of prison, to which he had been temporarily committed, the justices sternly replied that drunkenness was an ill argument "to justify any offence."[5] There seems to have been only one person indicted for intoxication

---

[1] Henrico County Records, vol. 1677–92, orig. p. 336.

[2] *Ibid*, vol. 1677–92, orig. p. 312.

[3] *Ibid*, vol. 1677–92, orig. p. 372; vol. 1688–97, pp. 133–4 Va. St. Libr.   [4] *Ibid*, vol. 1682–1701, p. 299, Va. St. Libr.

[5] *Ibid*, vol. 1677–92, p. 431, Va. St. Libr.

at the term of court held in April 1693; and at a later term held in the same year, only two were presented for the same vice.[1]

The authorities during the Seventeenth century appear to have been fully determined to repress as far as possible the evil habit of swearing. Under the Acts of 1619, a freeman or the head of a family, who, after three warnings, persisted in his profanity, was to be fined five shillings for the benefit of his parish church; and if the person guilty happened to be a servant, he was to be severely flogged unless his master consented to pay a fine equal to the one imposed upon a freeman for the same offence.[2] The law of 1631 required that, for every oath a person uttered, he should be mulcted in one shilling; and by the Act of 1657–8, such a person, if he had been sentenced for the same offence on three separate occasions, was to be rendered incapable of holding any public office.[3] If the person guilty was a servant or under age, then by the terms of this Act also, unless his fine was paid by his master or parents, he was to be punished in the discretion of the district magistrates or county justices.[4] Under the military regulations prevailing in 1674–5, a soldier who persisted in swearing after he had been convicted of it at least three times, was compelled to ride the wooden horse.[5]

In the course of 1685, Abram Womack, of Henrico,

[1] Henrico County Records, vol. 1688–97, pp. 407, 536, Va. St. Libr. The innkeepers, for allowing drunken disorder in their taverns, were frequently deprived of their licenses; see for an instance, Lower Norfolk County Records, 1646–51, p. 126.

[2] Minutes of Assembly, 1619, p. 27, *Colonial Records of Va.*, State Senate Doct., Extra, 1874.

[3] Randolph MS., vol. iii., p. 217.

[4] Hening's *Statutes*, vol. i., p. 433.

[5] Colonial Entry Book, Acts of Ass., 1674–5, p. 70.

who, at this time, was serving on the grand jury, presented at a session of the county court Thomas Wells and his wife for swearing "in a horrible nature"; and on the same occasion, Major Thomas Chamberlaine was indicted for the like offense.[1] Thomas Wells seems to have been inveterate in his indulgence in profanity; "I came to his house," Edward Stratton testified in 1686, "and I heard him singing with his servant wench and Indian boys and swearing several bitter oaths. I thought there had been several drunken men. And he and his wife doe make a common custom of swearing and cursing on the Sabbath day."[2] The only presentments entered by one grand juryman in Isle of Wight at a term of the county court held in 1688, was one against one person for "swearing God's wounds," and one against another for "swearing God's blood."[3] A few years afterwards, there were, at a single term of the Henrico county court, as many as ninety presentments for profane oaths; and in some of these cases, the same person was indicted at least three times for the like offence; among those included in the list of the guilty were men of such prominence in the Colony as William Randolph and Stephen Cocke, which proves that no favor was shown to any one, however powerful or influential, by the grand jury in their effort to put an end to the evil.[4]

Apparently, profanity was not so prevalent in some of the counties of the Northern Neck, for, in the course of one year, 1692, there were only two cases reported by the grand jury in Westmoreland.[5] The vice,

1 Henrico County Records, vol. 1677–92, orig. p. 336.

2 *Ibid.*, vol. 1677–92, orig. p. 371.

3 Isle of Wight County Records, vol. 1688–1704, p. 58.

4 Henrico County Records, vol. 1688–97, pp. 133–4, Va. State Libr.

5 Westmoreland County Records, vol. 1690–98, pp. 66, 67.

however, seems to have been so generally indulged in
in] Virginia, in spite of the vigilance of vestries and
grand juries, that, during this year, the Governor and
Council gave directions that the law for the prevention
and punishment of swearing and cursing should be read
at least once every two months from the pulpit of each
church and chapel-of-ease situated in the Colony.[1]
This action on the part of the highest authorities
evidently stimulated the county and parish officers
to extraordinary activity. In the course of the same
year, one hundred and twenty-two persons were indicted in Henrico for uttering "wicked oaths"; and
in the following year, sixty-eight; of whom John
Huddlesey was accused of "oaths innumerable."[2]
In 1692, forty persons were presented in Princess Anne
at the March term of the county court for common
swearing; and in 1695, fourteen.[3] In the course of
1694, thirty-nine persons were indicted in Henrico for
profanity. One of these, Ann Stop, was charged with
having been guilty of that vice at least sixty-five times.[4]

[1] British State Papers, B. T. Va., 1692, No. 123, Unassorted
Papers.

[2] Henrico County Records, vol. 1688–97, pp. 321, 322, 407, Va.
St. Libr.

[3] Princess Anne County Order Book, 1691–1709, pp. 34, 78.

[4] Henrico County Records, vol. 1688–97, p. 536. Ann Stop was,
at a later date, appointed administratrix of her husband's estate.

CHAPTER V

Public Morals: Bastardy and Slander

ONE of the most common offences against morality committed in the lower ranks of life in Virginia during the Seventeenth century was bastardy, the explanation of which fact is to be found in the number of women, who, in search of employment as agricultural and domestic servants, came over either free, or bound under articles of indenture drawn before the ship transporting them had left the shores of England. These women, as a rule, had belonged to the lowest class in their native country, and not all of them had received lessons such as to imbue them with the strictest principles of virtue. After their arrival in Virginia, their contracts rendered it difficult for them to marry. Having paid a very high price for their labor, their masters, not unnaturally, were opposed to their entering a relation which was quite certain to lead to interruptions in their field work, perhaps, at the very time their taking part in that work would be most valuable, if not wholly indispensable. Not only would the birth of children make it necessary for them to lie by for a month or more, but it might even result in their deaths, and the complete loss of the money invested by the planter in their purchase. Independently of these considerations, many of this class of women were exposed to improper advances on their masters' part as they were, by their situation, very much in the power of these masters, who, if inclined to licentiousness, would not be slow to use it. In the corn and tobacco fields, and in the barns, the female agricultural servants of English birth were also thrown into a very close and promiscuous association with the lowest class of men to be found in the Colony, and the opportunities thus constantly arising, no doubt, led to frequent immoralities; and the same was true of the social intercourse after hours of labor for the day were over; and also during the various holidays, including Sunday, which the servants and slaves enjoyed. The fact also that most of these women in emigrating from their native country had left all of their kins-people and early social ties behind must have had an important influence in weakening that sense of responsibility for their own conduct, which might have resulted in more self-control.

That servant women in Virginia during the Seventeenth century gave birth to so many bastards was not due to any lack of strictness on the part of the authorities in enforcing the laws designed to discourage this form of immorality. At a very early period, punishment was inflicted for incontinence even though the guilty parties had afterwards married, and their child had been born in wedlock.[1] Anthony Delamasse and Jane Butterfield, having been arrested in Lower Norfolk county, in 1642, for living unlawfully together, received each a round of thirty lashes; and they were thereafter kept separate until they had been legally united. John Smith, also of Lower Norfolk, was, for

[1] See Lower Norfolk County Records, Orders June 4, 1640. Nine such cases were presented in Lower Norfolk at the December term, 1654; see Records, vol. 1651–56, p. 114.

the same offence, compelled to contribute one hundred and fifty pounds of tobacco towards the erection of a pair of stocks in front of the court-house. During this year, a woman was convicted in the same county of having borne two bastards.[1] John Pope, of Accomac, who had been summoned for improper intimacy with a woman, was tried and sentenced to build a ferry boat for the transportation of people across Plantation creek; and should he fail to do so, he was to receive forty lashes on his bare back, and on the following Sunday acknowledge his fault in the parish church in face of the congregation.[2]

In a case of bastardy occurring in Accomac about this time, the father was required by the county court to go before the congregation of his parish church and confess his sin, whilst the mother was sentenced to be whipped until thirty lashes had been laid on her bare back.[3] Edith Tooker, of Lower Norfolk, having been found guilty of the same offence, was ordered by the justices to appear in her parish church at the hour of divine service. Clothed in a white sheet, she was led in after the worshippers had taken their seats; the clergyman began at once to urge her to repent of the "foul sin" she had committed; but she, turning a deaf ear to his admonitions, "did, like a most obstinate and graceless person, cut and mangle the sheet wherein she did penance." She was for this act condemned to receive twenty lashes, and commanded to appear again in a white sheet in the same church, on the following

[1] Lower Norfolk County Records, Orders Febry. 15, March 18, 1642.

[2] Accomac County Records, vol. 1632–40, p. 123, Va. St. Libr.

[3] *Ibid*, vol. 1632–40, p. 120, Va. St. Libr.

A like case is found in Lower Norfolk County Records, Orders Oct. 15, 1645.

Sabbath fortnight.[1]   During the same year, two other accused were, at the hour of divine service, required to take their stand, each on a stool placed in the middle aisle, where, in white sheets and holding white wands in their hands, they were forced to remain until the last hymn had been sung.[2]

A conviction for adultery in 1642 was followed by a sentence under which both parties to the crime were compelled to throw themselves on their knees in the judges' presence and implore forgiveness; and at a later hour, each had to submit to a severe flogging.[3] Occasionally, at this time, the court, relenting under the influence of an expression of "hearty contrition and sorrow" on the woman's part, directed the punishment to be foregone[4]; but generally, it was the man who escaped the whipping. For instance, in 1649, in a case of bastardy in Lower Norfolk, the mother was condemned to receive fourteen lashes, and the father to pay the cost of building a bridge across one of the creeks situated in that county.[5] By an order of the justices of Northampton in 1648, an adulteress was dragged through the water behind a boat passing between two previously designated points.[6]

After the middle of the century, the offence of bastardy became more frequent than ever owing to the rapid increase in the number of female domestic and agricultural servants who were imported into the Colony. The records of all the counties show this.

[1] Lower Norfolk County Records, Orders Sept. 6, 1641.

[2] *Ibid.*, Orders April 12, 1641.

[3] *Ibid.*, Orders Aug. 15, 1642.

[4] A case in Lower Norfolk County Records, Orders Febry. 16, 1645.

[5] Lower Norfolk County Records, vol. 1645–51, p. 131.

[6] Northampton County Records, vol. 1645–51, pp. 148–9.

Of the indictments entered at the December term of
the court of Lower Norfolk, in 1654, twelve were for
incontinence, although in three fourths of these cases
the children had been born in wedlock.[1]   In the course
of 1662, nine persons were indicted in York for the
same offence[2]; and, in the following year, at a single
session of court, fourteen in Accomac.[3]   In the latter
county, at one term of a later date, there were ten
indictments for bastardy; and in 1666, eighteen in
Northampton[4]; whilst, in 1684, the whole number
of the like presentments in that county amounted to
eight.[5]   In this year, as in 1688, later on, the indictments were confined to this one form of immorality.
In 1688, there were at least three servant women
residing under Col. John Custis's roof who had given
birth to illegitimate children.[6]   Bastardy does not
appear to have been a common offence in Henrico
at this time, as, between 1682 and 1697, only about
eleven cases were presented, and of the persons guilty
at least two were women of the African race.[7]   In
November 1695, there seem to have been only two cases,
and in June, only three presented in Essex county[8];

---

[1] Lower Norfolk County Records, vol. 1651–56, p. 114.

[2] York County Records, vol. 1657–62, p. 418, Va. St. Libr.

[3] Accomac County Records, vol. 1663–66, p. 23.

[4] *Ibid.*, vol. 1666–70, p. 169; Northampton County Records, vol.
1664–74, folio p. 30.   In 1677, nine cases of bastardy were presented by the church-wardens of Accomac; see vol. 1676–8,
p. 48.

[5] Northampton County Records, vol. 1683–89, p. 53.

[6] *Ibid.*, vol. 1683–89, p. 377.

[7] Henrico County Minute Book for 1682–1701.   Two incestuous
marriages in this county were, in 1694, reported to the Governor by
the clergymen; see Colonial Entry Book, vol. 1680–95, April 21,
1694.

[8] Essex County Records, vol. 1692–95, Orders Nov. 12, 1695.

and during the same year, only five were presented in Westmoreland.[1] In August, 1695, two women were indicted in Elizabeth City for sexual immorality; and in 1698, four.[2]

How serious had become the burden imposed upon the Colony by the maintenance of illegitimate children is shown by the petition offered in the House of Burgesses by Col. Lawrence Smith, of Gloucester county, in 1696, in which, after dwelling on "the excessive charge" that lay on the parishes "by means of bastards born of servant women," he asked that more stringent methods should be adopted in order to diminish the drain upon the tax payers' purses for their support; but the House, after considering the whole question, decided that the laws in force were sufficient to cover the whole ground of complaint[3]; and this, as we shall see later on when we come to treat of the Vestry's duties was a statement strictly accurate.

In addition to the different punishments inflicted for the various forms of incontinence which I have already touched upon, an Act was passed in 1657–8 depriving the person guilty, when of the male sex, of all right to deliver testimony in court, or to hold public office. The latter especially was a severe penalty in an age when there were few men of any importance in the community not anxious to fill some position in the administration of the Colony's affairs, local or general.[4]

The authorities, during the Seventeenth century, showed equal firmness and swiftness in punishing those guilty of slander and defamation of character,

[1] Westmoreland County Records, vol. 1690–98, pp. 66, 67.

[2] Elizabeth City County Records, Orders Aug. 19, 1695, July 18, 1698.

[3] Minutes of House of Burgesses. Sept. 28, 1696, B. T. Va., vol. lii.   [4] Hening's *Statutes*, vol. i., p. 433.

or of spreading false reports. In 1662, it was provided that any one setting afloat groundless rumours calculated to disturb the country's peace should pay a fine not to exceed two thousand pounds of tobacco, and be required to give bond for his good behaviour.[1] A wife convicted of slander was to be carried to the ducking stool to be ducked unless her husband would consent to pay the fine imposed by law for the offence.[2] There were other forms of punishment for it; in 1634, for instance, a woman who had defamed another to her face by applying to her one of the most opprobrious of terms, was compelled to beg forgiveness of the injured person at church in the interval between the first and second lessons, and to ask the congregation to pray for her, the guilty one, in order "that God might forgive her great sin."[3] Deborah Glasscock, of Lower Norfolk, having, in 1638, without any ground, brought an outrageous charge against Capt. John Sibsey, was sentenced to receive one hundred stripes on her bare shoulders and to implore his pardon, first, in court in the justices' presence and afterwards in the parish church during divine service.[4] Two years later, Mrs. Thomas Causon raised a cloud of scandal against Colonel Adam Thoroughgood's memory by publicly declaring that he had "paid slowly or paid not at all"; complaint having been lodged against her by his widow, she was arrested and ordered by court to beg Mrs. Thoroughgood's pardon on her knees in the court room; and also in the parish church of Lynnhaven after the first lesson of the morning prayer.[5]

Sometimes, after asking forgiveness of the victim of

[1] Hening's *Statutes*, vol. ii., p. 109.   [2] *Ibid.*, vol. ii., p. 166.
[3] Accomac County Records, vol. 1632–40, p. 22, Va. St. Libr.
[4] Lower Norfolk County Records, Orders April, 2. 1638.
[5] *Ibid.*, Orders Aug. 3, 1640.

the slander, the author was compelled to submit to a severe flogging. A case occurred in Lower Norfolk in 1646, in which the guilty person, having first received fifteen lashes on his bare back, was sentenced to wear in court a paper on his head inscribed with the name of the person wronged; and this paper was also required to be worn in the parish church during divine service; and also at a public meeting, to be held at Elizabeth River.[1] Some years later, a woman, residing in Northampton, was punished for defamation by being condemned to stand at the door of her parish church, during the singing of the psalm, with a gag in her mouth.[2] Deborah Heighram, of Lower Norfolk, was, in 1654, not only required to ask pardon of the person she had slandered, but was mulcted to the extent of two thousand pounds of tobacco. Alice Spencer, for the same offence, was ordered to go to Mrs. Frances Yeardley's house and beg forgiveness of her; whilst Edward Hall, who had also slandered Mrs. Yeardley, was compelled to pay five thousand pounds of tobacco for the county's use and to acknowledge in court that he had spoken falsely. Hall, it appeared, belonged to the social rank of a gentleman, and for this reason, the sentence was not accompanied by ignominious circumstances.[3] When Francis Manning complained to the justices of this county that his wife and himself were often "upbraided by their neighbours with scandalous speeches," the court publicly announced that, should the offence be repeated, those guilty of it should suffer corporal punishment.[4]

[1] Lower Norfolk County Records, vol. 1646-5, p. 15. Capt. Thomas Willoughby was the person slandered.

[2] Northampton County Records, vol. 1651-54, p. 170.

[3] Lower Norfolk County Records, vol. 1651-56, pp. 83, 84, 97.

[4] *Ibid.*, vol. 1656-66, p. 82.

It will be seen, from the various instances given
relating to the profanation of Sunday, drunkenness,
swearing, defamation, and sexual immorality, that, not
only were the grand juries and vestries extremely
vigilant in reporting these offences, but the courts were
equally prompt in inflicting punishments; and that the
penalty ranged from a heavy fine to a shameful exposure in the stocks or the parish church, and from
such an exposure to a very severe flogging at the
county whipping post.   There are many indications
that the justices, if they erred at all, erred on the side
of severity rather than of leniency.   When we consider on the one hand, the size of the Colony's population, and, on the other, the comparatively small
number of prosecutions for offences of this character,
in spite of the extraordinary watchfulness of the authorities, an impression is created that the communities of
Virginia, during the Seventeenth century, were pro-
portionately far more exempt from these forms of
viciousness than contemporary England itself.   This
impression is confirmed by the direct testimony on this
point of one of the most intelligent observers who
visited the Colony in these early times.

The country is full of sober, modest persons [wrote the
author of *Leah and Rachel*], and many that fear God and
follow that perfect rule of our Blessed Saviour to do as
they would be done by; and of such a happy inclination
is the country that many who, in England, have been lewd
and idle, there, in imitation of the industry they find there,
not only grow ashamed of their former courses, but abhor
to hear of them, and in small time wipe off those stains
they have been formerly tainted with; if any be known either
to profane the Lord's Day or his name, or be found drunke,
commit whoredom, scandalize or disturb his neighbour, or

give offence to the world by living suspiciously in any bad course,—there are for each of these severe and wholesome laws and remedies made and put into execution. I can confidently affirm that since my beinge in England, which is not yet four months, I have been an eye and ear witness of more deceits and villainies (and such as modesty forbids me to utter) than I either ever saw or heard mention made in Virginia in my one and twenty years abroad in those partes.[1]

---

[1] Hammond in *Leah and Rachel*, p. 16, Force's *Hist. Tracts*, vol. iii.

CHAPTER VI

The Parish: How Formed

THE parish was the local unit for the administration of the religious affairs and the promotion of the moral health of the community. As one of the ordinary local divisions of England, it was established in Virginia at an early date; such a division existed in the Colony certainly in 1623, for, in the course of that year, it was provided by an Act of Assembly that a public granary should be erected "in every parish" to secure the people against the pangs of a general famine.[1]

Now, as at a somewhat later period, the determination of the boundaries of a new parish had, no doubt, to be finally approved by the General Assembly itself[2]; in 1642, we find this body instructing the justices of Isle of Wight to divide the county into two parishes along such topographical lines as popular convenience demanded; and when the limits of each had been carefully defined, to make a full report to the General

[1] Hening's *Statutes*, vol. i., p. 128. When the country was laid off into shires in 1634, each shire was divided into parishes, and also into precincts or boroughs for the constables; see Hening's *Statutes*, vol. i., p. 224. This probably signified merely a readjustment of the area of the existing parishes.

[2] Robinson Transcripts, pp. 226, 230. In 1639, Cheskiack and Lawne's Creek parishes were laid off by order of the General Assembly.

Assembly for confirmation.[1]   And in the course of the next year, this body, which had directed that the new county of Northampton should be laid off into two parishes, formally approved the determining lines adopted by the county court.[2]

This method of establishing a new parish was suggested by practical wisdom; in laying off the boundaries of such a parish, the questions to be considered embraced, not only the country's configuration, such as the presence of large streams and wide tidal creeks, but also the extent to which the population was either concentrated or dispersed.   Only persons residing within the limits of the proposed parish were thoroughly informed as to either, and in leaving the determination of boundaries to them, most frequently perhaps as represented by the bench of county justices, the General Assembly followed a course that assured the division most promotive of public convenience.

The parishes about 1643 spread over such a wide area of ground as to give rise to complaints that the services in the churches were neglected, and that the number of persons present at them was steadily declining.   In reality, it was not possible for a large proportion of the parishioners to attend owing to the great distance to be traversed, or wide streams or inlets, often swept by storms, to be crossed.[3]   In order to create a remedy for these physical disadvantages, the policy of dividing all the large parishes was systematically carried out in every case in which the size

[1] Hening's *Statutes*, vol. i., p. 279.

[2] *Ibid.*, vol. i., p. 249.   The name "Northampton ' was substituted for "Accomac."   Later on, Northampton county was divided, and its upper part was designated as "Accomac County."

[3] *Ibid*, vol. i., pp. 251, 347.

of the population justified it. In 1643, three parishes
were, with the approval of the General Assembly,
erected in Upper Norfolk county,[1] and a few years later,
the inhabitants of Upper Chippoak were permitted
to lay off a new parish, provided that they paid the
dues already assessed against them for the support of the
clergyman residing at Jamestown, and the special tax
imposed for "finishing and repairing" the church
situated at that place.[2] When, during the early part
of the Puritan Supremacy, New Kent became a county,
the parish of Marston was established within its boundaries.[3] In the course of the same year, the county of
Lancaster was divided into two parishes, the determination of whose respective lines seems to have been
referred by the General Assembly to the popular voice,
for it is stated that, by the justices' order, the inhabitants of all the country lying within the area of the
proposed new parishes were summoned to meet at a
designated place, there to agree upon boundaries that
would be convenient to each set of parishioners.[4] It
was perhaps possible, in such a case, for a county
court, of its own motion, to adopt certain lines of
division as a purely tentative step, but to leave their
acceptance to the popular vote. Whether the county
should be laid off in parishes by the pole, or by number
of acres, was generally decided by the people alone; and

---

[1] Acts of Assembly, 1643, MS., Clerk's office, Portsmouth, Va.

[2] Hening's *Statutes*, vol. i., p. 347.

[3] Randolph MS., vol. iii., p. 256.

[4] Lancaster County Records, vol. 1652–56, p. 152. About 1680,
the inhabitants of Pamunkey Neck petitioned the General Assembly for authority to establish a separate parish. A part of the
Neck had previously been embraced in St. Peter's parish. The
petition was granted; Assembly Orders, 1680, Colonial Entry Book,
vol. lxxxvi.

on their expressing a preference for a division by the pole, the county court would enter an order that this course should be followed.[1]

About 1656, the burden of providing for a minister was so heavy that the people inhabiting some of the newly formed counties were very dilatory in taking the steps necesssary for the erection of new parishes; which led the General Assembly to pass an Act requiring that all such counties should be at once laid off in parishes; that the determining lines should be agreed upon by the majority of the population; and that these lines should be confirmed by the subsequent action of the county court.[2]

Occasionally, it was found that the union of two parishes into one would greatly promote the religious welfare of the people, as well as reduce public expenses. Under these circumstances, the appeal for a change was, about the middle of the century addressed to the House of Burgesses, which, during the whole period of the Commonwealth, possessed the controlling voice in every branch of public affairs; for instance, in 1656, the inhabitants of Nutmeg Quarter begged that body to merge them in Denbigh parish as being contiguous; and the General Assembly, promptly acting upon their prayer, sent an order to the court of the county in which Denbigh parish was situated, to submit the question of consolidation to the popular voice; and should the majority be favorable to that course, to carry it out.[3]

At a later period in the century, the appeal for throwing two parishes into one seems to have been

[1] Lancaster County Records, vol. 1656–66, p. 56.

[2] Hening's *Statutes*, vol. i., p. 469.

[3] Acts of Assembly, 1656, Randolph MS., vol. iii., p. 269.

made to the Governor and Council; thus, in 1691, Major John Robins and Mr. Thomas Harmanson, Burgesses from Northampton, petitioned those officials sitting in their ecclesiastical capacity, to make one parish of the two situated in that county; they based their prayer upon the ground that each of the two parishes was too small separately to support a clergyman in comfort and keep the church in repair, but that joined together, their combined inhabitants could afford to pay a high salary to the one minister who would serve for both, and preserve the single parish church in a sound condition. The Governor and Council seem to have thought that the request fully reflected the popular wish, for, apparently without ordering a general vote, which would have shown this beyond doubt, they gave directions for the two parishes to be consolidated, to be known thereafter as Hungar's parish.[1] A few years afterwards, the inhabitants of Sittingbourne parish dwelling on the southern side of the Rappahannock appealed to the Governor and Council to require a division of that parish, but this body declined to allow the step proposed to be taken unless the petitioners should agree to unite with the nearest parish situated on the same side of the river.[2]

Sometimes a parish that had once been fully organized sank, for a time at least, if not permanently, out of practical existence. There were generally several causes for this; such a cause was the presence of a soil that proved, after a short or long period of cultivation, incapable of further production on a scale sufficient to support a considerable number of people. A second

[1] Northampton County Records, vol. 1689–98, pp. 117–118.
[2] Orders, June 14, 1694, Colonial Entry Book, vol. 1680–95.

cause was extreme unhealthiness arising from the existence of a great area of swamp land, which spread abroad over the entire face of the surrounding country an invisible but deadly cloud of miasma. And, finally, a parish situated on the irregular line of frontier was not infrequently depopulated for many years during the course of an Indian War by fear of those savage warriors, who, brandishing the tomahawk in one hand and the torch in the other, carried ruin and death into every dwelling-house in their path not yet emptied of its inmates.[1] As soon as one of these periodical conflicts came to an end by the destruction of the Indian foe, or the signing of a treaty of peace, the white people not only returned to their former homes, but also began to hew down right and left the trees of the forest growing beyond the old settlements; parishes, which it had previously been unsafe to inhabit owing to their remoteness, came in time to be situated far within the chain of outer plantations, and the continuity of their organization was never again interrupted by apprehension of Indian invasion.

It was estimated that the number of parishes in Virginia in 1661 did not exceed fifty; nearly half a century later, in consequence of a disposition to consolidate existing parishes with a view to diminishing public expenses, the number had fallen off to forty nine.[2] As a rule, each parish fronted on a stream for a great distance up and down, but its boundary lines perpendicular to the stream ran back into the country only a few miles. The parish took this shape from its conformity to the situation of the group of plantations embraced in its area. Not infrequently, it was divided into enor-

---

[1] British Colonial Papers, vol. li., No. 101.
[2] Campbell's *History of Virginia*, p. 371.

mous halves by a wide river or broad inlet of the Bay.[1]
The presence of such a body of water, which had to be
crossed by any one travelling to the parish church,
should he happen to reside on the opposite side, had
a tendency to diminish the parish's prosperity, and so
soon as the size of the population justified it, a division,
as we have already pointed out, always took place.

Every parish was laid off into precincts.   This was
done by the vestry, who were authorized by an Act of
Assembly to create as many such divisions as the needs
of their parish seemed to demand.[2]

[1] *Virginia's Cure*, p. 4, Force's *Historical Tracts*, vol. iii.
[2] Henrico County Records, Orders March 1, 1699.

CHAPTER VII

Parish Government: The Vestry

THE administration of the affairs of each parish was in the control of a local body known in Virginia, as in England, as the Vestry. Each of the vestries was composed of the foremost men residing in the parish represented by it, whether from the point of view of intelligence, wealth, or social position. To the power derived from an office of acknowledged authority, there was added the great personal weight given by large possessions, force of character and intellect, and the very best education which England or Virginia afforded. It is rare to note in the county records the name of a vestry-man who, in signing documents, was only able to make his mark.[1] Many vestry-men enjoyed the further distinction of being members of the county court, the House of Burgesses, or the Executive Council. It does not seem strange to discover that even so powerful an individual as the Governor himself was generally at great pains to be conciliatory in his bearing towards the vestries, not only because they had practical control of their communities, and, through their representatives, of the colonial

[1] Apparently, Robert Todd and John Clarkson, of York parish, in 1647, were unable to write, but this does not follow positively from their making their marks, as they may have been physically disabled; see York County Records, vol. 1638–48, p. 275, Va. St. Libr.

Assembly, but also because their family connections in England were often able to affect favourably or unfavourably his standing with the persons to whom he owed his appointment, and upon whose good will his continuance in office depended.

In the long run, the vestries proved themselves to be, of all the public bodies in the Colony, the most tenacious of their right of independent action, and in their contentions with Governor, Commissary, and clergy invariably turned up the victorious party. Thoroughly understanding the local interests of their parishes, they showed, as a rule, a determination to support these interests, whether or not their conduct was opposed to immemorial English customs, or brought them in direct conflict with the most influential personages of the Colony. In the firmness and persistency with which they, on so many occasions, refused to be guided by anything but what was called for by the welfare of their community, they revealed themselves as the earliest defenders to spring up in Virginia of the principle of local administration free from all outside interference. Chosen by the people, they were truly the representatives of the people within the sphere to which their jurisdiction was confined; and the example set by them had a powerful influence in nourishing the popular form of government.[1]

Even more controlling was the influence which the vestrymen exercised from a social point of view. As the first gentlemen in the county, apart from the prestige they derived from being the principal guardians

[1] It was only during the last years of Berkeley's administration, when the influence of the reaction first set in motion in England under the restored Stuart dynasty seemed to overwhelm so many land-marks of freedom, that the vestries showed themselves to be out of sympathy with popular feeling.

of public morals, they were looked up to as the models of all that was most polished and cultured in their respective parishes. It was one of the happiest features of that early society that each community possessed in its vestry a body of men prompted as well by every instinct of birth, education, and fortune, as by every dictate of their official duty, to set the people at large a good example in their personal deportment and in their general conduct. To their influence is directly traceable a very large proportion of what was most elevated and attractive in the social life of the Seventeenth century; and to that influence, we are, in no small degree, indebted for the character of the distinguished men of Virginia who cast such renown over the great era of the Revolution.

Broadly speaking, the vestry's jurisdiction extended to the repression of all forms of immorality, the care of the indigent, and the administration of the affairs of the Church. In church government, as we shall see later on, the vestry's power, during certain periods of the Seventeenth century, ran very much ahead of the power of the same body in England, but, in a general way, it may be said that their respective jurisdictions covered nearly the same ground. Before entering into a detailed description of the various duties performed by the vestry in Virginia, it will be necessary to inquire as to the manner in which the members were chosen.

The earliest reference to the existence of a vestry in the Colony is to be found, perhaps, in the statement contained in a letter of Sir Thomas Dale to a clergyman in London, that, during his administration, the affairs of the Church were conducted by "the minister and four of the most religious men."[1]   Whether these men

[1] See Hamor's *Discourse* for Dale's Letter.

were known by the name of vestry or not, they exercised substantially all the powers ordinarily incident to that body.   They were, perhaps, not the first to be chosen for this purpose, but from the date of their selection, there is little room for doubt, there was always a small band of persons picked out of the congregation to aid the clergyman in carrying on the business, and in advancing the general welfare, first of the church at Jamestown, and, afterwards, of each additional church as soon as it was erected.   There was no custom prevailing in England more likely to have been followed in the Colony than this simply because it had a pressing motive in practical necessity.   In a community in which, under the operation of the plantation system, the inhabitants were very much dispersed, it required constant vigilance to hold each congregation together; and this could only be effectively shown by an organisation like the vestry, whose first duty it was to maintain the prosperity of their particular church.   It is not surprising to find in the earliest of the surviving county records frequent references to the existence of vestries.   Certainly by 1635 the name was in common use in Virginia to signify a body of men who had control of the church affairs of their parish.[1]

Who appointed the members of the vestry?   During the period that immediately followed the coming together of the first Assembly in 1619, this seems to have been done by the monthly court, certainly at times.[2]

[1] See Accomac County Records, Orders Sept. 14, 1635.   An order of the county court of Lower Norfolk, adopted May 2, 1641, is expressed in such a manner as to justify the inference that the vestry of Sewell's Point church had been established previous to 1640.   We find a reference to a vestry of that date in Robinson Transcripts, p. 14.

[2] *Ibid.*, Orders Sept. 14, 1635.

By 1641, the parishioners alone appear to have exercised this power, for in the course of that year, the General Court instructed the clergyman in charge of the church at Jamestown to issue a general notice to the inhabitants of the county that a meeting of all the people would be held at that place on a specified date to choose a vestry.[1] This manner of selecting was, in 1644, confirmed by an Act of Assembly, which provided that the choice should be determined by a majority of voices; and the same Act required that ample notice should be given by the clergyman and churchwardens to enable all the parishioners to be present on the appointed day.[2] The utmost care was to be taken that only men thoroughly fitted by ability, character, and estate to fill so responsible a position should be named.[3] In 1666, the court of Accomac ordered the reader of the parish church situated in that county to announce several Sundays in succession that the parishioners were expected to meet on a designated date at Mr. Thomas Fowke's house, and there choose the members of the new vestry.[4] We find the same court in 1670 confirming the election of vestrymen, recording their names and administering to them the oaths of allegiance and supremacy.[5]

By the provisions of an Act passed by what was known as Bacon's Assembly, vestrymen were to be chosen in mass at least once in the course of every three years; and they were always to belong to the rank of freeholders.[6] This body had, by this time, grasped extra-

[1] General Court orders, Robinson Transcripts, p. 235.
[2] Hening's *Statutes*, vol. i., p. 291.   [3] *Ibid.*, vol. i., pp. 240–1.
[4] Accomac County Records, vol. 1666–70, folio p. 14.
[5] *Ibid.*, vol. 1671–3, p. 174; Hening's *Statutes*, vol. ii., p. 25.
[6] Hening's *Statutes*, vol. ii., p. 356.

ordinary power, and the requirement that all the members should be reelected together at definite intervals was designed to lessen this power by making the vestry more dependent on the people. Each vestry had assumed the right to fill all vacancies at its board by a vote of its own members apparently without submitting at intervals to a reelection of the whole body by the popular voice, and had thus become self-perpetuating. In the long list of grievances presented by nearly all the counties to the Commissioners who were settling the disturbed affairs of the Colony after the failure of the Insurrection of 1676, one of the most vigorously expressed was that condemning this encroachment upon the parishioners' rights and earnestly praying that it should be corrected. The complaint of Isle of Wight went so far as to request that, not only should all the members of every vestry be elected once every thirty-six months, but also that no member of the preceding vestry should be eligible for reelection when the next choice had to be made.[1] This proposition was impracticable, but it shows to what an extraordinary point the abuses prevailing during the last year of Berkeley's administration had been pushed in every branch of the Government, local as well as central. At a time when the General Assembly persisted in sitting for half a generation without a single general election, and exhibited in all their proceedings the arbitrary spirit caught from the reactionary rulers of the Mother Country, it was to be expected that local bodies like the vestries, largely composed as they were of the same men, would display a similar determination to trample upon regulations, which, by requiring their repeated reelection as a body, made them dependent on popular favor.

[1] Winder Papers, vol. ii., p. 183.

The power of self-perpetuation without popular election at intervals, to which apparently they had no real claim, at this time, either in law or custom, seems to have passed from the vestries with the colony's pacification.   As early as 1684, we find the county court of Rappahannock designating the twenty-second day of November as the date for the "free election" of the members of the vestry of North Farnham parish. The people were directed to assemble for that purpose at the parish church, there to choose one half of the members from the upper parts of the parish, and the other half from the lower.   This was the only restriction upon the right of selection by the popular voice.[1]   In accordance with this mandate of the county court, the inhabitants of the parish met at the appointed place, elected the members of the vestry, and returned their names to the justices at their next session; not so much, it appears, to be approved, as to be entered among the permanent records.   The court promptly impowered the new vestry to lay the parish levies.[2]

Should no election take place at the first popular meeting, the county court proclaimed a date for a second one.   In 1692, the justices of Rappahannock appointed a day for the inhabitants of North Farnham parish to assemble, but when the day ended no vestry had been chosen.   This fact was reported to the court, which proceeded to appoint a second date for the election; but, in the meanwhile, it directed that this order should be read in the parish church on two successive Sundays.   In anticipation of a choice being made, Capt. William Barber, Capt. Alexander Swann, and Mr. Thomas Glasscock were named by the justices

[1] Rappahannock County Records, Orders Nov. 7, 1684.
[2] *Ibid.*, Orders Dec. 21, 1685.

to administer to the new vestrymen the oaths of
allegiance and supremacy, as well as the oath to execute
properly all the duties of their office.[1]

After the county of Richmond was formed from
Rappahannock, dissatisfaction arose because its court
had removed the persons chosen from that part of
Rappahannock, before its division, to represent it in
the vestry of North Farnham parish, and had then
ordered the election of new vestrymen. The Governor
and Council, to whom this complaint was made as the
final arbiters in all ecclesiastical disputes, instructed
the justices of Richmond to return to the Secretary's
office a full account of their proceedings respecting
these new vestrymen, on which a judgment might be
based; and this command was at once complied with
by the members of the court.[2]

Sometimes, the original order for the election of a
new vestry came from the Governor and Council, but
perhaps only after some controversy had been settled
by these officials sitting as an ecclesiastical court;
for instance, in 1691, we find the Lieut.-Governor and
the Council instructing the county court of Northampton to appoint a day for the people of the parish to
meet and choose a vestry. Only a small number of
persons assembled, and it was decided to defer the election to a later date; when that date arrived, the new
vestry was chosen "by subscription of the major part
of the inhabitants" of the county who were present.[3]

The county court was impowered to order the election
of a new vestry should this be shown to be advisable.

---

[1] Richmond County Records, Orders July 2, 1692.

[2] The complainants were Capt. William Taylor, John Lloyd, and
John Taverner; see Orders April 29, 1693, Colonial Entry Book,
1680–95. See also Richmond County Records, Orders July 14, 1693.

[3] Northampton County Records, vol. 1689–98, p. 117.

In 1697, a petition was presented to the justices of
Elizabeth City by William Mallory and John Sheppard,
in which they prayed for such an election; the justices
were equally divided in opinion, and the petition for
that reason alone seems to have failed.[1]

At the end of the century, the vestries were chosen
by the suffrage of the freeholders and householders;
but in the intervals between the elections of the entire
body by a popular vote, the vestrymen had power
to fill any vacancy in their board caused by death,
resignation, or removal from the parish; and this
power they had, no doubt, always enjoyed, as it was
called for as well by the necessities of parochial business
as by the convenience of heads of families, who could
hardly have been summoned for a new election every
time such a vacancy occurred.[2]

It is probable that, from a very early date, the number of persons composing a vestry was limited to
twelve; by an Act passed in 1660, it was expressly
declared that the membership should not exceed this
number[3]; and such continued to be the law until the
close of the Seventeenth century.[4] The meetings of the
vestry were held at least twice in the course of each
year; and the minutes of their proceedings were very
frequently incorporated with those of the proceedings
of the county court.[5] Very often, the members of a

[1] Elizabeth City County Records, Orders Nov. 18, 1697.

[2] Present State of Virginia, 1697–8, Section xi.; Beverley's *History
of Virginia*, p. 211. For vestry's power to fill vacancies as early as
1648, see Lower Norfolk County Orders Aug. 10, 1648; Lower
Norfolk County Antiquary, vol. ii., p. 15.

[3] Hening's *Statutes*, vol. ii., p. 25.

[4] Present State of Virginia, 1697–8, Section xi.

[5] For instances, see Lower Norfolk County Antiquary, vol. ii.,
p. 15.

vestry came together in obedience to a special order
issued by that court; for example, in 1662, the sheriff
of Northampton received instructions from the justices
to summon the "gentlemen of the vestry to meet at
ye towne church on the following Monday at eleven
o'clock"[1]; and in the same year, the vestry of Lynnhaven parish, in Lower Norfolk, were directed by the
court of that county to convene at their accustomed
place of meeting on a designated day.[2]   In cases of this
kind, there was, no doubt, urgent business touching the
parish's welfare which the justices thought ought to be
attended to at once.   In 1666, the vestrymen of the
parish situated in Accomac were summoned to the
next session of the county court with a view to following "ye order of public affairs"; this was probably to
enable them to acquire a more intelligent understanding of the public needs before they undertook to make
the bye-laws which they had been impowered to adopt.[3]
The same year the members of the two vestries established in Lower Norfolk were directed by the county
court to hold a meeting at the court-house for the
same purpose[4]; and during 1671, they were again
summoned to the same place in order that they might
consult with the justices "about several businesses
concerning ye welfare of the county."[5]   These "businesses" doubtlessly related particularly to matters
in which the purely moral health of the community was more or less involved.   The regular
session of the vestry seems to have been ordinarily

[1] Northampton County Records, vol. 1657–1664, folio p. 167.
[2] Lower Norfolk County Records, vol. 1656–66, p. 344[2].
[3] Accomac County Records, vol. 1666–70, folio p. 15.
[4] Lower Norfolk County Records, vol 1666–75, p. 4[2].
[5] *Ibid.*, vol. 1666–75, p. 63[2].

held at the home of one of its members; perhaps at the home of each member in turn; but it was also very frequently held (more probably in the summer) in the parish church.[1]

[1] "Deposition of Thomas Moundfort saith that ye very day Mr. Benjamin Read, late of this County, did die, there happened to be a vestry appointed at York Church and your deponent going there etc"; York County Records, vol. 1690–4, p. 255; see also Orders May 2, 1641, Lower Norfolk County Records. The following entry has many resembling it in the county records: "A meeting of Vestry of Elizabeth River Parish called to meet at the house of Lawrence Phillips, &c"; 1648, Lower Norfolk County Records, vol. 1646–51, p. 82.

CHAPTER VIII

Parish Government: Duties of Vestry

WHAT were the duties performed by the vestry? The first great duty of the vestry as a body seems to have been to appoint the clergyman of their parish. To this, reference will be made at length at a later stage in our inquiry. Their second appears to have partaken somewhat of a judicial character, as it involved an investigation into those cases of drunkenness, adultery, and the like moral offences which they were authorized to present, if well grounded, through the churchwardens to the county court for final prosecution. In an entry appearing in the Northampton records for 1648, there is found a long list of depositions taken originally at a meeting of the vestry called together to consider the question of the innocence or guilt of a prominent citizen's wife who was accused of infidelity to her husband. The verdict was unfavorable to her, and she was presented to the county court by the minister and churchwardens of the parish acting under instructions from the vestry; the depositions taken before the latter body were read in court; and the woman was a second time convicted, but now for the first time sentenced.[1] In a trial of a case of this kind, whether initially before the vestry, or finally before the justices, the churchwardens seem

[1] Northampton County Records, orig. vol. 1645–51, pp. 148–9.

73

to have acted the part of prosecutors. There is no evidence in the county records to show that every case of a grave moral offence presented by these officers to the county court was preceded by a formal inquiry before the vestry, as in the case occurring in Northampton, but it is probable that such an inquiry was sometimes held when there was any very serious ground for doubt; in undertaking it, the vestry would have been simply following, within their own jurisdiction, the example set by the grand jury in investigating the circumstances of a case to see whether there was a sufficient basis for an indictment.[1]

The third great function performed by the vestry as a body was to lay the parish levy. As early as 1640, there is found in the records of Lower Norfolk an order of court commanding the inhabitants of the county to obey an order of the vestry of Lynnhaven parish, requiring each person to bring to certain designated places three bushels of corn to be used in meeting the expenses of that parish. The tax was paid in such a dilatory way that the justices had been compelled to intervene to enforce a strict performance of the obligation.[2] In 1641, it was provided by an Act of Assembly that a vestry should be appointed in every parish of the Colony for the express purpose of laying levies and making assessments with a view to raising the funds needed to pay the ministers' salaries, to repair the church edifices, and to cover all other parochial charges as they arose.[3] In the following year, these funds were increased by the addition to them of all the fines

[1] See hereafter in Chapters on Legal Administration an account of the Parish Court in Henrico county.

[2] Lower Norfolk County Records, Orders Aug. 3, 1640.

[3] *Va. Maga. of Hist. and Biog.*, vol. ix., p. 53.

collected as a penalty for swearing.[1] The vestries, in the course of 1658, were empowered to settle, according to the conclusions of their own judgment, all matters relating to their parishes and parishioners, and this included the independent exercise of their own discretion in apportioning the levies.[2] An act passed in 1662 again confirmed their right to do this,— they were again authorized specifically to collect taxes for building and repairing the churches and chapels-of ease, for maintaining the minister, for buying and improving glebes, for paying salaries to readers, clerks and sextons, and for such "other necessary duties for the orderly managing of all parochial affairs."[3]

The vestry usually met in October to lay the levy, as, by the time that month had rolled around, the tobacco crop, having been housed and cured, was in a condition to be exported. A list of all the expenses incurred for parochial objects was made, and their sum increased by the percentage allowed for collection; the whole, which was always calculated in pounds of tobacco, was then divided by the number of tithables

[1] Accomac County Records, vol. 1640–5, p. 169, Va. St. Libr. "It is ordered by this Court that Mr. John Wilkins shall be amerct. 30 lbs. of tobacco for swearing a blasphemous oath in the face of the Court, to be desposed of at the next vestry."

[2] Hening's *Statutes*, vol. i., p. 433.

[3] *Ibid.*, vol. ii., p. 45. The following is an example of the parish levy; it will be found in Northampton County Records, Orders Nov. 5, 1668:

To Mr. John Taylor 8,000 lbs.

To ye Churchwardens for nails, timber and carrying in ye timber of ye church 4.425 lbs.

To ye French Doctor for looking after Tom Spelman 400 lbs.

To ye French Doctor for curing ye woman's leg 700 lbs.

To Richard Smith 2,000 lbs.

To Mr. Clayton 6,000 lbs.

To Mr. Hutchings and other charges 4,200. lbs.

residing in the parish. In this way, the proportion which each had to pay was arrived at.

During the period when the vestries claimed the right of self-perpetuation, without any election by the people, a suspicion was spread that these bodies did not act with the strictest fairness and honesty in making the annual assessments; this led to the passage of an Act impowering the freeholders and housekeepers of each parish to choose six among their own number, distinguished for sobriety and discretion, to occupy seats at the vestry board, and to take part with its members in laying the parish taxes; and should the freeholders and housekeepers neglect to appoint such representatives, or the representatives themselves fail to be present at the meeting of the vestrymen, then the latter were authorized to proceed without them.[1] As this law was renewed by the General Assembly in the following year, it would appear that it had given satisfaction.[2] As soon, however, as the vestry assumed once more a popular character (which took place before many years had gone by), the need of these assistants must have passed away with the restoration of public control over that body, and the renewal of the voters' ability to change its membership, should they have good reason for doing so. There always remained the right of appeal to the General Assembly whenever the tax payers desired an immediate remedy against a parish levy considered by them to be oppressive; for instance, in 1699, the citizens of one of the parishes of Lower Norfolk laid a strong protest against their vestry's last assessment, before the Committee of Propositions and Grievances of the House of Burgesses,

[1] Hening's *Statutes*, vol. ii., p. 396.
[2] Colonial Entry Book, 1676–81, p. 161, Acts Febry. 20, 1677.

which immediately referred the petition back to the justices of that county, with instructions to make a careful inquiry as to whether the complaint was well grounded.[1]

In a large number of instances, the amount of the parish levy <u>exceeded that of either the county or the public.</u> The following relative proportions of the parish and county levies, drawn from the Elizabeth City county records for the last decade of the Seventeenth century, are fairly representative of the relative proportions of these levies throughout the Colony at this time:—in 1692, the parish levy amounted to 22.138 pounds of tobacco in a total of 36,096 pounds; in 1693 to 22.130 in a total of 56,606; in 1696, to 20.768 in a total of 50,292; in 1698, to 20,500 in a total of 29,019; and in 1690, to 43.832 in a total of 50,292.

In laying the levy, it was in the vestry's power to exempt any parishioner from taxation for parochial uses on the ground that he was disabled by age or some physical defect from working in the fields. Such action on this body's part seems to have led quite invariably to exemption from the county levy, provided that it was attested to by the clerk of the vestry; it was by this means that Robert Russell, of Henrico, who had been afforded relief from the parish levy in 1697 because of senility and impotency, obtained a like relief from the county levy; and the same privilege was allowed Hagar, a free Indian woman residing in Henrico also, on the score that she was a very sickly person.[2] In-

[1] Minutes of Assembly, May 10, 1699, B. T. Va., vol. lii. A report of the results of the inquiry had to be returned to the clerk of the House.

[2] Henrico County Records, Orders June 1, 1697, April 1, 1698. The attestation in both cases was made by the clerk of Bristol parish.

numerable cases of a similar character might be given.

When a dispute arose as to the extent of the vestry's local jurisdiction, the point was reserved for the decision of the county court. In 1660, there came up for settlement the question as to where the tithes of a family, all the members of which resided in one parish, but some of whom worked in another, should be paid; should the tithes of such a family be divided between the two parishes, or should they be turned over to the parish where the common dwelling house was situated? The dwelling house of Mrs. Elizabeth Jones stood in Hampton parish, but some of her tithables were engaged in planting in Middleton parish; but, it would seem, they nightly returned to her home. The court decided that Mrs. Jones must pay to the vestry of Hampton parish the whole amount of the parochial tax levied on her.[1]

[1] York County Records, vol. 1657–62, p. 262, Va. St. Libr.

CHAPTER IX

Parish Government: The Churchwardens

A LARGE part of the most important work performed by the vestries was performed by them, not as a body, but through their direct representatives, the churchwardens. The duties of these officers were carefully defined as early as 1619 in the Acts passed that year by the first Assembly to convene in Virginia, an evidence that, even at this date, such officers were appointed for the churches then in existence.[1] How were they chosen in these early years? It would appear that, in 1632, this was done at a public meeting.[2] By a law adopted in 1641, it was provided that two churchwardens should be annually selected in every parish, but without describing specifically the manner in which the choice should be made.[3] Six years afterwards, at a time when vestries had been long established in the Colony, we find the justices of Lower Norfolk "nominating and appointing" William Lucas and Francis Land to be churchwardens

[1] See Minutes of Assembly, 1619, p. 27, State Senate Doct., Extra, 1874. There are no references in the minutes of this Assembly to vestries. Mr. Edward Ingle in his admirable monograph *The Colonial Institutions of Virginia* suggests that the four assistants to the minister in the time of Dale were churchwardens.

[2] Ingle's *Colonial Institutions of Virginia*, p. 168.

[3] *Va. Maga. of Hist. and Biog.*, vol. ix., p. 53. Reenacted in 1642–3; see Hening's *Statutes*, pp. 240–1.

for Lynnhaven parish, and Roger Williamson to fill
the same office in the other parish situated in the
county.[1]   Only two years later, it is stated that John
Hill and William Crouch were, on October 2, "elected"
churchwardens for the parish of Elizabeth River; and
they were directed by the county court to attend its
next term in order to take the oath of office.   There
seems no reason to doubt that, in this case, the choice
was made by the vestry.[2]   In 1652, two churchwardens
were named in Northampton by the justices and "ye
parishioners present" at the session of the court[3];
this constituted practically an election by popular voice;
and it is probable that the same method was not infrequently employed throughout the period of the
Puritan Supremacy in Virginia.   If such was the
method in force during this interval, an Act passed,
after the Restoration, in the winter of 1661–2, put an
end to it by requiring that two churchwardens should
be chosen by the vestry of every parish,[4] and this
continued to be the law down to the end of the century.
The churchwardens were named once a year, and the
members of the vestry served in rotation in order to
share equally the burdens of the office.[5]

The oath which, during the Seventeenth century,
the churchwarden was required to take throws much
light on the various duties expected to be performed
by any one holding this office.

[1] Lower Norfolk County Records, vol. 1646–51, p. 36; see also
Lower Norfolk County Antiquary, vol. ii., p. 13.   In 1644, the
county courts were authorized to call churchwardens to account if
they neglected their duty; see Hening's *Statutes*, vol. i., p. 291.

[2] See Lower Norfolk County Records, vol. 1646–51, p. 88; Lower
Norfolk County Antiquary, vol. ii., p. 87.

[3] Northamption County Records, orig. vol. 1651–54, folio p. 86.

[4] Hening's *Statutes*, vol. ii., p. 45.

[5] Beverley's *History of Virginia*, p. 211.

By the terms of the oath used in 1632, it was incumbent upon the churchwarden to present all persons leading a profane and ungodly life, such, for instance, as common swearers, blasphemers, violators of the Sabbath, drunkards, fornicators, slanderers, and backbiters; all disturbers of the congregation in church; and all masters and mistresses failing to catechize the young and ignorant dependent on them.[1]

The oath used in 1643 was very much broader in its scope: by its terms, the churchwarden was required, first, to present all who, to his knowledge, had been guilty of uttering "wicked" oaths, violating the Sabbath, profaning the name of God, or abusing His Word and Commandment, contemning His Holy Sacraments, or anything relating to His worship, committing adultery, fornication, drunkenness or defamation, or remaining away from divine service; secondly, to return a correct account of all collections made in accord with the vestry's assessments; and finally to disburse the amount of these collections in obedience to the vestry's orders.[2]

Under an Act passed in 1662, the churchwardens were also required by the general terms of their oath to keep the church edifice in good repair; to purchase the books needed for the registry of births and deaths; and also the communion cloth and napkins, and the cushions for the pulpit.[3]

---

[1] Hening's *Statutes*, vol. i., p. 156.   [2] *Ibid.*, vol. i., pp. 240–1.
[3] *Ibid.*, vol. ii., p. 52. "The grand jury having presented the Parish of Sittingbourne for not entertayning a minister, or providing a minister or reader, and for not keeping their Church in due Repair, the Court hath ordered that the Sheriff of their County or his deputy doe summon the churchwardens of the said parish in behalf of the Parish to appeare at ye next Court held for this County there to answer ye Sd. Presentment"; Rappahannock County Records, Orders January 5, 1690.

The oath prescribed for churchwardens in 1664 was in substance the same as that prescribed in 1662; it only required in addition that they should see that all the ceremonies and rites performed in the parish church should conform to the "orders and canons of the English Church"; and that the liturgy for the administration of the sacraments should be in harmony with the Book of Common Prayer.[1] The oath used in 1696 followed the general tenor of the preceding one.[2]

To whom were the churchwardens' presentments for the different moral offences made? Under an Act of Assembly passed in 1639, it was provided that these officers should make their presentments to the monthly courts; and at this time, therefore, their jurisdiction in the matter of such offences corresponded almost exactly with that of ordinary grand jurymen.[3] After a presentment was entered, the monthly court issued its warrant requiring the accused to appear at the next term in order to defend himself against the charge.[4] The Act of 1662 directed that churchwardens should, twice a year, first, in December, and secondly, in April, submit to the justices in writing a report of all "such misdemeanors as to their knowledge, or by common fame" had been committed while they filled the office; and they were also impowered to summon to the next session of the court the witnesses on whose testimony

[1] Northampton County Records, vol. 1664–74, p. 1. This oath was, no doubt, the one taken by churchwardens throughout the Colony.

[2] Colonial Entry Book, vol. lxxxix, pp. 181–2. The oath was taken before the county justices; Northampton County Records, vol. 1657–64, p. 106; York County Records, vol. 1657–62, p. 302.

[3] Acts of Assembly, Janr'y 6, 1639, Randolph MS., vol. iii., p. 231.

[4] Lower Norfolk County Records, vol. 1646–51, p. 122.

this report had been based.[1]   Here again we find that
the churchwardens were expected to supplement the
duty imposed on grand jurymen; save only that their
jurisdiction did not extend as far as felony.

One of the most important duties of churchwardens
growing out of their relation to the presentment and
punishment of moral offenses was to see that the
parish was saved from expense in cases of bastardy.[2]
When a female servant gave birth to a child, the father
of which was her master, they were authorized to sell
the mother for a period of two years; and the sum of
tobacco thus obtained was paid over to the parish.[3]
Sometimes, however, they compelled the father to
give bond that he would protect the parish against any
outlay on account of the mother and child while the
woman remained in his service.[4]   In the cases in which
the bastard was born of a free English mother and
a negro father, the churchwardens would order the
woman to pay fifteen pounds sterling within one month
after the birth of her child; and if she were unable to
do so, she was sold for a term of years to the person

---

[1] Hening's *Statutes*, vol. ii., p. 51.

[2] The first step towards effecting this seems to have been to
present the case of bastardy to the county court.   "Whereas complaints hath been made to me by ye churchwardens of this our
parish of Southwarke that Jane Sudley, a woman servant belonging
to William Carpenter, is lately delivered of a bastard child, and is
likely to be chargeable to sd. Parish, these are, therefore, to require
you to attach ye body of ye said Jane Sudley to bring her before me,
and my fellow Justices on Monday next at ye Wareneck about
11 o'clock"; Surry County Records, vol. 1684–86, p. 7, Va. St. Libr.
When the woman was convicted, the fact was reported to the
vestry of the parish, who then directed the churchwardens to take
the steps referred to in the text; see Henrico County Minute Book,
vol. 1682–1701, p. 139, Va. St. Libr.

[3] Colonial Entry Book, 1681–84, Acts of 1660.

[4] York County Records, vol. 1657–62, p. 324, Va. St. Libr.

offering for her the largest amount. If, on the other hand, the mother was a servant, the churchwardens waited until the expiration of her indentures and then disposed of her to the highest bidder for a period of service to last five years.[1]

It was always in the power of the master of the guilty woman, if not himself the father of her illegitimate child, to prevent her sale by voluntarily paying such a sum on her account as would remove all risk of the parish incurring expense through her misconduct; for instance, about 1686, Mr. Alexander Dornphin, of Rappahannock, confessed judgment to the church-wardens of St. Mary's parish, for that parish's use in the amount of five hundred pounds of tobacco, the fine imposed on Ann Palmer, his servant, for bastardy. A like case occurred in the same county in the course of 1690.[2] In both cases, the servants were required to reimburse their masters by an extension of their terms of indenture; and no doubt this compensation was, in 1696, also granted to John Collion, of Essex, who, of his own motion had bound over his whole estate to save the parish from any expense to it that might arise from one of his servants having given birth to a bastard.[3] And a like bond was exacted of John and Matthew Williamson, who resided in the same county, because they had recently imported several women known to be of lewd character.[4]

The county courts, however, exercised a close supervision over the action of the churchwardens in

[1] B. T. Va., 1691, No. 29.

[2] Rappahannock County Records, vol. 1686–92, orig. pp. 125, 252, Va. St. Libr.

[3] Essex County Records, Orders June 10, 1696.

[4] *Ibid.*, Sept. 10, 1697.

dealing with women of blown reputation to see that they were not treated with unnecessary harshness. In 1693, Elizabeth Paine was ordered by the church-wardens of York parish, for some offence committed by her, to leave the plantation where she had been living; she at once appealed to the justices of the county for permission to remain, as she had ground there prepared for a crop, which, she said, would be lost to her and her "poor children," should she be forced to abandon it. The court granted her full liberty to stop on the plantation until the tobacco had matured and been cut; and all persons disposed to interfere with her were commanded to refrain from doing so under the penalty of a heavy fine.[1]

The churchwardens were impowered to bind out, until he was thirty years of age, every bastard un-provided for; and if they neglected to do so, they ran the risk of being prosecuted in the county court.[2] Their jurisdiction also extended to all orphans who were lacking in means of support. In a case of this kind, it seems to have been usual to place the child with a planter or tradesman under articles of indenture to serve until he or she had arrived at the age of twenty-one, at which time the term of apprenticeship came to an end.[3] Such an orphan frequently received from the parish a certain sum in the form of tobacco to cover the ex-pense of apparel; in 1691, for instance, a girl who had been bound out to Daniel Neech, a citizen of Northamp-ton, through him petitioned the court of that county

[1] York County Records, vol. 1690–94, p. 287, Va. St. Libr.

[2] B. T. Va., 1691, No. 29; Middlesex County Records, vol. 1680–94, p. 5.

[3] Surry County Records, vol. 1645–72, p. 386, Va. St. Libr. In this case, the orphan was apprenticed until he should reach the age of twenty-four years.

to allow her five hundred pounds of tobacco in order to clear the parish of all further charge for her clothing; and this appeal was approved by the justices.[1] The churchwardens were also required to report to the county court the existence of every case in which parents were unable to afford their children a decent maintenance; and under these circumstances, they were authorized to bind these children out for a long term of years in which to acquire skill in a trade.[2] Their jurisdiction also extended to those cases in which the parents were not only very indigent, but also disposed to encourage their offspring in bad courses. In 1692, John Higgleby, of Henrico, was reported to the justices of that county as "an idle and lazy person," whose children derived their only support from what he was able to beg, or they to purloin. Having himself refused to bind them out as apprentices to tradesmen, the churchwardens were instructed by the court to do so, should they find that he continued to lead the life of a vagabond, without making any endeavour to secure for his sons and daughters an honest subsistence.[3] It was particularly incumbent upon these officers to keep under their supervision the treatment which the boys and girls they had bound out received from their masters, and of all cases of neglect or cruelty to give the county

[1] Northampton County Records, vol. 1689–98, p. 93. In 1645, the county court of Lower Norfolk directed the churchwardens of Lynnhaven parish to report to the vestry the amount of tobacco they had collected in the parish for the maintenance of an orphan, at that time in the custody of one of its inhabitants; see Orders June 16, 1645.

[2] Northumberland County Orders Aug. 19, 1691. In this case, Thomas Seddon, Jr., a child only a year old, was, with his father's consent, bound out to John Bird until he should reach his majority.

[3] Henrico County Records, vol. 1677–92, orig. p. 427.

court prompt information; in such a case, an inquiry was at once instituted by the justices; and if the charge was found to rest on good ground, not only was the master punished, but the child was transferred to another person so as to remove him from all chance of again becoming the victim of the same harshness.[1]

In a general way, it may be said that it was the churchwardens' duty to call attention to all cases of extreme poverty. The aged pauper was as much an object of their care as the most youthful orphan entirely lacking in means. The benevolence of wealthy citizens had, as we have seen, established in some of the parishes a fund for the maintenance of the helpless poor, but the number of parishes enjoying such a fund was necessarily comparatively small. The poor who were wholly without resources were almost everywhere directly dependent upon the vestry's aid, as extended through the churchwardens. As there was no such establishment in the parish as an almshouse, the pauper was supported at the parish's expense by boarding him at the home of some citizen willing to receive him for a sum agreed upon beforehand. Sometimes, the compensation assumed the form of an exemption from public and county levies; such was the return made to Francis Youell, of Henrico, who, at the solicitation of Bristol parish, had brought a "poor and impotent" person into his house under a contract with the vestry to support him.[2] Generally, however, a specific sum in tobacco was annually granted in the parish levy to anyone who,

[1] Richmond County Orders Aug. 2, 1693; Lower Norfolk County Records, vol. 1646–51, p. 120.

[2] Henrico County Minute Book, 1682–1701, p. 267, Va. St. Libr.

at any time during the previous twelve months, had taken care of a pauper. Very many instances of this kind are recorded. For example, in 1658, James Whiting, of York county, received a considerable amount from the vestry for his trouble and expense in looking after a "poore woman" who had died in his house, where she had been living during nearly three weeks.[1]   Again, in 1687, Hannah Moore, of Northampton, being entirely without means to afford her relief in her distress, was placed in the home of Thomas Lucas, with whom the churchwardens of Hungar's parish had contracted for her comfortable support in return for an amount to be allowed at each levy.[2] Sometimes, the sum annually received for the care of a pauper was estimated as high as two thousand pounds of tobacco.[3]

Beverley, commenting on the provision made for the indigent in Virginia at the end of the century, declares, with undisguised pride, that the pauper was not taken care of "at the common rate of some countries, that gave but just sufficient to preserve the poor from perishing, but the unhappy creature was received into some charitable planter's house, where he was at the public charge boarded plentifully."[4]   In writing these words, it is evident that Beverley had England in mind. The Colony was in a position to make a much more liberal provision for the destitute to be

[1] York County Records, vol. 1657-62, p. 101, Va. St. Libr.

[2] Northampton County Records, vol. 1683-89, p. 344.

[3] "Ordered that Dr. Robert Boodle doe keep Bridgett Press, an impotent woman, with sufficient diett, washing, lodging, and apparell until ye next vestry laying the parish levy, for which ye sd. Boodle is to have 2000 pounds of tobacco"; Middlesex County Records, Orders Febr'y 3, 1689/90.

[4] Beverley's *History of Virginia*, p. 223.

found in her different parishes than the Mother Country could do for hers, first, because food was so abundant in Virginia that the average expense of maintaining a pauper in a private house, where he obtained as much to eat as the members of the family, was almost always small; and secondly, because the number of paupers in the Colony was at no time large. During the Seventeenth century, the cost of food in England was generally high as compared with its cost in Virginia; and there were few English parishes not greatly burdened with poor persons entirely dependent on the parish rates for a subsistence. The opportunities for earning a livelihood in the Colony were too numerous to allow the creation of an onerous class of paupers in its different communities resembling the class that taxed so heavily the pecuniary resources of the English people. The happy circumstances which made it so easy, comparatively speaking, to support what poor did exist in Virginia operated to diminish their number by throwing open to all persons the door to at least a moderate degree of prosperity. So urgent was the demand for agricultural laborers throughout every period of the Seventeenth century that a man or woman in the possession of sufficient strength to plant and hoe corn and tobacco, or even to strip the tobacco when ready to be placed in the hogshead, never lacked employment sufficiently remunerative to afford good lodgings and an ample supply of food.

As a rule, only persons both physically disabled and entirely devoid of resources of their own sought the alms of the parish.[1] Sometimes, however, the church-

[1] Parish aid seems to have been sometimes extended only to meet one form of expense, such, for instance, as rewarding a physician

wardens afforded relief to wives, who, with their
children, had been turned out of doors by their husbands to depend for subsistence on charity. Mary
Lawrence, of Accomac, having (in 1676) complained
to the county court that her husband had driven her
into the road and refused to maintain her, the justices
entered an order that she should be returned to her
home; and that, if an inquiry should show that her
husband was a vagabond, he was to be seized and hired
out for a term of years for her and her child's support,
but, in the meanwhile, the latter two were not to be
allowed by the churchwardens to suffer for lack of food.[1]
In 1688, Mr. Samuel Peachey, of Rappahannock, on
behalf of North Farnham parish, reported to the
justices of the county court that Thomas Clutton had
stolen out of the county, and that his wife, whom he
had left behind, was so old and deaf that, unless the
remnant of her husband's estate was sold for her benefit, she would be thrown on the parish for a subsistence.
The court gave directions that an inventory of Clutton's
property should be at once taken in the churchwardens'
presence; that these officers should act as trustees of
whatever estate was found; and that it should be
expended by them towards the support of the deserted
woman.[2]

The collection of the amount of tobacco imposed

---

for the cure of a pauper's "sore leg" and the like; or providing
food without at the same time providing lodgings. For a case of a
single physician's fees for medical attendance on the poor amounting in one levy to two thousand pounds of tobacco, see Middlesex
County Records, vol. 1673–80, folio p. 148.

[1] Accomac County Records, vol. 1676–78, p. 12. Another case
of non-support will be found in York County Records, vol. 1694–97,
p. 348, Va. St. Libr.

[2] Rappahannock County Records, vol. 1686–92, orig. p. 94.

by the parish levy on all tithables in order to meet
the parish expenses, or the supervision of such collection, was one of the most important of all the duties
performed by the churchwardens as the agents of the
vestries. As early as 1643, an Act of Assembly required that an annual meeting of the ministers and
churchwardens of each county, in the nature of a
visitation according to the orders of the Anglican
Church, should be held after Easter before the commander and commissioners of the county's court;
and that, at this visitation, the churchwardens should
hand in a true and full report of all the collections and
disbursements which they had made in conformity
with the parish levy.[1] Where one of them had advanced his own tobacco to meet urgent parochial
expenses, he was to be saved from loss by having
returned to him an amount exactly equal to what he
had paid out.[2] The churchwardens of each parish
were authorized to issue a warrant of distraint against
the goods and chattels of all persons failing to pay
the parish taxes; we find this power exercised by them
in Accomac as early as 1632[3]; and they were also
authorized to issue a writ of attachment against
the general estate of any one guilty of the same delinquency. This process was used in 1663 by the
churchwardens of Elizabeth River parish against
Thomas Lambert's property in order to enforce a debt
of this kind amounting to three thousand pounds of
tobacco.[4] When the refusal to pay the parish tax

[1] Acts of Assembly, 1643, MS., Clerk's Office, Portsmouth, Va.;
see also Hening's *Statutes*, vol. i., pp. 240–1.

[2] Lower Norfolk County Records, Orders June 15, 1646.

[3] Accomac County Records, Orders Jan'y 7, 1632.

[4] Lower Norfolk County Records, vol. 1656–66, p. 360².

was based on some legal ground, these officers seem
to have had recourse to a formal suit to test the strength
of the claim; such a suit was in 1682 entered in Henrico
county court against Major Thomas Chamberlaine
for the sum of four hundred and fifty pounds of tobacco,
assessed by the vestry against him in laying the parish
levy[1]; and numerous cases of this kind appear in the
records.

As time lapsed, it became increasingly the rule for
the churchwardens to leave to the different county
sheriffs the task of gathering in the parish dues.[2]
There were several reasons for this:—first, in collecting
the county taxes, it required no additional exertion
or expense on the latter officers' part to collect the
parish dues also, as they were payable at the same
time; and secondly, should this duty be performed by
the churchwardens, who were generally among the
wealthiest and busiest planters in their community,
they would be forced to abandon their regular employments for the time being, at great risk of pecuniary
loss and personal inconvenience. It was because the
parish dues were so often collected by the sheriff that
the county court frequently directed the vestry to hold
a meeting for the purpose of laying the parish levy,
as this would prevent any delay on the sheriff's part
in collecting all the taxes, which could only be done
successfully at one period of the year.[3] Sometimes,
the vestry would petition the county court to allow
the sheriff to collect the parish dues; this occurred, in

[1] Henrico Minute Book, 1682–1701, p. 166, Va. St. Libr.; see also
York County Records, vol. 1694–97, p. 226, Va. St. Libr.

[2] Present State of Virginia, 1697–8, section relating to vestry;
Culpeper's Report, 1681.

[3] See Elizabeth City County Records, vol. 1684–99, p. 45, Va. St.
Libr.

1661, in Hungar's parish, in Northampton; the vestry of that parish requested that, not only should the sheriff collect the parish taxes, but that he should also distrain in all cases of delinquency.[1] Originally, it was customary for the inhabitants of Lower Norfolk to bring their parish dues, in the form of tobacco and corn, to certain places previously designated by the churchwardens; but this occasioned such general inconvenience, that, about 1671, the county court gave orders that the sheriff should collect the whole amount in the manner usual with the county taxes.[2] So thoroughly were the collections made by the sheriffs towards the end of the century, that Beverley informs us that the tobacco due the minister was delivered at the parsonage, or the nearest landing, all packed in hogsheads ready for immediate shipment.[3]

The churchwardens were assisted in the performance of their general duties by two officers known as sidesmen or questmen, who were especially interested in looking out for persons whose conduct made it necessary that they should be subjected to civil or ecclesiastical discipline. The sidesmen were also useful in keeping a vigilant eye on the condition of the poor.[4]

[1] Northampton County Records, orig. vol. 1657–64, folio p. 115.

[2] Lower Norfolk County Records, Orders July 15, 1671.

[3] Beverley's *History of Virginia*, p. 212.

[4] Meade's *Old Churches, Ministers, and Families of Virginia*, vol. i., p. 146, Phila. edition; *William and Mary College Quart.*, vol. iii., p. 174.

CHAPTER X

Parish Church: How Built

THE first religious services held in Virginia were held at Jamestown under an old sail cloth only a short time after the voyagers of 1607 had landed. The sail cloth was tied to the trunks of three or four large oaks or cedars, and as thus spread out afforded an ample shelter from the rays of the sun. The walls of this improvised sacred edifice were made of rails mauled from timber procured on the spot; the seats, of the round and unhewn logs; and the pulpit, of a bar of wood nailed to two trees. When the sky became overcast and rain fell, the services were held in a large tent brought over from England. Such were the simple makeshifts for a church building used by the English after the foundation of their first permanent settlement in America.[1]

It was not long before a much less primitive church edifice was erected; but even this new building was looked upon as temporary in its character. It was in fact neither elaborate nor substantial. It was made apparently of roughly sawn planks or unhewn logs, in the shape of a barn; the roof was covered with rafts, sedge and earth; and so, we are informed, were the walls; while the weight of the whole rude structure

---

[1] *Works of Captain John Smith*, Arber's edition, p. 165.

rested upon crotchets.[1] This edifice was destroyed
by fire within a few months after it was completed.[2]
Captain Newport had by this time returned to the
Colony with the First Supply, and as soon as this
catastrophe occurred, he set his mariners to work
to build a second church.[3]

The new edifice was, no doubt, of larger dimensions
than the one that had recently been consumed by fire,
for in length it extended sixty-four feet; in width,
twenty-four. This church was still standing when
De la Warr arrived at Jamestown. As this Governor
was moved by extraordinary religious zeal, it was
natural that one of the first acts of his administration
should be not only to put the old building in a state
of thorough repair, but also to make additions to it
that greatly improved its appearance. The interior
at least must have presented a very pleasing aspect;
—the whole chancel was constructed of the timber
of cedar trees; and of the same beautiful and sweet
smelling material, which was extremely abundant in
the surrounding forest, was also made the pulpit, the
pews, and the window frames. The communion
table consisted entirely of black walnut, whilst the
baptismal font had been skilfully hewed and carved
out of a single block of wood. The windows were
sufficiently numerous to let in a great flood of light;
and, as noted with admiration at the time, were of a
character to permit their being shut or opened without
difficulty as the state of the weather required.

The chancel and the interior walls were kept decor-
ated with the many beautiful flowers found growing

[1] *Works of Captain John Smith*, Arber's edition, p. 165.
[2] *Ibid.*, Richmond edition, p. 170.
[3] Brown's *First Republic*, p. 57.

in such profusion in the thickets of the neighbouring
woods; there could be no clearer proof of the loving
interest taken in the church than was shown in thus
adorning it from day to day while the wild flowers
lasted; and, no doubt, when the frosts of November
had destroyed all these blooms, branches of ever-
greens, like cedar, pine, and holly, were used to take
the place of the dogwood, the sweet bud, the daisy, the
clematis, and the arbutus. A steeple rose from the
west end of the church; and within it were suspended two bells, which the sexton regularly rang at
ten o'clock in the morning and at four in the afternoon,
the earliest sound of church bells to call Englishmen
to worship in the New World. It reveals the destructive influence of the varying climate,—now
extremely hot or extremely cold, now excessively dry
or excessively humid,—that this building, which was
far from being unsubstantial, had sunk into such a
condition of disrepair by the time of Dale's arrival
in 1611, that it was found to be in imminent danger
of falling to the ground.[1]

The religious spirit of Dale was revealed in the fact
that, after he had chosen Henrico as the site of a new
settlement, one of the first tasks he undertook as soon
as he had erected the palisade and watchtower, a
measure of defense, was to build a wooden church;
this edifice was designed to be only temporary, for
while it was in the course of erection, the foundations
of a brick structure were laid, which however were
never pushed to completion.[2] It shows how perish-

[1] Dale to the Council in England, May, 1611, Brown's *Genesis of
United States*, vol. i., p. 492.

[2] A Briefe Declaration, p. 75, *Colonial Records of Va.*, State
Senate Doct., Extra, 1874. *Works of Captain John Smith*, vol. ii., pp.
11, 12, Richmond edition.

able these early wooden churches were that, on Argoll's arrival at Jamestown in 1617, the church edifice there had become such a ruin that the people were forced to hold religious services in a storehouse.[1]

It was in this year that Mrs. Mary Robinson, a pious and philanthropic lady of England, bequeathed two hundred pounds sterling for expenditure, in part at least, in the building of a church for the Indians' use; in her will, she directed her cousin, Sir John Wolstenholme, who seems to have acted as her executor, to exercise his own judgment as to where this church should be placed; but he was required to pay over the gift for the purpose designated within a period of two years after her death. The General Court of the London Company ordered a memorial of her name and her benefactions to be hung on the walls of the room in which they held their usual meetings, whilst they sent instructions to all the clergymen residing in Virginia to commend her in their prayers to the favour of God.[2] With the fund thus obtained, a church was erected in Smith's Hundred.[3] The great massacre of 1622, which so completely altered the friendly relations of the settlers with the savages, no doubt put a sudden stop to all plans which might then have been under advisement for the building of additional churches for the Indians' benefit.

When Governor Yeardley arrived at Jamestown in 1619, he found a church in use by the people of that place which had been built by themselves without

---

[1] *Works of Captain John Smith*, vol. ii., p. 33, Richmond edition.
[2] For will of Mrs. Robinson, dated Febry. 13, 1617 (O. S.) see Brown's *First Republic*, p. 275; see also Abstracts of Proceedings of Va. Co. of London, vol. i., p. 29.
[3] Brown's *First Republic*, p. 286.

any assistance from persons residing elsewhere. As this edifice is stated to have been fifty feet in length and twenty in width, its dimensions were, by a number of feet, smaller than the dimensions of the church in which De la Warr and Dale had worshipped, although the population of Jamestown must have increased in the interval. The wooden church erected at Henrico when Dale had founded a town there had, by this time, fallen into a state of complete dilapidation. Apparently, there were no church edifices in existence on the other plantations in spite of the fact that many of these plantations contained numerous inhabitants; the religious services held there were quite probably conducted in private residences,[1] for, only four years later, an Act was passed requiring a house or room to be set apart exclusively for religious exercises in every settlement where "the people used to meet for the worship of God"; a custom which, no doubt, prevailed wherever the number of persons made up more than one family.[2]

It was provided by law in 1631–2 that the inhabitants of every parish should contribute an amount sufficient to build a church on a site selected by the clergyman and the churchwardens, and that, if the county justices neglected to compel the parish officers to carry out this order when disregarded, they were to forfeit fifty pounds sterling.[3] Seven years later, the Governor and Council, acting in their ecclesiastical capacity, gave instructions apparently to the county court and the local military commander to supervise

---

[1] A Briefe Declaration, p. 80, *Colonial Records of Va.*, State Senate Doct., Extra, 1874.

[2] Hening's *Statutes*, vol. i., p. 123.

[3] Acts of Assembly, 1631–2, Randolph MS., vol. iii., p. 216.

the erection of a church in the upper parts of Lower Norfolk; and the county court was required to enforce these instructions, should the contractors fail to carry out their agreement. The choice of the exact site for the building was, in this case, it seems, left to the commander and justices, and not to the clergymen and churchwardens of the parish, although it is quite probable that the wishes and opinions of the latter were fully consulted. The edifice had been completed only in part when Captain John Sibsey and Henry Sewell were appointed by the county court to procure mechanics to finish the work, the cost of which was to be met by a special tax to be paid by the people.[1]

Whilst the expense of erecting a church was not infrequently covered in part by the fines assessed by the county court as the penalty for the commission of various offenses,[2] yet the chief method of raising the necessary funds continued, during the whole of the century, to be the imposition of a tax, which fell, like the ordinary items in the county and parish levies, on the people at large. It is probable, however, that this tax was generally confined to the tithables residing within the bounds of the parish in which the church

---

[1] Lower Norfolk County Records, Orders Nov. 21, 1638. Under the authority of the Act for establishing ports, passed in 1654, the justices of Lower Norfolk county selected the plantation of William Shipp on Elizabeth River as the place where to build a new church and lay off a new market. Land belonging to Mrs. Yeardley situated on Lynnhaven River was chosen as the site for the second church, and also for the second market; Lower Norfolk County Records, Orders July 16, 1655; see also the Lower Norfolk County Antiquary, vol. iii., p. 32.

[2] In 1638, David Winley, of Accomac, was fined one hundred pounds of tobacco for slander, which was devoted to the erection of a new church; Accomac County Records, vol. 1632-40, p. 112, Va. St. Libr.

was to be built. In 1640, an order was issued by the
justices of Lower Norfolk that the inhabitants of the
particular area of country beginning at Mr. Peter
Porter's house and ending at Captain Thomas Willoughby's, should contribute, for repairing and finishing the
parish church, one bushel of corn and twenty-four
pounds of tobacco per poll. Special gifts of one hundred pounds of tobacco each had already been received
for this purpose from Mr. Cornelius Lloyd and other
wealthy citizens.[1] The building of this church had
been greatly delayed by want of nails and other iron
work, but these articles were in the end furnished by
one of the parishioners, who further showed his interest
in the edifice's completion by promising to give it his
personal labor for the space of a fortnight.[2]

An Act of Assembly, which had confirmed the
boundaries laid off for Lawne's Creek parish, relieved
the inhabitants of Chippoak and Hog Island of the
payment of one half of their dues to the clergyman
at Jamestown, provided that they contributed to the
fund for the erection of the new church at that place.
For this, the parishioners of James City had already
been assessed.[3] In 1642, the people of Hog Island

[1] Lower Norfolk County Records, Orders March 15, 1640.
When the parish covered a very wide area of ground, there was
sometimes a private arrangement between the inhabitants of one
half of it and the inhabitants of the other half to aid each other
in building two churches, one for each half of the parish. This
occurred in Fairfield parish in Northumberland County in 1696;
see Minutes of Council, Oct. 9, 1696, B. T. Va., vol. liii.

[2] Lower Norfolk County Records, Orders July 6, 1640. At this
time, there were parish churches at Lynnhaven and Sewell's Point;
and an order had been issued to build a chapel-of-ease at Elizabeth
River; see Lower Norfolk County Records, Orders Aug. 3, 1640,
May 2, 1641; also Lower Norfolk County Antiquary, vol. i., p. 143.

[3] Robinson Transcripts, p. 230.

were released from the obligation of making such a contribution because it was held that they resided too far away from the town.[1] To the church at Jamestown, as to so many others, private individuals had made liberal gifts to ensure its early construction. This fact we learn from a letter addressed by Governor Harvey and his Council to the Committee of Plantations in England, in which it was stated that, previous to January, 1639–40, they had not only presented out of their own purses a large sum to be expended for this purpose, but had induced numerous shipmasters and planters to imitate their example.[2] The edifice had not been finished by 1642, for, in the course of that year, the General Court entered an order touching its completion.[3]

About 1656, so many parishes were without an edifice for religious services that it was found necessary to pass an Act providing for the removal of the deficiency. It was ordered that every person residing in a parish lacking such an edifice and also a clergyman, should pay annually into the county court's hands the sum of fifteen pounds of tobacco, to be used towards the erection of a parish church, and the purchase of a glebe as a means of insuring a comfortable support to whatever minister should be called to fill the vacant position.[4] A few years later, it was recognized that so general a law as this might work a great hardship in the parishes occupied by a population

[1] Hening's *Statutes*, vol. i., 277.

[2] British Colonial Papers, vol. x., 1639–43, No. 5. In his will, dated 1636, William Beard left 500 lbs. of tobacco to a "new Church at James City," *i.e.* towards its construction; *Va. Maga. of Hist. and Biog.*, vol. xi., p. 148.

[3] Robinson Transcripts, p. 236.

[4] Randolph MS., vol. iii., p. 263.

both small and impoverished on account of the barrenness of the soil, the unhealthiness of the plantations, or some other cause of a like blighting nature; in a case of this kind, the parish was to be consolidated with one adjacent, and the inhabitants of the former of the combined parishes were to be required to build only a chapel-of-ease, in which the usual services were to be held.[1]

One of the different forms of oppression inaugurated during the period when the vestries, following the example of the Long Assembly, sought to perpetuate themselves without submitting to an election by the popular voice, was to levy a public tax for the erection of new churches when the old had, by mere carelessness, been suffered to fall into a state of neglect, though capable of restoration by the expenditure of a small amount. In 1675, the inhabitants of Accomac complained bitterly to the county court that such a charge had been imposed on them at a time when there was a church in the parish going to ruin merely because it had been half finished; and that until this was completed, it was contrary to "law and reason" to start building another one, especially when they had already been mulcted to "the utmost of their abilities."[2]

As we have seen, gifts from private citizens to aid in the erection of a new church were not uncommon previous to the middle of the century. After that time, such gifts became more frequent owing to the growth of population and the great increase in the wealth of individual planters. About 1660, a large amount of tobacco was contributed to the building of a church in Upper Machodick parish, in Westmore-

[1] Hening's *Statutes*, vol. ii., p. 44.
[2] Accomac County Records, vol. 1673-76, p. 362.

land county, by Nathaniel Jones, and also by one of
his kinsmen who was interested in advancing the
religious welfare of the people.[1]   Before a public levy
was laid for the construction of the church at Middle
Plantation in 1678, voluntary donations were solicited
of the parishioners, and in response to the appeal,
John Page and Thomas Ludwell each subscribed
twenty pounds sterling, and Philip Ludwell and Col.
Thorp each ten, whilst numerous citizens contributed
respectively five pounds sterling.[2]   Thomas Ludwell
showed special generosity, for, under the provisions
of his will, he left, for the same general purpose, thirty
pounds sterling,[3] a sum that had a purchasing power
of about seven hundred and fifty dollars in modern
currency.   The entire cost of building the church at
Middle Plantation was stated by Culpeper to have
been eight hundred pounds sterling, which represented
an amount equal in value to twenty thousand dollars
at least.[4]

In 1682, Robert Everett, of York, made a gift of five
hundred pounds of tobacco towards the erection of a
new church in Poquoson parish.[5]   Lieut. Gov. Nicholson, who was conspicuously generous in contributing
to the like objects, wrote, in 1690, to the justices of
Lower Norfolk, to remind them that they "should
not allow him to be disappointed in paying what he

[1] Westmoreland County Records, vol. 1653–72, pp. 122, 170.

[2] Meade's *Old Churches, Ministers, and Families of Virginia*, vol.
i., p. 146, Phila. edition.

[3] Will of Thomas Ludwell, *Waters's Gleanings*, p. 719. This money
was to be employed "towards building a church in Virginia."

[4] Colonial Entry Book, 1681–5, pp. 173–4. Culpeper stated this
in his report to the Board of Trade in 1683. The amount seems so
large that it is possible there was some mistake. See also *William
and Mary College Quart.*, vol. iii., p. 172.

[5] York County Records, vol. 1675–84, orig. p. 447.

had promised" towards the completion of one of the churches of that county then in the course of construction; and a few years later, he subscribed twenty pounds sterling to the fund which was to be expended in erecting a similar building at Yorktown.[1] The presentation of a site for a new edifice of this kind was not an infrequent àct of liberality on the part of wealthy planters; in 1658, Joseph Croshaw, of York, granted in fee simple, not only the ground on which the new church of Marston parish was to stand, but also a considerable additional area to serve as a yard; James Calthorpe, of Poquoson parish, made, in 1688, a similar gift; and their example was followed by George Barrow, of Sittingbourne parish, in Rappahannock.[2]

A contract between the churchwardens of Hungar's parish, in Accomac, and Simon Thomas, a carpenter, preserved among the records of that county, gives no doubt, a fairly accurate idea as to the method followed in building parish churches towards the close of the Seventeenth century. Under the terms of this agreement, the projected edifice was to extend forty feet in length and twenty-five in width. Its framework, which was to be constructed of wood, was to be supported by blocks cut from the trunks of the locust as a tree especially remarkable for the durability of its fibre even when exposed to the most trying variations of weather. This skeleton frame was to be covered with planks of the finest quality, whilst the

[1] Lower Norfolk County Records, vol. 1686–95, p. 145; York County Records, vol. 1694–97, p. 323, Va. St. Libr.

[2] York County Records, vol. 1657–62, p. 104; vol. 1687–91, p. 453, Va. St. Libr.; Rappahannock County Records, vol. 1656–64, orig. p. 309.

braces, studs, and rafters were to consist of seasoned oak. The ceiling of the old church, which must have still been in a sound condition, was to be transferred bodily to the new, and in reconstructing it, care was to be taken that it should "rest upon arches underneath the roof." These arches the carpenter agreed to build. The churchwardens, as the agents of the vestry, bound themselves to furnish the entire number of nails which would be called for in building the church; to supply the carpenter and his assistants with all the food they would need; and to transport to the site of the projected edifice whatever timbers would be required. Thomas, on his side, agreed to devote his attention to the work until it was completed, without allowing himself to be diverted by other tasks of the like nature, and without intermitting his labor except on "some great occasion"; and even this was, on no account, to draw him away from the church for a period longer than seven days. By way of compensation, he was to receive ten thousand pounds of tobacco, which represented a sum equal in modern values to about two thousand dollars.[1] Thomas seems to have been employed to erect more than one church, for, in 1681, he is found engaged in building an edifice of this kind in Northampton county.[2]

The great majority of the churches built in Virginia during the Seventeenth century were built of some

[1] Accomac County Records, vol. 1678–82, p. 240. As soon as a new church was finished, a committee was appointed by the county court to view it and make a report; see Lower Norfolk County Records, vol. 1656–68, p. 228; also Lower Norfolk County Antiquary, vol. iii., p. 103.

[2] Northampton County Records, vol. 1679–83, p. 187. The dispute referred to in this entry may have been connected with the new church in Hungar's parish alluded to in the preceding authority.

endurable variety of wood. There were a few, however, made of brick; such was the character of the material entering into the construction of the edifices at Middle Plantation and Jamestown. The church at Smithfield, which still stands in its original beauty and solidity, was also built of brick, and forms perhaps the most admirable specimen of ecclesiastical architecture in Colonial Virginia surviving to the present day. That fine structure, which recalls in its general aspect both within and without, so many of the ancient parish churches of England, bears silent testimony to the thorough organization reached at a very early date by the religious establishment in the Colony. It is hard to realize that a building like this, which would now appear more congruous if found standing in the valley of the Thames, or the Severn, in the midst of immemorial yews, was erected very probably within thirty years after the foundation of Jamestown. It offers very striking proof of the fact already dwelt upon, namely, that, from the very beginning, the settlements in Virginia resembled more the long established communities of England than the communities of a new country as conceived of by us in the light of our knowledge of the modern American frontier.[1]

One of the most frequent items in the list of expenses provided for in the parish levy was the cost of repairing the parish church from time to time. Sometimes, the outlay on this score was very heavy; in one case

[1] See Mr. R. S. Thomas's exhaustive article on the old brick church near Smithfield in Va. Hist. Soc. Collections. In 1695, a brick church was standing near Princess Anne courthouse; see Princess Anne County Order Book, 1691–1709, entry for Sept. 12, 1695. In that year, an order was entered for the building of the new courthouse "on the land belonging to the Brick church."

reported in Lower Norfolk in the course of 1656, it amounted to nearly seventy-five hundred pounds of tobacco[1]; and in other cases which might be mentioned the outlay was almost as large. A parish might well consider itself exceptionally fortunate should it have received from some benevolent testator a sum sufficient to meet the expense of repairing its church; such was the happy condition, in 1658, of the parish of Martin Brandon, to which John Sadler, a wealthy merchant of London, had left for this purpose a quantity of goods valued at twenty pounds sterling.[2] Nor was the need of renewal confined to the edifices built of such perishable material as wood:—in 1699, William Broadribb and Edward Travis, churchwardens of James City parish, petitioned the Governor and Council for public assistance in restoring the walls and pews of the church at Jamestown to their original sound condition.[3]

The principal seats in each church seem to have been held by the families of the wealthiest planters residing in the parish. The right to the exclusive enjoyment of a whole pew for an indefinite period was often granted in return for substantial aid in building the church itself; such was the reward which John Page and Edmund Jennings received for their generous contributions towards the construction of the church at Middle Plantation; such also Mr. Kendall for subscribing one thousand pounds of tobacco for the removal of the church in Hungar's parish to a new site.[4] Sometimes, the holder of a pew obtained his

[1] Lower Norfolk County Records, vol. 1656–66, p. 32.

[2] *Va. Maga. of Hist. and Biog.*, vol. vii., p. 211.

[3] They also requested aid in building a steeple; see Minutes of Assembly, May 17, 1699, B. T. Va., vol. lii.

[4] Northampton County Records, vol. 1689–98, p. 251. Mr. Kendall was on this occasion the only contributor.

right of permanent possession by having it built at his own cost; such was the manner in which Col. John Custis, of Northampton, acquired the one he occupied in his parish church; he seems to have paid Simon Thomas, the carpenter who erected the edifice, several head of live-stock and a large cask of cider to construct for him a pew, which, of all the pews, should be situated the nearest to the chancel.   In seeking to be so placed, Custis was either vain and desired to own the most conspicuous seat on account of the prominence it would give him in the eyes of the congregation, or he was deaf and wished to be in close range of the pulpit and reader's desk.[1]

[1] "The deposition of Thomas Lucas saith that in September last at ye raising of ye new church, Mr. John Custis came thither and spoke to Simon ye carpenter to make him a pew in ye sd new Church, telling him he would give him . . . tobacco.   Ye said Simon made answer yt he would not take tobacco to build it but had rather take creatures.   Said Custis made answer yt he would give creatures to choose, and ye sd Custis desired to have ye first pew in ye church . . . and farther ye sd Custis bade ye sd Simon to send to his house and he would give him a thirty or forty gallon cask of Cyder to drink ye next day."   Northampton County Records, vol. 1679–83, p. 187.

CHAPTER XI

Parish Church: Plate and Ornaments

THE plate and ornaments belonging to many of the churches during the Seventeenth century were both handsome and costly. Among the properties of St. Mary's, founded at an early date in Smythe's Hundred through the benevolence of Mrs. Mary Robinson, there were a silver communion cup, two chalices of the same precious metal, one white damask communion cloth, and several variegated carpets of damask with silk fringes. These different articles had been presented to this church after Mrs. Robinson's death by a benefactor who refused to reveal his identity; their fine quality was shown by the fact that they were valued at twenty pounds sterling, equal to about five hundred dollars in purchasing power. They appear to have been, for some years, left in Governor Yeardley's care; and when he died, were delivered by his widow into the possession of the General Court sitting at Jamestown.[1] A second benefactor, who was equally successful in concealing his name, presented to the Treasurer of the London Company for use in the chapel of the College projected for the education of

[1] General Court Orders, Febry. 9, 1627-8, Robinson Transcripts, p. 72; British Colonial Papers, vol. i., Doct. 46. Some of this plate is now in the possession of the vestry of the P. E. Church at Hampton, Va., and forms one of the most interesting relics of Colonial Virginia in existence.

Indian youths, a silver cup and plate for the wine and bread in the celebration of the communion; and also a carpet of crimson velvet and a table cloth of linen damask.[1]

Gifts of communion plate, or bequests of large sums to be invested in that form, were not confined to the period of the Company:—there are many instances of the like benefactions recorded of later times. In 1643, William Burdett presented the parish in Northampton by will with five pounds sterling for the purchase of a cup and plate for use in the celebration of the communion service[2]; and his example was followed, in 1654, by William Hawkins, of York, who directed that fifteen hundred pounds of tobacco belonging to his estate should be reserved for the purchase of a silver flagon, to be inscribed with his name and delivered to the churchwardens of York parish for use in the sacraments.[3] Three years later, Simon Overzee, of Lower Norfolk, placed in the hands of the churchwardens of Lynnhaven parish "a parcell of plate" which he had bound himself to buy for the benefit of the parish.[4] Dorothy Balridge, by will, in 1662, ordered her executors to obtain in England, at an expense of two thousand pounds of tobacco, "a bowle or cupp and chalice," and having seen that her name was engraved on each piece, to present them to the church of Appomattox parish situated in Westmoreland county.[5] Ten years afterwards, Christopher Lewis,

[1] Abstracts of Proceedings of Va. Co. of London, vol. i., p. 13; British Colonial Papers, vol. i., Doct. 46.

[2] Northampton County Orders, July 4, 1643.

[3] York County Records, vol. 1633–94, p. 65, Va. St. Libr.

[4] Lower Norfolk County Antiquary, vol. iii., p. 51. He was required to do this by order of Court.

[5] Westmoreland County Records, vol. 1653–72, p. 189.

of Surry, bequeathed to the churchwardens of South-
wark parish a silver flagon capable of holding two
quarts of wine; and about the same time, George
Watkins, of the same county, by will reserved a part
of his personal estate for the purchase of a piece of
silver plate for use in the church of Lawne's Creek
parish.[1] In 1677, George Jordan, also of Surry, left
by will to his parish church a baptismal bason of
silver valued at three pounds sterling.[2]

Argoll Blackstone, of York county, in 1686, instructed his executors to invest the proceeds from the
sale of one hogshead of tobacco in the purchase of a
wine bowl, which was to be engraved with his name
and presented to the vestry of York parish for use at
the communion table.[3] George Spencer, of Lancaster,
showed even greater liberality, for, in 1690, he directed
that twenty pounds sterling, or five hundred dollars,
of his estate at his death should be expended in the
purchase of communion plate for the altar of St.
Mary White-chapel in that county.[4] A few years
later, a large silver plate was presented to Bruton
parish by Governor Andros. The church in this
parish was the beneficiary of several other gifts for use
in the celebration of the sacraments; for instance, in
1694, Mrs. Kate Besouth bequeathed the vestry ten
pounds sterling for the purchase of an additional piece
of plate, on which her name was to be engraved.
Mrs. Alice Page, in 1698, made to the same church a
gift of one pulpit cloth and a velvet cushion of the

[1] Surry County Records, vol. 1671–84, pp. 54, 56, Va. St. Libr.
[2] Will of George Jordan, Surry County Records, vol. 1671–84,
p. 296, Va. St. Libr.
[3] York County Records, vol. 1687–91, p. 121, Va. St. Libr.
[4] Lancaster County Records, vol. 1690–1709, p. 11.

finest quality.[1]   Other articles for practical use were presented by generous testators; for example, in 1697, Thomas Cocke bequeathed one thousand pounds of tobacco to the churchwardens of Henrico parish, with the request that they should expend it in obtaining from England a bell, which was to be hung up in the parish church.[2]

In all those cases in which private liberality had failed to provide a communion service, the churchwardens were required by law to procure the necessary plate, and for this purpose, they were ordered to set aside a certain proportion of the parish levy annually until a sufficient amount had been accumulated.[3] Under an Act passed in 1662, they were also required to purchase for use in each church one large Bible and two Common Prayer Books, a communion cloth and napkins, a pulpit cloth and cushions, and also a bell with which to summon the people to worship.[4]   On at least one occasion, the King of England himself made a present of sacred volumes to the churches in Virginia; this occurred in 1683, when there were delivered in the royal name, through the Bishop of London, forty two sets, each of which consisted of a folio Bible and Common Prayer Book in calf, the Homilies, the Canons, the Thirty Nine Articles, and the Table of Marriages.[5]

As the parish church was generally situated at some distance from the nearest plantation settlement, its surroundings not infrequently came to have a neglected

---

[1] *William and Mary College Quart.*, vol. iii., p. 173.

[2] Henrico County Records, vol. 1688–97, p. 686, Va. St. Libr.

[3] Acts of Assembly, 1662, Colonial Entry Book, vol. lxxxix., p. 5.

[4] *Ibid.*, p. 5.

[5] October 24, 1683, Colonial Entry Book, vol. 1681–85, p. 263.

air, especially in summer, when, owing to the rapidly alternating humidity and dryness, the weeds sprang up and spread with wild luxuriance everywhere. It was sometimes found necessary to make special provision for the destruction of these weeds; in 1641, all persons in Accomac who had failed to conform to a general order requiring them to carry arms whenever they went abroad, were punished by the county court's compelling them to go to the parish church on the following Saturday, there to cut away all the foul growth obstructing the yard about the building as well as the different bridle paths leading up to it.[1]

As early as 1623–4, ample provision was made by law for laying off a burial plat in the neighbourhood of every settlement; and again, in 1639, the county court was required to choose a "convenient parcel of ground" for a public graveyard wherever one did not already exist.[2] In both years, there is reason to think that a site was chosen near the parish church in accord with the custom which had prevailed in England from a very early period. Such a burial lot, however, was much less used in Virginia than in the Mother Country. In consequence of the remoteness of most of the plantations from the parish church, the habit sprang up in the Colony at an early date of burying the deceased members of a family in the garden attached to their dwelling house; and this habit has continued down to the present times. Owing to the extraordinary vicissitudes through which the colonial homes of Virginia have passed, in consequence of the numerous changes in the political, social, and economic condition of the community, few of these private burial grounds

---

[1] Accomac County Records, vol. 1640–45, p. 88, Va. St. Libr.
[2] Hening's *Statutes*, vol. i., p. 123; Robinson Transcripts, p. 219.

have escaped entire obliteration; nor would their fate have been very different had they formed a part of a public graveyard connected with one of the churches of the Seventeenth century, for only a very few of these edifices were able to withstand the destructive influence of the same far reaching changes succeeding each other at long intervals.

Great care was taken from an early period that there should be public highways running to the parish church, and that they should be kept in good condition. An Act of Assembly, passed in 1665, required that these highways should be at least forty feet wide; that no logs or stumps should be allowed to remain in their beds; and that the bridges along their course should not be suffered to fall out of repair.[1] It was perhaps this necessity of maintaining permanently a free and safe passage to the parish church which gave the colonial vestries their jurisdiction over the public thoroughfares. Numerous controversies arose over the question of a right to use a bridle path leading to church, and it frequently became imperative for the county court to settle a dispute of this kind.[2] The first attempt to block a bridle path which had been

[1] Northampton County Records, vol. 1664–74, p. 9.

[2] *Ibid.*, vol. 1674–79, p. 269.

"Whereas at a court held for this County May, the 10th Anno 1676, In the difference depending then between John Chilton and Isaac Wall plts. and Nicholas Wren, deft., concerning a Bridle-way to their parish Church, It was there ordered for the determination of the said difference that a way should be forthwith layd out by Mr. Thomas Haynie, Mr. Fortunatus Sydnor, John Custis and William Hatcher, and make report thereof to the Court, who upon their said report doe find the way which leads from Nicholas Wren's to the old Road is the best way, being a Ridge and but one swamp on the way, it is, therefore, advised etc;" Lancaster County Records, Orders Sept. 13, 1676.

long used by the public without their right of enjoyment being attacked, was promptly rebuked by that body, and if repeated, was put an end to for good by a more decisive interference still.[1]

[1] Essex County Records, Orders May 10, 1694.

CHAPTER XII

The Clergy : How Procured

AMONG the clergymen of the Anglican Church, who, during the Seventeenth century, occupied pulpits in Virginia, not one, so far as is now known, was a native of the Colony. Some had been born and educated in Scotland, but a very much larger number had emigrated from England, where they had first seen the light, and where they had also received their first lessons in letters and theology. What had induced these men to abandon the country in which alone they could, if possessed of great talents, look forward to securing the highest honors in their profession? In a general way, it may be said that there were two influences leading the great majority to settle in Virginia: first, in order to acquire a benefice in England, the clergyman must obtain the favor of some person or institution having the right of preferment, and it was no easy task for a young divine lacking in powerful connections to commend himself to the goodwill of the individual or the corporation entitled to name the next incumbent of a vacant rectorship; secondly, the condition of the clergy residing in the rural districts of England during the Seventeenth century was not distinguished for such comfort, prosperity, and honor as to make removal to the Colony always appear a step distinctly disadvantageous.

If the picture drawn by English historians of the

condition of the great body of the English rural clergy (who constituted the vast majority of the members of their profession) during the Seventeenth century, be correct, then the situation of the average occupant of a pulpit in Virginia was far more happy and fortunate; and the only ground for surprise is that more of the young English divines did not emigrate to the Colony. We are informed that, in ten instances out of eleven, the English rural ministers of the gospel stood in a position hardly superior to that of a menial servant. A very large number either lacked a benefice at all, or the benefices they held did not afford a decent living; and under these circumstances, they considered it a reason for congratulation, should they be able to obtain a room in the garret and a seat at the table of some great landowner. In this situation, the clergyman, if a man of strong self-respect, was exposed to various forms of mortification hardly compensated for by the bed, food, and pittance in money he received as a private chaplain. Should he be advanced to some living in his patron's gift the chances were that it would not assure an income sufficient to meet the expenses of a growing family, and in consequence he would be compelled to act as a common labourer on his own glebe. His children, we are told, were in no better position than the children of the peasantry attending his church; the boys assisted in ploughing the land, and the girls became seamstresses and ladies' maids; it followed that the family of the average clergyman enjoyed no advantages which raised them high above those sections of the community represented by small farmers and upper servants.[1]

[1] Macaulay's *History of England*, Chap. iii. After allowing for the rhetorical exaggerations of this historian, the substance of

In spite of this thriftless condition of so large a proportion of the English rural clergy, the demand for
their services in Virginia could never be fully supplied.
This fact was not due to the supineness of the colonial
authorities.   From the foundation of the settlement
at Jamestown until the close of the century, there was
a standing invitation to English divines to remove to
the Colony as a field of labor in which their services
were urgently called for.   Rev. Alexander Whitaker,
writing to Rev. William Crashaw in 1611, begged him
to send at once over-sea such "young, godly, and
learned" ministers of the Church of England as were
lacking in employment at home.   Young men, he
declared, were the "best and fittest" for Virginia;
there was no need there of those who gave an exalted
significance to ceremony; nor was there any room for
those who did not follow a clean and scrupulous life.
What was wanted were men of discretion, scholarship,
and zeal joined to practical knowledge.[1]   In February,
1619–20, there were only five clergymen residing in
the Colony, though at that time it was populous enough
to be divided into eleven boroughs.   The smallness
of this circle led the London Company to ask the
Bishop of London to supply for the vacant pulpits
such a number of clergymen as would be needed to
supplement the appointments to be made by the

---

the testimony brought forward by him, and confirmed by the
investigations of other writers, shows at least that the general
condition of the English rural clergy at this time was one of great
pecuniary narrowness.   A remarkable tribute to Macaulay's
knowledge of English history in the Seventeenth century was paid
by the late Lord Acton, a man "fraught with all learning," in one of
his letters to Mr. Gladstone's daughter recently published.

[1] Whitaker's Letter, Aug. 9, 1611, Brown's *Genesis of the United
States*, vol. i., p. 499.

members of the Company itself.[1] The different in-
ducements held out must have led the required number
to settle in Virginia, for only a few years after the
Company had taken a successful step to render the
glebes profitable, we find it stated in a public paper
issued by this body that a "store of ministers" had been
imported into the Colony at the Company's expense.[2]

In 1629, Governor Harvey, just before he set sail
for Virginia, in a letter addressed to the Privy Council,
after touching at length on the Colony's crying need
of "able and sufficient" ministers, strongly urged that
six "grave and conformable" ones should be immediately sent out without cost to themselves for transportation, and furnished with the entire number of
books they would have to use in instructing the people.
And again, in 1631, after he had arrived at Jamestown,
he earnestly repeated his request, perhaps because the
Privy Council, whilst approving his first proposition,
had declined to bear the clergymen's expenses in
crossing the ocean.[3]

A few years after this petition was submitted, a
number of divines, deprived of their benefices in
England by the triumph of the Puritans, emigrated
at their own cost to Virginia, where they were received
with a hearty welcome. The author of *Virginia's
Cure*, who went out to the Colony about the time
the persecution of the loyal ministers began in the
Mother Country, lauded the great love which the
planters bore for the "stated constitution of the Church
of England," whether relating to its form of govern-

---

[1] Abstracts of Proceedings of the Va. Co. of London, vol. i., p. 45.

[2] *Ibid.*, vol. ii., p. 188.

[3] British Colonial Papers, vol. v., Nos. 22, 23; Randolph Ms., vol.
iii., p. 259.

ment or manner of public worship:—"we had the advantage of liberty to use it constantly among them," he wrote, "after the naval force had reduced the Colony under the power, but never to the obedience, of the usurpers"; and he goes on to contrast the fortunate condition of the Colonial church with the unhappy state of the church in England.[1] It was evidently thought by these emigrating clergymen that they had found in Virginia at least a land where the spirit of toleration prevailed, and where sermons might be delivered, and the lessons read, without fear of rude soldiery thrusting themselves into the pulpits to silence the preacher. Berkeley's heart turned with fondness to all things associated with the King's faithful supporters in the Civil Wars, but there was probably something more than this excusable prejudice which led him, in 1671, when he had grown to be an old man, to compare unfavorably the ministers then occupying the parsonages of the Colony with those "divers worthy men" whom the "persecution in Cromwell's tyranny" had driven to Virginia in search of an asylum.[2] These men were not young or unsuccessful divines who had come over in a spirit more or less of adventure and speculation, but clergymen of tried talents, and of ripe experience in their calling, who had been forced out of their pulpits practically at the point of the sword and bayonet.

Apparently, the demand for "able and sufficient" clergymen of the Anglican Church was as great in Virginia during the Puritan Supremacy as during any period of equal length in the Colony's history in the Seventeenth century. When, in 1655, Captain Thomas

---

[1] *Virginia's Cure*, p. 22, Force's *Historical Tracts*, vol. iii.

[2] Hening's *Statutes*, vol. ii., p. 517.

Willoughby was about to set sail "towards New England," he received a letter, signed by seven of the principal citizens of Lower Norfolk, in which he was requested to engage a preacher to serve in the parish; and as a means of securing a "godly and honest" man, whose abilities were "above distrust," Willoughby was impowered to offer an annual salary of ten thousand pounds of tobacco.[1]   In the following year, Mr. Moore, of New England, was invited to become the minister of the same parish; and should he accept, he was promised the transportation to Virginia of himself and his family without personal cost, with "present entertainment" on his arrival, a convenient residence, and continuance in the position as long as he should find in it contentment and satisfaction.[2]

It reveals the extraordinary pains the Colony's authorities were at to secure competent divines to fill the different vacancies among the parishes, that, in 1650, the General Assembly declared that, should a shipmaster or merchant import a clergyman into Virginia without any agreement with him touching the payment of his expenses, then such shipmaster or merchant should receive by the public levy, to reinburse him for his outlay, twenty pounds sterling, either in the form of a bill of exchange or of twenty thousand pounds of tobacco.   The parish in which the clergyman who had emigrated under these circumstances settled was required to raise this amount to assure its not falling on the taxpayers of the Colony at large.[3]

[1] Lower Norfolk County Records, vol. 1651–56, p. 158; Lower Norfolk County Antiquary, vol. iii., p. 31.

[2] *Ibid.*, vol. 1656–66, p. 29; Lower Norfolk County Antiquary, vol. iii., p. 33.

[3] See Hening's *Statutes* for 1656; also *Virginia's Cure*, p. 18, Force's *Hist. Tracts*, vol. iii.

It was with a view to securing a more certain means of supplying all vacant pulpits in the Colony that, in 1660–1, the project of establishing a college in Virginia was considered by the General Assembly.   In the Act passed for giving form to this project, it was declared that, owing to the great distance between Virginia and the Mother Country, it would perhaps be impossible to draw from England the entire number of divines needed to afford the people " those great blessings that always attend on the service of God"; and that steps ought to be taken for the education in the Colony itself of the "able and faithful" clergymen for whom so much room already existed.   And in a subsequent Act, the Assembly again declared that one of the principal ends sought for in the proposed college was to provide an "able and successive ministry"; and the people were urged to subscribe large sums of money or tobacco for its early erection.[1]   Had this institution been founded and carried to such a pitch of development that native Virginians aspiring to the priesthood could have acquired in it the necessary training in theology, there would still have remained an obstacle of importance to overcome:—there was no bishop in the Colony to ordain such candidates; and in order to pass through that ceremony, they would have been compelled to visit London to receive the blessing of the Bishop of that city, in whose diocese the Colony lay. This would have caused a double expense, namely, the expense of the outward and the return voyage, whilst the clergyman of English birth who came over ordained had only to meet the cost of the voyage to Virginia; this fact would, in the long run, have placed the native Virginian, anxious to become a divine of the Church

[1] Hening's *Statutes*, vol. ii., pp. 25, 37.

of England, at a serious disadvantage in competing with the imported minister.[1]

The very year in which the project of the college was broached, Rev. Philip Mallory was dispatched to England for the purpose of arranging that a greater number of English clergymen should be sent out to the Colony,—a step in accord with the pressing appeal of the General Assembly, which had already written directly to the King to solicit his personal influence with the Universities of Oxford and Cambridge to induce them to furnish Virginia at once with all the ministers needed to fill the vacant parishes.[2]   This appeal probably led to little from a practical point of view, for, only five years later, the lack of clergymen in the Colony was so great that the author of the pamphlet, *Virginia's Cure*, was moved to propose to the Bishop of London, as a certain means of meeting the want, that Parliament should establish in the two English Universities fellowships to be held only by persons who had bound themselves, after an enjoyment of seven years, to emigrate to Virginia, there to serve as ministers of the gospel during a period of seven years more; at the end of which time they were to be at liberty to return to England, should they prefer to do so.   This plan of

[1] According to the historian Campbell, the General Assembly never expressed a desire for the settlement of a Bishop in Virginia. He attributes the failure of that body to do so to the popular recollection of the cruelties practised by the English prelates in the past, but the omission was much more probably due to a natural reluctance on the Assembly's part to increase the public burdens by having to vote a large annual salary for the maintenance of such a dignitary.   In 1697, Nicholas Moreau, in a letter to the Bishop of Coventry, urged the appointment of a Bishop for the Colony, but the suggestion seems to have made no impression; see Perry's *Hist. Coll. American Colonial Church, Va.*, p. 31.

[2] Hening's *Statutes*, vol. ii., pp. 31, 34.

securing an annual supply of pastors for the Colony, which seems to have been a practicable one, was apparently never acted on.[1] It was a fit of disappointment, following, perhaps, upon the indifference shown in England when some such scheme as this was broached, which led Thomas Ludwell, in the course of the same year, to write to Secretary Arlington:—"I could heartily wish that my Lord of London and other great clergymen would take us a little more into their care for our better supply, since ye utmost of our incouragement will invite none to us."[2]

In 1680, the Council requested the Governor, as the only hope of filling all the pulpits of Virginia, to beg the Bishop of London to furnish the vacant parishes with "able, godly, and orthodox" ministers, of whom four should be sent over-sea by the very next shipping, and not less than two dispatched every year thereafter.[3] Half a decade later, Fitzhugh declared that there still existed in the Colony a pressing need for "able, faithful, and sober pastors."[4] During Nicholson's administration, some years later, a determined effort was made to procure such pastors from England; and so great was that Governor's zeal as a churchman that he cheer-

[1] *Virginia's Cure*, p. 10, Force's *Hist. Tracts*, vol. iii.

[2] Letter of Ludwell, Sept. 17, 1666, Winder Papers, vol. i., p. 209.

[3] Colonial Entry Book, 1680–95, p. 45.

In 1680, each of the three parishes in Nansemond was occupied by a minister. Of the four parishes in York, but one was vacant; of the four in New Kent, none; and the same was true of Gloucester. On the other hand, there was only one minister to supply the four and a half parishes of Charles City county, and only two the four and a half parishes of James City. Lancaster and Northumberland were each divided into two parishes, and there was but one minister in each county to supply them; and this was also true of Stafford, Warwick, and Henrico, the last of which counties was divided into one and a half parishes. British Colonial Papers, vol. lx., No. 410.

[4] Letters of William Fitzhugh, May 18, 1685.

fully bore all the expenses of a newly arrived clergyman until, on his earnest recommendation, the vestry of some vacant parish extended this clergyman a call.[1] Writing in 1697, Commissary Blair stated that there were then only twenty-two ministers to look after the spiritual interests of fifty parishes; the explanation of which great disproportion was to be found in the fact that a considerable number of these parishes were too impoverished to support a separate pastor.[2] Only three years later, Nicholson declared that there was still room in Virginia for six or eight additional divines; but that, although the want was one keenly felt, the people appeared to be extremely averse to the appointment of any more Scotch or very young clergymen, for there were several of both sorts, he added, "who hath caused a great dissatisfaction in ye country."[3] Nicholas Moreau has recorded that the ministers of Virginia at this time were, for the most part, Scotchmen, a fact due quite probably to the influence of Commissary Blair, who belonged to that nationality.[4]

One of the reasons most strongly and persistently urged for the foundation of the institution afterwards known as William and Mary College was that it could be made a "seminary for a Church of England ministry," the principal argument, as we have seen, so earnestly advanced in 1661, when a similar project was under discussion. Now, as at that earlier date, no native Virginian could legitimately act as a clergy-

---

[1] Blair's Memorial, Perry's *Hist. Coll. Amer. Colon. Church*, vol. i., p. 11.

[2] Perry's *Hist. Coll. Amer. Colon. Church*, vol. i., p. 11.

[3] Letter of Nicholson, May 27, 1700, Fulham Palace, Unbound MS. relating to Virginia.

[4] Letter of Moreau to Bishop of Coventry, Perry's *Hist. Coll. Amer. Colon. Church*, vol. i., Virginia, p. 31.

man unless he had been regularly ordained, and this
could only be accomplished by a voyage to England, a
journey which, from the heavy expense it imposed,
would have always discouraged many young men,
born and residing in the Colony, from turning to the
study of theology with a view to a calling in life.
As early as 1643, the General Assembly passed an
Act declaring that no pastor should be allowed to
officiate in Virginia who was unable to produce a
testimonial to prove that he had received ordination
from some Bishop in England.   The object of this law
was asserted to be to preserve the doctrine and discipline
of the Church in its original purity and unity, and to
insure the proper administration of the Sacraments.
It was again enacted in 1662.[1]   Thomas Ludwell, a man
thoroughly informed as to the ecclesiastical affairs of the
Colony, writing in 1666, stated that no one was permitted to perform all the functions of a minister of the
gospel in Virginia who was not in orders.[2]   As a rule,
the clergymen securing charges there had been ordained
by the Bishop of London, as the Colony had from
its foundation been subject to the jurisdiction of that
see.[3]   In the instructions received by Howard on his
appointment to the Governorship, he was expressly
forbidden to prefer a minister to a benefice unless he
could present a certificate over the Bishop of London's
signature testifying to the fact that he was "conformable to the doctrine and discipline of the Church of Eng-

---

[1] Hening's *Statutes*, vol. ii., p. 46.

[2] Ludwell to Lord Arlington, Winder Papers, vol. i., 209.

[3] Ludwell to Lord Arlington, Winder Papers, vol. i., p. 209; see
also British Colonial Papers, vol. xx., Nos. 125, 125, i. The Bishop of
London's jurisdiction was due to the fact that Virginia was originally
colonized by the London Company.

land"; and that, in his life and conversation, he was not open to the accusation of "ungodliness."[1]

In spite of these strict regulations, irregularities in appointments sometimes crept in, owing to the constant demand for clergymen to fill the vacant pulpits of the Colony. In 1680, Jonathan Davis, although not a qualified minister, "assumed to himself the liberty of the pulpit" in Poquoson parish, which really belonged to the Rev. John Wright; and the dispute between them was only settled by its reference to the Governor and Council sitting as an ecclesiastical court.[2] George Hudson, in 1695, was severely reprimanded by the same court because he had failed to secure a license from the Bishop of London authorizing him to preach, but as he was able to show that his ordination was strictly correct, he was not deprived of the right to serve as a pastor.[3]

A very common way of supplying the want of a clergyman in a vacant parish was to appoint a deacon. Godwyn, who seems to have judged everything relating to the church in Virginia with a prejudiced eye, in consequence of his indignant disapproval of the vestries' independent spirit, wrote with scorn of these "lay priests of the vestries' ordination," who, he asserted, made up nearly two thirds of the whole number of

[1] Instructions to Howard, Colonial Entry Book, 1685-91, p. 33.

[2] Minutes of Council, June 23, 1680, Colonial Entry Book No. 86. "Whereas one Mr. David Richardson, our late minister, for want of orders was found not orthodox, and, therefore, we hired him from year to year (to supply the place of minister so far as the laws of England and this country could make him capable) until we could supply ourselves with an able, orthodox divine, and for-asmuch as Mr. Isaac Key did present etc, this writing to certify him to the Governor for induction."—Northampton County Records, vol. 1674-79, p. 137.

[3] Minutes of Council, April 15, 1695, Colonial Entry Book, 1680-95.

pastors residing in Virginia. "They are the shame and grief of the rightly ordained clergymen," he exclaimed, " deacons to undermine and thrust out Presbyters, to administer Sacraments, and to read the Absolution."[1]

During the last decade of the century the see of London was represented in Virginia by a Commissary. The object of such a dignitary's appointment was, according to the English law, to supply the Bishop's office in the outlying parts, situated within his jurisdiction, which the prelate himself could not conveniently reach. The Commissary, however, did not possess the power either of ordination or confirmation, and his principal duty consisted simply of making visitations to the different parishes and reporting to his superior his conclusions as to their needs.[2] Previous to 1690, the Bishop of London had been represented in the Colony by Rev. William Semple, who, however, had received no regular commission.[3] In 1690, Rev. James Blair was appointed the first Commissary[4]; he had arrived in Virginia five years earlier, had first settled in Henrico county, but later on had become the incumbent of the pulpit at Jamestown, which he continued to hold while filling the representative office.[5] Blair was by birth a Scotchman, and had received his education in a Scotch University. His salary amounted annually to one hundred pounds

[1] *Godwyn's Negro's and Indian's Advocate*, p. 167 et seq.

[2] Hawks, p. 73.

[3] Campbell's *History of Virginia*, p. 345.

[4] His Commission was read in Council, June 4, 1690; see Colonial Entry Book, 1680–95, p. 354. A circular letter of Nicholson, addressed to every sheriff in the Colony, informed them that, in the spring of 1691, Blair would make a visitation to the different parishes; Colonial Entry Book, 1680–95. This letter was dated, 1690.

[5] Orders, April 26, 1695, Colonial Entry Book, 1680–95.

sterling payable out of the fund of the quit-rents,[1] but it seems to have been received irregularly, for, in 1698, a warrant, signed by the Governor, was delivered to the Auditor requiring him to pay four hundred pounds sterling to Mr. Blair, the sum due for the preceding four years.[2]

Blair, though able and aggressive, failed to invest the position of Commissary with any real power or influence. The Bishop of London acknowledged that the people of Virginia were, on the smallest occasion, disposed to contemn and slight his representative's authority; and this prelate was, therefore, made the more solicitous that the Commissary should continue to occupy a seat in the Council as a means of securing for him a larger degree of popular consideration and respect. His characterization of Blair as a "discreet man who would give no offense" does not appear to have been very discriminating, for Blair had not been long settled firmly in his office before he came into violent conflict with Nicholson on the subject of the claim made by the latter that he, (the Governor,) was the mouthpiece, not only of the King, but also of the Bishop of London in the Colony,—a claim that official based on a statute passed as early as 1643, at which time there could have been no representative in Virginia, save the then Governor, of the head of the diocese.[3] Blair also undertook to interfere in several cases of

[1] B. T.Va. Entry Book, vol. xxxvii., p. 261; see also B. T.Va., 1698, vol. vi., p. 347.

[2] The payment was made by express orders of the King, and covered a period ending July 11, 1698; Minutes of Council, Feb. 25, 1698, B. T. Va., vol. liii.

[3] See Letter of Bishop of London to Sir Philip Meadows, B. T. Va., 1698, vol. vi., p. 339; McIlwaine's *Struggle for Religious Toleration in Va.*, p. 9.

moral offenses, such, for instance, as incestuous marriages, which came within the ecclesiastical jurisdiction
of the ordinary courts.   Promptly called before the
Governor and Council, he was rebuked, and the cases
were referred to the courts for prosecution.[1]

[1] See *Memorial of Virginia Clergy*, dated sometime after 1693, an
imperfect paper at Lambeth Palace, Cod. Misc. No. 954.   On one
occasion, while Blair, who was then the incumbent of the pulpit at
Jamestown, was suffering from a severe attack of sickness, the
churchwardens of the parish requested Governor Andros to procure
a qualified minister to fill the place temporarily.   Andros not only
consented to do this, but also expressed his willingness to remunerate
the substitute out of his own pocket.   It was claimed afterwards
that Blair gave his leave to the new appointment, but if so, he soon
changed his mind, for he was reported as saying that neither the
King nor the Governor had, under these circumstances, the authority to appoint a clergyman to preach; and that it might be of as
ill consequence as it was in the reign of King James.   Not content
with speaking thus, Blair declared that it was entirely unnecessary
for a clergyman seeking a parish in the Colony to produce to the
Governor the certificate of his ordination.   For these bold utter-
ances, he was temporarily suspended; Orders April 26, 1695,
Colonial Entry Book, 1680-95.

CHAPTER XIII

The Clergy: Their Tenure

THE right of induction belonged to the Governor. This power was conferred by an Act of Assembly passed as early as 1643, and it was reconferred by an Act passed in 1662. In the instructions given to Nicholson when appointed to the highest office in Virginia in 1698, the authority to collate to benefices was granted to him just as it had previously been granted to Howard and Andros.[1]

The vestry, on the other hand, possessed the right to choose a minister for their parish and to present him to the Governor for induction. In England, the right to choose and present lay, not with the vestry, but with the patron of the living, who might be either a person or a corporation, like one of the great Universities. Only during the brief existence of the Proprietary form of government established in Virginia by the temporary grant to Arlington and Culpeper was the power of presentment withdrawn from the vestry and reserved, somewhat as in England, to special individuals, who, in this case, happened to be the Proprietaries themselves.[2] Practically, throughout the

[1] B. T. Va., vol. vii., p. 168; see also B. T. Va. Entry Book, vol. xxxvi., p. 112.

[2] Randolph MS., vol. iii., p. 320. The Act of 1643 declared that it

Seventeenth century, <u>the vestry was the controlling</u> power in filling the vacant pulpits; and, as we shall see, they, in no small measure, by a boldness unknown in the ecclesiastical history of England, really emancipated themselves from the undoubted right of the Governor to induct.

The most important of all the early Acts of Assembly touching the vestry's power to present for induction a clergyman of their own election was that of 1643, in which it was declared that they should have the authority to choose their own minister with the approval of the commander and justices of the county court, if residents of the parish; but if not, without such approval. This last provision was, no doubt, in most cases nominal, as each parish of a county, even when there were as many as three parishes, is likely to have included among its inhabitants at least one third of the members of the county bench. The statute of 1643 probably conferred on this body a power which had previously perhaps been only exercised by the inhabitants of the parish at large, for in 1640 it is recorded that the people of Lower Norfolk assembled and chose Mr. Thomas Harrison as their minister.[1] After the passage of the Act, the vestry alone, in some instances certainly, made the original choice and continued

---

should be "lawful for the Governor for the time being to elect and admit such a Minister as he shall allow in James City parish, and in any parish where the Governor and his successors shall have a plantation; provided that he or they shall enjoy that privilege only in one parish where he or they shall have such a plantation"; Acts of 1642–3, MS. Clerk's Office, Portsmouth, Va.

[1] Hening's *Statutes*, vol. i., p. 242. The words of the statute are: "choose ministers who are to be recommended to the Governor and so by him admitted." See also Lower Norfolk County Records, Orders May 25, 1640.

to do so, but not without regard to public endorsement, as many cases show. In 1649, in Lower Norfolk, for example, Sampson Calvert was selected, with the approval, as the law required, of the commander and the members of the county court, and also, it would appear, with the full consent of every freeman residing in the parish.[1] It is possible that, after a selection had been made by the vestry, the name of the clergyman was submitted informally to the consideration of the parishioners, without, however, there being necessarily any legal obligation to do so. In 1655, James Doughty was chosen in this more or less popular manner in Northampton county; and, in 1657, Samuel Cole, in Lancaster, apparently by the popular voice alone.[2] Not in-

---

[1] Lower Norfolk County Records, vol. 1646–51, p. 115; Lower Norfolk County Antiquary, vol. ii., p. 63.

[2] Northampton County Records, vol. 1654–55, p. 117; Lancaster County Records, vol. 1654–1702, p. 141. The following is interesting as showing the terms of an ordinary contract between a clergyman and his parishioners: "Agreement made and concluded at ye house of Mr. Henry Corbyn on the 17th of November, 1657, between Samuel Cole, clerk, and ye major part of ye inhabitants of ye p'sh of Lancaster in Rappah River, sheweth imprimis that ye said Samuel Cole doth promise, agree, and engage with ye sd p'sh of Lancaster to serve them in ye office and function of minister every other Sabbath so long time as he shall remain in ye Colony; that he will fulfil, p'form, and duly officiate all Christenings, burials, marriages, churchings, and whatsoever else is proper to his office and ministry in ye sd. parish. It is agreed and concluded by ye Samuel Cole and ye major part of ye inhabitants now mett together that a church shall be built with all convenient speed on Mr. Boswell's Point, and that ye vestry now made choice of shall take care for effecting ye same. Lastly, it is agreed and concluded ye sd inhabitants of ye p'sh of Lancaster aforesaid to pay unto ye sd Samuel Cole ye full sum of four thousand pounds of tobacco in cash yearly, and every year so long as ye sd Saml. Cole shall serve and officiate in ye office and function of minister in ye sd p'sh; likewise to agree with ye inhabitants of ye p'sh for ye settling of a glebe and buying a house for ye sd Mr. Cole's better conveniency

frequently, the vestry would elect a candidate whose
merits had been warmly recommended by the Governor; such were the circumstances under which Samuel
Eborne was, in 1688, advanced to the assistant rectorship of Bruton parish, but the vestry was careful to
limit his term to seven years; and just before this period
expired, they passed a resolution fixing one year as the
time to be covered by the incumbent's term thereafter.
Reelected on this basis, Eborne declined to accept the
position.[1]

In a new country like Virginia, it was impossible
for such a system as that governing the appointments
to livings in England to spring up. There was no
influence accompanying the division and settlement
of the virgin soil (so long at least as the community
was subject directly to the Crown), to create a circle of
patrons,—such as had existed almost immemorially
in the Mother Country,—in whose disposal every benefice in the Colony would rest. Had there been, as time
went on, any influence at work to create such a circle,
it would have been anticipated by the necessity,
which arose almost in the very beginning, of leaving
the choice of the minister to some public body like
the vestry; and once this right had been secured by

---

to officiate and serve both p'rishes of Lancaster and Pianketank;
for ye p'formance hereof ye sd. Saml. Cole and those underwritten
by consent as aforesaid have interchangeably subscribed ye Day
and year above written."

                                    " SAML. COLE.

"The Underwritten, chosen for vestrymen of Lancaster Parish,
Peter Montague and 13 others."

See Lancaster County Records, vol. 1654–1702, p. 141.

[1] Meade's *Old Churches, Ministers, and Families of Virginia*, vol. i.,
pp. 148–9, Phila. edition, 1889. The reason given by Eborne for
declining was the state of his health.

such a body, there was no probability that it would pass to separate individuals resembling the patrons of the English benefices, however wealthy and influential. Each vestry acquired the power to appoint its own minister; the next step was to appoint him, should they so desire, only from year to year; and this every vestry was able to accomplish by refusing to present him to the Governor for induction, for, as soon as inducted, the minister could claim a life tenure in his pulpit, and like the English clergyman occupying a living by his patron's gift, he became at once independent, from a legal point of view, of his congregation's favor or disfavor. He could be suspended by the Governor and Council sitting as an ecclesiastical Court, for neglectful and unbecoming conduct, but could be removed only by an Act of the General Assembly.[1]

It is no reason for surprise that the custom prevailing so generally in the Colony of placing the minister as it were, on probation from year to year by refusing to present him to the Governor for induction, should have excited the hostile criticism of all the persons anxious to establish universally in Virginia the English freehold tenure simply because it would have made every clergyman practically independent of his vestry. Godwyn, with characteristic intemperance, described this body as a "plebeian junta"; and the expression in common use "to hire a divine" stirred in him extraordinary indignation. He accused the Virginians of seeking, by the appointment of lay readers, to evade the support of regular ministers as a heavy charge on their purses; and declared that, where a pulpit was occupied, the parishioners treated the minister "how they please, paid him what they list, and discarded

[1] Hening's *Statutes*, vol. i., p. 242.

him whenever they had a mind to it." "All things
that concern the Church and religion in Virginia," he
exclaimed, with increased bitterness, "are delegated to
the mercy of the people." [1]

However wide of the mark, according to our modern
ideas, may appear Godwyn's heated attack upon a
manner of engaging and remunerating divines which
has continued, from that day to this, to be followed
in our country, there can be no doubt, that the probational tenure of most of the clergymen in the Seventeenth century was the chief reason for a fact which
often appears inexplicable in the light of the substantial advantages the Colony had to offer throughout
that period, namely, the reluctance of the English
divines to emigrate thither. Godwyn declared that the
Virginians were the enemies of the clerical profession;
and the same impression was unquestionably wide-
spread among members of the calling in England, simply
because, owing to the clergymen's forced dependence on
the vestries, they were supposed to be in a state of
absolute servitude. The evil consequences of the
probational tenure from the minister's point of view
are clearly stated by several writers. Blair, for instance, asserted that it prevented divines of superior
talents from either coming to Virginia at all, or, after
they had once arrived, remaining there long; that
it discouraged the clergyman from improving his
glebe, or even purchasing a plantation of his own;
that it diminished his ability to intermarry with a
woman of the better sort; and finally, that it had a

[1] Godwyn's *Negro's and Indian's Advocate*, p. 167 et seq. Morry-
son, who was sent, in 1675, to England as one of the Colony's agents
to secure a new charter, denounced Godwyn's pamphlet as a "viru-
lent libel," and Godwyn himself as a "fellow" and an "inconsiderable wretch"; Neill's *Va. Carolorum*, p. 343.

tendency to cultivate in him a mean, base, and mercenary spirit, because any reflection upon vices which members of his vestry might be addicted to might raise up a faction opposed to continuing him in his place.[1]

The authors of *The Present State of Virginia, 1697–8*, offered almost precisely the same objections:—they declared that the probational tenure kept out of Virginia all the superior persons among the English clergy who were fully informed of it, and that those who came over in ignorance of such a custom, soon had reason to regret their settlement over-sea owing to the high hand shown by the vestries in using their power; that the ministers residing in the Colony, having only a precarious hold on their pulpits, felt no interest either in keeping their parsonages in repair, or in improving their glebes; and that they were unable to attack every form of vice for fear lest they might unintentionally offend some influential member of the vestry. Practically, the clergyman was simply a chaplain whose tenure of his living was dependent on an annual agreement renewable at the option of a small body of men.[2]

It was natural that the Bishop of London for the time being should be greatly impressed by these arguments. In 1698, the then prelate, in a letter addressed to Sir Philip Meadows, touching instructions to Governor Nicholson, declared that the Virginians often took a minister on trial, but from year to year failed to present him, thus depriving him of all legal claim to the payment of his salary; and that they also

[1] Blair's Memorial concerning Gov. Andros, 1697, Perry's *Hist. Coll. Amer. Colon. Church, Va.*, vol. i., p. 15.

[2] *Present State of Virginia, 1697–8*, Section xi. It is probable that Blair wrote this section.

gave the vestry the power to discharge him, should they see fit to do so. Information of this state of absolute dependence coming to England, divines of "ingenuity" were unwilling to place themselves in it, and, therefore, declined to emigrate to Virginia to fill the unoccupied pulpits. As a remedy for the supposed evil, the Bishop proposed that the Governor of the Colony should be impowered to collate to a vacant place immediately upon a lapse, the appointment to be made subject to the Bishop's confirmation or rejection within a period of six months, and to the King's without any limit as to time. As if he thought there might after all be some practical reason for the vestries' reluctance to present ministers for induction, he, in concluding recommended that the probation of a clergyman who had gone out to Virginia, and found employment there, should be restricted to one year; and if, at the end of that time, he afforded satisfaction, his tenure should be made permanent by induction.[1]

No official in the Colony is more likely to have sympathized with the views of those favoring the rigid enforcement in Virginia of a universal rule of presentment and induction than the Governor. It was to his interest to respect and support the Bishop of London's wishes to the utmost; and it would have been only natural also had he shown a determination to retain his right of induction in every case. Although the Governor possessed the power of inducting of his own motion a minister whom the vestry had deferred presenting, there is no instance recorded of his having exercised this power; and this fact is only explicable on two hypotheses: first, he was afraid, for political

[1] Letter of Bishop of London to Sir Philip Meadows, Aug. 11, 1698, B. T. Va., 1698, vol. vi., p. 339; see also June 20, 1698, p. 287.

reasons, to interfere with the vestries' freedom; or, secondly, he was convinced that, in making the tenure probational, these bodies were acting with necessary prudence and caution.   It is quite probable that this was the opinion entertained by all the Governors[1]; and if so, it seems to have been well grounded, although the undoubted effect of the uncertain tenure was to discourage the emigration of English clergymen to Virginia.

The principal reason for the growth of the custom of employing a minister from year to year on a salary annually agreed on, instead of presenting him at once for induction, which would have given him a permanent legal claim to his living and the payment of his dues, was that the vestry was thus able to protect the parish against the appointment of men who might, after a short experience, prove either intellectually unfit or morally unworthy.   It should be remembered that the persons filling the pulpits during this early period were natives, not of Virginia, but of England, and that when they settled over-sea, they had still their personal reputations to make there.   A very large proportion, when they left the Mother Country, were still so young that they had hardly had time to attain a standing which, before their arrival, might have been favorably reported in the Colony by Virginians returning home from England.   At best, these emigrating clergymen

[1] Culpeper, in his report dated 1681, wrote: "The Parishes paying the minister themselves have used to claim the right of presentation whether the Governor will or not, which must not be allowed, and yet must be managed with caution"; Campbell's *History of Virginia*, p. 331.   If Culpeper, who was by no means politic, felt it necessary to be circumspect in dealing with the subject and to advise prudence on the part of the English authorities in interfering, it was likely that the other Governors would show even greater reserve.

could only show certificates from the Bishop of London to the effect that they had led lives free from every form of licentiousness, but whether these documents really reflected their true dispositions was a question which the vestries might well have desired to leave to the test of time. Had the men occupying the Virginian benefices in the Seventeenth century been drawn entirely from the Colony; had they first seen the light and passed their whole previous existence there, a fact which would have given an opportunity to all to understand their characters and weigh their conduct before they were called to the sacred responsibilities of the pulpit, it is quite probable the probational tenure, so much complained of by ministers of English birth, would never have been gradually introduced, or at least would never have become so general. Certainly, the objection to that custom entertained by divines educated in England would never have been advanced so earnestly by them had they been natives of the Colony. Had they been sons of the foremost citizens and relatives of all the leading families of their parishes, and reared in the Colony from their earliest childhood, they would have felt that they could rely on their vestries with implicit confidence for just treatment because that treatment would have been largely influenced by long-standing kindness for themselves personally.[1] The clergyman from England was in a very different situation from this: he entered the com-

---

[1] They would have been disposed to accept such a tenure the more readily because they would have been accustomed to hearing of it from early childhood. Much of the opposition shown by the clergyman of English birth arose from the fact that he had been familiar with a different system; and English pertinacity in clinging to what was deemed to be a right was also partly accountable for this opposition.

munity as a stranger to all, without one tie of blood to bind him to any family in his parish, his moral disposition yet to be discovered, and his intellectual capacity yet to be tried. If he was to win his vestry's goodwill, he was to do so by the force of his own individuality entirely disassociated from all those extraneous influences which would have played such a part in his favor had he been a native of Virginia.

As a matter of fact, the whole character of the probational tenure was well adapted to foster in a clergyman all those qualities most urgently required in a man in his position. He was made by it more energetic, more faithful, and more circumspect in his conduct; and when a pastor on trial exhibited all these qualities, there is no reason to think that he had any ground of complaint. Beverley, who understood thoroughly the sentiment of the clergymen towards the close of the Seventeenth century, states that the only grievance of which they were heard to speak was the precariousness of their livings, but that even this was no real cause for dissatisfaction, as it was rare that one was dismissed without having been guilty of some provocation not to be condoned; and that when discharged, unless his life had been "abominally scandalous," he found no difficulty in securing at once another benefice owing to the eagerness of every vestry, should the pulpit of their parish be vacant, to engage a minister to fill it. No qualified clergyman, he added, ever returned to England for want of preferment in Virginia.[1]

In their reply to a memorial of the Clergy submitted to Governor Andros in 1696, the House of Burgesses declared that the inhabitants of the Colony held a pastor of "good life and conversation" in the highest esteem;

---

[1] Beverley's *History of Virginia*, p. 213.

and that so far from being addicted to disagree with such a one, they were disposed to make use of every inducement in their power to retain him. No pastor, they asserted, was really hopeless of obtaining induction; and it was only reasonable, they added, that a vestry should be well satisfied before taking a step which would give their clergyman a free-hold in his benefice.[1]

The minister failing to secure induction enjoyed, by force of his agreement with the vestry, all the pecuniary advantages possessed by one who had been inducted.[2] Apart from the uncertainty of his tenure, which, as

---

[1] B. T. Va., vol. vi., p. 108. The statement made by the House of Burgesses that induction was not uncommon is confirmed by the testimony of Beverley in his *History* (p. 213), and also by various entries in the records. Clergymen known to have been presented for induction were Isaac Key, of Northampton County (see vol. 1674–9, p. 137); Benjamin Doggett, of Lancaster (Robinson Transcripts, p. 257); and Jacob Ware of St. Peter's parish in New Kent (see Orders of Council, March 23, 1692, Colonial Entry Book). Among the ministers who became involved in controversies with their vestries were Rev. Cope Doyley and Rev. John Monro. In 1695, Doyley, who was the incumbent of Denbigh parish in Warwick county, having been shut out of the church by one of the churchwardens and the late clerk, appealed for redress to the Governor and Council. The churchwardens could show nothing against him; on the contrary, it was proven that for several years past Doyley had borne himself well in his life and faithfully in his ministry; and the Board therefore recommended him for continuance (see Minutes of Council, Febry. 13, 1695, B. T. Va., vol. liii.). Rev. John Monro, of St. John's parish, King and Queen county, having charged the vestry with nailing up the door of his church (1695) to bar him out, they stated in their own defense to the Governor and Council, before whom they had been summoned, that they had done this only to keep out the cattle, and that the door was not opened when Monro attended to perform service, because they thought the parish vacant. Minutes of Council, May, 1695, Colonial Entry Book, 1680–95.

[2] Meade's *Old Churches, Ministers, and Families of Virginia*, vol. i., pp. 367, 368, Phila. edition, 1889.

we have seen, was practically removed by faithful conduct, the average clergyman in Virginia was in a better position, from a worldly point of view, than the average member of his calling residing in the rural districts of England. It is true that he was shut out from all hope of preferment, a hope that exercised a powerful influence in restricting the emigration to the Colony of the most talented and ambitious young men who had obtained orders, but in place of a mere aspiration for advancement, which, with the majority of those entertaining it in the Mother Country, proved entirely illusory, there were numerous solid advantages every clergyman in Virginia bearing himself decently, was absolutely sure of acquiring.[1] Not only could he rely with confidence on securing a benefice, something which the English divine was by no means certain of, but the remuneration for his services taken as a whole, —salary, parsonage, glebe, and perquisites,—was such as to relieve him of all anxiety about the support of his family. Moreover, there does not appear to have been any public sentiment hostile to his undertaking to increase his income by producing tobacco for his own profit on an estate he had either rented or purchased. In a community in which a successful planter enjoyed the highest degree of consideration, it was not

[1] An unbound MS. among the Fulham Palace Collections entitled *Propositions to Improve the Clergy of Virginia* has the following to say about the effect on that clergy of the absence of preferments: "By means of their equality, they, *i.e.* the Virginia livings, are very ill calculated to distinguish and encourage men of parts and diligence, who ought to be spurred on by hopes of better preferment, and not left to fare equally with the most negligent and blockish." The writer of this paper declared that it was more satisfactory for a clergyman to receive £40 salary in England, where the benefice was sure and there was a hope of promotion, than £80 in Virginia, where the tenure was uncertain, and there was no hope of advancement.

at all improbable that the minister showing great talent as a manager found that, instead of this fact diminishing his influence as a pastor, it enabled him to push his moral homilies in the pulpit all the more closely home. Having ocular proof of his capacity to grow tobacco better than most of his neighbors, his congregation would perhaps have been the more inclined to repose confidence in his knowledge of his real calling.

CHAPTER XIV

The Clergy: Their Remuneration

A STATED salary was paid the clergyman from a very early period in the Seventeenth century. In the instructions which Governor Yeardley received from the Company in 1618, before going over to Virginia, he was ordered to see that, for the maintenance of the incumbent of every living in the Colony, contributions in one form or another equal in amount to two hundred pounds sterling (five thousand dollars in purchasing power) should be raised annually out of the profits of the different farms situated within the bounds of his charge; and should good reason for it arise later on, that this sum was to be increased.[1] This income was to be exclusive of what he could obtain by the cultivation of a glebe of one hundred acres attached to his parsonage. When, the same year, the Company dispatched over-sea a clergyman to officiate in the Colony, they granted him, not only a salary of forty pounds sterling a year, but also fifty acres of land in fee simple.[2]

Extraordinary pains were taken to ensure the payment of the minister's salary. The first Assembly

[1] Instructions to Yeardley, 1618, *Va. Maga. of Hist. and Biog.*, vol. ii., p. 158. An Act to this effect was passed by the first Assembly.

[2] Abstracts of Proceedings of Va. Co. of London, vol. i., p. 12.

145

convening in Virginia adopted measures directed towards that end; and a few years later, the same body passed an Act requiring that no planter should dispose of his tobacco crop before the share of it due the clergyman of the parish had been delivered, and that, if he disobeyed this command, he should forfeit double the amount of that share. As if they deemed this by itself an insufficient protection of the clergyman's interests, the Assembly provided for the appointment of special officers, upon whom was imposed the duty of collecting his salary out of the "first and best corn and tobacco" that should be gathered.[1] No one could claim exemption from the payment of his proportion of the levy for the minister's support. Those persons who were settled in Virginia before Sir Thomas Gates's last arrival were relieved of the burden of all other public charges, but they were required to pay the church dues, including the minister's salary, just as if they were so many citizens who had come in only within the last few months.[2] The very members of the Governor's Council, who enjoyed such an extraordinary privilege in the way of freedom from public taxation, were expected to contribute their share to the clergyman's maintenance.[3] And the like was also exacted

[1] Hening's *Statutes*, vol. i., p. 124.

To ensure performance of duty by the clergyman, it was enacted that, should he absent himself without excuse from his church for a period exceeding two months, he should forfeit one half of his salary; and that if his absence extended to four months, he should forfeit, not only the whole of his salary, but also his living; Hening's *Statutes*, vol. i., p. 123.

[2] Laws of Assembly, Febry. 1623/4, British Colonial Papers, vol. iii., No. 9. Every person who worked in the ground, no matter what his 'quality or condition," was, by this law, to be considered as a tithable; see Hening's *Statutes*, vol. i., p. 144.

[3] Colonial Entry Book, 1606–62, p. 223.

of the poor even when they were so disabled that the vestry of their parish had granted them certificates for presentation to the county court to secure relief from the county levy.[1]

A law adopted in 1623/4 fixed the clergyman's salary at ten pounds of tobacco and a bushel of corn for each tithable; and in 1631, it was enlarged by permitting him to claim every twentieth new-born calf, kid, and pig, a very important addition to his income at a time when all kinds of livestock were increasing with extraordinary rapidity. The tobacco and corn were to be delivered at whatever place he should designate as the one most convenient to him; and whoever failed to bring his share was to forfeit double the amount due.[2]   The county court was especially jealous that these provisions for the minister's support should be strictly enforced, In 1632, Rev. William Cotton, of Accomac, complained to the justices of that county that the churchwardens, though often urged by him, had neglected to collect his tithes in full; the court at once responded by requiring warrants to be issued against all persons who had defaulted, by which they were compelled to pay twice as much in corn and tobacco as they were originally liable for.[3] And this was no uncommon instance.

By an Act of Assembly passed in 1632/3 for the establishment within the cultivated area of the Colony of a system of warehouses, to which the entire crop of

---

[1] Hening's *Statutes*, vol. i., p. 242.

[2] Acts of Assembly, Feb. 21, 1631/2, Randolph MS., vol. iii., p. 216. The provision about the calf. kid, and pig was repealed in 1633; see Hening's *Statutes*, vol. i., p. 221.

[3] Accomac County Records, vol. 1632–40, p. 11, Va. St. Libr.; see also p. 44 of same volume. See Northampton County Records, vol. 1651–54, p. 73, for case of Rev. Thomas Higby.

tobacco produced each year was to be brought previous
to its shipment to England, the salaries of the clergymen were, before the settlement of any other debts,
to be paid out of the quantity of that commodity thus
annually collected; and authority was given them to
appoint their own agents, who were, at the doors of
these storehouses, to receive what was due.[1]   A few
years later, it would appear that each minister, out of
his income derived from the tax of ten pounds of tobacco imposed on each tithable person, was expected
to remunerate both the clerk and the sexton of his
church.[2] In 1640, there was a special levy of one bushel
of corn per poll allowed for these two officers' benefit,
in addition to the fixed proportion of tobacco which the
minister was required to pay them.[3]

Even at this early date, should there be a special
reason for it, the minister's salary could be increased
much beyond the sum designated by law; for instance,
in 1640, the county court of Lower Norfolk gave directions that every tithable residing within the area
of country situated between the plantations of Peter
Porter and Captain Thomas Willoughby should contribute ten shillings, as well as twenty-four pounds of
tobacco, towards the payment of the minister's dues.[4]
This allowance, perhaps temporary only in character,
was made the very year in which the General Assembly,
in order, as was stated in the Act, to rectify the con-
fusion growing out of the constant disputes between
pastors and their parishioners over the subject of
salaries, renewed the provision of one bushel of corn

[1] Acts of Assembly, February 1, 1632, Randolph MS., vol. iii., p.
223; Hening's *Statutes*, vol. i., p. 207.

[2] Hening's *Statutes*, vol. i., p. 226; Randolph MS., vol. iii., p. 230.

[3] Robinson Transcripts, p. 22.

[4] Lower Norfolk County Antiquary, vol. i., p. 141.

and ten pounds of tobacco per tithable, adopted some years before as we have seen, for the support of clergymen.[1]   The tobacco was to be delivered November 20, and the corn, December 19; and two bushels of this grain unshelled were to be accepted as equal to one bushel shelled.[2]

The inhabitants of the parish in which the church at Sewell's Point was situated, in a contract with Rev. Thomas Harrison in 1640 agreed to pay him an annual salary of one hundred pounds sterling as long as he occupied that pulpit.   The parish seems to have been laid off into three districts, in each of which several of the wealthiest citizens, acting for themselves and the remaining tithables, guaranteed the contribution of their proportionate share of this amount.[3]   It shows the scrupulous regard for the clergymen's interests prevailing in the Colony at this time, that, whenever a pastor having two parishes was unable to attend to all his duties in consequence of the great area he had to traverse, he was nevertheless not permitted to suffer any diminution in his salary because the inhabitants were occasionally compelled to rely upon some other minister to baptize or preach.[4]

Again, in 1646, the vestry exercised the power of advancing the tax for the minister's support beyond the ten pounds of tobacco per tithable allowed by law, special authority for which had lately been granted by the General Assembly whenever a parish's population had been so cut down that the ordinary rate afforded the clergyman an insufficient maintenance.

[1] Robinson Transcripts, p. 22.

[2] Hening's *Statutes*, vol. i., p. 242.

[3] Lower Norfolk County Records, Orders May 25, 1640.

[4] Hening's *Statutes*, vol. i., p. 290.   The words of the statute were "without prejudice to the incumbent."

In many parishes, there had been a large reduction in the number of inhabitants in consequence of the great massacre by the Indians which had recently taken place.[1] The vestry seems to have also possessed the right to increase the rate of payment in tobacco in consideration of not imposing at all the rate in corn; in 1649, by the provisions of the contract between Rev. Sampson Calvert and the vestry of Elizabeth River parish, that clergyman was to receive thirty instead of ten pounds of tobacco per tithable, but he was to give up his legal claim to the usual amount of grain. The use of a boat to transport him to his church every Sabbath was also assured him free of expense to himself.[2] Occasionally, the levy for the minister's support rose to fifty-three pounds per poll; but, in some of these cases, it is possible that there were arrears covering the whole of the previous year.[3]

The pecuniary advantages enjoyed by the clergyman were, in 1656, substantially increased by the exemption of himself and six of his servants from the payment of public dues.[4] This Act was renewed two years later. Thomas Teakle and Francis Doughty, the two ministers occupying the parishes on the Eastern Shore, having been taxed as usual, they succeeded, on the authority of this statute, in obtaining a full reimbursement; and when in the following year, the

[1] Hening's *Statutes*, vol. i., p. 328.

[2] Lower Norfolk County Records, vol. 1646–51, p. 115. In 1656, the levy in this parish for the minister's support had been reduced to fifteen pounds of tobacco per tithable; see Lower Norfolk County Records, vol. 1656–66, p. 33.

[3] The churchwardens of one of the parishes in Northumberland county were, in 1655, ordered to distrain for that amount; see Orders June 30, 1655.

[4] Randolph MS., vol. iii., p. 268.

regular levy was laid, their names were omitted.[1]
In 1672, Rev. John Farnefold, of Fairfield parish, in
Northumberland, paid for himself and five servants
the rates imposed on all tithables; but on his making
complaint to the county court, this body entered an
order that the amount should be returned to him out
of the proceeds of the next county levy.[2]   The existing law was modified during the session of 1676, when,
under the influence of the movement headed by Bacon,
so many abuses relating to public taxation were corrected; it was then enacted that, in all future assessments, the clergyman could claim relief from the
payment of public and county dues for himself, but,
should there be other tithables in his family, he was as
to them to be subject to the rule applicable to the
ordinary citizen.[3]   This provision had its origin in the
idea that, when a clergyman was so easy in fortune as to
possess a number of servants capable of adding by
their work to his income, there was no reason why he
should not bear at least such a share of the public
burdens as would be in proportion to the product of
these servants' labor.   And this view seems to have
been altogether equitable.

As a means of ensuring a support for the clergymen
who should be induced to settle in parishes long re-

---

[1] Northampton County Records, vol. 1657–64, folio p. 26.
Doughty complained, in 1660, that his tithes had not been delivered, and thereupon the county court issued an order that the
inhabitants of his parish should assemble in their precincts, and that
all who could not show a discharge should be required to make
payment; Northampton County Records, vol. 1657–64, folio p. 66.
The trouble in this county arose from its division into two parishes,
which made it difficult for its people to support two preachers; see
Records, vol. 1689–98, pp. 117–18.

[2] Northumberland County Orders, Aug. 21, 1672.

[3] Hening's *Statutes*, vol. ii., p. 357; see also vol. ii., p. 392.

maining vacant because impoverished, the General Assembly, in 1660–1, urged the vestries of these parishes, not only themselves to subscribe to the fund required, but also to use their influence to cause all other citizens of means to contribute as much as they could afford.[1] In the following year, it was expressly provided that the minister's salary should be paid in the country's "current commodities" in a quantity estimated to be worth as a whole not less than eighty pounds sterling. These commodities were to consist of corn and tobacco, —the corn to be rated at ten shillings a bushel, and the tobacco at twelve shillings a hundred pounds. It was always allowable for any one to pay his share of the minister's salary in the form of bills of exchange on England; but it is not probable that this was frequently done, although the permission was specially granted by the terms of the same statute.[2]

Thomas Ludwell, who had enjoyed the best opportunities of acquiring a thorough knowledge of the condition of the church in Virginia, declared in 1666 that there were few parishes failing to pay their incumbents each year an amount smaller than one hundred pounds sterling.[3] By the levy of Fairfield parish in 1679, not less than thirteen thousand, three hundred and thirty-three pounds of merchantable tobacco was assessed for the benefit of the Rev. John Farnefold, the divine who, at this time, was in the possession of that living.[4] At two pence a pound, the sum of tobacco which had to be raised for him was worth in the market about one hundred and eight pounds sterling, but it

[1] Hening's *Statutes*, vol. ii., p. 37.

[2] *Ibid.*, p. 45.

[3] Letter of Ludwell to Arlington, Winder Papers, vol. i., p. 209.

[4] Northumberland County Records, Orders Oct. 22, 1679; see also Oct. 20, Nov. 17, 1680.

was probably not quite so valuable as this. Only a
few years afterwards, Culpeper, in his general report
on the state of Virginia, declared that a living should
carry with it a salary of at least eighty pounds sterling,
but owing to the low price tobacco had fallen to, the
fixed quantity allowed the minister would not then,
as a rule, assure so large an amount. In those parts
of the Colony where the variety of the plant known as
Orinoko was cultivated, his salary at this time hardly
exceeded forty pounds sterling a year; and in those
parts where the sweet scented variety, a more profitable kind, was cultivated, sixty pounds. As soon,
however, as the price of tobacco would rise, the clergymen's salary would assume its original proportions;
and if that price went up above the average figure on
which the original allowance was based, then the sum
the clergyman would receive for his services would run
very considerably ahead of eighty pounds sterling.
At the time when Culpeper was writing, there were only
four parishes in the Colony containing livings that paid
the minister so large an amount; one of these was
situated at Middle Plantation; two were situated in
Gloucester county; and the fourth in Westmoreland.
That the parish in Westmoreland was as lucrative as
this, was, it seems, due in part at least to the private
contributions or personal influence of its wealthiest
and most distinguished citizen, Nicholas Spencer, the
Secretary of the Colony and a zealous churchman; and
the presence of citizens as powerful, affluent, and religious in the other parishes perhaps told equally to the
advantage of the clergymen filling those livings.[1]

In 1684, the salary of Rev. James Porter, who oc-

[1] Report of Culpeper to Board of Trade, 1683, Colonial Entry
Book, 1681–85, p. 174.

cupied one of the parishes situated in Lower Norfolk, was fixed at ten thousand pounds of tobacco and one hundred bushels of corn. As he died before the second year of his incumbency was completed, the vestry declined to pay his representatives more than seventy-five hundred and eighty-eight pounds of tobacco; but allowed six hundred pounds as a fee to the clergyman who preached his funeral sermon. A suit was entered by the executors for the additional amount required to make up a whole year's salary; and it shows the disposition of the county courts to favor the minister's cause, unless patently wrong, that this claim was approved after the cost of the funeral sermon had been deducted.[1] Rev. Thomas Teakle, of Northampton, seems to have received the same salary.[2]

Fitzhugh, writing in 1690, ventured the statement that the salary at that time paid a clergyman in Virginia was "large and comfortable"; and that twenty pounds sterling, or its equivalent in tobacco, was always granted the newly arrived minister to reimburse him for the expenses entailed by his voyage from England.[3] The clergy of the Colony, in an address to the English authorities, the following year, did not give so favorable a character to their condition, although it is not improbable that they were seeking to make out as bad a case for themselves as they could

[1] Lower Norfolk County Records, Orders Nov. 17, 1684. In 1655, Capt. Willoughby was authorized by one of the parishes of Lower Norfolk County to secure a minister at an annual salary of ten thousand pounds of tobacco; see Lower Norfolk County Antiquary, vol. iii., p. 33.

[2] In 1688, Teakle entered suit for the payment of the combined salaries due him for 1684 and 1685, equal in amount to twenty thousand pounds of tobacco; Northampton County Records, vol. 1683–89, p. 393.

[3] Letters of William Fitzhugh, Aug. 20, 1690.

without stretching the truth too far. They declared that by law they were entitled to a salary of eighty pounds sterling, payable in tobacco at the rate of twelve shillings per hundred pounds of that commodity, which would bring the amount due them to twelve or thirteen thousand pounds. Instead, however, of the hundred pounds being worth twelve shillings, as it was at the time the salary was fixed, it was worth only six, owing to the enormous increase in the quantity of tobacco produced following upon the growth of the native population, and the large importation of negroes, all of whom were at once set to working in the fields. Many of the clergymen (so the address went on to say), finding that they could not live comfortably on the salary they received, had returned to England, and their representations had prevented ministers there, who had proposed going out, from emigrating in order to fill the vacant parishes.[1]

In their reply to this address, the Virginia Council merely asserted, what there is reason to believe was strictly true, that the condition of the Colony's ministers was as good as that of the body of the English clergy.[2]

William III, about 1691-2, evinced an extraordinary

---

[1] B. T. Va., 1691, No. 73. At a later date, as will be seen from a subsequent statement in the text, the Burgesses showed that the fluctuation in the prices of tobacco frequently operated very much to the clergymen's advantage; as frequently indeed, as to their disadvantage. An additional reason given in the ministers' address for the low price of tobacco at this time was the high customs in England, and the large quantity of the commodity produced on the Rhine and in other parts of Europe. The address was adopted "pursuant to ye earnest desires of the clergy at their general meeting in ye year 1690." Such was the statement made in a petition of the clergy to Andros in 1696; see B. T. Va., vol. vi., p. 105.

[2] April 24, 1697, B. T. Va., vol. vi., p. 81.

interest in the improvement of the Virginian clergymen's pecuniary condition; he not only directed the
General Assembly to assure the payment to each of a
competent salary, in the form of either coin or tobacco,
but also ordered a special inquiry to be set on foot as to
whether the numerous laws passed for their better
maintenance had been carefully enforced.[1]   By the
provisions of the Act for Ports, one third of the tax
imposed by that Act on all skins and furs exported was
to be disbursed for the support and encouragement of a
"learned and pious" clergy; and this object was to be
accomplished by distributing the sum obtained from
this source equally among all the persons following the
clerical profession.   Again, by the provisions of the Act
for the suppression of drunkenness, swearing, and similar moral offences, one third of the amount accruing
from the fines and forfeitures paid by the guilty persons
was required to be devoted to the same purpose.

The King was not content with ordering, for the
clergy's benefit, the strict enforcement of these various
laws; he even went so far as to instruct the Governor
of the Colony to afford relief to the poorer ministers by
diverting to them the revenue derived from the quit-
rents, provided that, after three years' test, it was found
that this revenue could be spared from the immediate
wants of the central administration.   At a later date,
the pastors complained that they had been prevented
from securing any advantage from the King's recommendations by the authorities' success in inventing
new means of exhausting the surplus from this source
when it had been accumulated; that instead of disburs-

---

[1] Orders of Council, Sept. 1, 1693, Colonial Entry Book, 1680-95.
For Andros's Proclamation requiring a stricter enforcement of these
laws, see Henrico County Records, vol. 1688-97, p. 442, Va. St. Libr.

ing it, according to the royal intention, among the different ministers, they had spent it, partly in erecting unnecessary fortifications, and partly in assisting New York to carry on a campaign against the Indians.[1]

Andros, under the pressure of the royal commands, in April, 1695, urged the House of Burgesses to make suitable provision for the clergy's support; but that body in reply again declared that the ministers had no just reason for complaint; and that the laws already passed for their maintenance were sufficient for the purpose.[2] In the following month, however, they adopted a proposition to grant to each pastor an annual salary of 13,333$\frac{1}{3}$ pounds of tobacco. When this proposition was submitted to the Council sitting as an Upper House, they amended it by fixing the salary at sixteen thousand pounds of tobacco, a very considerable increase; and the Lower House assented when the change in the original allowance came before them for acceptance or rejection.[3] In the revision of the laws, the Assembly of its own accord agreed upon sixteen thousand pounds of tobacco as the regular salary of each clergyman; but it would appear that Andros refused or failed to give his approval. Having been criticized for his conduct, he sought to induce the Assembly to renew its provision; and this it consented to do; but in the new Act, the ministers were not granted the advantage

[1] The complaint of the clergy will be found in a Memorial preserved at Lambeth Palace; see Cod. Misc., No. 954.

[2] Colonial Entry Book, vol. 1682–95, no page. In his petition about Governor Andros, Blair declared that this official had been ordered by the King as early as 1692 to bring the question of the ministers' salaries before the Assembly, but that he had failed to do so. Andros probably agreed with the House of Burgesses that the clergy had no reasonable ground for dissatisfaction on this score.

[3] Minutes of Assembly, May 16, 1695, Colonial Entry Book, 1682–95.

of cask, as they had been in the old; and besides, they were compelled to pay a larger fee for collection. It was estimated that these two new forms of expense entailed a reduction of thirteen per cent. in the total amount of their salaries.[1]

When, in 1696, the clergy again complained that they could only, as a rule, obtain six shillings for their tobacco per hundred pounds, although, in the payment of their salaries, every hundred pounds received was rated at twelve shillings, the House of Burgesses replied by saying that the planter's profits were subject to the like fluctuations in the price of the commodity; and that this price did not always remain at six shillings per hundred pounds, was shown by the fact that, in this very year when the clergymen were so discontented, an hundred pounds was selling at the rate of sixteen to twenty shillings.[2] We are informed by Beverley that, in the parishes cultivating sweet-scented tobacco, the amount which, near the close of the century, was delivered to each minister was not infrequently worth at least twenty shillings for every one hundred pounds of the sixteen thousand allowed by law; and that, taken as a whole, it assured him, from year to year, as much as the ordinary planter could derive from the arduous labours of one dozen slaves. At the time when this was written, each clergyman was entitled to have the tobacco due him for his annual stipend brought to him stored in hogsheads ready for immediate shipment abroad.[3]

It will be seen, by an examination of the previous paragraphs, that two facts were brought out clearly

[1] Blair's Memorial, 1697, Perry's *Hist. Coll. of American Colonial Church*, Virginia, vol. i., p. 10. For Act fixing salary at 16,000 lbs. of tobacco, see Hening's *Statutes*, vol. iii., p. 151.

[2] B. T. Va., vol. vi., pp. 105, 108.

[3] Beverley's *History of Virginia*, pp. 211, 212.

about the salaries paid the clergymen during the
Seventeenth century:—first, that the General Assembly
evinced an unvarying determination to make as liberal
a provision for this purpose as the Colony could afford;
and, secondly, that the stipend of the minister in
Virginia was fully as large as that of the average divine
in the far more wealthy communities of the Mother
Country during the same period.

But the clergyman's remuneration was not confined
to his salary.   In addition to the annual payment of a
fixed sum of tobacco, he enjoyed certain perquisites,
which went far in swelling the amount received from
the public for his maintenance.   The most important
part of this supplementary income was derived from
preaching funeral sermons and performing marriage
and burial services.   As early as 1631, each minister
was impowered to charge two shillings and sixpence for
the marriage service, and one shilling for the burial.[1]
Twelve years afterwards, the fee allowed for the marriage service, when banns had been published, was
forty pounds of tobacco, and one hundred when a
license had been obtained.[2]   We learn from a statement made by the House of Burgesses in 1696 that the
fee which the clergyman had the right to charge at this
time amounted to twenty shillings, or two hundred
pounds of tobacco[3]; and this is confirmed by Beverley's
testimony as to a marriage following a license; but if
the ceremony had been preceded by the publication
of banns, the fee was limited to five shillings, or fifty
pounds of tobacco.[4]

[1] Acts of Assembly, Randolph MS., vol. iii., p. 216.
[2] MS. Laws of Va. 1643, Clerk's Office, Portsmouth Va.
[3] B. T. Va., vol. vi., p. 105.
[4] Beverley's *History of Virginia*, pp. 211, 212.

In 1644, Rev. John Rosier was, by order of the Northampton county court, paid three pounds and two shillings for having performed a marriage and a funeral service in the family of Dr. John Holloway.[1] When a body was interred in the chancel of a church in York county, the clergyman was impowered to demand a fee of five pounds sterling, or one thousand pounds of tobacco.[2] A fee of one thousand pounds of the same commodity was, in 1645, received by Rev. Thomas Harrison for performing the burial service over the graves of Mr. and Mrs. Sewell of Lower Norfolk, and for preaching a sermon in their memory.[3] William Hodgkin, of Rappahannock, bequeathed, in 1671, five hundred pounds to the clergyman who should pronounce the funeral sermon over his body; and this was probably the amount usually allowed for this purpose at this time.[4] The regular fee for a funeral sermon delivered in the church at Middle Plantation about 1683, was fixed at two pounds sterling, or fifty dollars in modern values[5]; and this was the amount received by the minister, who, in the course of that year, preached a sermon in Henrico county in Francis Eppes's memory.[6] In 1684, one of the parishes situated in Lower Norfolk allowed a fee of six hundred pounds of tobacco for a funeral sermon delivered in memory of a former pastor.[7] About eight years later, the elder Nathaniel Bacon bequeathed five

[1] Northampton County Records, Orders April 10, 1644.

[2] *William and Mary College Quart.*, vol. iii., p. 172.

[3] Lower Norfolk County Records, Orders for 1645.

[4] Rappahannock County Records, vol. 1664–73, p. 65,Va. St. Libr.

[5] *William and Mary College Quart.*, vol. iii., p. 172.

[6] Henrico County Records, vol. 1677–92, orig. p. 258.   Rev. Mr. Ball was allowed out of the Eppes estate ten shillings for a funeral sermon, delivered perhaps in memory of a child who had been a member of that family.

[7] Lower Norfolk County Records, Orders Nov. 17, 1684.

guineas to Rev. Stephen Fouace in consideration of his
preaching his funeral sermon; but in leaving so large a
sum for this purpose, Bacon was perhaps influenced by
a feeling of personal friendship.[1] Nevertheless, we learn
from a statement of the House of Burgesses made in the
course of 1696, that a clergyman about this time very
often received for delivering a funeral sermon as much
as one thousand pounds of tobacco, which, at twelve
shillings a hundred pounds, would represent a fee equal
in value to six pounds sterling.   The total perquisites
from this source of some of the ministers were estimated at four thousand pounds of that commodity.[2]

The incomes of many pastors were increased by the
fees they received for reading prayers during the sessions of the General Assembly.   Rev. Cope Doyley, for
having performed this service in 1695, was allowed five
pounds sterling out of the revenue derived from the
tax on liquors; and a like remuneration for similar
services was, at the same time, granted to Rev.
Samuel Eborne.[3] The Assembly always ordered a fee
to be paid to every clergyman who had been asked to
deliver a discourse before its members; fifteen pounds
sterling were, in 1698, divided up among those who had
preached on such an invitation[4]; and in the following
year, there were distributed among the numerous
ministers who had appeared under these circumstances
before the House during the present and the last session,
not less than one hundred pounds sterling, at the rate
of ten pounds sterling to each.   This large sum was

[1] York County Records, vol. 1690–94, p. 154, Va. St. Libr.

[2] B. T. Va., vol. vi., pp. 105, 108.

[3] Minutes of Assembly, May 16, 1695, B. T. Va. vol. liii.; see also
Hening's *Statutes*, vol. ii., p. 392.

[4] Minutes of Council April 26, 1698, B. T. Va., vol. liii.

delivered to Commissary Blair to be handed over in equal proportions to the persons designated to receive it.[1]

Sometimes, a clergyman was the beneficiary under the will of a wealthy parishioner; in 1690, Rev. John Bertram was bequeathed the sum of five pounds sterling by George Spencer, of Lancaster; and in 1693, Rev. James Wallace, five hundred pounds of tobacco by Thomas Taylor, of Elizabeth City county.[2]

[1] Minutes of Assembly May 3, 1699, B. T. Va., vol. liii.   We find the following in Hening's *Statutes*, vol. i., p. 549 :—"Ordered that Mr. Peter Lonsdale and Mr. Philip Mallory be desired to preach at Jamestown the next Assembly."

[2] Lancaster County Records, vol. 1690–1707, folio p. 11: Elizabeth City County Records, vol. 1684–99, p. 251, Va. St. Libr.

CHAPTER XV

The Clergy: Glebes and Parsonages

IN addition to his regular salary and his fees for the performance of various services, the clergyman was, during his incumbency, entitled to the use of a glebe. As early as 1619, a plantation of one hundred acres was, for this purpose, set apart in each of the newly created boroughs; and the Company took such extraordinary pains to provide laborers for the tillage of these lands that, at a session of the General Court in the following year, it was stated that at least fifty tenants for them had already been sent out to Virginia.[1] A large proportion of the area of soil embraced within their boundaries must, at this time, have been highly productive, as there had not yet been cultivation sufficient to exhaust the fertility resulting from the deep layers of decayed wood and leaves. In 1625, the date of William Claiborne's survey, the glebe lying at the point where the Chickahominy River emptied into the James contained one hundred acres, whilst the one situated in the vicinity of Newport's News contained as many as two hundred.[2] The

---

[1] Abstracts of Proceedings of Va. Co. of London, vol. i., p. 66. It was at first decided to transport to Virginia six tenants for each of the three most important glebes, namely, those attached to the lands assigned respectively to the College, the Governor, and the Company; for each of the other glebes, the Company agreed to send out three tenants, provided that each settlement where a glebe had been laid off would furnish an additional three.

[2] Randolph MS., vol. iii., p. 185.

Assembly, in 1639, directed that the glebe lands of Cheskiack parish should cover an area of not less than two hundred acres.[1]   It is probable that this number was allowed by law to be attached to every parsonage, for when, in the following year, Rev. Thomas Hampton petitioned the General Court that he should be granted one hundred acres, in addition to the one hundred at that time forming his glebe, the judges, assenting, gave orders that the new patent should be laid off at a point back of the old.[2]

By the instructions given to Berkeley in 1642, the Governor of the Colony was required to see, not only that the area of each existing glebe was increased to two hundred acres, whenever it fell short of that number, but also that, during the next three years, every parishioner, either with his own hands or his servants', assisted his pastor in working this ground so as to bring it to a proper state of cultivation.   This probably applied only to those glebes which had recently been laid off, and which were, no doubt, overrun with thick woods.   It was expressly ordered that every glebe should be chosen as near as possible to the parsonage; and that it should be made up of the most fertile soil the surrounding country afforded.[3]

It seems to have been in the vestry's power as early as 1647 to dispose of the existing glebe should they have cause to think that they could secure another marked by a finer quality of soil.   Such sales, perhaps, occurred very often, for, under the system of cultivation pre-

---

[1] Robinson Transcripts, p. 226.

[2] *Ibid.*, p. 22.   The patent was made out to "Mr. Hampton and his successors."

[3] Instructions to Berkeley, 1642, *Va. Maga. of Hist. and Biog.,* vol. ii., p. 281.

vailing throughout the century, the land was soon reduced in fertility, unless situated in the alluvial bottoms along the banks of the streams. The area of the glebe was small, and there was not much virgin ground to draw upon after that area had been tilled by a succession of clergymen. At an early date, as we have seen, instructions were given by the authorities that each new glebe should be laid off in the most favored locality, because so much more likely there to endure a long course of working without serious injury; if, however, the land after a few years began to show unmistakable signs of exhaustion, no recourse was left the vestry but to sell it to some wealthy planter of the neighbourhood anxious to enlarge his forests or his cattle range, and buy a second glebe where the soil promised a longer retention of its original excellence.[1]

By a law adopted in 1660–1, every parish occupied by a sufficient number of tithables was required to have a glebe attached to the parsonage; and this glebe was to be furnished with all the necessary buildings; and also fully stocked with cattle and hogs. Whenever a parish was inhabited by too few persons to allow such a serious outlay, it was to be annexed to the nearest parish possessing population and general resources sufficient to permit it to own a glebe and to keep it in good condition.[2]

By the instructions given to Berkeley in 1662, it would appear that the glebe's area was thereafter to be cut down to one hundred acres.[3] The reason for

[1] In 1647, a sale of one of the glebes in York County was made to Mr. Peter Rigby; see Records, vol. 1638–48, p. 274, Va. St. Libr.

[2] Hening's *Statutes*, vol. ii., p. 30.

[3] Randolph MS., vol. iii., p. 276. This regulation, it would appear, was intended to apply only to the glebes to be created after these instructions were given.

this change is obscure, unless all fertile lands situated within the body of the Colony had been steadily rising in price with the growth in wealth and population; such a reason, however, had no application in the outlying parishes, where so large a proportion of the lands, being still covered with forest, were practically without any value.

When a clergyman had vacated his pulpit, the glebe, in the interval before his successor's election, was sometimes cultivated by an agent of the vestry. In 1648, Rev. Mr. Harrison, of Lower Norfolk, having refused to administer the sacraments, deliberately deserted his ministerial office owing to his conversion to Puritanism. The glebe attached to his parsonage was at once placed in charge of John Norwood, who was required to give an account of the profits.[1] As a rule, the glebes, under these circumstances, seem to have been rented; such at least was the disposition made of one in Henrico county in 1685, in which year, Thomas Cocke, Jr., was summoned to court to answer for tending, contrary to law, tobacco seconds growing on land belonging to the parish living.[2]

Devises of ground for use as a glebe were not uncommon on the part of benevolent testators. About 1638, Mr. Cooper, of Isle of Wight county, left a part of his estate for this purpose[3]; and thirty years later, Thomas Foote, of York, by will directed that, should his sons not live beyond their twenty-first birthday, his "entire seate of lande" was to pass to New Poquoson parish, to be converted into a glebe for the support of a

[1] Lower Norfolk County Records, vol. 1646-51, p. 82.
[2] Henrico County Records, vol. 1677-92, orig. p. 313; see also Isle of Wight County Records, vol. 1688-1704, p. 269.
[3] Isle of Wight County Records, vol. 1688-1704, p. 269.

minister.[1] In 1671, Zachariah Cripp, of Gloucester, made a gift of three hundred acres to Ware parish, situated in that county, to serve the same end.[2]

Numerous instances occurred in which the glebe was stocked with cattle and hogs by the generosity of persons residing in the same parish, or interested in its welfare. John Sadler, joint owner with Richard Quiney of a great patent at Merchant's Hope, bequeathed to the parish lying there, for the use of the minister occupying its pulpit, his herd of cows, from which it was expected that a large income would be annually obtained.[3] At a later date, Nathaniel Jones, of Westmoreland county, made a similar though less valuable present to the parish of Machodick for the like purpose.[4] Before the close of the century, these gifts for the improvement of the glebes' value must have represented a very considerable sum, for Beverley informs us that they included, not only cattle, horses, hogs, and the like, but also slaves; and that a minister in vacating his living was required to account for this livestock only to the extent of their number when he entered on the glebe. In other words, he was permitted to appropriate any surplus as if it had, from the beginning, belonged to him absolutely.[5]

The general condition of the glebes at the end of the century is presented in two different lights in a controversy which at that time arose between certain clergymen and the House of Burgesses. In 1695, when Andros, acting under instructions from the King, urged

1 York County Records, vol. 1664–72, p. 242, Va. St. Libr.
2 General Court Records, vol. 1670–76, p. 54.
3 *Va. Maga. of Hist. and Biog.*, vol. iv., p. 316.
4 Westmoreland County Records, vol. 1653–72, p. 122.
5 Beverley's *History of Virginia*, p. 211.

the Assembly to make more comfortable provision for the ministers, that body asserted that, as a rule, the area of lands embraced in the glebes belonged to the most fertile soil in Virginia; that in many instances, these glebes spread over as much ground as four hundred or five hundred acres, and in some, over as much as eight hundred or a thousand; that they had been improved by the planting of orchards, the building of fences, and the laying off of pastures,—all in addition to the presence of the ordinary farm houses; and that, taken as a whole, the glebes were so valuable that the minister occupying any one of them was in as good a pecuniary condition as a gentleman owning a fine plantation and twelve or fourteen servants.[1]

Blair and fourteen of his associates among the clergy, in their reply to this statement of the House, declared that the description of the glebes' condition which it contained was "ornamental" because, first, there was no glebe at all in many of the parishes; secondly, in several, the minister was deprived of its possession; thirdly, the glebes actually occupied and enjoyed were not fitted for the clergymen's "commodious reception and accomodation" whether one considered the houses, the orchards, or the other conveniences; and, finally, if one glebe was taken with another, the income annually derived from this source by each pastor would not exceed forty or fifty shillings.[2]

[1] Colonial Entry Book, April 30, 1695, vol. 1682–95. As previously shown in the text, this statement was confirmed by the testimony of Beverley in his History.

[2] B. T. Va., vol. vi., p. 105. There are numerous entries in the records which show incidentally that many glebes were occupied by a succession of ministers; for example, from a deposition of an aged citizen of Isle of Wight in 1697, we learn that the glebe in that county had, in the course of sixty years, been in the possession of

The Burgesses were greatly incensed by this reply, which they characterized as "malitious, untruthful and unjust." As to the charge that some parishes were lacking in a glebe, they declared that this was the minister's fault as he had, under the provisions of the existing law, a right to have a glebe laid off and assigned him as soon as he entered his living; and as to the detention of glebes, that but one instance had occurred, which was due to the fact that the minister in possession had committed such waste that the vestry had been compelled to deprive him of its use.[1] As to the physical condition of the glebes, the House's claim that they were as well appointed in the way of buildings and other improvements as the average plantation of the Colony, was, no doubt, strictly correct. If there were signs of dilapidation in some cases, it was to be laid chiefly at the door of the ministers themselves, either because they were deficient in capacity for practical management, owing to inexperience or special traits; or because, having reason to doubt their vestries' good will, they allowed their probational hold on their livings, which created the impression that they might at any moment have to vacate the land, to discourage them from keeping their glebes in good condition. Blair himself, as we have seen, had asserted that this indifference to their improvement was one of the most unhappy results of the clergymen's uncertain tenure. Where, however, the minister was not only sure of his vestry's favor, but also, as a lover of tidiness, reluctant to allow his glebe to fall into a state of neglect, there is no ground for

---

at least three. This glebe was finally leased and sold; see Isle of Wight County Records, vol. 1688–1704, p. 269.

[1] B. T. Va., vol. vi., p. 108.

thinking that the complaints of Blair and his fellow-signers obtained either his silent sympathy or his open encouragement.

Perhaps, the first parsonage erected in Virginia was the one built at an early period in the Colony's history for the Rev. Mr. Whitaker. It was situated on the western side of the James River, at a point opposite Henricopolis. Smith described the house as a "fair framed" structure, although, at the time this was written, it had not yet been finished. It seems to have been known by the name of Rock Hall.[1] Many years later, there was a parsonage standing further down the river at Martin Brandon, as we learn from the bequest which John Sadler, a merchant of London, made for its repair.[2]

It was the General Assembly's custom in directing a new parish to be laid off, to give instructions for the building of a parsonage on the glebe assigned to it; such was the course followed when, in 1639, the new parish of Cheskiack was created.[3] It was perhaps by force of this general provision that Rev. William Cotton, in 1635, presented to the county court of Accomac an order from Jamestown requiring a parsonage to be erected on the glebe which he held; and the court, having appointed a vestry, there being none at the time, commanded them to carry out this order.[4] The dwelling-house built represented very probably the average size of the residences occupied by the clergymen:—it extended forty feet in length, and eighteen in width; and between the floor and the wall

[1] *Works of Captain John Smith*, vol. ii., p. 12, Richmond edition.
[2] *Va. Maga. of Hist. and Biog.*, vol. iv., p. 316.
[3] Robinson Transcripts, p. 226.
[4] Accomac County Records, Orders Sept. 14, 1635.

plates, there was an interval of nine feet. A chimney was constructed at each end of the house. A partition raised near the middle of the floor divided the interior into a set of rooms:—on the one side, a chamber; on the other a study, kitchen, and buttery. In the garret above, there were perhaps additional rooms for the family's use.[1]

If the contingency anticipated by Stephen Charlton in his will in 1654, occurred, the minister then holding one of the livings on the Eastern Shore was much more commodiously situated in the way of a residence and glebe:—Charlton directed that, should his daughter, who appears to have been an only child, die without issue, then the mansion in which he dwelt as well as the outbuildings, orchards, gardens, and the surrounding dividend of land lying immediately on Nassawaddox Creek, should become the property of the parish, to be reserved indefinitely for the support of a clergyman of the Church of England.[2]

In some of the parishes, the minister's residence was more spacious than the parsonage erected in Accomac for the Rev. William Cotton. We discover, through the inventory of his personal estate, that the dwelling-house of Rev. Rowland Jones, besides a passage or hallway and a kitchen, contained two chambers for Mrs. Jones, one perhaps occupied as a sleeping-room,

[1] Accomac County Records, vol. 1632–40, p. 43, Va. St. Libr. Culpeper in his report of 1681, stated that "in most of the glebes there are houses good enough as they think, to answer the law." The parsonage built in Accomac county for Cotton's occupation was the typical residence of the average citizen of the Colony.

[2] Northampton County Records, vol. 1654–5, p. 57. It is probable that this condition went into effect, as the daughter seems to have died without heirs not long after her clandestine marriage referred to elsewhere.

the other as a sitting; a chamber and a study for the use of Mr. Jones himself; a parlor, which also perhaps served as a dining-room; a room situated above the porch; a chamber reserved for guests; and a chamber attached to the kitchen, where, no doubt, one of the servants slept.[1]

Some of the clergymen, especially if they happened to be unmarried, preferred to engage board with a neighbor rather than to reside alone in the parsonage. In 1658, Simon Barrows, of Lower Norfolk, petitioned the court to allow him in the next levy one thousand pounds of tobacco, which he claimed to be due him for providing "diet" for Rev. George Alford, the minister holding the benefice of Lynnhaven parish.[2]   Rev. George Hopkins and his wife seem to have spent at least three years as lodgers in Captain West's home during the time Hopkins was the incumbent of one of the livings situated in York county.[3]

In every parsonage, however small in dimensions, there was always one room reserved as a private study for the minister in writing his sermons; and this was, no doubt, the apartment in which he also received his callers.   It was here too that the volumes he owned were stored away on shelves.   All the clergymen, as one of the requisites of their calling, had been carefully educated, and were familiar with books; when they came over to Virginia, they brought with them at least the different works in which they had been grounded while pursuing a course in theology before becoming candidates for holy orders.

---

[1] *William and Mary College Quart.*, vol. iii., p. 246.

[2] Lower Norfolk County Records, vol. 1656–66, p. 183; Lower Norfolk County Antiquary, vol. iii., part i.

[3] *William and Mary College Quart.*, vol. iii., p. 181.

Some of the libraries belonging to ministers in the Colony were, in number of volumes, very respectable for that age. In 1645, the collection in the possession of Ralph Watson, who is designated in the records as "clerke," contained as many as thirty "great books" in folio, and fifty smaller ones in quarto. The two sets made up a total of eighty. Now if by "books" titles were meant, as was generally the case, then these eighty books represented, at an average of two volumes to the title, not less than one hundred and sixty volumes; and that they were well chosen is proven by the fact that the larger proportion were written in the Latin language, the language used by the greatest scholars of that age.

In the year in which an inventory was taken of the Watson collection, an inventory was also taken of the collection of Rev. George Hopkins, described as composed of old volumes.[1] In 1656, Rev. Robert Dunster, of Isle of Wight county, bequeathed all his books to his wife,[2] whilst, in 1678, Rev. Amory Butler, of Rappahannock, by will left his library, as well as his sermons and other papers, to his brother, Rev. William Butler, who held the living of Washington parish. His executors, however, were to exercise the privilege of selecting, each for himself, any three works they respectively preferred.[3]

Rev. Robert Powis, of Lower Norfolk, owned in 1652 thirty-two works, which, in the proportion of two volumes to the title, represented a collection of sixty-four volumes.[4] In his will, offered for probate in 1682,

[1] *William and Mary College Quart.*, vol. iii., p. 181.

[2] Isle of Wight County Records, Wills for 1656.

[3] Rappahannock County Records, vol. 1672–82, p. 64, Va. St. Libr.

[4] Lower Norfolk County Antiquary, vol. i., p. 105; Lower Norfolk County Records, vol. 1651–56, p. 37.

Rev. Benjamin Doggett instructed his executors to purchase a "great cheste" in which his books were to be packed and shipped to England, where they were to be sold for the benefit of his heirs.[1] The library of Rev. Thomas Perkins, of Rappahannock, was inventoried as containing three large parcels of books, one set of which was covered with parchment or paper; the remainder, no doubt, with calf. Three of the works that had belonged to him were so handsomely bound, and perhaps also so beautifully illustrated, that, after his death, they were appraised at the large figure of four hundred and fifty pounds of tobacco, whilst the total value of the library was estimated at one thousand and ninety-two pounds, about one seventh of the value of the entire personal estate. In considering this collection, it should be remembered (and the same is true of all the other collections yet to be mentioned) that the appraisement took into account only the physical condition of the books, and that a low calculation of their value, from that point of view, does not convey any real idea of their value from the point of view of their contents or their rarity.[2] The collection of Rev. William Scrimgour, who resided in Westmoreland, was entered in the inventory of his estate as worth as much as ten thousand pounds of tobacco, which, at twopence a pound, would bring its value in modern currency to two thousand dollars at least, no mean sum to be invested in books by a divine of that age, and perhaps not surpassed by the value of the libraries owned by the great bulk of the English clergy. The library of Rev. Mr. Scrimgour may not have been

[1] Lancaster County Will Book, 1674–89, folio p. 81. Among the items of his inventory was "one trunke of bookes."

[2] Rappahannock County Records, vol. 1677–82, orig. p. 28.

larger than that of Rev. Mr. Perkins, or more desirable
from a literary or theological point of view, but because
the majority of the volumes had been more recently
published or bought, their physical condition called for
a higher appraisement when an inventory of them was
taken.[1]

The books arranged on the shelves of Rev. Rowland
Jones's study were appraised in the inventory of his
personal estate at fourteen pounds sterling, or three
hundred and fifty dollars in modern values. In a
chest standing in one of the chambers were stored
away a number of volumes so dilapidated that they
were entered as worth only fifteen shillings. But the
largest and choicest library in a clergyman's possession
during this period was the one owned by the Rev.
Thomas Teakle, who filled a benefice on the Eastern
Shore. To his son, Mr. Teakle bequeathed fifty-two
works written in English relating to religious subjects,
and also thirty-four written in Latin, whilst his daughter, as her share, received sixty similar works in English
and thirty-one in Latin. This library contained about
one hundred and nine books treating of theology and
kindred topics, or a total, perhaps, of two hundred and
fifty volumes ranging over this general field alone.
There were also forty-eight books, probably embracing
as many as one hundred volumes (the larger number

[1] Westmoreland County Records, vol. 1691–99, folio p. 52. The
Scrimgour personalty was appraised at 61,303 pounds of tobacco;
the value of the books, therefore, amounted to one sixth of the
estate. Scrimgour is improperly entered as "Scrimmington" in the
List of Parishes and Clergymen in 1680 printed in the *Colonial
Records of Virginia*, State Senate Doct., Extra, 1874. It is an old
English family name generally spelled "Scrimgeour." In 1659, the
inventory of the personal estate of William White, clerke, of York
county, included "His Bookes"; see York County Records, 1657–62,
p. 152, Va. St. Libr.

written in Latin), devoted to the discussion of the various branches of the medical science. The varied character of the whole collection showed that Mr. Teakle possessed unusual catholicity of literary interests. The two extremes were perhaps best represented, on the one side, by his copies of Horace and Lucretius, and on the other, by the treatise entitled the *Picture of a Papist and Presbyterian Unmasked*. The library also contained Burton's *Anatomy, Civil and Military Aphorisms*, Grotius's *Laws of War*, and other similar works.[1]

[1] Accomac County Records, vol. 1692–1715, p. 146 et seq. The titles of the Teakle collection fill ten pages folio of the Accomac Records. In some instances, one title represented as many as nine volumes.

CHAPTER XVI

The Clergy: Their Estates

THERE are numerous proofs that many of the clergymen were in possession of a considerable amount of property, either inherited or accumulated out of their professional incomes by strict economy. In the muster of 1625, Rev. Greville Pooley was entered as the owner of two agricultural servants, one of whom was twenty-one years of age, the other sixteen; his livestock consisted of one cow and one pig; and he had eight barrels of corn stored away for future consumption. That he was not unprepared for defense in case of an Indian assault is shown by the fact that he owned one "armour," three swords, and three fixt peek. The minister residing at Elizabeth City at this time was the master of three servants; but his livestock seems to have been limited to three goats; and his fund of grain to ten barrels of corn. He possessed no arms.[1] In 1635, Rev. Thomas Butler, of Denbigh parish, obtained a patent to one thousand acres of land, and Rev. George White to two hundred.[2] Rev. George Keith, for bringing in fourteen persons, including himself and his wife, at his own expense, received a grant in Charles River, afterwards York county, of eight hundred and

[1] See Muster of Jan'y 20–Febry. 7, 1625, British Colonial Papers, vol. iii., No. 35.
[2] Virginia Land Patents for 1635.

fifty acres.[1]   Rev. Willis Higby, pastor of the parish
which included Mulberry Island, was presented with
a plantation of two hundred and fifty acres by the
General Assembly as a proof of the public appreciation
of his pious life, and as an inducement to others to
follow in his footsteps.[2]   Rev. Thomas Hampton, by
the importation of six persons at his own cost,
obtained in 1637 a patent to three hundred acres situated on the Nansemond River.[3]   Only six years afterwards, Rev. John Rosier, of Northampton, leased to
Robert Wyard his plantation and dwelling-house,
together with two servants; and Wyard was also to
have the use of nine milch cows, the poultry, the
household furniture, and other articles.   For the
whole, he was to pay a rental of six thousand, five
hundred pounds of tobacco.   It is evident that this
was Rosier's private property, for had the plantation
been really the glebe, the vestry, not he, would have
been renting it.   We find him, at a later date, bringing
in servants at his own expense; no doubt, to till land
at that time in his possession.[4]

The inventory taken of the estate of Robert Powis in
1652 disclosed that he was the owner of no inconsiderable amount of property.   His personalty, which alone
was valued at nearly twelve thousand pounds of
tobacco, included, in addition to a large quantity
of household furniture and utensils, eighteen head of
cattle and seven head of swine, and also a number
of debts due him.   He also possessed a boat, for he

---

[1] *Va. Maga. of Hist. and Biog.*, vol. iii., p. 279.

[2] Tyler's *Cradle of the Republic*, p. 151.

[3] *Va. Maga. of Hist. and Biog.*, vol. vi., p. 191.

[4] Rosier seems to have retained one room in the house for his
own use; Northampton County Records, Orders Febry. 10, 1643;
see also Orders July 28, 1645.

seems to have resided directly on the water. In his will, he gave orders that sixteen of his herd of cattle should pass to his daughter, who at this time, was living in the Mother Country; and should she prefer to remain there, these cattle were to be sold for tobacco, to be shipped for her benefit either to England or Holland. To one friend, he bequeathed a hogshead of that commodity; to another, a heifer and three barrels of corn; whilst to his only son, Robert, he devised the remainder of his estate.[1] John Gorsuch, of Lancaster, who is described in the records as a "professor in divinity," possessed at his death valuable interests in England; and in 1656, his two sons obtained an order of court permitting their sister to act as curator of this English property.[2] Rev. William Thompson, of Surry, in 1664, purchased from William Morton of New England one "p'cell or necke of land" situated in New London; and in the following year, he sold a tract of land which he owned in Virginia; and again another tract in 1673. The assessment of 1675 showed him to be the owner of eight tithables, the second largest in the county.[3]

[1] Lower Norfolk County Records, vol. 1651–56, p. 37; see also Orders Jan'ry 15, 1651, Dec. 21, 1652; Lower Norfolk County Antiquary, vol. ii., pp. 124, 126. For four years, Powis, who had been inducted for the whole of Lower Norfolk performed all the ministerial functions for the county, and yet received no compensation for his "great pains, travel and endeavors." The vestry, in 1648, paid him one year's full tithe in tobacco and corn. Mr. Powis, and, no doubt, there were others like him, refuted in his conduct the charge against the clergy of the Colony made in 1658 by a Quaker witness in Northampton County, who said: "the ministers who come into this Country were raveninge wolves and hungry dogges and would preach no longer than they were fed"; see Northampton Records, 1657–64, f. p. 27.

[2] Lancaster County Records, vol. 1656–66, p. 7.

[3] Surry County Records, vol. 1645–72, pp. 253, 281; see also vol. 1671–84, pp. 43, 136, Va. St. Libr.

Rev. John Gwyn in 1672 claimed the right under the law as a clergyman to be exempted from the payment of all public taxes due for himself and his six tithables, a working force that compared very favorably with the like force possessed by the average citizen of the Colony.[1]   That Rev. Thomas Doughty, of Rappahannock, was a large property holder is shown by the conveyances he made to his wife in anticipation of a long journey he was about to start upon at that time.[2]   Rev. Amory Butler bequeathed to friends, not only a number of valuable books, as we have seen, but also several legacies, one of which amounted to as much as two thousand pounds of tobacco.   The remainder of his estate passed to his nephew.[3]   Rev. Robert Parke, of Surry, owned a grist mill situated in that county and also several slaves.[4]   Rev. John Waugh, of Stafford parish, in 1675, sold a tract containing two hundred and fifty acres, perhaps only one part of the land belonging to him; and a few years later, Rev. John Ball, rector of Varina parish, in Henrico, is found presenting various kinds of livestock to his step-children.[5]   The personal estate of Rev. Thomas Perkins, of Rappahannock, was, in 1684, valued at seventy-four hundred and seventy-six pounds of tobacco.   It is interesting to note that it included one canonical and one cape gown, a dimity and a plush coat, a silk waistcoat and girdle, and two dimity waistcoats, three periwigs, a pair of silver buttons for breeches, and also a pair of shoebuckles.   As he seems to have left no household furniture, it is probable that,

---

[1] General Court Records, vol. 1670–76, p. 137.

[2] Rappahannock County Records, vol. 1668–72, p. 40, Va. St. Libr.

[3] *Ibid.*, vol. 1672–82, p. 64, Va. St. Libr.

[4] Surry County Records, vol. 1671–84, pp. 291, 391, Va. St. Libr.

[5] Henrico County Records, vol. 1677–92, orig. p. 217.

during his incumbency, he had resided in the parsonage belonging to his living.[1]

Rev. John Lawrence, who had preached for some time in Maryland, where (so he declared with evident complacency) the "Roman Catholics could not endure him," died at Point Comfort, in 1684, and his will revealed the fact that he had made a Mrs. Benson, his nurse during his last illness, the chief beneficiary of his personal estate. His bequests to her included a large quantity of gold and silver, jewels and rings. Lawrence, who had graduated as a master-of-arts at one of the English Universities, had owned considerable property in the parish of St. Martins in-the-Fields, in London.[2] In 1686, Rev. James Blair purchased from William Byrd land situated in the parish of Varina in Henrico county.[3] Rev. Rowland Jones, who died about 1689, left personalty which alone was valued at four hundred and forty pounds sterling, about eleven thousand dollars in our modern currency. He was the owner of ten slaves, and, in addition, forty-one head of cattle, twelve horses, thirty-six sheep, and a great number of hogs. His residence contained a large quantity of household furniture and kitchen utensils. Among the different articles belonging to his personal estate was one hundred and thirteen pounds of pewter appraised at a figure as high as four pounds and fourteen shillings. The number of livestock owned by Rev. Rowland Jones shows that he was also the proprietor of a very considerable area of land.[4]

[1] Rappahannock County Records, vol. 1677–82, orig. p. 28.

[2] Lower Norfolk County Deed and Will Book, 1675–86, p. 182.

[3] Henrico County Records, vol. 1677–92, orig. p. 420. Blair at his death is said to have left £10,000 to his nephew John Blair, President of the Council; see *Va. Maga. of Hist. and Biog.*, vol. vii., p. 155. [4] *William and Mary College Quart.*, vol. iii., p. 246.

The property in the possession of Rev. Thomas Teakle, who died about 1695, was even more valuable. To Margaret, a daughter, he devised a plantation, with the right of annually making a thousand gallons of cider from the apples produced in the home orchard, and to her, he also bequeathed three slaves; to his daughter Elizabeth, two and a plantation; and to his daughter Kate, the like. His son John was to receive three slaves and the remainder of his lands. The residuary estate was required to be apportioned equally among three of his children, who were mentioned by name; thus to John, there was to go one share consisting of clothes, linen, household utensils and similar articles, valued at ninety-five and a half pounds; a second share was to go to Elizabeth and a third to Kate, valued respectively at one hundred and eighteen pounds and seventeen shillings. Among these three children were to be divided fifty-four head of cattle and thirty-nine head of sheep, and quite probably a large number of hogs, — animals not always included in the inventories owing to the wild state in which they roamed the forests. Mr. Teakle seems also to have left a considerable sum in the form of ready money: — to his son, he bequeathed Spanish coin equal in value to four pounds and fifteen shillings, and also a purse of ten shillings in English gold; and Elizabeth too was to receive the same amount. His daughter Margaret does not appear to have benefited under the will to the same extent as the other children, either because she, as perhaps the oldest of them, had been partly provided for in her father's lifetime, or because she had given him offence by escapades like the dance, which, as we saw, brought down on her so much of the paternal displeasure.[1]   The whole estate, personal and real, of Mr. Teakle very probably fell little short of fifty thousand dollars in our present values.[2]

The preceding instances, which do not embrace all that might be gleaned from the few county records of the Seventeenth century surviving to the present day, indicate that there were a large number of clergymen in the Colony at that time who possessed a very considerable amount of private property.   If this property had been purchased by them with money brought from England, then it would appear that Virginia offered advantages even in the eyes of the English divines not absolutely dependant on their calling for a subsistence, a fact that would controvert the repeated statements of interested observers like Blair and Godwyn that the uncertain tenure of the livings in the Colony discouraged without exception the superior clergy from emigrating.   But it is more probable that most of the estates held by the ministers were accumulated by careful management after their arrival in Virginia, which would go to show that the income obtained in following their profession there was not so meagre after all.

There are numerous proofs that many of the clergymen were active men of business.   In 1643, Rev. John Rosier gave a bill for so large a sum as thirty pounds sterling; and that confidence was felt in his practical judgment is proven by the frequency with which he appears in the records as having served

[1] See Bruce's *Social Life of Virginia in the 17th Century*, chapter xii.

[2] Accomac County Records, vol. 1692–1715, f. p. 98, 138 et seq. In 1683, Mr. Teakle brought three young negroes to the county court to have their ages adjudged.   These he had very probably recently bought; see same records, vol. 1682–97, p. 26.

as either an appraiser or an arbitrator.[1]   Rev. John Wright, who held the living of Poquoson parish in York, on at least one occasion gave a bond for one hundred and forty pounds sterling, on account of some transaction in which he had been engaged.[2]   Rev. Thomas Higby served as the attorney in Virginia of Elizabeth Dodsworth residing in the English county of Middlesex.[3] Rev. Andrew Jackson, some years later, was named by James Phillips in his will as the guardian of his son, and curator of the whole of his personal and real estate. Jackson was to receive thirty per cent. of the profits in compensation for his trouble.[4]   In 1697, Rev. James Wallace was chosen by George Willocks, "late of Perth Amboy in New Jersey," to act as his representative in recovering all sums due him in Virginia, Maryland, and Carolina; and if necessary to cast his debtors into prison.[5]   Wallace seems to have found, at least in one instance, the collection of these outstanding amounts a dangerous undertaking, for while seeking to carry out his principal's instructions, he was assaulted at Kikotan at the court-house door by Colonel Armistead and his son.[6]   Rev. Thomas Teakle, probably the wealthiest clergyman residing in Virginia during the Seventeenth century, was constantly acting as trustee and executor, a tribute as well to his integrity as to his talents for business.

---

[1] Northampton County Records, Orders Febry. 10, 1643; July 28, 1645.

[2] York County Records, vol. 1684–87, p. 12, Va. St. Libr.

[3] Northampton County Records, vol. 1654–55, f. p. 39.

[4] Lancaster County Records, Orders Jany. 3, 1689.

[5] Elizabeth City County Records, vol. 1684–99, pp. 128, 487, Va. St. Libr.

[6] See an imperfect paper preserved at Lambeth Palace, Cod. Misc., No. 954, paper 65.

In some cases, the minister found himself in court in a character perhaps less creditable:—for instance, in 1647, Rev. Robert Powis was the defendant in a suit for seven hundred and thirty-three pounds of tobacco; and Rev. William White, in 1657, for seventeen hundred pounds. White seems to have left his family in a situation of great poverty on account of the number of claims in Virginia and England alike against his estate.[1]   About 1684, Rev. Samuel Dudley, of Rappahannock, was required by an order of court to pay to Colonel William Lloyd thirty-eight hundred and fifty pounds of tobacco.[2]

[1] Lower Norfolk County Antiquary, vol. ii., p. 14; Lancaster County Records, vol. 1656–66, p. 46.

[2] Rappahannock County Records, Orders Oct. 1, 1684.

CHAPTER XVII

The Clergy: Their Duties

BEFORE entering upon an inquiry as to the general character of the clergymen of Virginia during the Seventeenth century, it will be of interest to touch briefly on the nature of their ordinary duties. As early as 1619, they were required to make a report of all christenings, burials, and marriages occurring in their parishes in the course of a year.[1] This duty, by the Act of 1631–2, was imposed on them apparently in association with the churchwardens; but as late as 1686, it seems to have been again imposed on them alone.[2] Every pastor under the provisions of the same Act was ordered to instruct all the young persons belonging to his congregation in the Ten Commandments, the Lord's Prayer, the Catechism, and the Articles of Belief; and should a parent fail to send his child to the church at the time appointed, namely, the half hour before evening service, then he was to be called before the county court and censured. This is an additional indication of how minute was the supervision exercised by the justices over everything promotive as well of

[1] Minutes of Assembly, 1619, p. 26, *Colonial Recs. of Va.*, State Senate Doct., Extra, 1874.

[2] Hening's *Statutes*, vol. i., pp. 155–7; Proclamation of Governor and Council, Colonial Entry Book, vol. 1680–95, p. 227. The law of 1657–8 required the vestry to keep a registry book for this purpose; see Hening's *Statutes*, vol. i., p. 431.

the moral as the material welfare of the community.
By an Act passed in 1640, the minister was ordered to
catechize, not only all the children living in his parish,
but also all the servants; and in performing this duty
it would seem that he could cause his pupils to repair
to the church nearest to them to receive instruction,
and if there was more than one, he had to traverse the
whole of his parish in order to visit each church until
all had been taught.[1] He was also required to visit
the sick, to administer the sacraments three times a
year, and to baptize infants.[2]

It was provided by law, in 1641, that there should be
an annual meeting of all the ministers and churchwardens of the Colony; that it should be held at Jamestown; and that the Governor and Council, in their
character very probably of an ecclesiastical court,
should be present. This meeting, which was to take
place immediately after Easter, was to be in the nature
of a visitation as formulated by the orders of the
Church of England.[3] No doubt, on this occasion,
the general condition of the Colony's religious affairs
was fully gone over, the needs of the different parishes
carefully canvassed, and plans adopted for advancing
the moral welfare of the people. Moreover, such a
meeting afforded the clergymen (who had few chances
of being thrown together in consequence of the dis-

[1] *Va. Maga. of Hist. and Biog.*, vol. ix., p. 52. The catechism
was to extend to the "fundamental points of the Christian Religion."
It was to be held on Sunday afternoon throughout the interval
between March 1 and November 30, the period of the year when
the atmosphere was at its mildest, and the children were in the
least danger of exposure to inclement weather.

[2] Randolph MS., vol. iii., p. 216; Hening's *Statutes*, vol. i., pp.
157, 290.

[3] *Va. Maga. Hist. and Biog.*, vol. ix., p. 53.

tances between their homes) at least one opportunity
each year of becoming well acquainted with each other;
of forming new and reviving old friendships; and of
acquiring a deeper zeal in performing all the duties
of their sacred calling. This personal association,
though necessarily brief, must have been highly re-
freshing and stimulating for a body of men who,
during the remainder of the twelve months, led a
rather secluded life in their remote parsonages.

The minister's duties in 1644 were perhaps unusually
heavy, for at this time some of them at least were in
charge of two parishes; and some even of three.[1]
Every clergyman, after the Restoration, was required
to deliver at least one sermon a month in the chapel-of-
ease, should one be situated in his parish; on each
remaining Sunday, he was to preach in his parish
church; and twice in the course of the year (instead of
thrice as formerly), he was to administer the Sacrament
of the Lord's Supper. The service each Sabbath was
now perhaps rarely held more than once during the
twelve hours, as the distance which most of the people
had to traverse in order to attend at all would have
made it impossible for them to wait for the second
sermon without exposing themselves to the certainty
of being overtaken by night far from home. Indeed,
there were many persons in most of the parishes dwelling so remotely from the church edifice that they were
unable to reach it in time for the sermon delivered in
the morning. The length of the journey when it was to
be made by land, the dangers of storms when to be
made by water, excessive heat in summer, heavy
snows in winter, and flooded streams in spring,—all

[1] Hening's *Statutes*, vol. i., p. 290.

served to thin the ranks of the congregations. Had the minister considered it to be his imperative duty to visit constantly all those families residing in his parish who were prevented from being present Sunday after Sunday in the parish church, then but little time would have been left him to administer to the spiritual wants of the remainder of his flock.[1]   It is quite probable, therefore, that he was forced to content himself with an occasional tour through those parts of the country, embraced within the boundaries of his living, which were difficult of access. This obstacle of remoteness was foreseen as early as 1632–3, and as a partial remedy for it, the General Assembly, that year, authorized the clergymen having large parishes to appoint deacons to read prayers in the neighborhoods lying far from the parish church.[2]

In the minister's absence from his regular pulpit, whether due to sickness or an imperative call elsewhere, the clerk was, by the nature of his office, impowered to read the lessons.[3]   The minister, however, was very frequently assisted in the performance of this duty by some person specially appointed. By an Act passed in 1660–1, it was provided that, should a parish be unable to secure a clergyman to preach in the parish church every Sunday, a "grave and sober citizen of good life and conversation" should be chosen to read the lessons on the intervening Sabbaths.[4]

Some of the ministers preferred a reader to an ordained assistant. About 1675, Rev. Robert Parke, a

---

[1] Virginia's Cure, pp. 4–6, Force's Hist. Tracts, vol. iii.

[2] Hening's Statutes, vol. i., p. 208; Randolph MS., vol. iii., p. 223. A fixed sum was allowed the deacons thus appointed.

[3] MS. Laws of Va., 1643, Clerk's Office, Portsmouth, Va.

[4] Hening's Statutes, vol. ii., p. 47.   This remained the law until the end of the century; see Beverley's History of Virginia, p. 210.

young divine, on arriving from England, became the guest of Mr. Randall Holt, who resided on Hog Island, a part of Surry county. During his stay there, he preached in the church at Lawne's Creek in the absence and without the consent of the regular pastor, Rev. William Thompson; and so favorable was the impression made by him, that it was soon whispered about that he would be an acceptable person to fill the pulpit of the lower parish church on those Sundays when Mr. Thompson would be required to officiate in the upper parish church. It was arranged by the vestry that a meeting of the citizens should be held on an appointed day, and that Mr. Parke should be requested to deliver a sermon on that occasion with a view to his becoming the assistant pastor. When Parke appeared, he was forbidden by the sheriff to occupy the pulpit. Mr. Thompson, it seems, had complained to the Governor and Council, sitting as an ecclesiastical court, and obtained an order prohibiting Parke's appointment to serve as his curate. The feeling of resentment aroused in the people who had assembled was so strong that it was with difficulty that the sheriff was able to disperse them.[1]

[1] Surry County Records, vol. 1671–84, p. 124, Va. St. Libr. It would be inferred from Thompson's defiance of the wishes of the congregation of the lower parish church, that he was an inducted minister; that is to say, one who had a freehold title to his living, and, therefore, one who was practically independent of his parishioners' favor. His conduct seems to reveal the arbitrary spirit in which it was always possible for a clergyman so placed to take advantage of his permanent position; and serves to illustrate further the Virginians' wisdom in refusing to induct all their pastors. Had Thompson been engaged from year to year, his desire to stand in well with his vestry would, perhaps, have caused him to submit to an appointment apparently called for by the people's religious welfare. See, however, an entry in the Surry County Records (vol. 1671–84, p. 124, Va. St. Libr.) showing the extraordinary esteem in which he was held. This is referred to later in the text.

In 1680, when the Colony was divided into about forty-eight parishes, there were only three served by readers alone; this is to be inferred from the fact that there were, at this time only three parishes lacking in clergymen.[1] But eleven years later, the number of vacancies was perhaps much greater, for the Council then considered it necessary to issue an order that a reader should be chosen wherever such a vacancy existed.[2] In 1691 also, Capt. Hugh Campbell, in a petition to the Governor, stated that the inhabitants of certain parts of Isle of Wight, Nansemond, and Norfolk counties, dwelling as they did at an extraordinary distance from churches and chapels-of-ease, were seldom able to be present at public worship; and that, as it would promote a more Christian manner of life among the people thus cut off, should some one be appointed in each of these places to read prayers and a sermon every Sunday (especially in winter when it was impossible for them to make the long journey to the nearest parish church), he was ready to convey a plantation of two hundred acres in area for the support of such a reader in each place; and that should the plantations he proposed to deed away for that purpose be inconveniently situated, then he would be ready to give six thousand pounds of tobacco for the purchase of that extent of ground wherever it should be thought to be more proper to buy it. This generous offer was accepted by the Governor; and the courts of the three counties were directed to take all the necessary steps to carry out Campbell's pious design. Nicholson, with that impulsive public spirit and burning zeal for advancing the church's welfare so characteristic of him,

[1] British Colonial Papers, vol. lx., No. 410.
[2] Henrico County Minute Book, 1682–1701, p. 294, Va. St. Libr.

promised to give all the fees that, in the future, would be due him in these counties for marriage and tavern licenses, towards defraying the different expenses involved in establishing this endowment.[1]

Though the Colony's population was far more dispersed than that of England, and the character of its society necessarily more provincial, not so much from its remoteness from the society of the Mother Country as from the entire absence of cities, towns, and even villages, nevertheless, the general field of work to which the Virginian clergymen were confined must have been very similar to the field in which the English clergymen labored in the different English shires. On the whole, the life led by them was even more onerous, owing to the greater size of their parishes. In England, as the result of the greater concentration of the people, the parish did not cover any extraordinary extent of ground; and it followed that it was not difficult for the minister to traverse it even on foot, in a comparatively short time, in visiting the sick among the members of his congregation, in administering comfort to the afflicted, or in distributing gifts for the relief of the poor. In Virginia, on the other hand, the parish generally spread over such a wide area, and the number of inhabitants were, as a rule, so sparse, that the clergyman required the aid of a horse in getting from house to house; and even that means of locomotion did not always assure a rapid conveyance owing to the badness and circuitousness of most of the roads. The duty of visiting his parishioners could be performed, not in a few hours, as in England, but very often only in a couple of days. Each journey was attended with great

[1] Norfolk County Records, Orders Jan'y 27, 1691; see also Lower Norfolk County Antiquary, vol. i., p. 65.

fatigue, and at certain seasons, with extraordinary discomfort, and even danger, to horse and rider. Nor was he likely in those secluded plantation communities to have the tedium of the trip relieved by the occasional companionship of acquaintances by the way, or by exchanging greetings with travellers coming up from a direction opposite to the one in which he himself was going. But when the journey's end was reached, the Virginian clergyman received perhaps an even more hearty welcome than he would have received in an English home, because a visit from the minister was in the Colony a rarer event. If he was a man enjoying the esteem of his parishioners,—if he was also attractive in deportment and agreeable in conversation,—it can be easily seen that the hearts of the family he was stopping with would have gone out to him with an almost unbounded hospitality.

CHAPTER XVIII

The Clergy: Their General Character

IF we consider as a body the ministers who performed the various duties of their calling in Virginia during the Seventeenth century, there is no reason to think that they fell below the standard of conscientiousness governing the conduct of the English clergymen in the same age. The early history of the New World was adorned by no nobler group of divines than that group which gives so much distinction, from the point of view of character and achievement alike, to the years in which the foundation of the Colony at Jamestown was permanently laid. Among the company setting out for Virginia with the expedition of 1606 was Rev. Robert Hunt, a man who, as Governor Wingfield, his friend and companion, declared, "was not anywise to be touched with the rebellious humors of a popish spirit, nor blemished with the least suspicion of a factious schismatic."[1] The ships were, by unprosperous winds, detained six weeks in sight of the English headlands; and during this entire time, he lay so sick that his recovery was looked upon as impossible. The vessel bearing him waited for a change of weather at a point in the Downs hardly twenty miles away from his old home, and yet neither his proximity to that beloved spot, nor the illness weighing him down, nor

[1] *Works of Captain John Smith*, p. xci., Arber's edition.

unjust reflections and imputations leveled against him, could move him to abandon an enterprise in which his whole soul had been embarked. All these influences tugging so persistently at his heart to persuade him to turn upon his course, "all," exclaims his historian, with ardent admiration, "could never force him so much as a seeming desire to leave the business." The secret and wily plots under way to defeat the action would have been successful had he not, by his patience, pious warnings, and faithful and unselfish example, quenched the "flames of envie and dissension."[1] His discriminating glance detected John Smith's high and useful qualities; when the fellow councillors of that bold and impatient spirit would have shut him out of their body, it was the "good doctrine and exhortation," the sound common sense and eloquent persuasions of the devoted clergyman, which reconciled the perilous differences and led to Smith's admission to his rightful place at the board.[2] A fire broke out among the inflammable huts at Jamestown and destroyed Mr. Hunt's library, and every article he possessed except the clothes he was then wearing; but not one word of dissatisfaction or repining was heard to escape from his lips, though the loss, especially of his books, must have fallen heavily on his spirit. Remaining in Virginia until his death, he, throughout his whole pastorate, directed his thoughts and energies exclusively towards advancing the Colonists' spiritual welfare. Whilst he lived, so an eye witness declared, he so "comforted the wants and extremities" of the settlers that all their hardships seemed easy enough to bear as compared with what they had afterwards to undergo when he was

[1] *Works of Captain John Smith*, vol. i., p. 150, Richmond edition.
[2] *Ibid.*, p. 152, Richmond edition.

no longer on earth to teach them by word and example how to endure their sufferings with heroic patience and fortitude.[1]

Rev. Richard Buck, who succeeded Hunt, was a graduate of Oxford, and when the question of his appointment to Virginia arose, was earnestly recommended as a man zealous and faithful in his calling; and this encomium was fully confirmed by the entire history of his pastorate from the first hour of his arrival in the Colony.[2]

Rev. Alexander Whitaker, who left England about the same time,[3] was the son of one of the most celebrated preachers of that age; had won at Cambridge the degree of master-of-arts; and had filled a benefice in a northern shire with such untiring devotion to its duties that he had succeeded in securing the hearty approval and deep love of his parishioners. In the possession of a large salary that more than supplied him with all that he needed; with the assured prospect of even more lucrative preferment and far greater distinction in the church,—nevertheless, well born, well educated, well placed as he was, he voluntarily left his "warme neste" (to use the expressive phrase of Rev. William Crashaw), and, to the amazement of his kindred and friends, passed oversea to "help to bear the name of God to the Gentiles."[4] What did he himself say of the heavy task he had undertaken at a sacrifice of all personal ease and promotion?

[1] *Works of Captain John Smith*, p. 959, Arber's edition. Wingfield declared that he always "took such notes in writing of Mr. Hunt's sermons as his capacity could comprehend"; Brown's *First Republic*, p. 31.

[2] *Purchas*, iv., p. 201. Buck came out with Sir Thomas Gates.

[3] Whitaker came out with Dale in 1611.

[4] Brown's *Genesis of the United States*, vol. ii., pp. 614–15.

"My coming to Virginia," he wrote, "has been prosperous, and my continuance here hath been answerable. I think I have fared better for your prayers and the rest. Though my promise of three years' service to my country be expired, I will abide in my vocation here until I be lawfully called hence." And there, in the zealous performance of his duties, he remained until accidentally drowned in the James River. In forming the "hard but heroical" resolution of going out to Virginia, he was aware that he would be confronted with innumerable perils to his personal safety; and in meeting death upon the waters, while perhaps on an errand of sympathy and consolation, he had only come to that premature end by the shock of fate which he doubtless anticipated in giving up his quiet parsonage amid the peaceful scenes of an English parish.[1]

Rev. Mr. Glover, a contemporary of Whitaker, did not survive so long; and, like Whitaker, paid with his life for his zealous self-sacrifice in settling in Virginia. He was one of the numerous victims of the new country's extraordinary unhealthiness before the plantations had spread out widely; so long, however, as his health permitted, he is described by one who was deeply interested in the Colonists' religious welfare at that early period as giving "his soule to Christ Jesus, under whose banner he went to fighte, and for whose glorious name he undertook the danger." Glover was a graduate of Cambridge, and by his faithful conduct while holding livings in Bedford and Huntingdon shires had come to be greatly reverenced and beloved. Like Whitaker, however, though perhaps past his youth, he felt that he was

[1] Brown's *Genesis of the United States*, p. 500; *Works of Captain John Smith*, vol. ii., p. 22, Richmond edition; Neill's *Virginia Company of London*, pp. 75, 76, 82, 100.

called to that wild and remote field of labor oversea; and he put aside every hope and comfort in his native land in his determination to obey. He gave up his life to the cause, apparently without one word of repining or lamentation, except perhaps that the work in which his heart was centred should be cut short by his death.[1] Well might the eloquent Crashaw, in dwelling with fervent admiration upon the firm resolution, the unyielding patience, the indefatigable zeal, and the indifference to suffering of these early clergymen, exclaim: "The ages to come will eternize your names as the Apostles to Virginia."[2]

In 1616, when Dale left the Colony to return to England, the pastors then occupying pulpits there were Wm. Wickham, who resided at Henricopolis; Alexander Whitaker, at Bermuda Hundred; Richard Buck, at Jamestown; and Mr. Meese, at Kikotan.[3] Wickham, it appears, had never been ordained, but after the death of Mr. Whitaker, owing to the smallness of the number of clergymen surviving, he was, it seems, impowered by the Archbishop of Canterbury, at the request of Governor Argoll, to administer the sacraments.[4] Two years later, Governor Yeardley reported that there were then (1619) only five pastors in Vir-

[1] Brown's *Genesis of the United States*, p. 619; Anderson's *Colonial Church*, p. 225.

[2] Anderson's *Colonial Church*, p. 238. One of the most learned and eloquent tributes ever paid to the zeal and piety of these early clergymen will be found in the address delivered by Mr. R. S. Thomas before the convention of the P. E. Church at Petersburg, Va., in 1898. This is one of several contributions, equally interesting and valuable, which Mr. Thomas has made to our knowledge of the church in Colonial Virginia.

[3] Campbell's *History of Virginia*, p. 117, Phila. edition.

[4] See Letter of Governor Argoll, June 9, 1617, Randolph MS., vol. iii., p. 137.

ginia; and of these five, but three had received orders. Of the two who had never been ordained, one, Samuel Maycock, was a scholar of Cambridge University.[1] Francis Bolton, who filled first the living at Elizabeth City, and afterwards the one on the Eastern Shore, having, in 1621, been highly recommended to the Company for piety and learning, had been gladly accepted as the minister for appointment to the earliest vacant pulpit in the Colony. He seems, at one time, to have officiated as the rector of the church at Jamestown, the most important in Virginia; here he succeeded Rev. Hawte Wyatt, a brother of Governor Wyatt, and himself a graduate of an English university with the degree of master-of-arts.[2] Rev. Robert Staples, who emigrated in 1622, was a man of such remarkable qualifications that twenty conspicuous English divines had united in urging the Company to secure his services as a pastor for one of the Virginian benefices.[3] Rev. Thomas White, who went over about the same time proved himself to be so zealous and untiring in the performance of his duties, that the Governor and Council addressed a letter of special thanks to the Company for having dispatched to them so useful a minister.[4] At a later date, the authorities did not

[1] Brown's *First Republic*, p. 327; Neill's *Va. Co. of London*, p. 138. The three ordained clergymen were Rev. Richard Buck, Rev. Mr. Meese, and Rev. Mr. Bargrave. William Wickham and Samuel Maycock had not been ordained.

[2] Abstracts of Proceedings of Va. Co. of London, vol. i., p. 135.

[3] *Ibid.*, p. 166. The Company supplied both Rev. Robert Staples and Rev. William Leete with £20 respectively to meet the cost of their clothes and books, and to defray the charges of their voyage to Virginia.

[4] Randolph, MS., vol. iii., p. 166. Among the clergymen residing in Virginia in 1623 were Greville Pooley at Fleur de Hundred; Hawte Wyatt at Jamestown; David Saunders (Sandys) at Hog

content themselves with simply commending a divine who had set a lofty example to his fellow clergymen; in 1635, as we have already stated, they bestowed on the Rev. Willis Higby a grant of two hundred and fifty acres for his "faithful paines" in pursuing his calling, and for the quiet and pious life with which he had "seconded his doctrine."[1]

From the middle of the century to the end, as from the beginning to the middle, a large proportion of the clergymen were not only graduates of English universities, but also men of more or less distinguished social connections in England. Morgan Godwyn, at one time, in charge of the living of Marston parish adjoining Middle Plantation, was the great-grandson of a chaplain of Queen Elizabeth, afterwards promoted to the bishopric of Bath and Wells. His grandfather had filled the see of Hereford, whilst his father had died an archdeacon.[2] Rev. Philip Mallory, who had won the degree

---

Island; and George Keith at Elizabeth City; see *Colonial Records of Va.*, State Senate Doct., Extra, 1874, p. 37. About fifteen ministers arrived between 1618 and 1623, among them William Bennett, Jonas Stockton, Mr. Hopkins, Mr. Pemberton, and Henry Jacob. Rev. Robert Pawlett also came over in this interval; he seems to have been also a physician and surgeon.

[1] Tyler's *Cradle of the Republic*, p. 151. Among the clergymen residing in Virginia in 1680 were Benjamin Doggett, Charles Davies, Mr. Dudley, Mr. Scrimgour, William Butler, John Waugh, John Farnefold, John Ball, Paul Williams, John Clough, Rowland Jones, Thomas Vicars, John Gwyn, John Sheppard, William Sellick, Thomas Taylor, William Williams, Robert Carr, Thomas Hampton, Robert Parke, William Housdon, John Gregory, John Wood, Henry Parkes, Thomas Teakle, John Lawrence, and James Porter. The following clergymen signed a memorial to Governor Andros in 1696:—James Blair, Cope Doyley, James Sclater, William Williams, Henry Pretty, Joseph Holt, Geo. Robinson, John Batte, Andrew and John Monro, Charles Anderson, Francis Fordyce, Jonathan Saunders, Jno. Alexander, and John Wallace.

[2] Neill's *Va. Carolorum*, p. 342.

of master-of-arts at one of the universities, was both the son and the brother of a dean of Chester, and had himself occupied a vicarage in County Durham before emigrating to Virginia; the personal esteem and confidence in which he was held, as well as his high reputation for ability, were shown by his selection in 1661 as the agent to be sent to England to advance the interests of the colonial Church; and in the same year, the General Assembly paid a warm tribute to his zealous and faithful conduct in performing his duties as a clergyman. Rev. Thomas Hampton was a bachelor-of-arts of Corpus Christi College. His family, like that of Mallory, had been intimately associated with the English Church; he himself was the son of a vicar; and a brother had long occupied the same office. Rev. Thomas Harrison, who, after acting as Berkeley's chaplain, was converted to the Puritan faith, was appointed, on his return to England, the chaplain of Henry Cromwell, a proof of his high standing as a man of talents and devoted piety. Rev. Justinian Aylmer was the grandson of an archdeacon of the same name, and there is reason to think identical with the Justinian Aylmer, who, in 1657, graduated from Oxford University with the degree of bachelor-of-arts. Rev. Rowland Jones, like so many others of the clergy who settled in Virginia, was sprung from a family prominent in the Church. His father was a vicar. Jones himself had enjoyed all the advantages of education which Merton College could afford. Rev. John Clayton, before removing to the Colony, had been vicar of Crofton Warwick; he was a graduate of Oxford University, a member of the Royal Society, and a student in the natural sciences of remarkable attainments. The book which he wrote touching the various natural features of Virginia is one of the most valuable and entertaining composed in the Seventeenth century on the same or a kindred topic. Rev. James Blair had graduated from the University of Edinburgh as a master-of-arts, and was a man of such conspicuous ability, and such extraordinary vigour of character, that, in addition to serving as a clergyman, he filled many honorable and responsible positions, — was commissary of the Bishop of London, member of the Council, and President of William and Mary College.[1]

Robert Hunt, Richard Buck, Hawte Wyatt, and Francis Bolton, previous to 1630, and Justinian Aylmer, Rowland Jones, John Clayton, John Clough, and James Blair, after that date, were incumbents of the pulpit at Jamestown. That we are more familiar with their lives than with those of the same number of men who, during the same period, occupied, one after another, the same benefice in some other part of Virginia, is due only to the fact that they were associated with the history of the political capital and social centre of the Colony. Outside of the great towns of England, or the wealthiest and most populous of the English rural parishes, there was, in the course of the century, perhaps no single English living filled by a succession of clergymen superior to this body of men in combined learning, talents, piety, and devotion to duty; and yet there is no reason to think that the ability, zeal, and fidelity of these ministers who occupied the pulpit at Jamestown were overshadowing as compared with the same qualities in the clergymen, who, one after another, occupied any of the more important benefices in York,

[1] I am indebted for most of the preceding details to Mr. Tyler's *Cradle of the Republic*, a work full of interesting information obtained by original research; see page 87 et seq.

Surry, Elizabeth City, or Gloucester counties, or the counties situated in the Northern Neck, or on the Eastern Shore. Among these clergymen towards the end of the century were such men as Rev. Bartholomew Yates and Rev. Peter Kippax, who were both bachelors-of-arts of Brasenose College, Oxford; Rev. Cope Doyley and Rev. Emanuel Jones, bachelors-of-arts of Merton and Oriel Colleges; Rev. St. John Shropshire, who had won the same degree at Queen's College[1]; Rev. James Clark, distinguished for culture as well as for piety; Rev. William Thompson, described in a public paper as an orthodox, faithful, and painstaking minister, who led a quiet, sober, and exemplary life, and was of a "conversation becoming his function unreprovable."[2]

All the surviving records of the Seventeenth century go to show that, whatever, during that long period, may have been the infirmities or unworthy traits of individual clergymen, the great body of those officiating in Virginia were men who performed all the duties of their sacred calling in a manner entitling them to the respect, reverence, and gratitude of their parishioners. There were two influences quite sure to have made a deep impression even on those members of the profession, should there have been any, who were disposed to lead unbecoming lives:—first, that general attitude of hostility to all forms of dissoluteness which must have prevailed among the great majority of the ministers themselves, because, if for no higher reason, it was the only means of preserving the exalted position of their order; and, secondly, the force of public

[1] *Va. Maga. of Hist. and Biog.*, vol. viii., pp. 59–63. Rev. David Lindsay of Northumberland county was the son of a Scotch baronet and King-at-arms. See *William and Mary College Quarterly* for 1907.
[2] Surry Country Records, vol. 1671–84, p. 124, Va. St. Libr.

sentiment, which was not likely to have judged over-leniently the bad conduct of those holding themselves out as the moral teachers and exemplars of the people. We have already seen how extremely active the grand juries and churchwardens were in presenting all persons guilty of immorality, and in this action they were simply reflecting the general temper of the community, which was certain to have been especially quick to condemn a clergyman's offenses because so much more injurious and pernicious in their influence. As early as 1631–2, when the Colony was still in its infancy, and the force of public opinion not yet as powerful as it was destined to become with the growth of population, the General Assembly passed an Act declaring that no divine should set an evil example by drinking or playing dice or cards; and again in 1643, it was provided that, should a clergyman conduct himself in a manner unbecoming his profession, the Governor and Council should punish him either by suspension or the infliction of such other penalty as their judgment suggested.[1]

If the clergyman who, by nature was inclined to be lax in his conduct had no other reason for self-restraint, his absolute dependence upon his vestry for his continuation in his place must have influenced him powerfully to act with prudence and circumspection. There is no evidence to show that that body was disposed to

[1] Hening's *Statutes*, vol. i., p. 157; MS. Laws of Va., 1643, Clerk's Office, Portsmouth, Va. An Act of Assembly passed in 1677 fixed the penalty of acting "scandalously" at the loss of half a year's salary; see Colonial Entry Book, 1675–81, p. 160. Governor Nicholson was instructed to use the "best means for the removal of any person already preferred who should appear to give scandall either by his doctrine or his manners"; see Instructions to Governor Nicholson, B. T. Va. vol. vii., p. 168.

consider an unworthy life on the part of their minister a matter of no great concern to themselves. There may have been times when they allowed an anxiety to keep the pulpit of the parish occupied to induce them to retain a pastor whose courses they had reason to criticise, yet we have the testimony of the author of *Leah and Rachel*, a careful observer of the condition of the Church in the Colony, that, even under these circumstances, they "still endeavoured for better" in his stead, and succeeded in obtaining him.[1] There are likely to have been few clergymen who would deliberately defy their vestry's disapproval when they were aware that the inevitable consequence, however delayed, was dismissal as soon as that body was able to secure a substitute. If a minister's conduct had been "abominably scandalous," we learn from Beverley that he found it far from easy to acquire another living; and this fact, which was clearly known to every member of the same calling, must have served as a powerful check upon any one who otherwise would have been indifferent to his vestry's displeasure. The room for employment outside of the plantation was not so great that a clergyman, with the most ordinary sense of discretion, could afford to run the risk of losing the only means of subsistence which at the time was in his reach. Let him give offense to his vestry by an im-

---

[1] "There came thither such as wore black coats and could babble in a pulpit, roar in a tavern, exact from their parishioners, and rather by their dissoluteness destroy than feed their flocks. Loath was the country to be wholly without teachers, and, therefore, rather retain them than be destitute; yet still endeavors for better in their places, *which were obtained*, and these wolves in sheep's clothing by their Assembly questioned . . . and some forced to depart the Country. Then began the Gospel to flourish." *Leah and Rachel*, p. 9, Force's *Hist. Tracts*, vol. iii.

proper life, and at once, owing to his uncertain tenure, the bread that went to the support of himself and his family, might, at the end of the annual contract, be taken away.[1]

It is probable that the "loose lives and ungodly conversation" laid by the intemperate Godwyn at the door of some of the Virginian divines of these times was merely a not unnatural distaste for the morbidly austere standards of Puritanism affected by that writer, standards that dismissed as unbecoming in a clergyman all those innocent gratifications in which the Church of England saw no real harm unless pushed to an extreme. The very ministers against whom Godwyn brought this charge in the spirit of a Bunyan or a Mather, who were outraged by the ringing of bells or the kissing of one's wife on Sunday, were perhaps the very persons whom Berkeley, a zealous Anglican, long afterwards eulogized as the "worthy men" driven by "Cromwell's tyranny" to Virginia.[2] Among the almost innumerable instances of disputed wagers in horse racing, card playing,

---

[1] As the Virginian clergyman's title to his benefice was subject to a contract renewable from year to year, he was, as the world goes, much more likely to have acted discreetly and becomingly than the English clergyman who held his living by a freehold tenure, a fact that made him practically independent of his congregation. We are referring only to those men in the Colony and Mother Country whose conduct was not governed by the highest motives alone.

[2] Godwyn's *Negro's and Indian's Advocate* was dedicated to Cromwell. Whilst breathing humane sentiments, this remarkable pamphlet is animated by much of that spirit which objected to bear baiting, not because it hurt the bear, but because it gave the spectators pleasure. For Berkeley's statement, see Hening's *Statutes*, vol. ii., p. 517. Berkeley declared on the same occasion that the ministers were well paid, and "by my consent," he added characteristically, "should be better if they would pray oftener and preach less."

and the like preserved in the county records, there is apparently not one in which a clergyman is entered as a party to the suit; and there is also but one case apparently in which a clergyman of those times participated even indirectly in a horse race.[1] And yet it was not at all opposed to what was thought becoming in the Anglican clergymen of that age to take part in those sports in the open air, and in those pastimes within doors which were enlivened by liberal betting.

[1] We find such a distinguished clergyman as Rev. James Blair serving as endman in a horse race which took place in Henrico county; Henrico County Minute Book, vol. 1682–1701, p. 268, Va. St. Libr.

CHAPTER XIX

The Clergy: Individual Offenders

WHAT were the serious offenses with which individual clergymen during the Seventeenth century were charged or of which they were convicted?

Perhaps the first minister to become involved in serious trouble was Rev. Anthony Panton, the rector of York and Cheskiack parishes. He was accused of having assumed towards Governor Harvey an attitude of such insolence and contempt as to encourage mutiny; and also of having denounced Secretary Kemp as a "jackanapes"; as a poor and proud fellow who tied up one of his locks with a ribbon "as old as Paul's"; and lastly as an officer unfit for his place, who was certain to be dismissed like his predecessor. A further charge brought against Panton was that he had counterfeited in a burlesque spirit a letter from the Archbishop of Canterbury. He was sentenced to pay to the King a fine of five hundred pounds sterling; to make public submission in every parish of the Colony; and to be deprived of the right to claim or acquire any property there. Finally, he was condemned to permanent banishment from Virginia; and should he return, he could be shot down on sight by the first citizen who saw him.

A sub-committee of the Privy Council made an investigation of the charges against Panton on his complaint after his arrival in England. In their report, they declared that they had received many "good testimonies" that he was an able preacher, diligent in his calling and without scandal in his life; that there was no proof that he had counterfeited a letter from the Archbishop of Canterbury; that, though the mutinies he was said to be guilty of were represented as extending over five or six years, the entire time covered by his residence in Virginia, yet only ten months previous to the date of his sentence, Harvey had presented him with a living, and in the document attesting the appointment, had commended him for his learning, conformity to the Church of England, pious spirit, and industry in his office.   The Privy Council instructed the new Governor, Wyatt, to institute a careful inquiry into the circumstances of the case; and in the meanwhile, they suspended that part of Panton's punishment requiring his permanent banishment from Virginia.   When the case came up before Wyatt and the Council sitting as the General Court, Kemp was summoned before them, but, without answering Panton's interrogatories, took ship for England, carrying off with him all the original depositions, on the strength of which the clergyman had been condemned. The Court, deciding in Panton's favor, ordered that thirty-four hundred and ninety pounds of tobacco should be paid him out of the fund derived from the sale of Governor Harvey's property remaining in the Colony.   This was the amount belonging to Panton which had been seized immediately after his conviction. The combined action of the Privy Council and the General Court showed that Panton had been one of the numerous victims of Harvey's arbitrary and grasping spirit.[1]

A charge brought against Rev. Thomas Hampton in 1646 was perhaps equally groundless. Having been appointed the guardian of the two orphan children of John Powell, of York, and curator of their estates, he removed one of them and most of the latter's property from that county without making the necessary provision for the support of the second orphan, who was left behind. On petition, he was deprived by order of court of the care of both children. There is no record of Mr. Hampton's defense, but as he continued to be one of the most prominent and useful clergymen residing in the Colony, it is probable that there was sufficient justification for his action to preserve his reputation for upright conduct unblemished.[2]

In 1649, Rev. Sampson Calvert, the incumbent of Elizabeth River parish in Lower Norfolk, was convicted of having committed adultery with the wife of Lawrence Phillips. Having, in a paper presented to the county court, declared his "hearty contrition" for so "foul an offense," he was ordered to read this confession on two successive Sundays in church to the assembled people. Phillips and his wife were, on each occasion, compelled to stand up in sight of the congregation with placards attached to their heads, on which were written an expression of great sorrow and a prayer for general forgiveness.[3] Ten years later,

---

[1] Randolph MS., vol. iii., p. 225; British Colonial Papers, vol. x., 1639–43, No. 32; Robinson Transcripts, pp. 185–6. When Panton was banished from the Colony, John Rosier succeeded him as the rector of York and Cheskiack parishes.

[2] York County Records, Orders Nov. 26, 1646.

[3] Lower Norfolk County Records, vol. 1646–51, p. 129. Phillips had no doubt been in complicity with his wife's dishonor.

a clergyman was sentenced by the General Court for immoral relations with a servant girl.[1] In 1654, Col. Edmund Scarborough, a man of rash and hasty temper, brought a double charge of adultery and poisoning against Rev. Thomas Teakle, but subsequently withdrew the accusation of adultery entirely, whilst that of the poisoning was shown to be equally unworthy of consideration. Mr. Teakle held his living forty years longer, one of the most respected as well as one of the most learned clergymen in the Colony. Vigorous, outspoken, and fearless, it is no cause for surprise to find that, on several occasions, he was a target for keen animosity. In the very year that Scarborough attacked him with such unjustifiable bitterness, Mary Powell, who was probably Scarborough's informant, was sentenced to receive twenty lashes, and to be banished from the county, because she had uttered a number of scandalous and abusive speeches in his detraction, which were proven to be altogether unwarranted in fact.[2]

In 1684, Samuel Mathews declared publicly that Rev. Mr. Ball, the clergyman occupying one of the livings situated in Henrico county, was "fitter to make a hangman than a minister." This disparaging remark, though it carried not even a hint of specific accusation, was promptly resented, and Mathews was indicted by the grand jury.[3] At a later date, Rev. John Bolton, who married the widow of Nicholas Spencer, the late Secretary of the Colony, became the victim of a plot directed against his reputation by an Irish woman and her accomplices; but the charge, after careful investigation, was shown to be without any ground. Mr.

[1] Robinson Transcripts, p. 242.
[2] Northampton County Records, vol. 1654–55, pp. 23, 94.
[3] Henrico County Records, vol. 1677–92, orig. p. 294.

Bolton was fully acquitted, and the woman ordered to be severely whipped.[1]   In the course of the same year, he excited the county court's displeasure by acting in what appeared to be an arbitrary and presumptuous manner in taking possession of the estate of Rev. Mr. Scrimgour, who had died at the home of Mrs. Bolton, but he justified his conduct by showing that by will all of Scrimgour's property had been bequeathed to Mrs. Bolton's first husband and that as Mrs. Bolton's second, he was simply exercising his undoubted right to its control.[2]

Rev. David Lindsay was brought into court on several occasions, but for trivial offenses carrying no criminal intent, although amounting to a breach of propriety.   In one instance, he refused to deliver up a small bill after its payment by his debtor; in another, he married two servants without their having obtained the consent of their owners, or showing that a license had been granted, or the banns published; and in a third, he withdrew a petition from the clerk's office without asking the justices' permission.   In the first instance, he probably had some justification to offer, though not tenable in law; and in the second, he secured his release by proving that, at the time, he was not aware of the requirements of the statute; having come from the land of Gretna Green, he might well have deemed it no serious wrong-doing to dispense with all those formalities usually preceding the marriage ceremony.   In taking the petition from the office, he was quite probably following a habit only too general even in these early times.[3]

In 1695, Rev. Stephen Gregg, of Abingdon parish in

[1] Westmoreland County Records, Orders July 26, 1694.

[2] *Ibid.*, vol. 1690–98, folio p. 122.

[3] Northumberland County Records, Orders Nov. 21, 1657; see also vol. 1652–66, p. 211.

Gloucester county, became involved in a heated controversy with his vestry, which ended with his expulsion. When an explanation of this summary course was demanded, that body justified themselves by asserting that Gregg had been guilty of misdemeanors. Gregg complained to the Governor and Council, sitting as an ecclesiastical court, that a general statement of this character was highly injurious to his reputation as a man and clergyman, and he stoutly declared that he was ready to defend himself against all imputations. The vestry then charged him specifically with the crime of sodomy, and the court directed the Attorney-General to investigate the grounds of the accusation.[1]

One of the most remarkable instances of an unworthy clergyman appearing in the records of the Seventeenth century was that of Rev. Samuel Gray, who seems to have been a man of flippant and choleric impulses rather than of criminal. Gray was a nephew of the wife of Sir Edward Wood,[2] and was of such prominence in the community at one time as to become, it would seem, a trustee of William and Mary College. In 1698, having been greatly incensed by his slave, a mulatto boy, running away, he ordered him when caught to be severely flogged. On the culprit's kneeling before him to implore his pardon, Gray struck him a blow that brought the blood, and threatening to brand him with a red hot iron, did apply such an instrument, but not sufficiently long to hurt seriously. The boy was then bound to a tree, and while being whipped by a fellow slave, was accidentally struck in a vital part and killed. Gray was soon arrested and tried, but was acquitted,

[1] Orders of Council, May 14, 1695, Colonial Entry Book, vol. 1680–95.

[2] See letter of Lady Wood in B. T. Va., 1698, vol. vi., p. 373. Sir Edward Wood lodged in Somerset House.

although his conduct was loudly condemned. "I would not have had it happen in my family for three times his price," exclaimed the clergyman, "but," he added with callous resignation, "such accidents will happen every now and then." All the depositions relating to the case were ordered by the court to be returned to the Secretary's office for review by the Governor and Council, an evidence that the justices, should they have erred in their acquittal of Gray, desired it to be corrected by that body sitting as the final Court of Appeal.[1]

In 1699, Gray appeared again, but in a light that was only discreditable to his sense of dignity and discretion. In the course of that year, he sent to Speaker Carter, of the House of Burgesses, a copy of verses described as being "scandalous, libellous, and very reflective on the Government"; they are said to have satirized the King, the late Queen Mary, the Governor of the Colony, several eminent citizens, and the College of William and Mary. An acquaintance of Gray's testified that Gray had stated to him that the verses had been "put in his pocket by some idle rascal or other at Jamestown"; but when summoned before the Council he confessed to the authorship. Imploring that body's pardon for his offense, it was granted, but only after the verses had been solemnly submitted to the examination of the Attorney-General.[2]

[1] Middlesex County Records, Orders 1694–1703, p. 236.

[2] Rev. John Gourdon (Gordon) was Gray's accomplice in this undignified escapade. Both were probably very young. Gourdon was the incumbent of Wilmington parish, and in 1695 was not allowed by his congregation to preach, no very surprising step. We also find Gray complaining that he was deprived of the same privilege; see Lambeth Palace MS., Cod. Misc., No. 954, paper 65; Minutes of Council, June 2, 6, 22, 1699, B. T. Va., vol. liii.; Minutes of House of Burgesses, May 31, 1699, B. T. Va., vol. lii.

CHAPTER XX

Struggle to Enforce Conformity

DOWN to the passage of the famous Act of Toleration by Parliament in the reign of William and Mary, there was, with the exception of the brief period during which James the Second granted freedom of worship to all sects, a determined and persistent attempt on the part of the government of the Colony to enforce in religious belief and services a rigid conformity with the doctrines and ceremonies of the Church of England. One of the General Assembly's most important duties was to enact legislation designed to protect the Established Church against dissent and schism; and an equally important duty of the General Court in its ecclesiastical capacity, was to punish those guilty of defying this legislation by entertaining religious tenets and following rules of worship not authorized by the Anglican canons.[1]

From the foundation of Jamestown, the English Government showed great solicitude that conformity should be strictly maintained. As early as 1606, when instructions were drawn up by the King for the guidance of those having the first expedition in charge, an in-

[1] Thomas Ludwell, writing to Secretary Arlington in 1666, stated that "Quakers and all other non-conformists are tried before the General Court at Jamestown"; see British Colonial Papers, vol. xx., Nos. 125, 125, i.

junction was laid on the President, Council, and minister that, not only should the "true word and service of God be preached, planted and used" in the projected Colony, both among the English settlers and the savages, but that this word and service should be "taught and performed" according to the doctrines and rites of the Church of England alone.[1] In order to ensure universal conformity, the Divine and Martial Laws of 1611 required that every man and woman then residing in Virginia, or who should hereafter arrive, should make a candid confession of religious belief; if found deficient in religious knowledge, then he or she, as the case might be, was directed to apply at once to the minister for the proper instruction; and should the person fail to do so without excuse, then the penalty was to be one whipping for the first offense, two for the second, and for the third a daily whipping until compliance was proven.[2]

In the instructions given to Governor Wyatt in 1621, he was ordered to maintain in Virginia the form and spirit of the "Church of England as near as may be"[3]; and, in 1639, he received further instructions to regulate the religious affairs of the people by the English ecclesiastic laws and statutes.[4] In 1641, Berkeley was enjoined by the English Privy Council to see that "God Almighty was duly and daily served" according to the framework of religion represented by the Anglican Church; and in 1662, when he had been restored to the Governorship, this order was repeated.[5]

---

[1] Instructions to Virginia Company of London, 1606.

[2] *Divine and Martial Laws, 1611*, p. 17, Force's *Hist. Tracts*, vol. iii.

[3] Randolph MS., vol. iii., p. 161.

[4] Colonial Entry Book, 1606–1662, p. 213.

[5] *Ibid.*, 1606–1662, pp. 219, 266.

The effect of these instructions was seen in numerous Acts passed by the General Assembly at different times during the century. As early as the session of 1623–4, this body declared that all religious services held in Virginia should be required to follow as closely as possible "the canons in England, both in substance and circumstance."[1] That this law reflected the settled determination of all the higher authorities of the Colony at this time is shown by the Governor and Council requesting that the French and Walloon Protestant families, proposing to remove oversea, should not only take the oaths of allegiance and supremacy, but also agree to conform in their religious worship to all the Anglican rules.[2] In 1629, the General Assembly ordered every clergyman occupying a living in Virginia to give the strictest obedience to these rules or submit to severe punishment[3]; and again in 1631, the same body passed an Act to enforce the most rigid observance of the "canons and constitutions of the Church of England."[4] Twelve years later, it was provided that not only should all ministers conform to these canons and constitutions, but that all persons dissenting should leave the Colony.[5]

The oath which the churchwardens were required to take in 1664 shows how firm the General Assembly continued to be in its determination to maintain conformity. "The ceremonies and rites," that oath declared in referring to the service in the church, "shall be according to the orders and canons of England, and the Sacraments shall be performed according to the

[1] Hening's *Statutes*, vol. i., p. 123.
[2] British Colonial Papers, vol. i., Doct. 55.
[3] Acts of Assembly, March 24, 1629, Randolph MS., vol. iii., p. 214.
[4] Randolph MS., vol. iii., p. 216.
[5] Hening's *Statutes*, vol. i., p. 277.

Book of Common Prayer."[1]   At a meeting of the
Council held in 1691, a complaint was made that some
of the vestries were retaining ministers who had departed from the rules and doctrines of the Anglican
Church; and a command was promptly issued that no
pastor should be allowed to hold a living who refused
to comply with the regulations of that Church.[2]   Nicholson, in vacating the Lieut.-Governorship of the Colony in 1692, declared emphatically that the people of
Virginia were faithful to the Church of England; and
the general correctness of this statement was confirmed
by Andros who succeeded him.[3]   When Nicholson
returned to the Colony a second time, he was impowered
to remove any pastor whose doctrines gave rise to
"public scandal"; and thereafter no minister was to
be admitted to a pulpit who was unable to show a
certificate from the Bishop of London to the effect
that he conformed to the tenets and discipline of the
Anglican Church.[4]

"Public scandal," as the term went, seems to have
been easily aroused in some quarters by very slight
departures from the requirements of the ecclesiastical
laws.   For instance, in 1668, a violent controversy
arose between Rev. Francis Doughty and two of his
vestry, John Catlett and Humphrey Booth, because
Doughty, in performing divine service, had been guilty
of "abstraceons from chants."   This was only one of
several delinquencies on his part hinting of non-conformity.   In taking the oath as a clergyman, he had

[1] Northampton County Records, vol. 1664–74, p. 1.

[2] Order of Council is recorded in Henrico County Records, Orders
May 15, 1691.

[3] B. T. Va., 1692, No. 128; Council Orders Sept. 20, 1692; Colonial
Entry Book, 1680–95.

[4] B. T. Va., vol. vii., p. 168.

not only declared himself to be a true son of the Anglican Church, and confessed his belief in its Articles of Faith, but had bound himself to act consistently with all its various canons down to the least important.[1] The justices of Rappahannock, where Doughty's living was situated, were ordered by the General Court, to which, in its ecclesiastical capacity, complaint had been made, to try the charges against him. The issue must have been contrary to his wishes, for in a document recorded in the county he expressed his determination to transport himself out of the Colony of Virginia into some other country and climate that might prove more favorable to his "aged, infirm, and disordered body." His wife was, however, unwilling to depart, as she found Virginia "best agreeing with her health"; and she also could not make up her mind to leave her children, who were probably grown and settled.[2]

There was not the slightest toleration for religious views which seemed to give countenance to heresy.

---

[1] Westmoreland County Records, vol. 1655–64, p. 46.

[2] Rappahannock County Records, vol. 1668–72, pp. 40, 51, 119, 195, Va. St. Libr. There was a suggestion that Doughty had been somewhat lax in his personal conduct; in what direction it is not stated; and this probably explains his wife's refusal to accompany him in his self-banishment. As we have seen, he made a liberal conveyance of property for her support. The oath taken by Doughty as a minister was, doubtless, the one taken by all persons of his calling before entering upon their work. In 1668, Doughty was the paster of Sittingbourne parish. Rev. John Waugh, of Stafford county, seems to have thought conscientiously that neither license nor banns were necessary preliminaries to the marriage ceremony, whether required by law or not. In 1674, he was suspended for marrying a couple without receiving any proof that a license had been obtained or banns published; see Westmoreland County Records, vol. 1665–77, p. 217. He committed the same offence in 1699; see Minutes of Council, Dec. 19, 1699, B. T. Va., vol. liii.; also Letters of William Fitzhugh, Oct. 27, 1690.

William Robinson, of Northampton, declared in a public argument in 1657 that Christ was never beheld by "carnal eye"; in uttering these words, he was accused of having committed a felony; and for this, he was arrested and carried to Jamestown to be tried by the General Court. A friend of Robinson, who held the same opinion, boldly announced that, in its support, he was ready to forfeit his life, "thus sealing it with his blood"; he also was promptly arrested and imprisoned; and was not released until he had given bond for his good behaviour.[1] In the very year in which these prosecutions took place in Northampton, Joseph Whitby and his wife, of Surry, were brought before the justices accused of entertaining "heinous tenets"; and it was only after expressing their deep contrition for their sin, and promising to abstain from such errors in the future, that they obtained their discharge.[2]

There was a large number of persons residing in the Colony about 1660, who rejected the doctrine laid down in the Book of Common Prayer, namely, that by baptism the infant is regenerated with the Holy Spirit. This opinion on their part seems to have made them as a class the target for the sharpest denunciation; they were described as schismatical persons, as persons averse to "the orthodox established religion," and governed by the new fangled conceits of their own heretical inventions. Whoever refused to baptize his child was compelled to pay two thousand pounds of tobacco for the offense[3]; and so serious was a case of

[1] Northampton County Records, vol. 1657–64, folio pp. 13, 27. Robinson, as will be found later on, was a Quaker.

[2] Surry County Records, vol. 1645–72, p. 113, Va. St. Libr.

[3] Neill's *Va. Carolorum* p. 293; Hening's *Statutes*, vol. ii., p. 166. This doctrine as to not baptizing was held by the Quakers as well as by the Puritans.

this character considered to be that it frequently went up to the General Court for settlement; in 1675, for instance, that court issued an order requiring the father named in it to baptize his child at once[1]; and in the course of the same year, the county court of Lower Norfolk directed John Biggs to repair to the minister of his parish for a like purpose.   This he must have declined to do, as only a few months afterwards, he was fined thirty-five hundred pounds of tobacco under a judgment of the General Court, to which his obduracy had been referred for punishment.[2]   Heretical opinions about the doctrine of baptism were not restricted to laymen; as early as 1645, Rev. Thomas Harrison, of Lower Norfolk, who had become a Puritan, and who soon abandoned his pulpit in Virginia, was indicted by the grand jury because he refused to perform the sacrament of baptism according to the canons of the Church of England.[3]

[1] Robinson Transcripts, p. 262.
[2] Lower Norfolk County Records, April 16, Aug. 18, 1675.
[3] Lower Norfolk County Antiquary, vol. ii., p. 12.

CHAPTER XXI

Dissent : The Quakers

OF all the non-conformists found in Virginia during the Seventeenth century the most important, from the point of view of numbers, were the Quakers. The spirit animating the members of this remarkable sect, as well as the authorities who sought to repress them, was clearly illustrated in a few words passed in a trial occurring in the General Court in 1661 ; a small company of Quakers had been arraigned before that Court as recusants and in defending themselves, one of them boldly exclaimed: "Quaker consciences must obey the law of God, however they suffer"; to which one of the judges returned the stern but significant reply: "There is no toleration for wicked consciences."[1] But it was not simply a keen repugnance to supposed heresy which lay at the root of the determined opposition to this sect. There were certain features characteristic of Quakerism which were regarded, not unnaturally, as directly inimical to the welfare of

[1] Records of General Court, 1660–62, p. 82. All the original records of the General Court were burned when Richmond was evacuated by the Confederates in 1865. We are indebted for information about this colloquy to a memorandum by Mr. Bancroft, who had had an opportunity of examining these records before they were destroyed.

the community as a whole. First, the members of this religious body aroused suspicion and distrust because their meetings were so often held in the profoundest secrecy; it was not unreasonably concluded that, having undergone such persistent persecution they would, when they came together in this dark and furtive manner, be strongly inclined to devise schemes of reprisal and revenge. Secondly, the necessity of paying tithes for the support of the religious establishment always bore very heavily on the resources of the persons assessed for the parish taxes; if the secession of a large number of the members of each congregation was to be permitted because they claimed to be Quakers, and these schismatics were to be exempted from the levy for the minister's maintenance on the plea that they were required to provide for their own clergyman, then it can be seen that the burden of supporting the Established Church, already so onerous, would have become unendurable.[1] Thirdly, one of the most important of all the duties imposed on each citizen was the defense of the community in the hour of internal commotion or invasion from without; and this duty seemed to be peculiarly imperative in Virginia because there the plantations were so often exposed to the atrocities of Indian incursions; when, therefore, a sect arose which demanded freedom from military service, on the ground that its members were opposed to all forms of war, the authorities quite properly saw in this principle one that would certainly diminish the fighting force of the Colony (a matter involving the safety of every man, woman, and child in it), and the security of every

[1] See Dom. Chas. II, vol. 56, No. 134, p. 426. It was said at the time that "half of the parish would become Quaker" if only to escape the payment of the regular tithes.

interest of its different communities.[1]   Fourthly, disloyalty to the Church of England was thought to be
at bottom disloyalty to its head, the King himself;
dissent was a form of revolt and rebellion against all
established order, and unless checked with sternness
and determination might lead to universal disaffection
and its attendant horrors, anarchy and blood-shed.
One of the most remarkable rules of the sect was, in
ordinary intercourse, to show no formal respect to persons in authority; it can be easily seen how quickly, in
the suspicious state of the official mind, this singular-
ity would be seized on, and its significance exaggerated
into a deep seated hostility to the Government itself.

In the light of all these powerful reasons for opposing
the sect, the only ground for surprise is that the persecution was not pushed to a greater extreme.   And that
it was not, was probably due to the fact that there
was something in the Quakers' purely religious doctrines which made a strong appeal to the sympathies
of many influential persons.   The appeal to the lower
section of the population was far stronger, certainly
for a time.   Nor is this to be wondered at.   It should
be remembered that the great body of the people were
widely dispersed; that family after family occupied a
separate plantation in the company of a few servants
and slaves; that the life they led was, for the most part,
lonely and uneventful; that they were familiar with
nature in all those aspects so well calculated to make a
very melancholy impression on their minds, such as
the solitude of the boundless forests, the roar of the

[1] See case of Alexander Makenny, who, on being fined for not
attending muster said: "His conscience did not permit him to bear
arms"; Henrico County Records, vol. 1682–1701, p. 305, Va. St.
Libr.

primæval woods in high winds at night, the terrible tropical storms in summer, which seemed to overwhelm the whole landscape, the great falls of snow in winter, the mighty floods in spring. Apart from the silent influence of these great natural phenomena, death, whenever it occurred in one of those remote homes, must have predisposed the heart to religion far more than in a crowded community where enlivening events were constantly taking place to divert the thoughts from whatever was sad. The very monotony and uniformity of existence on the plantation from day to day made the ear turn the more anxiously to voices that were appealing to the strongest emotions of the soul. Loyal as the great mass of people were to the Church of England, as represented in their ministers and parish churches, there was nothing in the manner in which it imparted its religious consolations to vivify, from time to time, the religious instincts of its congregations in the spirit of the modern religious revival. Now this was precisely what the early Quakers did. They found in those thinly settled and remote communities a population strongly disposed by their situation to religious thought, and ready to fall almost headlong into indulgence of religious emotions as soon as that chord in their hearts was touched. The missionaries of the sect made a direct appeal at the very hearth. Religion dropped the formalities of the liturgy and spoke to the spirit in the language of every day. It became personal, urgent, irresistible. It is not at all improbable that nothing but the unpractical features of Quakerism prevented a far more general conversion to that faith than seems to have really occurred.

The first Quaker missionary to appear in Virginia

seems to have been Elizabeth Harris, of London, who, arriving in 1656, remained only one year, although very successful in making converts. After her departure, she continued her work by writing letters and sending numerous books to those disposed to adopt the doctrines of her sect.[1] About 1657, the seeds which she had sown were zealously nourished by two other missionaries, Cole and Thurston by name, who laboured in the same virgin ground with such extraordinary activity that they drew down on themselves an order from the Governor and Council, sitting as the General Court, to leave Virginia by the first ship setting sail. In the interval, they were cast into prison and deprived of pen and ink for fear lest they should still persuade many citizens to incline a favorable ear to their tenets; but, during the winter, they were released and permitted to seek a refuge in Maryland.[2] During 1657 also, William Robinson held conventicles in private houses on the Eastern Shore; and for allowing him this privilege, one well known citizen who sympathized with the sect to such a degree that he refused to heed the warnings of Col. John Stringer, the presiding justice of Northampton, was summoned before the county court and required to give bond not to repeat the offence.[3] Robinson seems to have spent fourteen months in the Colony with a single eye to spreading the peculiar doctrines of the Quakers; and in this work of propagation, was assisted with great energy by Robert Hodgson and Christopher Holden, among others. His mission was not confined to the Eastern Shore; he did not stop

[1] Weeks, pp. 13, 14. The Quaker sect was first heard of about 1647.

[2] Robinson Transcripts, p. 243[2].

[3] Northampton County Records, vol. 1657–1664, f. p. 12.

until he had visited all parts of the Colony; nor did he altogether escape the penalty of such extreme boldness, for at least six of the fourteen months covered by his sojourn in Virginia were passed in jail; to which he was committed as probably the only means of restraining his zeal. But this was a mild fate in comparison with what afterwards overtook him in New England, where he showed the same fearless persistency, for there, all other penalties having proven unavailing, he was forcibly quieted by the gallows.[1]

Among the missionaries following in Robinson's footsteps were Elizabeth Hooton, Joan Brocksoppe, Mary Thomas, and Alice Ambrose. It is quite probable that, in the eyes of the authorities and all other ardent supporters of the Established Church, the action of these women in going about like the field preachers of a later day was all that was wanted to confirm the general impression as to the revolutionary nature of the doctrines they advocated; it may well have been thought that the spirit of revolt had so inspired the hearts of persons belonging to the new religious order that it had induced even members of the female sex to throw off all their natural modesty and reserve, and manlike to wander about seeking whom to turn to their pernicious and dangerous notions. But perhaps it was the exhortations of these very female missionaries which secured the deepest lodgment in the breasts of that poor and ignorant class among whom, owing to their greater susceptibility to a passionate appeal to their emotions, the larger number of the converts to Quakerism were found, for it was in the sermons of these female preachers that the greatest tenderness and sympathy lurked, not infrequently associated with a degree of moving

[1] Neill's *Va. Carolorum*, p. 285.

eloquence unsurpassed in the sermons of the male preachers themselves.

In 1658, it was enacted that every Quaker should be banished from the Colony.[1] Already the General Court had entered an order prohibiting all masters of ships trading with Virginia to import any person of that sect; and in case they did so, commanding them to carry such person away at the first sailing.[2] The firm measures taken for the Quakers' repression at this time are the more remarkable because, during the Protectorate's existence, there seems to have been no spirit of intolerance shown for what, at a later period, was so severely punished as non-conformity. There was in the Colony at this time ample room for a body so much opposed to the tenets of the Anglican Church as the Puritans, but there seems to have been as little room as ever for the Quakers, simply because the principles and doctrines they advocated were looked upon as dangerous to all forms of civil administration, whether presided over by a King or an elected ruler. By 1659, so many of the inhabitants of York had been converted to the new sect's beliefs that the judges of the county court were greatly alarmed, not from a religious, but from a political, point of view; they declared that the seduction of so many indigent and grossly ignorant persons might end in "the disturbance of the country's peace and the country's government"; and they, therefore, commanded the sheriff and constable to attend wherever a Quaker was about to exhort the congregated people and to warn them to disperse; and also to forbid all owners of plantations to suffer such meetings to be held on their lands. And

---

[1] Hening's *Statutes*, vol. i., pp. 532–3.

[2] Robinson Transcripts, p. 243[2].

these officers were also directed to make a report to the
nearest justice of the peace in order that he might take
steps to prevent the repetition of such "routs and
unlawful assemblies."[1]

So determined were the Quakers to spread their
doctrines far and wide that they appear to have continued to defy openly the guardians of the law, for in
the course of the same year, the county court of York
found it necessary again to interfere, after a second time
denouncing the propaganda of the sect as "tending to
the dishonor of God, the seducing and misleading of
many of the inhabitants, and ye disturbance of ye
country's peace." Mr. Thomas Bushrod, a convert,
had requested Rev. Philip Mallory to arrange a conference between certain representatives of the Quakers
and himself; and to this, Mr. Mallory gave a ready
assent provided that the justices of the county court
did not disapprove of the step. When the latter's
consent was asked, they were at first content to express
the hope that the "proposed conference would prevent
for the future all occasion of frequent meetings and
unlawful assemblies, and would undeceive ye much
seduced and misled people, especially of this county."
As, however, they looked upon the conference as an
event of extraordinary moment, they would not,
though favoring it themselves, assume the responsibility of allowing it without first submitting the pro-
posal to the Governor and Council.[2]

This attitude of the justices of York county sup-
ports our surmise that no serious objection would, during the Puritan Supremacy, have been offered to the
Quakers' missionary zeal had it not been attended with

[1] York County Records, vol. 1657–62, p. 163, Va. St. Libr.
[2] *Ibid.*, pp. 170–1, Va. St. Libr.

a certain degree of disturbance which jeoparded the safety of the community. And so far was this disorder carried in all parts of the Colony, in spite of the Act banishing such persons from Virginia, that, in the winter of 1659–60, the General Assembly was moved to denounce the entire sect "as an unreasonable and turbulent sort of people," who, meeting in large congregations, daily proclaimed and taught "lies, miracles, false visions, prophecies and doctrines" tending to "destroy religion, laws, communities, and all bonds of civil society"; and who would leave it to the caprice of "every vain and vicious person whether men shall be safe, laws established, offenders punished, and governors rule." In order to bar from Virginia any additions from the outside to a sect whose teachings were thought to be so dangerous to the Colony's peace and welfare, the General Assembly imposed a fine of one hundred pounds sterling on every captain of a ship importing a Quaker; and every Quaker exhorter to be found in any county was to be arrested and imprisoned without privilege of bail until security had been given that he would leave the country and never again return; and should he, in spite of this warning, re-enter the Colony, he was to be prosecuted as a contemner of the laws, and banished a second time; and if he again came back, he was to be punished as an ordinary felon. As a means of discouraging all persons disposed to receive the Quaker missionaries in their homes, it was provided that, whoever gave private entertainment to a member of that sect, should be liable to a fine of one hundred pounds sterling, or twenty-five hundred dollars in modern values.[1] Severe as this law was, its harshness was less than that of the regulations touching Quakers pre-

[1] Hening's *Statutes*, vol. i., p. 533.

vailing in New England. It was not until the Quaker had been twice banished without further punishment that he was proceeded against in Virginia with any real sternness. In Massachusetts, on the other hand, he would have been severely flogged on his second appearance; and on his third, would have forfeited his life.

Under the influence of this more stringent Act, as well as of his own personal animosity against the Quakers, Governor Berkeley, in the following year, wrote to the sheriff of Lower Norfolk a letter in which he sternly reproached him with remissness of duty in not putting a summary end to the meetings of what he denounced as that "pestilential sect." "I charge you," the letter closed, "by virtue of ye power ye Grand Assembly has intrusted me with not to suffer any more of their conventicles."[1] That the statute did not always remain a dead letter in other counties is proven by the action of the justices of Northampton in 1660:—William Colbourne, having been arrested, and brought before them accused of showing hospitality to Quakers, and having boldly declared that he would continue to do so, the court ordered execution to issue at once against his estate for the collection of the fine of one hundred pounds sterling which they had sentenced him to pay.[2] It is probable that his defiant attitude led to the strict enforcement against him of the law, for, in the course of the same year, when Henry White and Thomas Leatherbury were summoned before the same justices for a like offence, the latter were satisfied with commanding the two to appear before the Governor and Council; in the meanwhile,

---

[1] Lower Norfolk County Antiquary, vol. iii., p. 102.
[2] Northampton County Records, Orders Jany. 28, 1660; also vol. 1657–64, p. 88.

they were discharged without their having been subjected to a fine. And the same step was taken by the court in the case of Ambrose Dixon. As we have already seen, one of the principal citizens of Northampton had been simply required to give bond that he would not again entertain William Robinson, perhaps the most conspicuous of the Quaker missionaries; this person was dealt with thus tenderly although it was known that he was constantly engaged in violating the statute forbidding the importation of members of that sect; under pretence of transporting them up the Bay to Patuxent, he would land them at Nassawaddox, where they were received by Leven Denwood. At this place there was a building, described as a "ten foot house," which was used as a church by the sect; and it continued to serve this purpose until it was converted into a barn for the storage of wheat.[1]

It is evident from the surviving records that the county court of Northampton at this time was disposed to be as lenient as the county court of York in the treatment of the Quakers; and at the bottom of this disinclination to be as harsh as the statute enjoined lay, in both cases, the same reasons, namely, a clear perception of what was good in the purely religious teachings of that sect, and the recognition of the ignorance of the class upon whom its peculiar doctrines had made the deepest impression. The justices could not fail to acknowledge, at the very moment they deprecated the economic and political consequences of a schism of this kind, that most of these missionaries were animated by a true religious zeal; and that it was not at all strange that so many unlettered and unthinking people should be persuaded to accept all

[1] Northampton County Records, vol. 1657–64, folio pp. 82, 84.

their principles. It was only in a case like William Colbourne's, who showed a thoroughly untractable and defiant spirit, that the justices seem to have been aroused to enforce the law in all its rigid requirements.

Conscious of their own innocence of harboring any design against the existing political order, the converts to Quakerism were disposed to resent with great bitterness the interference with their liberty of opinion and worship. This is shown by an interview which took place, in 1661, between Rev. Justinian Aylmer and Thomas Bushrod, perhaps the most prominent citizen of that faith residing in York county. Aylmer had gone on board of a vessel riding in York River to purchase a servant. Bushrod happened to be there also, and although Aylmer endeavored to avoid him, yet he came forward and heaped on the clergyman's head "scandalous, reproachful, and abusive language," such as "ugly, lying knave and rogue." Not satisfied with these opprobrious words, Bushrod further exclaimed:—"Rev. Philip Mallory and yourself are a couple of episcopal knaves"; and then added, with an air of defiance:—"The Quakers shall and will continue their meetings; they will meet the next Sunday; and my wife shall be there." He then challenged Mr. Aylmer or Capt. Augustine Warner, a member of the Council, or any other person in his hearing to "disturb them if they durst." In reporting this scene to the justices of the county court, Aylmer concluded with an expression which throws a vivid light on the combination of reasons lying at the bottom of the strong opposition in that age to the propagation of Quaker doctrines:—in openly daring Captain Warner or himself to interfere, Bushrod, Aylmer declared, "struck at Church and State at one stroke according to ye usual practice" of that sect. Another witness, present on the same occasion, deposed that, when Mr. Aylmer asked Bushrod to bring his wife to the parish church, Bushrod denounced the clergyman as a "blind priest"; and when reproved for such abuse of a minister in orders, he replied:—"They are all anti-Christs and proceed from ye Pope." "Mr. Warner," he added, turning sharply on that gentleman, "I will not meddle with you as a Councillor, but you are a rogue and a dog." A warrant was issued a short time afterwards for Bushrod's arrest, and he was commanded to appear on the following day at Mr. Reade's house, where the Governor, Council, and other magistrates happened to be holding a court. All the witnesses were also summoned to testify on the same occasion.[1]

The same year, Thomas Forby, a citizen of Lower Norfolk, was presented by the grand jury for permitting an assembly of Quakers to be held at his residence; and having been arrested for the offence, was, by order of the justices, escorted by the sheriff to Jamestown for trial by the General Court for "breaking and contemning ye law" established against that sect.[2] Isabel Spring, a woman whose home was situated in the same county, for having denounced Mr. Thomas Browne in opprobrious language because he had come to her house to prevent a meeting of the Quakers, was condemned to receive twenty strokes of a whip on her bare back, and to remain in the sheriff's custody until she should acknowledge her great fault on her knees in

[1] York County Records, vol. 1657–62, pp. 325, 328, 338–9, Va. St. Libr.

[2] Lower Norfolk County Antiquary, vol. iii., p. 105; Lower Norfolk County Records, vol. 1656–66, p. 302. See will of Felix Forby of England, *Va. Maga. of Hist. and Biog.*, vol. xii., p. 398.

the presence of the Court. As she promised to abstain from committing the same offence in the future, the corporal punishment was remitted.[1] In the following year (1662), several members of the Yates, Porter, and Whitehurst families, belonging to Lower Norfolk, and also Mrs. Emperor, wife of one of its most prominent and wealthy citizens, were summoned for attending a similar meeting. Berkeley was now Governor and it was due to his great activity that all those arrested were promptly brought to Jamestown for trial; in the course of the same year, a large number were arraigned before the bar of the General Court, and these, there is reason to think, included the persons taken up in Lower Norfolk county.[2] That the latter were not discouraged from assembling again when they had obtained their release is shown by the arrest of nearly the same individuals on the occasion of a meeting held in May of the following year at the house of Richard Russell, who was fined an hundred pounds sterling for allowing it to take place there. And in spite of this intervention of officers of the law, a second meeting was held in June; and a third in November.[3]

[1] Robert Spring was on one occasion indicted for absenting himself from church, which he had done, no doubt, because he was a Quaker in faith; Lower Norfolk County Records, vol. 1656–66, p. 368[2]; see also *ibid.*, pp. 305–6; Lower Norfolk County Antiquary, vol. iii., p. 105.

[2] Bancroft's *History of the United States*, vol. ii., p. 201. Mr. Bancroft quotes from General Court Records now destroyed. One of the recusants mentioned by him was named Owen or Owens. Among the Quakers arrested in Lower Norfolk County was Thomas Owens, and this identity of names seems to confirm the supposition that the Lower Norfolk County Quakers were among those arraigned in the General Court in 1662; see also Robinson Transcripts, p. 177.

[3] Lower Norfolk County Records, vol. 1656–66, pp. 360[2], 386; Lower Norfolk County Antiquary, vol. iv., p. 78; see also vol. iii., p. 146.

During the same years, the Quakers had been equally active in York county. In 1661, a proclamation had been issued in the name of Charles II, recently restored to the throne, in which a gracious pardon was offered to every member of that sect guilty of a breach of the laws relating to uniformity of worship; but a stern warning was given that a repetition of the offence would be visited with severe punishment. Berkeley promptly directed the attention of the judges of York to this proclamation. It seems that, in that county, as in Lower Norfolk, the most zealous and fanatical disciples of the Quaker missionaries were found among individuals of the female sex[1]; Berkeley in his communication, therefore, instructed the justices that all women, who, after the royal Proclamation had been read, should attend the Quaker assemblies and publicly declare their "schismatical and heretical doctrines and opinions" should be at once tendered the oaths of allegiance and supremacy by the nearest magistrate, and on their refusing to take these oaths, should be led away to prison. The Quakers were now holding secret meetings in the woods; and that these meetings were supposed to have a political as well as religious significance of an alarming character was shown by this order, for the oaths of allegiance and supremacy were generally used for the detection of political infidelity and disloyalty. Among the women who had joined the sect was Mrs. Mary Chisman, wife of a leading citizen, and it was reported to the court that she had been seen at these furtive assemblages in the forests in the company of several of her slaves. The attention of her husband and herself was called to the proclamation, and she was warned

---

[1] Seven women were among the persons arrested in Lower Norfolk County, December 15, 1662.

that, should she repeat her offence, her arrest would follow, while Chisman himself was ordered to keep his negroes and the members of his family away from such meetings.[1]

[1] York County Records, vol. 1657–62, p. 324, Va. St. Libr.

CHAPTER XXII

Dissent: The Quakers (*Continued*)

THE Quakers had now become so bold and active that the General Assembly deemed it advisable to pass additional legislation for their repression. In March 1661-2, it was provided that all the penalties of the Elizabethan statute, passed for the punishment of those failing to attend the services of the Established Church, should be put in operation with a view of stamping out Quakerism; for instance, all persons remaining away for the period of a month were to be mulcted to the extent of twenty pounds sterling, and for the period of one year, to the extent of two hundred and forty pounds.[1] That these penalties were really intended to be carried into effect is shown by the fact that, in 1663, three Quakers residing in Lower Norfolk were each fined twenty pounds sterling because they had refused to attend the parish church for four Sundays in succession.[2] And in the course of the same year,

[1] Hening's *Statutes*, vol. ii., Acts 1661-2. An Act, passed this year, imposed a fine of 200 lbs. of tobacco on each Quaker presented by the churchwardens of his parish for attending a religious meeting of his sect; see Hening's *Statutes*, vol. ii., p. 48.

[2] Lower Norfolk County Records, 1656-66, p. 363[2]. On the other hand, Richard Yates, Richard Russell, Anne Godby, John Porter, and Mrs. Mary Emperor, all zealous Quakers of the same county, were mulcted to the extent of only fifty pounds of tobacco for not attending church; perhaps, on a single occasion,

Ambrose London, of Northampton county, was fined
for the like offence one thousand pounds of tobacco;
but the punishment in his case was perhaps increased
because he appeared in court clothed in the peculiar
garb of his sect, and demeaned himself insolently in
replying to the justices' questions.[1] The fine for being
present at an assembly of Quakers was also strictly enforced; thus every one of the twenty-two persons attending the meeting held in Lower Norfolk in November,
1663, to which reference has already been made, was
required to pay two hundred pounds of tobacco as the
law prescribed.[2]

In the preamble to the statute passed in March
1662–3 (which was perhaps a re-enactment of a measure adopted in a previous year), it was stated that
the Quakers were now assembling in great numbers in
different parts of the Colony; that under the pretence
of religious worship, they were spreading terror among
the people and endangering the public peace; that they
kept up a constant and secret correspondence with each
other; and that they separated themselves from the
rest of the King's subjects and avoided the regular
congregations. The ship-master who had brought in a
Quaker was ordered not only to carry him away at the
first sailing, but also, during his sojourn in the Colony
to shut him up so closely that he could find no opportunity to proclaim his "seditious tenets."[3] The

---

however. At the same time, Porter was fined three hundred and
fifty pounds of tobacco for laboring in his tobacco fields on Sunday;
see Lower Norfolk County Records, vol. 1656–66, p. 396[2].

[1] Northampton County Records, vol. 1657–64, p. 188.

[2] Lower Norfolk County Records, 1656–66, p. 386; Hening's *Statutes*, vol. ii., p. 48.

[3] Hening's *Statutes*, vol. ii., pp. 181–3. It was provided by this
Act that every Quaker who should be indicted for having been

ground for suspicion against the sect was very much increased at this time by the conduct of John Porter, of Lower Norfolk. Porter, who was a member of the House of Burgesses, was reported by the sheriff of that county to be so well affected towards the doctrines of the Quakers that he opposed the baptism of children; he admitted the correctness of the charge, and when the oaths of supremacy and allegiance were tendered to him, declined to take them; and for this refusal was promptly expelled from the body.[1]

Whilst there is no evidence that the native Quakers, in spite of the bitter feeling against them aroused in the breasts of the authorities by their persistent contempt for the law, were treated with greater severity than was reflected in the imposition of a fine, yet it is not surprising to discover that the alien members of the sect, who came into the Colony and deliberately defied all the Acts passed for their exclusion and repression, were sometimes punished rather harshly; for example, in 1663, Mary Thompkins and Alice Ambrose, two female missionaries, who had, no doubt, been more than usually bold in trampling these statutes underfoot, are said to have been sentenced to receive thirty-two lashes apiece, and to be drawn to the pillory with a noose, having a running knot, tied about their necks.[2] The penalties inflicted, however, continued to have as

present at an assemblage of as many as five persons, over sixteen years of age, of his sect, should, for the first offense be liable to a fine of 200 lbs. of tobacco; for the second, to a fine of 500 lbs.; and for the third, be banished. Every ship captain convicted of importing a Quaker should be compelled to pay 5000 lbs. of the same commodity.

[1] Hening's *Statutes*, vol. ii., p. 198; Randolph MS., vol. iii., p. 282.

[2] Neill's *Va. Carolorum*, p. 299. The accounts of the sufferings endured by the missionaries must be received with some reservation, as there was a disposition to exaggerate the extent of the martyrdom in this as in other cases recorded in history.

little effect as before in either dispersing or restraining the Quakers. In but one instance does any person of that faith appear to have been frightened into renouncing the creed; this occurred, in 1663, in the case of Elizabeth Emerson, of Lower Norfolk; who, when arraigned in the county court, promised that, should her fine be remitted, she would abandon the sect, and thereafter refuse to attend their meetings.[1] Among those presented to the General Assembly by a jury of inquest sitting in Nansemond county in the course of this year, were several Quakers, who had declined to be present at the regular services in the parish church.[2] William Edmundson, a friend of George Fox, preached, in 1671, in Nansemond and Isle of Wight to numerous congregations in sympathy with his doctrines; and so powerful was the impression produced by him that, in 1675, a special order had to be issued for the suppression of all the local conventicles, most of which were probably confined to his followers.[3] There are indications that, during this year, the Quakers were also very active in making converts on the Eastern Shore. William Lewis and Samuel Young, of Northampton, declined to take the oath when impanelled on a jury, while George Johnson and Timothy Coe, of Accomac, were presented because, with numerous companions, they were in the habit of attending Quaker meetings, and probably exhorting the assembled people.[4]

[1] Lower Norfolk County Records, vol. 1656–66, p. 400. She was probably the wife of Nicholas Emerson, who was frequently fined for attending Quaker meetings.

[2] Sept. 10, 1663, Colonial Entry Book, vol. lxxxvi

[3] *William and Mary College Quart.*, vol. vii., p. 211; Robinson Transcripts, p. 262.

[4] Northampton County Records, vol. 1674–79, p. 46; Accomac County Records, vol. 1676–78, p. 48.

The most prominent Quaker in Henrico county at this time was John Pleasants, a planter of considerable wealth, and of a high reputation for sense and character. He had been convicted previous to 1679 for violating the provisions of the statute passed for the repression of his sect, but the sentence was not put in force. On his persisting in allowing Quaker services to be held in his house, he was warned that, if he continued to do this, execution would be ordered pursuant to the old judgment.[1] As Pleasants refused to desist, he fell a victim to what must have proved to him to be a peculiarly annoying form of persecution:—he and his wife were indicted for living together without the sanction of legal marriage simply because they had been united after the ordinary Quaker manner; and for their alleged illicit cohabitation, each was fined two hundred and forty pounds sterling on the ground that they constituted, not one couple, but two separate persons. In addition, a fine of twenty pounds sterling was imposed on each of them for every month they had respectively refrained from attending services in the parish church; a fine of two thousand pounds of tobacco for refusing to baptize their children; and also one for five hundred pounds for permitting conventicles to be held in or near their residence. Had the total amount of these double penalties been collected by execution on Pleasants's estate, it would have precipitated ruin upon his affairs; but fortunately for him, Culpeper intervened under the authority of the order recently promulgated in England granting liberty of conscience to all the subjects of the King.[2] That Pleasants en-

[1] Henrico County Records, vol. 1677–92, orig. p. 116. The English Conventicle Act, passed in 1664, imposed penalties on those taking part in religious meetings in private houses.

[2] Henrico County Minute Book, 1682–1701, p. 40, Va. St. Libr.

joyed the esteem and good will of the community in which he lived is shown by his election in 1692 to the House of Burgesses; but as he declined to take the required oaths, he was not allowed to occupy his seat.[1]

John Lend, a Quaker, who died in Henrico county about 1681, dated his will the "Tenth day of the Sixth Month 1679." As the witnesses, who belonged to the same faith, refused to prove the instrument by taking the usual oath, or the wife to follow the ordinary legal formalities, the justices had no other alternative but to place the estate in the hands of an administrator of their own appointment.[2] It shows how far the Quakers at this time carried their peculiar doctrines that one of this religious body residing in this county whose wife had been ravished by a negro refused to prosecute the criminal.[3] This man's daughter, when called upon to testify in a case in court, declined for conscience's sake to take the oath; put in jail, she begged the justices to excuse her delinquency; and on her father's humbly seconding her request, they remitted her fine and released her from prison in consideration of her tender years.[4]

The heavy pecuniary penalty for failure to attend

British Colonial Papers, vol. xlviii., No. 11. Culpeper's words were: "Pursuant to Instructions for liberty of conscience, I stopped execution against a Quaker, John Pleasants." The date of this letter was Sept. 20, 1683.

[1] *Va. Maga. of Hist.* and *Biog.*, vol. vii., p. 171. Notwithstanding the fact that Pleasants was a Quaker, he bequeathed his slaves to his children as if they were merely an important part of his livestock; see Henrico County Records, vol. 1677–92, orig. p. 328; also Orders, Oct. 1, 1690.

[2] Henrico County Records, vol. 1677–92, orig. p. 196. William Randolph was appointed.

[3] *Ibid.*, vol. 1677–92, orig. p. 194.

[4] *Ibid.* vol. 1682–1701, p. 109, Va. St. Libr.

services in the parish church could not, at this time, have been very strictly enforced, for, in 1685, Edward Thomas, of York county, a member of the sect, who had not shown himself there for the space of a whole year, was merely required to give bond for good behavior.[1]   The term, however, continued to be one of reproach with some sections of the population; in 1687-8, Henry Beacher, of Lower Norfolk, is reported to have said of one with whom he had quarreled:— "It would be better for that Quaker dog to go stark naked into a red hot oven than to put his foot on my plantation."[2]

One of the most important acts of the unhappy James the Second was to issue a "Declaration for Liberty of Conscience and Indulgence in Religious Matters."   The object of this was to assure toleration for the English Roman Catholics, but as its terms were general, it also afforded the same great privilege to every body of persons who had seceded from the English Established Church.   In 1687, Howard having received instructions from the Privy Council to proclaim the Declaration in Virginia,[3] the colonial Council ordered it to be done in every county with the loud beating of drums, the firing of cannons, and every other manifestation of popular joy.[4]   Under this Declaration, the Quakers obtained ample protection; and the quickness with which the Revolution of 1688 followed assured its continuation.   Whatever annoyance they suffered thereafter was precipitated only by a refusal to pay the parish tithes imposed upon every citizen for

[1] York County Records, vol. 1684-7, p. 114, Va. St. Libr.
[2] Lower Norfolk County Records, vol. 1686-95, p. 57².
[3] Colonial Entry Book, 1685-90, p. 122.
[4] York County Records, vol. 1687-91, pp. 77-9, Va. St. Libr. The same order was recorded in Henrico county.

the support of the Established Church. They now, for the first time, became a religious body acknowledged by all to have the right to hold their own religious services openly and unmolested, provided that they had conformed to the requirements of the Act of Parliament passed in 1688 and known as the Act of Toleration.[1] Quakers were now for the first time also permitted to devise ground as sites for meeting houses; for instance, in 1688, George Brickhouse, of Northampton, left to that sect an acre of land surrounding the meeting house already erected at Nassawaddox; and a few years later, Mrs. Judith Patrick bequeathed thirty shillings, perhaps for the repair of the same structure.[2] John Pleasants, in 1690, devised a "small parcell of land" situated in Henrico county as the site for a meeting house and a graveyard. There seems to have been already a meeting house standing on this land, erected quite probably at Pleasants's expense; and he now granted a fee simple title to the tract, together with the building.[3]

Aggressive and even opprobrious language on a Quaker's part was no longer considered to be sufficient ground for issuing a summons against him to appear before the General Court at Jamestown to stand his trial for the supposed outrage; in 1688, Edward Thomas, of York, one of the most zealous members of that

---

[1] So stated in the Proclamation recorded in 1690 in Henrico County Minute Book, vol. 1682–1701, p. 287, Va. St. Libr. The Act referred to in this Proclamation was entitled: "An Act for exempting their Majesties' Protestant Subjects dissenting from the Church of England from penalty of certain Lawes"; see Minutes of Council, March 7, 1690, B. T. Va. 1690, No. 14.

[2] Northampton County Records, vol. 1683–89, p. 400; vol. 1689–98, p. 435.

[3] Henrico County Records, vol. 1688–97, p. 154, Va. St. Libr.

religious body, denounced Rev. James Slater for speaking, in the course of his ministerial functions, what Thomas represented to be "blasphemous words." Slater contented himself with a civil suit to correct the injury which he alleged had been done him in his parochial charge. The jury entered a verdict for fifty pounds sterling in his favor; and in addition to having to pay this large amount, Thomas was condemned to ask Slater's pardon on two successive Sundays in the church of Bruton Parish, in the face of the congregation; and also in the justices' presence at the next session of the county court. Should he, however, fail to conform to this part of the sentence, the penalty was to be simply a fine, in deference presumably to Thomas's personal standing in the community.[1]

Not unnaturally, when the peculiar principles of their sect brought the Quakers to the point of denying their liability for the performance of certain civil duties, which were incumbent on all citizens independent of creeds, they continued to suffer what they very unreasonably looked upon as a form of persecution. It is probable that they made no effort to escape from the payment of their share of the parish assessment for the support of the Established Church, although, no doubt, they resented such a call on their pecuniary resources. Opposition to war in all its branches was one of their fundamental doctrines. Evidence exists that some were not content to evade militia service simply by the payment of a specified amount; a Quaker summoned in 1691 to attend the muster in Henrico county positively refused to submit to the penalty of the fine imposed on him when he asserted that his conscience forbade him to bear arms. The sheriff

[1] York County Records, vol. 1687–91, p. 232, Va. St. Libr.

promptly levying on his feather bed, rug, and blanket, the delinquent appealed to the General Court; but that body decided that he could only recover his property by paying the fine, or performing the military service required of him.[1] After the passage of the Toleration Act, no objection seems to have been offered when a Quaker declared before the justices his unwillingness to take an oath; he was permitted to affirm; and his testimony was then considered to be entirely valid.[2]

Although the position of the Quakers as a distinct sect entitled to hold religious meetings, to possess church property, and to adopt all necessary regulations for their own church government, was now secure, nevertheless, they had not yet succeeded in freeing themselves entirely from the evil consequences of the popular suspicions to which they had been exposed so long. This fact is brought out clearly by a proclamation issued by Nicholson and the Council in 1691. It was reported in Virginia that the Quakers of Pennsylvania had declared that, should the French and Indians come down upon their settlements armed with rifles, tomahawks, and torches, they would offer no resistance

---

[1] Henrico County Minute Book, 1682–1701, p. 305, Va. St. Libr. After the passage of the Toleration Act, Quakers were not mulcted for failing to attend the services in the parish church; *Va. Maga. of Hist. and Biog.*, vol. vii., p. 168. The fact that a person was "of another opinion," however, does not seem to have always exempted a delinquent; in 1691, a man was compelled to pay a fine in Lower Norfolk County although he had offered this as an excuse for his absence, probably because not believed; see Lower Norfolk County Records, Orders March 17, 1691. In this year Lower Norfolk county was divided into Norfolk and Princess Anne counties.

[2] See case of Thomas Browne and his wife, Northampton County Records, vol. 1689, p. 88.

to the incursion. On hearing of this remarkable speech, the authorities at Jamestown asserted that such supineness on the part of their northern neighbors would enable the enemy, not only to obtain in Pennsylvania all the provisions they would need in the proposed campaign, but also to find a safe place of retreat there after they had spread ruin and havoc through Maryland and Virginia. Recently (so the Governor and Council stated), there had been numerous assemblages of the Quakers in the latter Colony, in holding which they had failed to inform the local authorities of their action, or to fulfil the other directions of the Toleration Act. By means of such meetings, the French and Indians, should they once take possession of Pennsylvania, would have the amplest opportunity of learning about the condition of Virginia, and thus of carrying out their projected attack in the manner exactly adapted to assure its success. The Governor and Council, greatly alarmed by this anticipated concert between the Quaker inhabitants of the North and South, issued a proclamation warning those of Virginia to refrain from coming together in a general assembly unless they had complied with every requirement of Parliament; and above all, to send word to the nearest magistrate at once, should an emissary of Pennsylvania appear amongst them with a message from that Government. This magistrate was commanded to summon the stranger to his court immediately upon receiving the notification of his presence, in order to subject him to a strict examination as to the place from which he came, the object of his mission, and his point of destination; and should the replies be such as to confirm the magistrate's suspicions, then they were to be taken down in

writing, and in that form transmitted to the authorities at Jamestown.[1]

As late as 1699, the suspicions aroused by the Quakers
were far from being allayed. In the course of that
year, a complaint was made to the Governor and
Council of what was described as the "evil and seditious
practices" of this religious body; and so just was it
thought to be that Commissary Blair was ordered to
devise a plan by which these "practices" might be
prevented in the future. It was perhaps at Blair's
suggestion that every county was enjoined to return
to the Secretary's office a full and exact account as to
whether there were held within its boundaries any
public or private religious meetings other than those
of the Church of England, and if so, where they took
place, by whom they were licensed, and how many and
what persons attended them; but above all, a strict
report was to be made as to whether any strangers had
appeared, either as preachers occupying the dissenting
pulpits, or as men professing to be interested in the
success of some special religious mission.[2] As we have
seen, the Act of Toleration required that every Protestant sect which had seceded from the Church of
England should regularly present to the authorities a
statement as to the places where their religious services
were held. It was in conformity with the provisions
of this law that John Pleasants, for instance, offered,
in 1696, for record a paper showing that the Quakers
of Henrico county were, during that year, in the habit
of assembling in three different houses for religious wor-

---

[1] Henrico County Records, vol. 1688–97, pp. 192–3, Va. St. Libr.
The same proclamation is also recorded in York County Records,
vol. 1690–94, p. 27, Va. St. Libr.

[2] May 30, June 21, 1699, Minutes of Council, B. T. Va., vol. liii.

ship, namely, the public meeting house, the residence of Mary Maddox, and also the residence of himself.[1] In ordering the counties to make a general report as to the dissenters among the population, the Governor and Council were probably influenced by the feeling, which still lingered, that disloyalty to the Established Church, whether tolerated by the authorities or not, was a vague form of disloyalty to every branch of the established order; and that if a spirit of revolt or treason prevailed among any section of the inhabitants of the Colony, it should be looked for in that section which rejected the doctrines and discipline of the Church of England.

The Quakers of Virginia were to illustrate a truth so often illustrated in the same manner in the history of religious bodies:—they were to find that their sect derived more nourishment from persecution than it did from toleration; and that as soon as they were at liberty to make converts without having an organized and legalized opposition to overcome, their power to win over new schismatics steadily declined. At the end of the century, after ten years of freedom of worship and propagation, the number of their congregations had shrunk to three or four.[2] The persecution of the Quakers residing in the Colony had been only sharp enough to stimulate their numerical growth; had it been very harsh, they would probably have found no foothold in Virginia; and had it been very mild, their creed perhaps would not have proved so seductive to so great a company of persons. Neither harsh nor mild,

[1] Henrico County Records, vol. 1688–97, p. 353, Va. St. Libr.
[2] Present State of Va., 1697–8, Section xi. The expression is "three or four meetings of Quakers," by which congregations are evidently meant.

but only moderately severe, such persecution as there was tended to maintain the public interest in the new sect, directed continued attention to its doctrines, and made more conspicuous what was really excellent in its religious teachings. Apparently their keenest enemy, Sir William Berkeley was in fact the most useful friend of the Quakers; it was during his administration, and the administration of his successors who entertained the same hatred of all forms of heresy, that they flourished most; their prosperity declined so soon as the Governor was deprived of all real power to interfere with their meetings or oppose their principles. They played a prominent part in the history of the Colony during those decades of the century when strong efforts were made to repress them; they began to play a more and more obscure part as those efforts steadily relaxed in intensity.

CHAPTER XXIII

Dissent: The Puritans

IT was not until 1662 that the term "dissenter" became strictly applicable to Puritans, for it was not until this year that the great English Act of Uniformity, which was so radical and far reaching in its operation, was passed. This Act was the final upshot of the uncompromising influences separating the Puritan and the Churchman during the civil wars. There were numerous Puritan clergymen in the early history of the Church of England, and it was to this section that several of the most saintly divines who went out to Virginia, during the first years of the Colony, belonged.[1] Such were George Keith and Alexander Whitaker. It was Whitaker who expressed surprise that "so few of our English ministers that were so hot against the surplice and subscription" emigrated to Virginia, "where neither is spoken of." [2] That those

[1] Purchas, Book ix., ch. xi.

[2] The early tone of the Church of England was distinctly Calvinistic, and it was not until 1630 that a reaction set in. This was first observed in the English Universities, and as the leading exponents of the movement were earnest advocates of the extreme view of the Divine Right of the King, they received the recognition of the crown by promotion to bishoprics and livings. The Act of Uniformity, adopted in 1662, completed the elimination of Puritan influence from the Church of England. All ministers were, by this law, to be expelled from their benefices should they decline to accept the whole of the Book of Common Prayer.

persons who administered the Colony's affairs in the time
of the Company entertained no strong prejudice against
the Puritans even when their principles were pushed
to the extreme of separatism, is shown by the fact that
the Pilgrim Fathers received permission to make a
settlement within the boundaries of Virginia. As we
have seen, however, the General Assembly began as
early as 1623-4 to enforce a strict conformity with the
canons of the Church of England both in "substance
and circumstance"; the same measure was re-enacted
in 1631; and from this time, with the exception of the
interval of the Protectorate, down to the passage of the
Act of Toleration, the Puritans remained as much
under a ban as the Quakers themselves.

The first large congregation of persons, either
Puritans at the time, or to become Puritans later
on, to make a settlement in Virginia obtained patents
to land situated on the present Burwell's Bay. The
leader of this band was Edward Bennett, who was
accompanied by his nephews, Robert and Richard;
and Rev. William Bennett served as its first minister.[1]
The community established by this congregation,
known as "Edward Bennett's Plantation," showed,
during many years, their sympathy with the Puritan
doctrines and form of religious worship. In 1642, the
very year in which Sir William Berkeley, an ardent
and zealous follower of Laud, became Governor of
the Colony, Richard Bennett and others holding to
the same beliefs, who resided in Nansemond county,

---

[1] Abstracts of Proceedings of Va. Co. of London, vol. i., p. 93.
Campbell in his *History of Virginia* states that the first Puritans
arrived in 1619, and that a larger number would have followed had
it not been for a proclamation issued by Bancroft, Archbishop of
Canterbury.

sent a messenger to Boston in New England with letters requesting that ministers should be directed to go to Virginia to administer to the spiritual wants of the Puritan non-conformists there.[1] It was evident that the latter did not anticipate that any effort would be made at this time to interfere with their religious services; and that the same view was entertained by their friends in Massachusetts was shown by the readiness of the response in dispatching to Virginia William Thompson, John Knowles, and Thomas James, three Puritan clergymen of distinction. They carried letters of introduction to Governor Berkeley from Governor Winthrop.[2] Berkeley, however, was as bitterly hostile to the Puritans as to the Quakers, and as he was choleric and outspoken, he very probably gave these clergymen a very ungracious reception.

It was under his influence that, in 1643, an Act was passed which declared that, in order to preserve the Established Church's unity and purity of doctrine, every minister whatever residing in Virginia should conform to all of its canons. If any one refused to do so, then he was not to be suffered either to teach or to preach, whether in public or in private; and if he continued obstinate, he was to be compelled to leave the Colony. This statute, so unmistakable in its meaning, was Berkeley's formal reply to Governor Winthrop's letters handed to him by the three Puritan divines. Knowles and James soon became discouraged and returned to the more congenial atmosphere of New England; Thompson, who was stouter of heart, if not more zealous, lingered, and it seems, by his earnest and

---

[1] *Va. Maga. of Hist. and Biog.*, vol. iii., p. 54.

[2] Winthrop's *New England;* see *William and Mary College Quart.*, vol. xii., p. 56.

resolute spirit in defying all obstacles in his way, made numerous converts, including, among others, a son of Daniel Gookin. Cotton Mather, probably exaggerating the success won by Thompson in Virginia in the teeth of the hostile authorities, declared, in the language of poetical enthusiasm:—"A constellation of great converts there shone around him, and his Heavenly glory were." It shows the ease with which inferences can be drawn from a terrible catastrophe to support either side. of a religious controversy that the massacre of the whites by the Indians in 1644 was proclaimed far and wide by the Puritans as a judgment from God upon the persecution they had suffered, and by Churchmen as an evidence of the Deity's condemnation of their own sin in granting a refuge to the Puritans in Virginia.

At least one clergyman of the Established Church seems to have been deeply affected by the awful significance which the non-conformists had attributed to the massacre; this was Thomas Harrison, who at one time had acted as Berkeley's chaplain[1]; and there appears a certain poetical retribution in the fact that one so close to this redoubtable champion of Laud's doctrines should have become a convert under the influence of an argument which must have seemed especially outrageous to all good churchmen. The impetuous wrath of the hot-headed Governor when his spiritual adviser turned coat must have been even greater than when, at a later period, he confronted the youthful Bacon at

---

[1] See Fiske's *Old Virginia and her Neighbors*, where this fact is mentioned. In 1640, as already stated, Harrison was elected to a living in Lower Norfolk county, which he seems to have filled until 1648. His chaplaincy must have been coincident with the occupation of this pulpit, see Tyler's *Cradle of the Republic*, p. 139.

the door of the State-House. Harrison, as we have already mentioned, was in 1648, the minister occupying the pulpit in Elizabeth River parish, but was compelled to abandon that living because he refused to read the Book of Common Prayer as a part of the services, or to administer the sacrament of baptism.[1] Either he or others had preached with such extraordinary energy and zeal in Nansemond county that he was able to announce by letter to Governor Winthrop that he had made seventy-four converts; that nineteen persons "stood propounded"; and that numerous others were showing a favourable disposition.[2] In the end, he seems to have been required to leave Virginia not later than the date on which should sail the third ship departing after he was informed of the order. On his arrival in New England, he reported that he had left in the Colony a congregation of Puritans numbering at least one hundred and eighteen persons. He consulted with the magistrates and elders as to what course he should pursue;—whether he should remain in Massachusetts or return to Virginia. They declared that there was excellent ground for expecting a "far more plentiful harvest" than had yet been reaped from the fact that many members of the Council were leaning toward Puritanism, and that at least one thousand persons had been converted to its doctrines; it would, therefore, in their opinion, show great haste should the Puritan

[1] An Act passed in 1647 declared that no minister who had refused to read the Book of Common Prayer was entitled to the payment of tithes by his parishioners; see Hening's *Statutes*, vol. i., p. 341.

[2] Mass. Hist. Coll. Fourth Series, pp. 434-5. This letter was dated 1647. It is possible that Harrison occupied two pulpits at the same time, — one at Elizabeth River, and the other in the adjoining county of Nansemond. All the Colonial records of Nansemond have perished.

ministers abandon the field before the terms on which they could stay there became absolutely intolerable.[1]

Harrison's banishment naturally aroused opposition among persons of the same tenets. The Puritans were now supreme in England, and this fact induced some of his followers to send a petition to the Council of State, in which their former pastor was described as an able man of an unblemished life, who had excited the hostility of the Virginian authorities by his refusal to read in church the Book of Common Prayer. As Parliament itself had now prohibited the use of that book, it was only to be expected that this body would command the Governor of the Colony to allow Harrison to return to his ministry.[2] His zeal, however, does not appear to have carried him so far, for at no very distant date, he is found serving as Henry Cromwell's chaplain, a proof of the radical change which his religious opinions had undergone since he had filled the same office under Sir William Berkeley.

Harrison was followed in the Elizabeth River parish by Rev. Wm. Durand, who appears to have entertained the same religious views[3]; and in this, he was supported by some of the first men in his congregation, as well as by a large number of the plainer members; but this did not save him from being apprehended at the suit of the King, and being compelled, like Harrison, to vacate his pulpit. The influence of their Puritan doctrines remained, for, in 1649, Edward Lloyd and Thomas

[1] Winthrop's Journal, p. 334. This estimate of number was based on conjecture, as the northern Puritans themselves acknowledged. Winthrop's Journal in part will be found printed in *William and Mary College Quarterly*, vol. xiii., p. 54 et. seq.

[2] Interregnum Entry Book, vol. cxv., pp. 482–3.

[3] Durand seems to have followed Harrison to Boston.

Meares, justices of the county court, and six additional citizens of about equal prominence were indicted as "seditious sectaries" because they had refused to attend religious services in the parish church, or to hear read the Book of Common Prayer; and for this double offence, they were required to give bond to appear before the Governor and Council sitting as an ecclesiastical court at Jamestown.[1]

During the existence of the Protectorate, the Puritans had no ground for complaint; their party was now supreme; and by the irony of circumstances, they, in their turn, were in a position to harry those who had striven so persistently to curb their freedom of religious opinion and worship. Perhaps, they would have done this had not their number, after all, been too small to make persecution effective. By the eleventh article of the terms of surrender agreed upon in 1651, the Book of Common Prayer (to which, as we have seen, the Puritans specially objected) was to be allowed to continue in use for the ensuing year provided that the prayers for the King and royal government were omitted; and the ministers then in possession of livings in the Colony were not, during the same period, to be interfered with either as respecting the retention of their pulpits, or the payment of their accustomed dues.[2] If at this time a clergyman of Puritan leanings was to

[1] Lower Norfolk County Antiquary, vol. ii., pp. 14, 83; see also Lower Norfolk County Records, Orders, Aug. 15, Oct. 1, 1649.

[2] Randolph MS. vol. iii., p. 243. This condition prevailed in England also. During the Protectorate, the church buildings were considered to be the property of the parishes; and according to the wishes of the majority of the worshippers, the pulpit of each benefice could be filled by a clergyman of the Presbyterian, Independent, or Church of England faith. This system prevailed from 1654 to 1660.

be found among the Virginian divines, this arrangement protected him as fully as it did one conducting religious services in strict conformity with the Anglican orders and constitutions. But it was only a breathing spell which the Puritan minister enjoyed while the Protectorate lasted; he had been exposed to serious persecution, as we have seen, previous to the establishment of the Puritan Supremacy in England; as soon as that supremacy was overthrown by the restoration of Charles the Second, and a rigid Act of Uniformity passed by Parliament, the Puritans residing in Virginia became as distinct a sect of dissenters as the Quakers themselves, and the hand of repression fell upon them not less heavily than it had done before. Berkeley probably detested them more thoroughly than he did the Quakers; but they do not seem to have found the same nourishment in persecution, and either steadily declined in numbers, or were less disposed to cling publicly to their own doctrines.[1] The gap between them and the Established Church was far less wide, and time perhaps had a tendency to bridge it entirely. Whatever Puritans resided in the Colony towards the end of the century obtained by the Act of Toleration the same freedom of religious opinion and worship outside of the Established Church as had been bestowed on all other dissenting sects.

It does not seem strange to find that the Puritans failed to secure much foothold in Virginia during the course of the Seventeenth century. They were always a small and apparently never an influential body. It is quite probable that the only real differences dividing them from the other congregations were wholly religious

[1] For the Puritan emigration to Maryland, see Fiske's *Old Virginia and her Neighbors*.

in character, namely a rejection of the Book of Common
Prayer, and of the Sacrament of Baptism. If they
introduced into their social life all those sombre and
austere habits and customs prevailing in the theocratic
communities of New England, there is no proof of the
fact. All the influences at play in such a colony as
Massachusetts, for instance, tended, as time passed on,
to accentuate the harsher features of Puritanism, and
not the least powerful of these influences were those
springing from the soil and climate. In Virginia, on
the other hand, the Puritan found himself in a community where not one person in fifty surrounding him
was in sympathy with his religious creed, or his social
principles; there he was not sustained by the example
or the teachings of all his associates as he would have
been had he resided in Boston or Plymouth; but, on
the contrary, was far more likely to be pointed at as a
target of ridicule, or held up as an object of folly. The
general tone of the social life in which he moved
prompted him unconsciously to make the most of the
comparatively few pleasures offered in those narrow
bounds, whether they consisted of a glass of wine, a
dance, a game of cards, or a horse-race. The whole
tone of that life was generous, liberal, abounding, at the
very time that it was marked by reverence for religion
and respect for law. Not one Puritan in an hundred
perhaps could have preserved the sombre self-denying
spirit of his sect in the life of the secluded plantation,
which gave an exaggerated importance to the few
indulgences in the reach of the inhabitants. Insensibly,
the general tendencies of such a religious body planted
in Virginia must have been modified by influences like
these, so entirely hostile to the extreme severity long
distinguishing people of that faith in the northern

communities. It was perhaps due to this modification in their character that the Puritans of Virginia played no great role in the Colony even during the supremacy of their party in England.

CHAPTER XXIV

Dissent : Presbyterians and Papists

THE Presbyterian denomination did not appear in Virginia until all forms of religious persecution had come to an end. The founder of it in the Colony was Rev. Francis Mackemie. In 1699, he presented a petition to the Governor, in which he requested that official to issue a proclamation reasserting the right of all, under the statutes of England, to freedom of conscience, and prohibiting anyone from attempting to deprive any religious sect of the privilege granted them to worship after their own manner. Mackemie was called into the Council chamber, where he was informed by Nicholson that, during his administration, the dissenters should enjoy every liberty conferred by law provided that they refrained from disturbing the peace of the government; this, he added, was all the encouragement which they could or should expect; and if anyone undertook to interfere with that liberty, then he was to be prosecuted for such illegal molestation.[1]

The Presbyterians appear to have obtained some foothold in Norfolk county; this is shown by the fact that, in 1692, the justices of the local court authorized them to hold public worship in three places, where meeting houses had either been specially erected or set apart; one of which was situated on the Eastern

[1] Minutes of Council, April 28, 1699, B. T. Va., vol. liii.

Branch, another on the Western, and a third on Tanner's Creek,—a division that must have subserved admirably the convenience of the members.[1] The pastor in charge of these congregations was Rev. Josias Mackie.[2] In the year 1702, two years after the close of the Seventeenth century, there were only four Presbyterian congregations in Virginia; of these, two had their places of worship on the Eastern Shore, and two on the Elizabeth River, in Norfolk county.[3]

The opposition aroused by the course of the Quakers and Puritans, embittered as it generally was, did not, in intensity, approach the hostility felt towards all who acknowledged themselves to be Romanists. Both of the former sects, after the Restoration in England, were looked upon as more or less disloyal to the Government; but the only ground for this passing belief was based on

[1] Norfolk County Records, Orders June 22, 1692.

[2] *Va. Maga. of Hist. and Biog.*, vol. vii., p. 362. The following refers to the oaths taken by Mackie:—

"Whereas in the first yeare of the Reigne of William and Mary, King and Queene of England, Scotland, &c being the year of Our Lord one thousand six hundred, eighty and nine, the twenty-fourth of May, An Act of Parliament for exempting their Majties' Protestant subjects dissenting from the Church of England from penalties of certain lawes passed the Royal Assent; these are, therefore, to certify that Mr. John Mackie, Minister of the Gospell, hath this day appeared before us, Thomas Butt and James Willson, two of their Majties' Justices for this County, and hath performed the conditions and terms of toleration enjoyned Protestant dissenters by the late Act of Parliament for Indulgence, upon the performance whereof they are to enjoy the liberty therein granted, Viz: hath taken the oaths of the said Act enjoyned, and hath made and subscribed the declaration therein mentioned and within written, and hath also declared his approbation of and subscribed the articles of religion, excepting what are to be excepted, as is required by Act of Parliament, and also written within; Dated under our hands June 22, 1692.

THOMAS BUTT,   WILLIAM WILLSON."

[3] Campbell's *History of Virginia*, p. 371.

suspicion alone; and so far as action showed, had no substantial footing whatever. The religion of the papist, on the other hand, carried with it necessarily the absolute spiritual supremacy of the Roman See in the hearts of all who professed it. In denying that the King of England was the head of their Church, the dissenters did not attempt to set up another, and that too, a foreign potentate in his stead; this the papist openly did; and in that age, it was not unnaturally regarded as a step towards treason in temporal affairs. The Pope, who was denounced by the great body of the English people as Anti-Christ, was the head of the Roman Catholic Church, and his principal design was supposed to be to overthrow both the spiritual and the civil order in England; a member of that church was, therefore, regarded as scheming, so far as lay in his power, to promote the success of this design, presumably so dear to that head, who claimed his entire allegiance.

As early as 1609, the author of *Nova Britannia* declared that he detested the thought of "one person seasoned with the least taint of that leaven" becoming a settler in Virginia; and the same writer urged that, should such a person be found there, he should be transported home at the first opportunity. There was no hope, he exclaimed, of the colonists prospering with this "viperous brood" in their bosom, "who will eat out and consume the womb of their mother. Papists are ever plotting and conspiring to root you out. Believe them not, howsoever they swear, flatter, and equivocate." [1] It was carefully enjoined in the charter of 1609 that the oath of supremacy, which asserted the spiritual headship of the King of England over all his subjects, should be tendered to every one seeking to land

[1] *Nova Britannia*, 1609, p. 20, Force's *Hist. Tracts*, vol. i.

in Virginia[1]; and should anyone refuse to swear, he
should not be suffered to disembark. In October, 1629,
when Baltimore and his companions visited the Colony with the view of seating themselves there, they
were requested to take this oath, but being open
supporters of the Romish doctrines and ceremonies,
they declined to do so; and as the authorities, in their
turn, refused to omit the oath, Baltimore had no
alternative but to depart, a step which was to have
momentous and lasting political consequences.[2] In
a letter to the Privy Council, the same year, informing
that body of their action, with their reasons for it,
the Governor and Council declared that, "among the
many blessings for which we are bound to bless God . . .
there is none whereby we have been made more happy
than in the freedom of our religion which we have
enjoyed, and that no papists have been suffered to
settle their abodes amongst us." They implore the
King to confirm this freedom, and beseech the Privy
Council to use all their influence with their royal master
to have it permanently continued.[3]

The promptness and sternness with which casual
expressions attributing Romanist leanings to the King
were punished in the Colony as early as 1642 shows that
popery was held at this time in such indescribable
horror that to impute it to the sovereign was looked
upon as a form of treason. In the course of that year,
Stephen Reikes said in the hearing of several persons:—
"His Majesty was at confession with the Lord of

[1] Brown's *Genesis of the United States*, vol. i., p. 235.

[2] Randolph MS., vol. iii., p. 214. The authorities refused "to
decline from the prescribed form so strictly enjoyned and so well
justified by the pen of our late Sovereign," James the First.

[3] British Colonial Papers, vol. v., No. 40; Robinson Transcripts,
p. 48.

Canterbury." He was arrested and tried; and his words having been pronounced to be of a dangerous tendency, he was condemned, not only to pay a fine of fifty pounds sterling (equal to about twelve hundred and fifty dollars in modern values, a very large sum at that time), but also to sit in the pillory, with a placard attached to his breast proclaiming his offence.[1]

An Act of Assembly passed a few years later forbade any office in the Colony to be filled by a popish recusant; and it also directed that every priest of the Romish Church, who should find his way to Virginia, should be sent out within five days after his arrival.[2] How keen and determined was the hostility to all persons of that faith at this time is revealed by the strong effort made to prevent them from exercising the most ordinary fiduciary powers. In 1654, Edwin Conway, of Lancaster county, was by will appointed the overseer of an estate, which also included the guardianship of several children. An order of administration displacing him was granted to John Meredith and Walter Heard apparently on the single ground urged by Meredith that he was a papist. Conway, objecting strenuously to his own removal, protested that no step should be taken until the county court had had an opportunity to pass upon his right.[3] We find the same uncompromising antagonism cropping out at this time even in the usual articles of indenture; in the course of August, 1655, John Dodman, of Westmoreland, by the terms of his contract with Jane Duke, agreed to bring up her

[1] Hawks, quoting Hening's *Statutes*, vol. i., p. 552, states that this event occurred in 1642, at which time Berkeley, a warm admirer of Laud, occupied the office of Governor; see Hawks, p. 50; see also Robinson Transcripts, p. 28.

[2] Hening's *Statutes*, vol. i., p. 268.

[3] Lancaster County Records, Orders March 27, 1654.

son, just apprenticed to him, in the Protestant religion; and in doing this, he was to be careful that the boy should be taught the correct prayers, and also how to read the Bible and other pious books printed in the English language.[1] In 1663, John Montone, a native of France, who followed the calling of a physician in Northumberland county, in his petition asking for naturalization, declared emphatically that he utterly denied and abhorred the "rules and superstitious ceremonies of the Romish Church."[2] Montone belonged to the sect of Huguenots, with whom hatred of that Church was not a historical tradition transmitted from a past generation, but a sentiment created by recent spoliation and persecution.

A man bearing the name of Raymond, who asserted that he was a Romanist priest, was, in 1687, summoned before the justices of Lower Norfolk on the complaint of Hugh Campbell that he had married a couple without any license, or publication of banns. Raymond, however, was able, in defence of his act, to show a certificate from the clerk of Elizabeth City county announcing that the banns had been published there in the manner required by law. The justices, not being satisfied apparently with the fact that the marriage ceremony had been performed by a Romanist priest, demanded security of him to answer by a designated date to the General Court sitting at Jamestown; this security Raymond refused to give, on the ground that the King had lately, by proclamation, bestowed on all his subjects, regardless of sect or creed, entire liberty of conscience; and that under the protection of this new Declaration, the Roman Catholic priest had a

[1] Westmoreland County Records, vol. 1653-64, f. p. 52.

[2] Northumberland County Records, Orders March 8, 1663.

right to celebrate the Mass and the other rites of his
Church in any house in the Colony. This, Raymond
stated he had done in the homes of Mr. Charles Egerton,
Captain Robert Jordan, and Mr. Henry Riddick.[1]

At a session of the Council held in October, 1688,
Governor Howard, who was especially remarkable for
his subserviency to the King, informed this body that,
during his recent visit to the Eastern Shore, Colonel
Charles Scarborough had, in his presence, declared that
"His Majesty would wear out the Church of England."
"How wear out?" asked the Governor. "When there
are vacancies," Scarborough replied, "the King supplies
the places with men of other persuasions." Howard,
in an excess of indignant zeal, not only reproved
Scarborough for expressing such a sentiment, but also
summarily deprived him of his commission as a justice
of the county court. The Council approved the
Governor's action on the ground that Scarborough's
words tended to disquiet the Government, and were contrary to the spirit of the King's Declaration of Liberty
of Conscience; he was summoned to answer for them
before the General Court; but appears to have been
finally discharged without punishment.[2] Scarborough
was not the only person charged with disloyalty because
he openly condemned the policy inaugurated by the
shortsighted James for the advancement of the welfare
of the Roman Catholic Church in his dominions;
Edmund Bowman, a merchant of large fortune for that

[1] Lower Norfolk County Records, Orders Nov. 16, 1687. The
royal proclamation referred to by Raymond was apparently that
of Charles II, which was designed for the protection of the Roman Catholics, but created such opposition that it was soon
withdrawn; see Green's *Short History of the English People*.

[2] Colonial Entry Book, 1680–95, p. 302; Palmer's *Calendar of
State Papers*, vol. i., p. 21; Hawks, p. 72.

period, was called before the Council on a like accusation of criticising the King's conduct, whilst James Collins was thrown into prison, and heavily ironed for the same offence.[1]

The panic raised in England by the blind course of the infatuated monarch had its reflection in conditions prevailing in the Colony about the same time. In 1688, a report was spread abroad in Stafford county that the papists of Virginia and Maryland were conspiring with the most ferocious of the Indian tribes to butcher all the Protestants; and that ten thousand Senecas and nine thousand Nanticokes had already snatched up their arms and were rushing forward, by forced marches, on the war-path. So terrifying was the impression created by this report that a large number of families residing near the line of frontier fled from their homes without stopping to carry off any of their property, and took refuge in those parts of the Colony where they thought they would find, at least for a time, some safety from danger. Coincident with the news of the papist and Indian incursion, it was whispered abroad that the entire Council, as well as a very large proportion of the county justices, had been converted to Romanism, and were giving open assistance to these sanguinary foes.[2] Under the influence of the violent passions aroused by fear and suspicion, the people seized their guns and formed themselves into armed bands, which were, with great difficulty, prevented from breaking the peace. The chief instigators of this extraordinary disturbance were Rev. John Waugh, Burr Harrison, and John West, who asserted that they had received their first infor-

[1] *Va. Maga. of Hist. and Biog.*, vol. vi., p. 394.

[2] Suspicion was most strongly directed against Isaac Allerton and John Armistead.

mation of the terrible plot from a friendly Indian. They were arrested by order of court and carried on board of the guard-ship *Deptford* for safekeeping.[1]

The report as to the papist and Indian uprising also got abroad in the neighboring county of Rappahannock; here the principal instigators of the commotion soon following were William Gannock, William Heather, Timothy Davis, and George Lambert; who, arming themselves with swords and muskets, marched about beating drums for volunteers, and crying aloud that "there was now no King, no law, no government." Three members of the Council, John Armistead, Ralph and Christopher Wormeley, at least two of whom resided in that part of the Colony, in order to put an end to so dangerous a disturbance, arrested the chief offenders and cast them into jail.[2]

A wave of suspicion beginning in these violent scenes in the Northern Neck seems to have passed to other parts of the Colony, and everywhere the terror of popish conspiracies led to absurd reports. For instance, it was said openly in Accomac that George Nicholas Hack, a leading citizen, supposed to be a papist in his sympathies, had received a bull directly from the Vatican; and one witness went so far as to assert that he had seen this remarkable document with his own eyes; that it was a pardon for sins; and that it ran out to three or four sheets of printed matter.[3] This

---

[1] Colonial Entry Book, 1680–95, p. 319.

[2] *Ibid.*, i., 80–95, p. 320.

[3] Accomac County Records, vol. 1682–97, p. 172, Orders Nov. 21, 1689.

"Deposition of Richard Bally, that sometime towards ye fall of ye liffe, ye day not well remembered, in ye yeare 1688, Mr. Samuel Palmer and your deponent being att ye depont. house and discorsing of ye difficulty of ye times, ye sd. Palmer tould ye depont.

astounding credulity in the popular mind lasted long after all prospect of a Roman Catholic restoration had vanished with the final expulsion of James the Second. In 1694, a witness testified before the Court of Henrico that Edward Hatcher, appearing at his house late at night, had announced that Mrs. Banister had been found hanged to a tree by means of a tenter-hook stuck in her jaw, and that nine other persons had also been found near her dead, each one attached to a separate tree in the same manner. "This is like the papists' way," exclaimed the witness in horror. Hatcher who had either invented the whole story, or was repeating a groundless rumor, declared that it was the deed of the Indians, but he added:—"I believe there were either papists with them, or they were hired by papists."[1]

In 1691, Joseph Bridger, of Isle of Wight, following

---

that there was a great man in our county had a Bull from ye Pope already, which news startled ye depont., and made him desirous to know how 't was. Ye sd. Palmer replied 'it was Capt. Hack.' Ye Depont. asked ye sd. Palmer how he knew it; ye sd. Palmer said he saw it and red part or all of it. Ye depont. asked ye sd. Palmer what manner it runn. Ye sd. Palmer replied 'A Pardonn for sinns.' Ye depont. asked ye sd. Palmer whether it was written in hand or in print, and how much there was of it. Ye sd. Palmer answered it was in print, and about three or four sheetes of paper, and further more saith not." Another witness deposed that he heard Palmer say "after he had read it (the bull), Mr. Hack being by said: 'Well Mr. Palmer and how do you like it,' and Mr. Palmer said, 'I cannot tell how I like it for it is the first I ever see of them, nor I don't greatly care whether I ever see another, for I don't understand what belongs to Bulls,' but since I have considered to myself yt it was a Bull or a pardon yt he had from ye Pope, and, therefore, I think he must needs be a papist, or else he would never keep such a thinge in his house." A third witness said that "Mr. Hack had a Bull come in and that it had cost him £5." Capt. Hack was probably amusing himself at the expense of these witnesses.

[1] Henrico County Records, vol. 1688–97, p. 532, Va. St. Libr.

the example set by John Meredith in 1654, petitioned
the county court to issue an order that a certain child,
at that time in the custody of Peter Blake, of Nansemond, should be delivered into his possession. He
based his claim on the fact that, in addition to his
obligations as administrator of the estate left by the
child's mother, he was under a solemn engagement
before God to ensure for the child a Christian education;
and that this was impossible so long as he remained
under the control of Blake, who was a "professed papist
contemner, and slighter of ye public worship of God as
is established by ye law of England and Virginia."[1]
This petition seems to have met with a favorable
response.

A like spirit was shown by the courts in a case occurring in 1699, which also involved the care of a youthful
person.   In the course of that year, information reached
the Governor and Council that William Aylward, of
York, and Samuel Hill, John Read, and the elder and
also the younger John Lucas, of Warwick, who were
known to be men of "popish principles," had entered
into a conspiracy to carry a girl named Mary Brown
by force out of Virginia into Maryland, there to be
married to a Roman Catholic. The plotters were
commanded to appear before their respective county
courts, where the oath prescribed by Act of Parliament in place of the former oaths of allegiance and
supremacy, was to be tendered to them; and should
they refuse to take it, this fact was to be reported to
the Attorney-General, who was to be required to
prosecute them at the earliest opportunity.   Hill and
Read had obtained their appointment as the girl's
guardians by false representations, for, as popish

[1] Palmer's *Calendar of Virginia State Papers*, vol. i., p. 31.

recusants, they were incapable of serving in that capacity under the law.[1]

Among the prominent attorneys belonging to the bar of Stafford county in 1691 were George and Robert Brent; both were Roman Catholics; and the question arose, could a popish recusant legally practise law in Virginia? The case against them seems to have dragged along until 1693, when the two attorneys were again indicted by the grand jury. They sought to postpone the issue as before, but in this were not successful; the justices decided against them; and an appeal was taken to the General Court, with what result is unknown, owing to the destruction of the records. George Brent, in 1690, was acting as the Ranger-General of the Northern Neck by the appointment of the Proprietary, who, it would appear from this fact, did not share the almost universal hatred and distrust of the Roman Catholics prevailing in Virginia at that time.[2]

The animosity towards the papists must have been fanned by the Protestant clergymen if their actions were influenced by the oath they were required to take before they could obtain a license to preach. The oath administered to Rev. Josias Mackie who, as we have seen, had charge of the Presbyterian congregations of Norfolk county in 1692, shows how elaborate its provisions were. He swore, first, that there was no transubstantiation of the elements of bread and wine in the Sacrament of the Lord's Supper; secondly, that the invocation and adoration of the Virgin Mary, or any other saint, and the sacrifice of the Mass as then

[1] Minutes of Council, May 17, 1699, B. T. Va., vol. liii.
[2] Palmer's *Calendar of Va. State Papers*, vol. i., p. 76; *Va. Maga. of Hist. and Biog.*, vol. i., p. 123.

used in the Church of Rome, were superstitious and idolatrous; thirdly, that this declaration was made in the plain sense of the words as understood by English Protestants, without any dispensation granted him for the purpose by the Pope, or any hope of such dispensation; and, finally, that he did not think that he could be acquitted before God or man, or absolved of this declaration, should the Pope or any other person, or power whatsoever, annul the same from the beginning. In addition to this general oath, the Protestant clergyman was also required to swear that he abhorred as most damnable the doctrine that princes excommunicated by the See of Rome, or with its authority, could be deposed, or murdered by their subjects, without the commission of an abominable crime, for which they should suffer the extreme penalty of the law.[1]

In 1681, Culpeper informed the Board of Trade that, at the time he was writing, there was but one papist residing in Virginia.[2] No doubt, this was a gross understatement, as it was only a few years later that a Roman Catholic priest, Father Raymond, was found celebrating the Mass in the homes of several leading citizens of one county alone. The entire body of papists, however, could never have been important either in numbers or influence. The extraordinary distrust with which they were regarded would not have reached the proportions it did had it originated either in a purely historical knowledge of the conflict between Catholics and Protestants, or in any apprehension as

[1] Norfolk County Records, Orders June 22, 1692; Henrico County Records, vol. 1688-97, p. 403, Va. St. Libr.

[2] Colonial Entry Book, vol. cvi., pp. 309-11. Culpeper also stated that, at this time, there were in Virginia a sect of dissenters who called themselves "Sweet Singers."

to the supposed injury this small body unaided could inflict on the people of the Colony. But from the foundation of Maryland, the proximity of that Romanist Province imparted to the papists of Virginia a much more sinister character than would have distinguished them in the popular view had they been looked upon as standing alone. They would have still aroused a bitter prejudice in the popular mind, but it would have been a prejudice not aggravated by fear.

CHAPTER XXV

Atheism and Witchcraft

TO confess that one was devoid of any religious belief was, if possible, deemed to be even more heinous than to acknowledge oneself to be either a Quaker or a Papist. How slight were the grounds on which charges of atheism were brought was illustrated in the case of Wingfield, the first President of the Council and Governor of the Colony:—he was accused of practically denying the existence of God because he had failed to carry a Bible with him to Virginia. Wingfield, knowing how destructive of his reputation such an imputation would be unless refuted, defended himself by saying that, when he left his home in one of the English shires to go up to London, his Bible was sent to that city along with his other books, and there left in the care of a Master Croft, but the trunk containing it was broken open by a thief and rifled, and he presumed that the Bible was one of the things "beasiled," as it could not be found among his other books on their arrival in Virginia.[1]

[1] *Works of Captain John Smith*, Arber's edition, p. lxxxviii. By an Act of Assembly passed in 1675, with the view of establishing certain military regulations, it was provided that a soldier guilty of blasphemy in camp should be required to run, after the Indian fashion, the gauntlet of one hundred men, and if he persisted in the offense, his tongue was to be pierced with a red hot iron; Colonial Entry Book, vol. lxxxvi., p. 70.

In 1654, Edward Hill, when a candidate for the office
of Speaker of the House of Burgesses, was, without
ground, charged with being a blasphemer and an
atheist, and the accusation seems even to have been
investigated by the General Court.   But his acquittal
did not save him from further imputations on the same
score.   Hatcher, a delegate in the House over which
Hill was presiding at the time, boldly exclaimed during
a session of the Burgesses:—"The mouth of this House
is a devil." He was compelled to kneel and acknowledge
the impropriety of this speech; and his name was afterwards dropped from the roll.[1]   In 1683, Thomas
Newhouse, of Lower Norfolk, was accused of having
asserted before an assembly of people that "a great
part of the Bible was false."   He was arrested, tried by
the justices of the county, and at once sent on to the
General Court sitting at Jamestown.[2]   A large number
of persons were, on one occasion, indicted in Accomac
on the ground that, by their participation in a mock
marriage, they had made a scoff of the same holy
book.[3]

During the last year of the century, it was proclaimed
in an Act of Assembly that a denial of the existence of
the Deity or the Trinity, or an assertion that there were
more Gods than one, or that the Christian religion was
false, or that the Scriptures were of human and not of
divine origin, should subject the person guilty of such
an utterance, for the first offence, to incapacity to hold
public offices; and for the second, in addition to this
penalty, to disability to sue in a court of law, dis-

[1] Acts of Assembly, Nov. 20, 1654, Randolph MS., vol. iii., p.
236; Neill's Va. Carolorum, p. 237.

[2] Lower Norfolk County Records, Orders Aug. 15, 1683.

[3] Accomac County Records, vol. 1690–97, p. 37.

qualification to serve as a guardian or executor, and incapacity to accept any gift or legacy; and as a further punishment, he was to suffer imprisonment during a period of three years.[1]

The excess of incredulity as reflected in atheism was probably far less frequently observed in the Colony than the excess of credulity as reflected in the belief in witchcraft. There was perhaps not a single community in the civilized world of those times in which this form of superstition did not exist; in some, as in Massachusetts, for instance, the belief in witchcraft was carried so far that it led, as at Salem, to the judicial murder of numerous unhappy persons; the annals of Virginia bear no such stain, but this uncouth superstition, which had its birth in ignorance and malice, prevailed certainly among the lower section of her people throughout the Seventeenth century. Fortunately, it resulted in the infliction of no severer punishment than a flogging or a ducking; and even this punishment was imposed in only two cases whose record has survived, one of which occurred early in the following century.

Rev. Alexander Whitaker, one of the most accomplished men of that age, writing to Rev. William Crashaw in England, touched at some length on the "anticks" of the Indians. "All these things," he concluded with evident awe, "make me think that there be great witches among them, and that they are very familiar with the Devill."[2] As soon as the Colony's population began to increase very much, the "great witches" were not supposed to be confined entirely to the ranks of the savages; they had now appeared among the settlers

[1] Hening's *Statutes*, vol. iii., p. 168.
[2] Brown's *Genesis of the United States*, vol. i., p. 499.

themselves; but unlucky was the man or woman who, in a moment of passion, attributing to some neighbor the evil powers of a witch, was unable afterwards to prove the charge; the accusation was too serious in its consequences, should the person to whom such powers were imputed, be innocent, to be passed over without an inquiry. In 1641, Jane Rookins, in a quarrel with George Busher's wife, as the consummation of abuse denounced her as a witch. Mrs. Busher, resenting the charge, in her great fear lest it should bring down on her head a wave of popular rage, made a complaint to court of the wrong done her by the application to her of such a frightful word. Mrs. Rookins professed to have no recollection of having used it, but declared her readiness, should she have done so, to express her hearty penitence. The apology was accepted as sufficient, but the justices ordered her husband to reimburse George Busher for the expense he had been put to in prosecuting the case.[1]

In the course of 1655, the justices of Lower Norfolk stated from the bench that the reputation of several women residing in the county had been recently blackened and their lives jeoparded, by the "dangerous and scandalous speeches" of persons publicly accusing them of witchcraft. So great an outrage did the court consider this to be, that they entered an order that, should anyone bring a charge of this kind without being able to support it by his own oath, or the oaths of other witnesses, he was to forfeit one thousand pounds of tobacco.[2] During the same year, Rev. David Lindsay, of Northumberland, a clergyman who

[1] General Court Orders, Robinson Transcripts, p. 28.
[2] Lower Norfolk County Records, Orders May 23, 1655; Lower Norfolk County Antiquary, vol. iii., p. 152.

had emigrated from Scotland, a land where witchcraft flourished, accused William Harding of that county of sorcery; the case was submitted to a jury, who found him guilty in part of the crime laid at his door; the court promptly sentenced him to receive ten stripes on his bare shoulders, and then to be banished permanently from the county. Two months, however, were allowed him within which to take his leave, for it was evidently regarded as only right that he should be permitted to settle his affairs before his departure.[1] Three years later, Rev. Francis Doughty, emulating the zeal of Mr. Lindsay, had Barbara Winbrow dragged before the justices of Northampton, on the ground that she was notoriously bad in her life and conversation, and generally supposed to be "guilty of witchery." She had already been arraigned for sorcery before the General Court, but had secured an acquittal.[2]

The only case involving the infliction of the death penalty on anyone accused of this offence coming before the courts of Virginia during the Seventeenth century related to an incident occurring, in 1659, at sea. In the course of a voyage from England, Captain Bennett, an Englishman engaged in the trade with the Colony, hung at the yard's arm, quite probably at the clamorous demand of his superstitious passengers during the progress of a violent storm, an old woman

[1] Northumberland County Records, Orders Nov. 20, 1655. There were other charges besides witchcraft brought against Harding on this occasion, and it is possible that the conviction was for these other offenses, and not for sorcery. The expression is: "They (the Jury) found part of the articles proved by several depositions." Harding, like Barbara Winbrow, may have been notoriously "bad in his life and conversation," and his banishment may have been due to this fact alone.

[2] Northampton County Records, vol. 1657–64, p. 18; General Court Orders, Dec. 1, 1657, Robinson Transcripts, p. 243[2].

named Katharine Grady suspected of witchcraft; but when information as to this summary act was submitted to the General Court at Jamestown, he was immediately summoned before them to answer for it, a proof that they did not consider that a charge of sorcery against anyone would justify such an instant and such an extreme penalty.[1]

A law passed in 1655 would seem to show a determination on the General Assembly's part to discourage as far as possible the endless turmoil caused by charges and countercharges of witchcraft; they referred to such accusations as designed to bring "slander and scandall" upon the person held up as guilty; and they, therefore, provided a severe punishment for anyone who began them. From this it would be presumed that they themselves had very little faith in such imputations. That this statute was enforced is proven by the case of Anne Godby, of Lower Norfolk; in a moment of great passion, she denounced the wife of a prominent citizen as a witch, and for this her husband was compelled to pay, not only a fine of three hundred pounds of tobacco, the penalty for her contempt of the statute, but also all the costs of the suit, including the fees and expenses of the numerous witnesses.[2]

In 1665, Alice Stephens was brought before the General Court on a charge of witchcraft[3]; and in the course of the same year, a judgment was obtained in the same court against a woman who had made a similar charge against one of her neighbors.[4]

[1] Robinson Transcripts, p. 243[2].

[2] Lower Norfolk County Records, vol. 1656–66, p. 267. The statute is referred to in this court entry.

[3] Robinson Transcripts, p. 250.

[4] *Ibid.*, p. 256.

A difference having arisen in 1671, between Mrs. Neal and Edward Cole, residents of Northumberland county, Mrs. Neal, during the quarrel, gave utterance to a "kind of prayer" that "neither he nor any of his family might ever prosper." Shortly after this vindictive expression had passed her lips, Cole declared that all the people connected with his plantation fell ill, and that Mrs. Cole also was taken down with sickness, and had not yet been restored to health. All this, so he informed Captain Edward Le Breton, was due entirely to the influence of Mrs. Neal's curse. On another occasion, when his wife was confined to her bed, he had sent word to Mrs. Neal to come and visit her. At this time, it would seem, he was not aware of her evil powers, but fortunately, said he, in entering the house, she passed under a horseshoe nailed over the door, and this fact alone had led her, when she reached Mrs. Cole's side, to pray heartily for her recovery. That this was no groundless assertion was proven by her becoming malignant again as soon as removed from the benign influence of the horseshoe.[1]

About 1679, Alice Cartwright was accused in the court of Lower Norfolk of having cast a spell over John Salmon's child. A jury of women was at once impanelled, but as they reported that they had found no suspicious marks on her body to show that she was in commerce with witches, she was discharged as innocent.[2]

The delusion prevailed in those times that if the person who had fallen under the evil ban of sorcery was a heathen, Christian baptism would break the charm

[1] Northumberland County Order Book, 1666–72, folio p. 104.
[2] Lower Norfolk County Records, Orders Jan'y 16, 1678–9; Lower Norfolk County Antiquary, vol. i., p. 56.

and set him free. Not long before the Insurrection of
1676 began, under the leadership of the younger
Bacon, Colonel Mason captured the youthful son of the
King of the Doegs and carried him home. After
arriving there, it is alleged the boy lay in bed for a
period of ten days, his eyes staring and his mouth agape,
but with no sign that he was breathing, although his
body remained warm. Captain Brent, a Roman Catholic in faith, visiting him, perhaps out of curiosity,
pronounced him, after examination, to be bewitched,
and earnestly recommended that he should be baptized,
a remedy which, he said, he had often heard would at
once counteract the evil consequences of sorcery.
His advice was promptly followed, and the chronicler
of the incident sagely declares that the boy soon
recovered.[1]

In the commissions which the justices of the county
courts received on their appointment to office in 1691,
they were strictly enjoined to inquire, not only as to
all felonies, trespasses, and forestallings occurring, but
also as to all witchcrafts,—a crime against the safety
of individuals, and the peace of the community, as
serious in its nature (at least in the eyes of the Governor
drawing up these commissions), as any coming within
the Grand Jury's jurisdiction.[2] Nevertheless, after
this time, whilst the accusations of witchcraft brought
into court for investigation were numerous enough,
there seems to have been little disposition on the part
of justices or juries to affirm them by a favorable
judgment or verdict. A charge of sorcery was as

[1] T. M.'s *Account of Bacon's Rebellion*, p. 9, Force's *Hist. Tracts*,
vol. i.

[2] See Nicholson's Commission to the Northampton County Justices in 1691, vol. 1689–98, p. 98. See Commission of Essex County
Justices in 1692, vol., 1692–5 pp. 1, 2, Va. St. Libr.

easily provable in one case as in another, as in no case was there any ground at all for it to rest on; and that these officers of the law should have allowed such charges to be the subject of civil suit more often than of criminal prosecution, shows that they were beginning to disbelieve in them thoroughly.

This fact is illustrated in numerous cases. In 1694, William Eale accused Phyllis Money of having cast a spell over Henry Dunkin's horse and by making him start off suddenly lacerate his owner's leg; and he further declared that she had taught her daughter, who was Dunkin's wife, to be a witch, and that Mrs. Dunkin had in turn taught her husband to be a wizard. Not content with speaking these terrible words in Dunkin's house, Eale had repeated them again and again in other places. Phyllis protested that she had never been guilty of witchcraft, or of any "wicked and base acts" of that nature, but that in consequence of Eale's groundless charges, her neighbors had refused to "keep company" with her and her husband, and that they had been much injured in their credit and good name; and she even went so far as to assert that their lives had been in imminent danger. Had there been a strong belief in witchcraft among the justices of the county court, Phyllis and her husband would have been arrested on the original charge and prosecuted; instead, they were allowed to bring a civil suit, which amounted to no more than an ordinary action of defamation; and in the end failed to secure any damages.[1]

In the following year, Henry Dunkin was summoned to court in a civil suit for scandalous reflections on the reputation of John Dunkin and his wife, the most reprehensible of which were that Elizabeth Dunkin had

[1] Westmoreland County Records, Orders Nov. 1, 1694.

boasted to him that she was a sorceress; that she had bewitched his cow, and was herself regularly sucked by the Devil. This was a charge which, could it be proven, would have rendered her, by the provisions of the English law, liable to be burnt at the stake, an accursed and shameful death; such "damnable and wicked words" falsely attributed to her, Elizabeth alleged, were deliberately designed to destroy the good names of herself and her husband, to ruin them in their estates and fortunes, and to bring lasting discredit on their posterity. A short time after Henry Dunkin reported these words to have been uttered, he went to John Dunkin's house, and there heaped "atrocious and scurrilous names" upon Elizabeth, denounced her as a witch and her children as witches' imps, and ended by defying all her works of sorcery. The case was submitted to a jury, with a claim on John and Elizabeth Dunkin's part to forty thousand pounds of tobacco in damages; but that body returned a verdict allowing them only forty pounds of that commodity. It would appear from this that the members of this jury at least looked upon a charge of witchcraft as calculated to make so little public impression that it could not be regarded as a very serious form of defamation.[1]

A suit was brought by William Morris, of King and Queen county, in 1695, on the ground that his wife, Eleanor, had been accused of sorcery. Eleanor, in her testimony in court, stated that she had resided in Virginia thirty years, and that in the whole of that time was "never guilty of any conjuration, witchcraft, enchantment, or charm," but, on the contrary, her skirts had remained clear of all such offences, or even the suspicion of them. Notwithstanding this fact, Anne

[1] Westmoreland County Records, Orders Aug. 28, 1695.

Ball had gone about declaring in a very loud voice that Eleanor had been and still was a witch, and had ridden her during several days and nights until she was wearied nearly to death. The jury, instead of turning a credulous ear to such a charge, promptly acquitted Eleanor, and found Mrs. Ball guilty of defamation. Mrs. Ball seems to have been disposed to bring numerous accusations of the same character, for about the same time she charged Nell Cane with riding her twice.[1]

Princess Anne county, which was to become early in the Eighteenth century the scene of the most memorable trial for sorcery recorded in the colonial history of Virginia, seems to have been frequently agitated, towards the end of the Seventeenth century, by the machinations of supposed witches. The most conspicuous of these was Grace Sherwood, who was to win such lasting fame as an enchantress. She appeared in this character as early as 1698, in which year, she was accused by John Gisburne of casting spells. She evidently thought that the reputation of possessing such evil powers was not favorable to her personal safety, for she joined with her husband in suing Gisburne for defamation. As the jury decided against her, it would be inferred that, like the jury in the Dunkins' case, they did not deem a charge of witchcraft, from the very nature of it, entitled to any consideration. Anthony Barnes also brought a similar accusation against Grace:—he declared that she had ridden his wife one night, and then, in the shape of a black cat had slipped through the keyhole, or a crack in the door. Barnes being sued for slander, the jury again decided against Grace, perhaps because they looked upon the charges

[1] Essex County Records, Orders June 11, 1695.

as too absurd to carry weight in the minds of sensible people.[1] Some years afterwards, the same woman was sentenced to be ducked, ostensibly to test whether she was really a witch, but quite probably to punish her slyly for having become a serious nuisance to the public by the strife which she was so successful in stirring up.

The year in which Grace Sherwood was accused of witchcraft by Anthony Barnes, Anne Byrd, of the same county, was charged by Charles Kinsey with riding him from his house as far as Elizabeth Russell's; this led to a report that she was a sorceress; and so much disturbed was she and her husband by this reputation, that they brought suit against Kinsey and placed the damages at one hundred pounds sterling. The defendant admitted that he had used such words, but declared that Anne had appeared to him merely in a dream, or if he were really awake at the time, that it was a pure illusion. The jury after this explanation found in his favor, but they also found in favor of John Pitts (who had accused Anne of riding him along the sea-shore), although Pitts, instead of seeking to back out like Kinsey, persisted in saying that "to his thought, apprehension, and best knowledge, she did serve him so." In this case, as in the others already mentioned, the jury plainly considered the charge to be too improbable in itself to be received with credulity, and, therefore, the reputation of Anne Byrd could not have been really injured.[2] And yet about the same time, a jury of women were impanelled, on Captain William Carver's information, to examine Jane Jennings for witch spots, as she had been accused of being inti-

[1] Lower Norfolk County Antiquary, vol. ii., pp. 92, 93.

[2] *Ibid.*, vol. i., p. 20; Princess Anne County Records, Orders July 8, 1698.

mate with evil spirits and skilful in the arts of a sorceress.[1]

In re-examining the various cases of supposed witchcraft which I have enumerated as found in the surviving records of Virginia during the Seventeenth century, it will be seen that, in one instance only, that of William Harding of Northumberland county, was the accusation (and that in part alone) sustained by the decision of a court or the verdict of a jury. The convicted person in this case was simply banished, more probably because he was notoriously bad in his life or was looked upon as causing dissension, than because he was really considered to be capable of exercising evil powers. In all those other cases in which some one had charged another with being a sorcerer or sorceress, instead of the law officers accepting the imputation seriously, they had been satisfied either to impose a fine on the accuser for defamation, or to dismiss the case without allowing any damages at all. The impanelling of female juries to make a search for witch spots on the supposed sorceress' body was the only act that seemed to show any belief in this form of superstition on the part of that class in the community from which the different magistrates were drawn; but it is quite possible that this concession to popular ignorance was made because all the chances in such examinations were against the discovery of such spots. The tit sought for with the greatest eagerness was not one planted in the female body in the economy of nature, and the judges had sufficient knowledge of female anatomy to be willing to rely on the impossibility of finding it anywhere outside of the realm of the imagination.

[1] Lower Norfolk County Antiquary, vol. ii., p. 49.

The ancient superstition of stroking a corpse to discover whether the dead person had died by violence, or in the course of nature, was often exhibited in Virginia during this century. This was done at the inquest over the dead body of Panell Rynurse held in Northampton in 1655; at the jury's command, William Custis touched the inanimate face and ran his hand along the motionless form; and as no signs of life appeared in consequence, a verdict was brought in that the death had not been brought about by violent means.[1] A similar case occurred in Surry county in 1662; in this case, the body was a female servant's, and her master and mistress, who were suspected of having murdered her, were required at the inquest to stroke the corpse.[2] The idea in this, as in Rynurse's case, was that, if the person or persons touching the body were guilty, it would give some indications of returning life. A third case, involving a child's corpse is preserved in the records of Accomac. The supposed murderer here was also compelled to draw his hand over the body.[3]

[1] Northampton County Records, vol. 1654–5, folio p. 123.
[2] Surry County Records, vol. 1645–72, p. 205, Va. St. Libr.
[3] Accomac County Records, vol. 1678–82, p. 159.

Part II

Education

CHAPTER I

Sentiment in Favor of Education

THE physical conditions prevailing in Virginia throughout the Seventeenth century were not so favorable to popular education in the broadest sense of that term as those prevailing in New England. Almost the entire body of the latter colonies' inhabitants had their homes grouped together in the form of villages and towns, which, by concentrating the people of each neighborhood in one spot, made it practicable, at an early date, to carry out a scheme of instruction for each community. Virginia, on the other hand, was composed of a succession of plantations. The average area of the plantation acquired by patent previous to 1650 was about four hundred and forty-six acres; and after the middle of the century, about six hundred and twenty-eight.[1] It is probable that the average area of the landed estates owned in the Colony, should we combine the portions obtained by purchase, patent, and inheritance alike, fell little short of one thousand acres. Naturally, such large holdings had a strong tendency to disperse the population over wide reaches of country; there were comparatively few persons to the square mile, and it followed that, had a public school system been established, each schoolhouse would have been so

[1] See Bruce's *Economic Hist. of Va. in the Seventeenth Century*, vol. i., p. 528, et seq.

remote from the homes of most of the pupils that only
those who were supplied with horses, and whose labor
in the fields could be dispensed with by their parents,
could have regularly attended its course of instruction.
It was not as if the pupils were to be drawn from a
town or village, in whose centre the schoolhouse had
been built or from groups of thickly inhabited farms
to which the same structure was conveniently situated;
on the contrary, the pupils were so widely scattered that,
to accommodate them all, the number of schoolhouses
to be erected would have been out of proportion to the
number of children to be taught, and far in excess of
what each community could have afforded to construct,
if reliance had to be placed on the public purse alone.
In consequence of these facts, popular education did not
take the same deep root in Virginia as it did in New
England, where all the physical conditions, which alone
caused the difference, were so much more favorable.[1]

There was, however, no side of the plantation system,
as it prevailed in Virginia during the Seventeenth
century, which was hostile to the setting up of numerous private schools for the benefit of all possessing the
means to send their children to them. It would be
the grossest error to suppose that the Colony was lacking in such schools, or even in a public school here and
there resting on a private foundation; and that the
only facilities for tuition were confined to the members

---

[1] "Their (the Virginians) almost general want of scholars for
the education of their children is another consequence of their
scattered planting of most sad consideration, most of all bewailed
of parents there"; *Virginia's Cure*, p. 6, Force's *Historical Tracts*,
vol. iii. In seeking, for a special purpose, to show the evil effects
of this "scattered planting," the author of this pamphlet, there is
good reason to think, underrated the number of "scholars" *i.e.*,
competent teachers.

of a child's own family.   The interest felt in education
by the Virginians during that period was as strong as
during any period of Colonial history; the principal
reason for which is obvious:—at no period were the
leading people of the Colony's different communities
so much controlled by English influences in every department of their social and intellectual life.   Throughout this century, the most important citizens, with
few exceptions, had been born and reared in England;
the proportion of conspicuous persons of English birth
was far larger in the Seventeenth century than in the
Eighteenth; and as the members of this class of emigrants had, before they left their native country
received as a rule, the best instruction which that
country afforded in those times, it followed that they
attached a high value to education; that they used
their interest to promote by all feasible means its
advancement among their neighbors; and above all
that they showed a persistent determination that their
own children should, as far as practicable, enjoy all
its advantages.   Whilst there were no colleges, or even
high schools, in Virginia comparable to those in which
most of these emigrants had obtained their final course
of instruction, still there is no reason to think that the
general tuition secured by them for their own offspring
was very much inferior to that which fitted a large
majority of the Englishmen of that age for the ordinary
business of life.

The desire of the Virginian parents of these early
times to extend to their children opportunities of
acquiring some sort of an education comes to light in
numerous ways.   One of the most remarkable is the
provision for this purpose made in last testaments.
A few examples may be given.   One of the earliest

wills touching on this subject was that of John Waltham, of Accomac county, who died about 1640. Waltham left directions that, as soon as his son should reach the age of six, his "instructions of good learning" should begin; and with the view of affording that son the best education, he ordered his executors to confide him to some "good and godlye schoolmaster," selected with extraordinary care. From this, it would be inferred that schoolmasters were sufficiently numerous on the Eastern Shore, or at least in Virginia, at this time, to allow a considerable latitude of choice. It does not appear to be quite certain whether this boy was to be taught at his own home by a tutor, or to be removed to the home of his teacher, who would there also act as his guardian when not engaged with his studies. His father further enjoined that he should remain under this teacher's guidance until he had arrived at the age of eleven years; and to provide for all the expenses thus entailed, the executors were authorized to sell the entire annual increase, both male and female, of the cattle which the child had inherited. After his eleventh year had been passed, only the male cattle were to be sold for this purpose; and this sale was to continue until the boy had reached his eighteenth year, when his education was to cease, and he was to come into possession of all his property. In concluding, Waltham reiterated the request to his executors that they should hold the child in "their tender care, more especially in the particular care of his education, and breeding in the rudiments of good learning." [1] Throughout the will, it can be seen that the strongest desire animating the maker in drawing up this last expression of his wishes was that his son should enjoy some of

[1] Accomac County Records, vol. 1640–45, p. 38, Va. St. Libr.

those advantages of instruction which, in all probability, he himself had enjoyed in England before
emigrating to Virginia; and there is no word in the
whole of it to show that he felt any doubt that his
ample provision would fail to assure the anticipated
tuition simply because the Colony could not offer such
advantages.

A few years after Waltham's death, Nicholas Granger,
also of Accomac, followed his example in providing for
his daughter's education by setting apart for that purpose a definite number of cattle.[1] Sometimes this
was accomplished by a deed of gift in the donor's
lifetime; in 1647, for instance, Susan English, of York,
placed on record the present of a heifer to each of her
children, the male issue of which were to be delivered
to anyone providing the children with board, clothes,
and tuition. This case illustrates, in a remarkable
manner, so many parents' eagerness to obtain the advantages of schooling for their offspring, for apparently
this little herd of cattle formed the bulk of Mrs. English's possessions. The fact that she herself was unable
to write gives a touch of pathos to her solicitude.[2] In
1651, Robert Wilson, of Northampton, left directions
by will that there should be appropriated from his
estate for his brother's education thirty pounds sterling,
which represented in modern values about seven
hundred and fifty dollars, a very considerable sum to be
devoted to such a purpose, and one large enough to
assure instruction through several years. The boy
was to be taught how to read, write, and cast accounts,
with great ease.[3]

[1] Northampton County Records, vol. 1645–51, p. 93.
[2] York County Records, vol. 1638–48, p. 339, Va. St. Libr.
[3] Northampton County Records, vol. 1651–54, f. p. 13.

A father lacking in cattle, which might afford a steady annual income by the sale of their increase, sometimes provided for his child's education by requiring in his will that the proceeds from the labor of a slave should be set apart for that purpose; for example, in 1654, John Brown, of Northampton, ordered his executors to reserve the income derived from one of his negroes' work in the corn and tobacco fields, and to devote it to meeting the expense of tuition of the testator's son.[1] The benefits of such a provision, which was no small one in the light of an agricultural servant's value in that age, were not always confined to the children of the deceased; in 1654, Richard Vaughan who also resided in Northampton, bequeathed his entire estate to a family of blacks, probably his slaves, with instructions to his executors that its younger members should all be taught how to read.[2] And in the course of the same year, Thomas Wright, of Lower Norfolk, provided in his will for his children's enjoyment of the advantage of three years' instruction in school; which was probably designed as simply a continuation of the tuition they had been receiving in his own life time. During the whole of this period of three years, they were to reside on the plantation formerly possessed by their father; from this it is to be inferred that they were either to be taught by a tutor in their own home, or there was a private school situated sufficiently near for them to attend daily without inconvenience.[3]

Sometimes a father, in his last will, laid an express injunction on his oldest children to secure for his youngest the best opportunities for education offered

[1] Northampton County Records, vol. 1654–55, p. 86.
[2] *Ibid.*, vol. 1654–55, p. 102.
[3] Lower Norfolk County Records, vol. 1651–56, p. 134.

in the Colony; such was the case of Giles Taverner, of York, who, in 1655, after directing his two eldest sons to place the youngest at school, ordered that, for the payment of the expenses which this would impose, there should be appropriated the income from his "entire stock" for a period of two years.[1] Humphrey Clark, of Isle of Wight county, required his executors to keep the whole number of his agricultural servants together in one body, and to reserve one half of their labor's proceeds for meeting the cost of maintaining his son in the care of a competent teacher.[2] In 1657, Clement Thresh, of Rappahannock, in his will declared that all his estate should be responsible for the outlay made necessary in providing, during three years, instruction for his step-daughter, who, being then thirteen years of age, had, no doubt, already been going to school for some length of time. The manner of completing her education (which, it seems was to be prolonged to her sixteenth year) was perhaps the usual one for girls at this period:—she was to be taught at a Mrs. Peacock's, very probably by Mrs. Peacock herself, who may have been the mistress of a small school; for it was ordered in the will that, if she died, the step-daughter was to attend the same school as Thomas Goodrich's children.[3] Thomas Whitlock, also of Rappahannock, left directions, in 1659, that his son should be placed in the care of a teacher by his executors[4]; and the same year, Thomas Buck, of York, repeated the like directions in his will.[5] Samuel Fenn, who was also a citizen of

---

[1] York County Records, vol. 1633-94, p. 79, Va. St. Libr.

[2] Isle of Wight County Wills and Deeds for 1655.

[3] Rappahannock County Records, vol. 1656-64, orig. p. 74.

[4] *Ibid.*, orig. p. 91.

[5] York County Records, vol. 1657-62, p. 177, Va. St. Libr.

York, requested his executors to secure for his children the "utmost education which Virginia afforded"; and in order to provide an ample fund for this purpose, he enjoined them to sell the whole increase of his stock of cattle from year to year.[1] Edward Littleton, of Northampton, in his last testament contented himself with leaving instructions that his children should receive the most thorough and extensive tuition which their estates would allow them to pay for.[2]

In the course of 1666, Walter Bruce, of Nansemond, who had married the widow of Thomas Sayer, one of the most prominent citizens of Lower Norfolk, increased his stepchildren's estates by presenting them with a considerable number of cattle; four of these, during his absence from Virginia, his wife sold, and with the proceeds met the expense of sending a daughter to school.[3] By the terms of John Russell's will, his daughter was to continue to be educated until she should marry[4]; which her father perhaps presumed would occur when she should reach her sixteenth or seventeenth year; for, in those times, the majority of women found husbands generally before they had passed that age. Thomas Griffin, of Isle of Wight county, left, in 1669, directions for his executors to have his son of the same name placed in a teacher's care in order that he might learn how to read, write, and cast accounts; and should they fail to observe this injunction, they were required to deliver to him at least eight thousand pounds

---

[1] York County Records, vol. 1657–62, p. 248, Va. St. Libr.

[2] Northampton County Records, vol. 1657–66, p. 150

[3] Lower Norfolk County Records, vol. 1656–66, p. 438. Francis Sayer, a stepson of Bruce, was one of the justices of the county in 1671.

[4] "So long as she keepes herself without a husband"; *William and Mary College Quart.*, vol. iii., p. 154.

of tobacco[1]; which, no doubt, he was expected to use in covering the cost of the education his father wished him to receive. As a certain degree of discretion was to be exercised by him in the event that the executors were delinquent, it is probable that he had already arrived at his fifteenth year. Richard Jarratt, of Surry, who apparently could not himself write, though he may have been prevented, as was so often the case, by extreme sickness from signing his last will, left instructions similar to Thomas Griffin's for the education of his son. A like provision was inserted in the last testament of Edmund Howell of the same county; and in the last testament also of John Smith, of Essex; and of John Newell, of Westmoreland.[2]

In his will, drawn about 1667, George Ashall, of Lower Norfolk, apparently a tanner by trade, instructed his executors to sell thirty hides belonging to his estate and to expend the proceeds in "bringing his son up to school."[3] A few years afterwards, Thomas Gerrard bequeathed one thousand pounds of tobacco to meet the necessary outlay for "the learning and education" of a negro boy, who was either his illegitimate son, or a favorite body servant.[4] Robert Gascoigne, of Northampton, who had, by the terms of his will, divided his cattle among his children, made by the

[1] Isle of Wight County Records, vol. 1661–1719, p. 84.

[2] Surry County Records, vol. 1671–84, pp. 29, 372, Va. St. Libr.; Essex County Records, vol. 1692–95, p. 372, Va. St. Libr.; Westmoreland County Records, vol. 1690–99, p. 181.

[3] Lower Norfolk County Records, vol. 1666–75, p. 134.

[4] *William and Mary College Quart.*, vol. iv., p. 84. At a later date, Henry Wickliff, of Westmoreland county, instructed his executors to purchase of Mrs. Anne Washington two mulatto boys, probably his own children, the youngest of whom "was to be put to school until he could read English"; see Records of that county, vol. 1690–99, p. 186.

same instrument a gift of these cattle's male increase during a designated period, to his widow, provided that she should keep their son Robert at school until he had acquired a perfect knowledge of reading and writing; and their daughter Bridget also, until she could both read and sew with an equal degree of skill.[1]   Five years later, Charles Dunn, of York, devised his residuary estate to Robert Calvert, with directions to his executors to see that he was "well educated."[2]   William Rookings, of Surry, gave orders that the entire number of his slaves should, after his death, continue attached to his plantation with a view to the production of income sufficient, not only to pay off all the debts he had incurred, but also to cover the expense of providing "clothing and schooling" for his children.   The degree of instruction which he designed for his son seems to have differed somewhat from that he intended for his daughters:—the boy was "to be brought up to good education," whilst the girls were to receive merely "what education may be fitting for them," a rather vague definition, which the executors were at liberty to interpret according to their own discretion.[3]   In his will, bearing the date of 1679, John Waterson, of Northampton, declared that it was his "pleasure that his little son John should have three years' schooling"; and a similar provision was made the following year by Henry Hallstead, of Lower Norfolk.[4]   Two years later, Richard Albretton, who left a daughter, followed their examples.[5]   In every one of the preceding in-

[1] Northampton County Records, Orders April 20, 1675.

[2] York County Records, vol. 1675–84, orig. p. 90.

[3] Surry County Records, vol. 1671–84, p. 329, Va. St. Libr.

[4] Northampton County Records, vol. 1679–83, p. 67; Lower Norfolk County Records, vol. 1675–86, p. 200.

[5] York County Records, 1675–84, orig. p. 555.

stances, it is probable that the children, whose future instruction was so carefully arranged for, had already been receiving some instruction.

Peter Johnson, who resided in Rappahannock county, released his "son-in-law" from an indenture about 1680 on condition that he should take his brother-in-law or half brother Johnson's son, under his care until he should arrive at his twentieth year; in the meanwhile, the youth was to have, at the expense of his new guardian, the benefit of as "convenient an education" as could be given him."[1]   In the course of the same year, John Davenport, of Lancaster, by will directed that his two young horses should be devoted to meeting the cost entailed by his son William's "schooling."   The animals were probably to be hired out so as to afford an annual income; or they were to be used on the estate left by the testator in working designated fields of tobacco, the harvest of which was to be sold in order to carry out Davenport's intentions.[2]   Mr. Francis Pigott, of Northampton, seems to have been interested in the continuation of his son's education only to a point where he would be able to "read a legible hand and also to write one"; apparently a modest aspiration, but when realized one that would signify the acquisition of a very considerable amount of knowledge.[3]   In 1686, David Williams, of Isle of Wight county, instructed his executors to keep his sons under a teacher's care until they could read the Bible with facility; if the estate offered no easier or quicker way of furnishing the means to cover the expense of tuition, then a mare, which the testator had bequeathed to these sons,

---

[1] Rappahannock County Records, vol. 1677–82, orig. p. 17.

[2] Lancaster County Will Book, vol. 1674–87, p. 92.

[3] Northampton County Records, vol. 1683–89, p. 122.

was to be sold; and a like disposition was to be made of the same animal should there be income enough to insure their learning to read, but not to write.[1] About the same time, Prevost Nelson, of Northampton, in his will requested Rev. Thomas Teakle to take charge of his two sons and to see that they acquired the power to read and write "for the future benefit of their affairs, and the health of their souls."[2] Francis Pettit, of the same county, felt an even greater solicitude that his children should be educated:—he left directions that, should his widow be unable, out of her own income, to meet the expense of keeping the children at school, the plantation occupied by him in his lifetime was to be rented, and all the proceeds devoted to the cost of their tuition, until they should arrive at an age when they could, by their own labor, contribute to the fund which would be needed.[3]

Sarah Pigott, of Lower Norfolk, in framing her will in 1689 made her entire estate liable for the outlay required for her grand-daughter's education.[4] Michael Fulgham, of Isle of Wight county, about the same year, provided for the education of his children by instructing his executors to devote to this purpose the whole income to be derived from one of the plantations he had left to his heirs.[5] Sebastian Perrin, of Elizabeth City, in 1692 gave orders in his last testament that his cousin, to whom he had devised his property, should be "brought up to learning."[6] Francis Page, a member of one of the most distinguished families residing in the

[1] Isle of Wight County Records, vol. 1661–1719, p. 271.
[2] Northampton County Records, vol. 1683–89, p. 208.
[3] *Ibid.*, p. 350.
[4] Lower Norfolk County Records, vol. 1686–95, p. 99.
[5] Isle of Wight County Records, vol. 1660–1719, p. 307.
[6] Elizabeth City County Records, vol. 1684–99, p. 209, Va. St. Libr.

Colony, in his will requested Dudley Digges, his brother-in-law, who was acting as his executor, to bestow on his daughter the "best education which this country could afford."[1]

Nor was this desire to have their children grounded at least in the rudiments confined at this time to white persons; it extended even to the free blacks, who as yet made up but a small part of the African population. In 1693, Thomas Carter, of Northampton, a person of that race, ordered in his will that his three children should, after his death, be delivered to Thomas Gelding, to be held by him, evidently as agricultural laborers, until they were each nineteen years of age. The chief condition exacted of Gelding was that he should teach the young negroes how to read.[2]

In the course of the same year, Robert Harper, of Princess Anne county, a white planter, left directions that the entire income annually accruing from the sales of tobacco obtained from two of his plantations should be expended in the education of his three children. Although this income must have represented a very considerable sum, the extent of the tuition which he wished to have imparted does not appear to have been very ambitious,—each child, it seems, was to be taught until he or she could read "true English" with perfect ease; but the sons alone were to be instructed in the rules of arithmetic; and only in these rules "so far as would be needful for this country's affairs."[3]

[1] York County Records, vol. 1690–94, p. 170, Va. St. Libr.

[2] Northampton County Records, vol. 1689–98, p. 250.

[3] Princess Anne County Records, vol. 1691–1708, p. 52. William Moseley, of Princess Anne county, in 1699, left directions in his will that his children should "be brought up in such learning as is most useful and necessary for this country's affairs"; see Records, vol. 1691–1708, p. 226.

Colonel William Ball, of Lancaster, who died about 1693, inserted in his will a request that his wife should teach each of their youngest children until he or she should arrive at their sixth year; after which age, all were to receive instruction from their two eldest brothers. The mother's task was to be confined to imparting a knowledge of reading, writing, and the like simplest rudiments, whilst the brothers were expected to give tuition in the higher branches of learning.[1] In the following year, Mr. John Custis, of Northampton, made what must, in those times have appeared as a very liberal provision for the education of his grandson, who bore the same name as himself:—he left directions in his will that the proceeds from the labour of fourteen slaves should be devoted to meeting all the costs incurred for the boy's maintenance and tuition. This was probably designed for paying his expenses up to a certain age, during which time, he was expected to remain in Virginia, since a special provision in addition was made to cover his expenses during his stay in England, where his education was to be completed. Fourteen slaves formed a large and valuable working force at this early period; and the income to be derived from their production of tobacco alone was sufficient for the ample support and the thorough instruction of the youthful Custis.[2]

A prominent citizen of Essex county about this time enjoined in his will that his son should be sent to school when fourteen years of age, and kept there until he was eighteen; in this case, it is quite probable that the boy had already been receiving instruction at home, and that it was his father's wish that he should, when older,

[1] Lancaster County Records, vol. 1690–1709, folio p. 45.
[2] Northampton County Records, vol. 1689–98, p. 358.

enjoy the advantages of a more advanced tuition; which was only obtainable at a regular school.[1] Vincent Cox, of Westmoreland, provided in his will for his daughter's education during the first two years after she had passed her tenth year. In this case also, tuition away from home was evidently intended, as it seems improbable that her instruction in the rudiments had been so long deferred. His son was to receive tuition for one year only after he had reached the same age; he also, no doubt, had been taught up to a certain point, by some member of his family.[2]

[1] Essex County Records, vol. 1695–99, orig. p. 127.
[2] Westmoreland County Records, vol. 1690–99, folio p. 174.

CHAPTER II

Sentiment in Favor of Education (*Continued*)

THE wills of the Seventeenth century reflect hardly more vividly the general esteem in which education was held in Virginia at that time than the long series of orders adopted by the justices respecting the tuition of orphans who had been bound out under articles of indenture, or had been placed in the care of guardians. Over no section of the community did the county court exercise a more exacting supervision than over the children who had lost their parents by death; a special session of that body was held in each county at least once a year for the purpose of passing upon all matters relating to their welfare; and in no particular does that court appear to have been more scrupulous and jealous than in requiring that its commands as to education should be strictly carried out.[1] If the child was without property, and had to serve an apprenticeship to earn a livelihood, then a clause had to be inserted in his articles of indenture to compel his master or mistress to give him instruction in reading, writing, and arithmetic; and if, on the other hand, he had inherited an estate, which assured him an ample support without

[1] Beverley's *History of Virginia*, p. 209. For a special instance of this extraordinary care on the part of the county courts, see Westmoreland County Records, Orders July 27, 1692.

making use of the labor of his hands, then his education
was to be pushed so far as his income allowed.

A few illustrations of the spirit animating the county
court in its relation to the tuition of orphans may be
given. First, as to those possessing property. In
1638, George Ford, as the guardian of John Saker, of
York, was required by the justices of that county to
present an account of all the costs which he had so far
incurred in the boy's education. From this account,
it would appear that he had, for that purpose, paid
out, during the first year, two hundred pounds of tobacco, and during the second, one hundred and fifty.[1]
Eight years later, William Hawkins, as the guardian of
an orphan who had inherited a considerable stock of
cattle from his grandfather, was instructed by the
justices of York, in which county the parties resided,
to devote only the herd's male increase to his ward's
maintenance and tuition, as that would be amply
sufficient for both.[2] In the first of these cases, the
guardian was reimbursed for advances; but by an Act
passed in 1656, no person performing these duties
thereafter was to be permitted to receive an allowance
from court for himself for money paid by him for the
education of any child under his care, who was in
possession of sufficient property to meet that expense
out of his own income. The cost of his education, to
use the words of the statute, must be covered by the
"interest of the estate according to the proportion of
the estate."[3]   There are numerous proofs that the Act
was strictly enforced. In 1668, Captain John Scarbrooke
was directed by the county court of York to assume

[1] York County Records, vol. 1638–48, pp. 55, 61, Va. St. Libr.
[2] *Ibid.*, vol. 1638–48, p. 182, Va. St. Libr.
[3] Hening's *Statutes*, vol. i., p. 416.

charge of the person and property of Dorothy Tucker, an orphan girl, and to expend for her maintenance and instruction an amount that would be in due proportion to the value of her estate; but it must be drawn exclusively from the profits.[1] Ten years later, Morgan Bouldin, the stepfather and guardian of Elizabeth Longe, assured the justices of Northampton that he would, during the following two years, send her to school; which was probably done only after the court had reminded him that he was neglecting her education.[2] Sometimes, the orphan himself called the county court's attention to his guardian's dereliction in this respect; for example, in 1678, Thomas Bonnewell, of Accomac, informed the justices of that county that, in consequence of his stepfather having left the country, he was not receiving the tuition to which he was entitled by law; he petitioned that George Hope should be named as his guardian; and this was done on Hope's promising to secure for his ward the instruction he was so anxious to receive.[3]

It shows how numerous were the instances of bonds in which guardians bound themselves to educate the orphans in their care that, in one series of records alone, namely, those of Surry county, belonging to the interval between 1679 and 1684, a period of five years, there are to be found fifty documents of this kind entered. Each guardian in these and similar cases placed himself under a legal obligation, not only to deliver up the orphan's estate when he came of age, but also to have him taught in school "honestly according to his degree[4];"

[1] York County Records, vol. 1664–72, p. 283, Va. St. Libr.
[2] Northampton County Records, vol. 1674–79, p. 225.
[3] Accomac County Records, vol. 1678–82, p. 40.
[4] Surry County Records, vol. 1671–84, pp. 558–584, Va. St. Libr.

or to use another expression which was even more characteristic of the times : — "according to his quality." [1]

The county court was, if possible, stricter still in ordering a certain amount of instruction to be given to all orphans without any estate whatever, who had to be bound out as apprentices to obtain a livelihood. The provisions of the respective indentures of boys and girls differed as to the manner of their employment, but not at all as to the extent of their education,—the stipulations as to tuition were precisely the same in the case of both sexes. The indentures of Anne Andrewes, who lived in Surry about 1658, required her master to teach her, not only how to sew and "such things as were fitt for women to know," but also how to read, and apparently also how to write. [2] Dorothy Thorne, of the same county, was, in 1666, constrained by the terms of her indentures to serve her master, Charles Barham, during a period of six years; and he, in return, was to furnish her with the customary necessaries, and also to instruct her in the art of reading. [3] A like provision was, in 1678, inserted in the indentures of Winifred Young, of Lower Norfolk. [4] In 1690, a girl was bound out to Captain William Crafford, of the same county, under indentures which required him to teach her how to spin, sew, and read [5]; and in the course of the same year, Robert Monagan, of York, was also required by a like instrument to assure Rebecca Francis a full year's instruction "in reading the vulgar tongue." [6]

[1] Westmoreland County Records, Orders July 27, 1692.
[2] Surry County Records, vol. 1645–72, p. 121, Va. St. Libr.
[3] *Ibid.*, vol. 1645–72, p. 362, Va. St. Libr.
[4] Lower Norfolk County Records, Orders March 18, 1678.
[5] *Ibid.*, Orders Aug. 15, 1690.
[6] York County Records, vol. 1687–91, p. 514, Va. St. Libr.

The preceding instances, which might be greatly added to, <u>all show that the ordinary indentures of orphan girls were modelled on exactly the same lines; and that from the earliest to the latest case in the century, there was no omission of the provision requiring their education in the rudiments</u>. The same provision was, with <u>equal regularity, inserted in the indentures of all male apprentices.</u> When the term of service was to continue for a prolonged period, the obligation assumed in 1667 by Daniel Wyld, of York county, in entering into indentures with Valentine Harvey, was not unusual,—he promised, at his own expense, to keep young Harvey at school during at least three of the fourteen years agreed upon as the length of the apprenticeship. That the instruction was, in many instances, to be given by an experienced schoolmaster is shown by the condition of this instrument, which relieved Wyld only in case the parish should be without such a teacher.[1] This clause was inserted in order to save Wyld from incurring the cost of boarding the boy in the home of a schoolmaster residing at a distance, should there not be one near at hand to whom he could go for his lessons from day to day. In 1672, Eleanor Nash, of Lower Norfolk, in binding out her son, expressly stipulated that he should be taught how to read the Bible.[2] Edward Wood, who, a few years later, entered into indentures with a shoemaker of this county, was, by the provisions of that instrument, to be instructed in the art of both reading and writing; and a like clause was inserted in the indentures of William Pell, who, in 1685, was bound out to a carpenter residing in Rappahannock. The same benefit was to

[1] York County Records, vol. 1664–72, p. 202. Va. St. Libr.
[2] Lower Norfolk County Records, vol. 1666–75. p. 135.

be afforded Samuel Bennett, the apprentice of Robert Clarke, a cobbler of Northampton county.[1]

The extraordinary importance attached to the clause in indentures assuring the child's instruction in the rudiments of learning is revealed by a case that occurred in York. A dispute arose there, in 1681, between Mary Wilkinson and one Platt over the question of the tuition to be afforded the former's son while serving a term as Platt's apprentice; the mother insisted that the master should bind himself to "give the boy learning," whether or not it could be conveniently done; but Platt was only willing to agree to such instruction in case there should be a schoolmaster close at hand.[2] That the action of a master who had promised to have his apprentice taught was jealously watched is shown by a second instance occurring two years later; in 1683, a suit was entered by Alice Alvis, of Henrico, against Richard Ligon, in which he was charged with failure to "educate and maintain" her son in conformity with the provisions of the indenture; but the court decided that the allegation had not been sustained.[3] A similar case occurred, in 1685, in Rappahannock; Hawkins Snead, an orphan, complained to the county court that Captain Bloomfield was detaining him as a servant, although Major Thomas Hawkins (whose widow Bloomfield had married) had solemnly promised him a "liberal education." The justices having decreed

---

[1] Lower Norfolk County Records, Orders Aug. 15, 1682; Rappahannock County Records, April 1, 1685; Northampton County Records, vol. 1689–98, p. 525. Sometimes the indentures required that the boy should also be taught the Lord's Prayer and the Ten Commandments; see Elizabeth City County Records, Orders for 1694, p. 30.

[2] York County Records, vol. 1675–84, orig. p. 359.

[3] Henrico Minute Book, 1682–1701, p. 48, Va. St. Libr.

that Snead must continue in Bloomfield's service, he appealed to the General Court, evidently on the ground that, as Hawkins's representative, Bloomfield was legally bound to carry out Hawkins's promise to give a more extended tuition than apprentices were in the habit of receiving.[1]

The two orphan children of William Davis, of York, were, in 1687, bound out to a citizen of that county under indentures requiring him to keep them at school at least three years.[2] William Neale, an apprentice of William Leake, of Essex, was to receive tuition for a term of one year; and Thomas Jackson, an apprentice of Bernard Gaines, of the same county, for a term of two.[3] It will be seen from the provisions inserted in these three indentures that the length of the instruction to be given depended upon the agreement reached by the master and the parent of the child; and this was, no doubt, true in every instance of the schooling afforded under these circumstances. There seems to have been no general term prescribed either by law or custom.[4]

Among the persons residing in the Colony in the latter part of the Seventeenth century were a large number of youths, who, having been educated at Christ's Hospital in the City of London, had afterwards found employment as regular apprentices with different masters in Virginia. In 1692, the head of that great charity school complained that no letters from these

[1] Rappahannock County Records, Orders Aug. 5, 1685.

[2] York County Records, vol. 1687–91, p. 116, Va. St. Libr.

[3] Essex County Records, Orders Sept. 10, Nov. 10, 1698.

[4] The county court apparently contented itself with inserting in the indentures of an orphan the provision that "he should be put to school," without giving directions for how great a length of time; see case of John Clyborn in Henrico Minute Books, vol. 1682–1701, p. 196, Va. St. Libr.

youths were ever received in England; and under the influence of this reproach, the Governor and Council of the Colony addressed a communication to each county, commanding their several masters to see that the boys wrote at least twice a year to the authorities of the Hospital; and the justices were required to enforce this order.[1] These boys had, before leaving England, received such an extended course of instruction that they would have been, had they desired to follow that pursuit, fully competent to serve as schoolmasters themselves, provided that the tuition was not to be carried very far in the field of learning.

[1] See Order of Governor and Council in Essex County Records, vol. 1692–95, p. 188, Va. St. Libr.

CHAPTER III

How the Virginians were Educated: English Schools

WHO were the schoolmasters of the Virginians in the Seventeenth century, and where were situated the schools in which the young people of that day received instruction? It can be easily understood that the disposition of most parents would have been to send their children to England to be taught: first, because the Mother Country offered so many advantages of education to which the Colony could make no pretension; secondly, because there they would enjoy so many influences outside of the schoolroom which would broaden and liberalize their minds; and finally, because there also they would be brought into intimate association with all the members of their family connection who had not gone out to the plantations oversea. But even when a father possessed ample means to meet the expense of educating his children in England, several considerations made him hesitate to send them thither for that purpose, ardently as he might have it at heart. The voyage across the ocean in these early times was far more perilous than it is in this day of rapid transportation and innumerable lighthouses along every coast. The imagination of the colonists, accustomed to an easy and uneventful existence on their own estates, must have imparted to that voyage even greater terrors and dangers than really belonged to it. To leave a girl or boy with a sea-captain, however well known and respected in Virginia, to pass over that vast world of threatening waters in a frail sailing vessel must have seemed to most parents a step involving a fearful responsibility; and this state of mind was only confirmed when they thought of the long years to go by before they could hope to see their child again; of the months that it would require even to exchange letters with him; of the sickness that might overtake him among strangers; of the dissipations which might seduce him in his inexperience; and of the lack of some one who might lend him constantly a guiding and helping hand.

In spite of all these obstacles and drawbacks to the education of the wealthier class of young colonists in England, a very considerable number even in the Seventeenth century were sent over-sea to receive instruction in the foremost schools and colleges of the Mother Country. How great was that number can never be accurately known in consequence of the destruction of so many of the records that belonged to these early times. From entries here and there in the few surviving county records, we learn incidentally and by accident as it were, of some young Virginian of this period having enjoyed so extraordinary an advantage. Had all the private correspondence of the leading families of that century been preserved with the same care as the letter books of the elder William Byrd and William Fitzhugh, it would be seen that a greater proportion of the members of these families were educated in English institutions of different grades than is now generally supposed to have been the case.

One of the earliest of the young Virginians to receive

tuition in the Mother Country was Henry Sewell, of Lower Norfolk county; when quite young, he was sent over-sea, and seems to have attended school at Yarmouth.[1] Ralph Wormeley, the younger, who was born at Rosegill, the home of his father in Middlesex county, was, in 1665, matriculated at Oriel College, Oxford, when only fifteen years of age.[2] Col. John Catlett, of Rappahannock, left directions to his executors that all his children should be educated in England, and that the entire income from his estate should be expended in meeting the expense thus to be entailed.[3] In 1658, the son of Augustine Warner, who bore the same name as his father, was enrolled as a pupil in the Merchant Tailors' School in the City of London[4]; and probably at a later date attended a higher seat of English learning. John Lee, the eldest son of Col. Richard Lee, entered Queen's College as an upper commoner, and four years afterwards received the degree of bachelor-of-arts; after his graduation, studying medicine, he succeeded in obtaining the diploma of a Doctor of Physic. His brother, Richard, was also educated in England, and acquired such scholarship that, in after life, he was in the habit of writing marginal notes in his books indiscriminately in Latin, Greek, and Hebrew.[5] Richard Sturman, of Westmoreland, instructed his executors to send his children to England, where they were to receive as extended a course of

[1] Lower Norfolk County Records, vol. 1651–56, p. 79.

[2] *Va. Maga. of Hist. and Biog.*, vol. vii., p. 283. Col. Ralph Wormeley's sons Ralph and John both attended school in England, see *Va. Maga. of Hist. and Biog.*, vol. viii., p. 180.

[3] *Ibid.*, vol. iii., p. 63.

[4] Neill's *Va. Carolorum*, p. 419.

[5] *Lee of Virginia*, pp. 66, 70, 75. Dr. Lee's library was valued at 4000 pounds of tobacco. He died in 1674.

tuition as the income of his estate should permit.[1]
When John Cary set out for the Mother Country in 1671,
he was accompanied by his youthful brother-in-law,
Walter Flood, who was to be entered at an English
school as soon as they arrived on the other side.[2] Two
years afterwards, Mrs. Elizabeth Butler, of Rappahannock, gave very strict injunctions to her executors to
be careful to provide each year the amount of tobacco
needed to meet the expense of her children's education
in England, and also of the voyage when they returned
to Virginia. These children at the time when the will
was written were already receiving instruction in English schools, and it was their mother's wish apparently
that this instruction should be continued for many
years more.[3]

In 1674, Philip Chesney left directions in his will
that his two nephews, who were then, it would appear,
residing in England, should be sent up to London,
where they were to remain at school four years, and
then to go out to Virginia, to follow there such pursuits
as their aunt should consider best suited for them.[4]
Henry Perrott was entered as a student at Gray's Inn
in 1674.[5] In the course of 1680, the attorney in
Virginia of Hugh Williams, of Bristol, brought suit
against the stepfather of George Parker, of Northampton, to recover thirty-four pounds and ten shillings
due Williams for the instruction received by the young
man while passing three years in that city for that

[1] Westmoreland County Records, vol. 1653–72, p. 344. It
seemed to be Sturman's wish that his children should remain
permanently in England.

[2] Surry County Records, vol. 1645–72, p. 420, Va. St. Libr.

[3] Rappahannock County Records, vol. 1664–73, p. 65, Va. St. Libr.

[4] York County Records, vol. 1671–94, p. 93, Va. St. Libr.

[5] *William and Mary College Quart.*, vol. vi., p. 173.

purpose. In addition to tuition, Parker had been provided with board, lodging, and clothes.[1] About 1678, Elizabeth Godson, of Rappahannock, was in the charge of Thomas Roberts, a relative residing in the same county, who seems to have also acted as her teacher. In his will, drawn in the course of this year, Peter Hopegood, apparently her stepfather, left directions that she should remain at school at Mr. Roberts's until 1680, but in that year she was to be taken to England, there to continue her education under the guardianship of an uncle who had never emigrated.[2] Three years later, Dominick Rice, also of Rappahannock, instructed his executors to send his son Stephen, as soon as he was five years of age, to his grandfather's home in Ireland, where he was to be taught for such a length of time as his grandfather should approve.[3]

John Savage, of Northampton, provided in his will that a horse and mare, two steers and two cows, with their increase, should be reserved to create a fund for paying all the expenses to be incurred by his son Thomas in attending school in England. Savage, who possessed one of the largest estates, both in realty and personalty, held by any citizen of the Eastern Shore, seems to have attached an unusual value to education; in his will, he also provided for the tuition of his two daughters and a second son by requiring his executors to hire out three servants, apparently to the teacher to be engaged; the proceeds of their labour to constitute this person's remuneration for imparting the stipulated

[1] Accomac County Records, vol. 1678-82, p. 187.
[2] Rappahannock County Records, vol. 1677-82, p. 71, Va. St. Libr.
[3] *Ibid.*, vol. 1677-82, orig. p. 42.

instruction, which was to be continued during a period of five years. Since no arrangement seems to have been made for the completion of their education in England, it is probable that this particular advantage was enjoyed by the eldest son alone as the one supposed to represent the family first, and perhaps inheriting the bulk of the estate.[1]

The younger William Byrd, probably the most accomplished gentleman produced by colonial Virginia, after obtaining his earliest instruction at home, was sent by his father to Holland, which, in those times, possessed a high reputation especially for the opportunities it offered for a training in business. In 1685, he was receiving lessons from a tutor in England[2]; and that he made the most of the advantages thus afforded to acquire a thorough insight into his own language was shown by the extraordinary graces of his writings. His culture reflected the spirit of the most admirable literary schools of that day. Nor was he content with a learning restricted to ancient and modern belles-lettres. Before returning to Virginia in 1696, he became a student in the Middle Temple, and thus added a special knowledge of law to the literary and business information which he had already obtained. He was elected a member of the House of Burgesses a few months after the completion of his education, and that body had probably never before found in its membership a young man of more highly cultivated talents or more polished manners.

In 1692, while Byrd was perfecting in London his social and intellectual accomplishments, a son of Christopher Robinson, of Middlesex county, was also

[1] Northampton County Records, vol. 1674–79, p. 316.
[2] Letters of William Byrd, March 31, 1685.

at school there; and his father, who passed away in the course of that year, was careful to provide for the continuance of his son's studies by an order that fifty pounds sterling (equal in purchasing power to twelve hundred dollars in modern currency) should be reserved for the payment of his expenses.[1]   Henry Hartwell, the distinguished lawyer, who died in England, whither he had been called on colonial affairs, and where his last testament was drawn and registered, instructed his English executors to bring over his nephew of the same name, at that time in Virginia, and to see that he obtained the most thorough education which the English institutions of that day could offer. His tuition was to continue until he had reached his twenty-first year.[2]   John Custis, of Northampton, left directions in his will that one hundred pounds sterling should be set apart from his estate to meet all the costs incurred by his grandson in attending an English school.[3]   In one of his letters, William Fitzhugh stated that but for his finding an excellent tutor in the pastor of the Huguenot refugees who had settled near him, he would have sent his eldest son to England to be educated.[4]

[1] *Va. Maga. of Hist. and Biog.*, vol. vii., p. 19.

[2] Will of Henry Hartwell, Waters's *Gleanings*, vol. i., p. 314.

[3] Northampton County Records, vol. 1689–98, p. 359.   See paragraph in Chapter I., Part II., of the present History for the general provisions made by his grandfather for the education of this boy.

[4] Letters of William Fitzhugh, July 10, 1690.

CHAPTER IV

Private Tutors

A VERY large proportion of that section of the children of the wealthy planting class who received their education entirely in Virginia were indebted to private tutors for the greater part, if not for the whole, of their instruction before they came of age. Sometimes these tutors' task was confined to imparting a knowledge of the rudiments, whether of the English tongue or the ancient languages; more frequently, however, carrying their pupils into wider fields, they gave them all the education which, in those times, could be obtained outside the walls of advanced schools and colleges like those established in England. When his employer's children were numerous, the tutor found his hours fully occupied in teaching them alone; but in the Seventeenth century, as at later periods in the history of Virginia, it was frequently the custom for the neighbors' sons and daughters to join the boys and girls whose father had engaged such an instructor's services and all together to receive their lessons from him. These children from adjoining plantations generally walked or rode over daily to attend school; but sometimes, especially when they were kinsmen of the family employing the tutor, they remained for the session under the same roof as boarders.

The men who earned their livelihood as tutors in private families were obtained from different places. Some of them came directly from England. In 1652, Nicholas Haywood, of London, wrote to Nathaniel Pope, a resident of the Northern Neck, to inquire whether he would like to engage the services in this character of Samuel Motherhead, who was warmly recommended as fully equipped to teach Pope's children successfully. "He can write a very good hand," Hayward stated in his letter, "cypher very well, and be able to keep your accounts."[1] It will be seen from this that the private teacher was often expected to make himself useful in the house outside of the precincts of the schoolroom. William Reynolds, who resided in the same part of the Colony, mentioned in his will, dated 1655, that he had obtained a young man from York (presumably in Virginia) for the purpose of instructing his children. The consideration offered and accepted, was to furnish him, free of all charge, with "meat, drink, lodging and washing" during the period covered by the contract, and at the end of that time to grant him, without rent, for a term of three years, ground in which to plant tobacco and corn, and barns in which to store these crops when harvested.[2] About the time when this contract was made, John Johnson, of Northampton, agreed to take into his own home John Rogers's son, and to teach him to read and write with perfect ease; and he bound himself not to employ the boy in any department of work that would, in the slightest degree, withdraw his attention from his books. His education having been continued until his thirteenth

[1] This letter, which is recorded in Northumberland, is printed in *William and Mary College Quart.*, vol. xi., p. 171.

[2] Northumberland County Records, Orders November 20, 1655.

year, he was to be then sent, at Johnson's expense, either to England or to Holland, where he was to serve an apprenticeship in order to acquire a thorough knowledge of some handicraft which would afford him a certain livelihood.[1] In 1662, Robert Jones occupied the position of tutor in the family of John Hansford, in York county[2]; and it was to him, no doubt, that Major Thomas Hansford, who followed so bravely Bacon's fortunes and perished with so much fortitude, the noblest of all the victims of Berkeley's insane wrath, was indebted for his earliest instruction, and perhaps for some of that patriotic spirit which made him ready to sacrifice even life itself in resisting the tyranny of the selfish reactionaries then controlling the affairs of the Colony.

Elizabeth Charlton, the greatest heiress in North-ampton county, was, about 1662, when she was only twelve years of age, persuaded by John Severne to run away from Captain Jones's residence, where we are informed "she was in care for her education." Severne was condemned and severely reprimanded for having "stolen ye said Elizabeth from school."[3] His conduct was regarded as so scandalous that a special session of the county court was held to pass upon his offence, which was evidently aggravated in the justices' minds by the abrupt and permanent termination of the young lady's education, brought about by her flight.

---

[1] Northampton County Records, vol. 1651–54, p. 131. John Johnson is spoken of in a Northampton county deed as of "Graft in Holland"; see Bruce's *Economic History of Va.*, vol. i., p. 351.

[2] *William and Mary College Quart.*, vol. vi., p. 5.

[3] Northampton County Records, vol. 1657–64, p. 158. Severne seems to have induced Elizabeth Charlton to run away for the purpose of marrying not himself, but another person, to whose house she was first taken.

Elizabeth Charlton was probably attending school at Captain Jones's because a tutor was domiciled there, whose services also extended to the children of the nearest planters. As it was difficult for a girl to walk or ride backwards and forwards daily, it happened more frequently in their case than in the case of boys that their parents obtained board for them with the neighbor employing a teacher. For example, in 1663, Richard Burkland agreed with Richard Kellam, both being citizens of Accomac, not only to give his daughter lessons in reading and writing, and in casting accounts, but also to supply her with food, and apparently also to furnish her with lodging.[1] A few years later, Martha Willett, the daughter of a well-known planter of Northampton, the adjoining county, was placed under the care of Mary Coar, who, in consideration of one thousand pounds of tobacco, contracted to teach her for a term of one year.[2]

Francis Browne and his wife, who resided in Rappahannock, in conveying a tract of land to Richard Glover, in 1666, stated that a part of the consideration received from him was the one year's schooling which he had already bestowed on their daughter.[3] This was perhaps only the beginning of her course of instruction. It would seem that, like the young man from York employed by William Reynolds in the adjoining county of Northumberland, to whom we have already referred, Glover taught in the Brownes' home under promise of their remunerating him by a gift of land. In 1668, Henry Spratt, of Lower Norfolk, sued George

[1] Accomac County Records, vol. 1663–66, folio p. 6.

[2] Northampton County Records, vol. 1683–89, p. 118.

[3] Rappahannock County Records, vol. 1663–68, p. 77, Va. St. Libr.

Ashwell to compel the payment of fees due him for the tuition of Ashwell's son. As these fees included a charge for "diet," the boy, no doubt, had been boarding at Spratt's while attending school.[1] In this case, it is also quite possible that Spratt had not himself been the tutor, but that instruction had been given by a teacher in his employment.

Sometimes the planter's sons as well as daughters received tuition from female teachers; about 1693, for instance, Katharine Shrewsbury, of Richmond county, was, during eighteen months, employed in instructing the son of Richard Tompkins. Katharine seems to have made some pretension to medical knowledge, for on one occasion, she brought suit against Peter Foxon on the ground that she had restored him to health; but the court refused to sustain her claim.[2] The following year, John Waters, of Essex, sought, but failed, to obtain judgment against William Johnson charged with the breach of a contract requiring him to pay nine hundred pounds of tobacco in consideration of Waters's receiving into his house Johnson's nephew, William Tunstall by name, and teaching him how to write a legible hand. This also involved his learning how to read.[3] A far more competent and accomplished instructor was the pastor of the Huguenot refugees who, for several years, acted as the tutor of one of William Fitzhugh's sons. The boy seems to have boarded under this clergyman's roof, and as only the French language was spoken there, he soon came to use that tongue with as much facility as the one to which he was born. Among other studies,

---

[1] Lower Norfolk County Records, vol. 1666-75, p. 30.

[2] Richmond County Records, Orders May 3, 1693.

[3] Essex County Records, Orders May 10, 1694.

he was grounded in Latin; but even in this branch of learning he was taught in French text; about 1690, Fitzhugh requested one of his correspondents in London to forward to Virginia at once a French Latin grammar, a French and Latin dictionary, and three French Common Prayer books, all for the use of this son.[1] Referring to his younger daughters in his will, drawn about 1699, Henry Williamson, of Essex, declared that, should "they grow stubborn and not conformable to their elder sister and tutors, then they were to be put out to such tutors as they should think convenient for their further education."[2] It would appear from this order that the choice of new teachers was to be left to the younger sisters whenever they grew dissatisfied with the old.

Not infrequently, the tutor in a private family was a person under indentures. In the vicissitudes of those times, whether political or otherwise, many men of no common acquirements were compelled to earn a subsistence by hiring themselves out for the performance of different kinds of service. In the great body of agricultural labourers drawn to Virginia from the Mother Country, there were individuals who had failed in higher pursuits, or who, having become involved in trouble in their native land, were induced to seek a new home over-sea. Among these men, and even among the convicts, there were found some who had received an excellent education in the most respectable English schools, and who were, therefore, fully competent, from the point of view of knowledge at least, to instruct the young. This was well known to the planters. In the light of this fact, it is no cause for

[1] Letters of William Fitzhugh, July 10, 1690.
[2] Essex County Records for 1699, p. 81; see Williamson Will.

surprise to find, for instance, that John Carter, of Lancaster, a citizen of high standing, and one in possession of a large estate, left directions in his will that a servant should be purchased for the exclusive purpose of teaching his son Robert (afterwards the famous "King" Carter) "in English and Latin."[1] Thomas Hellier stated in his history of his own life that his master, who resided in Westover parish, had promised to employ him as a tutor for his children, and that he was not to be set to work in the fields except when there was an extraordinary demand for labor about the crops; and then only for a "short spurt."[2]

Sometimes, when the planter's family was a large one, he caused a schoolhouse to be erected for their use in the immediate vicinity of his residence; or it formed a part of the residence itself; which latter seems to have been the case with the schoolhouse situated at the home of Col. John Ashton, one of the wealthiest and most prominent citizens of Westmoreland county.[3] It was here that a tutor instructed the children, not only of Colonel Ashton himself, but also quite probably of many of his nearest neighbors. The relations between such a tutor and his employer often became strained; for instance, in 1678, Mr. Charles Leatherbury, who resided on the Eastern Shore, having fallen into a dispute with John Matts, forbade him to "tarry in his house"; and in consequence, Matts brought suit against him, apparently for a breach of contract. Matts is designated in the records as following the schoolmaster's calling, and it was only in that character

[1] *William and Mary College Quart.*, vol. vi., p. 5.
[2] *Life of Thomas Hellier*, pp. 10, 11.
[3] Westmoreland County Records, vol. 1665–77, p. 324.

that he seems to have had a cause of difference with
Leatherbury.[1]

[1] This reference will be found either in Accomac or Northampton
County Records, vol. 1678–82, p. 29. We find the following
reference to Matts in the Accomac records: "Deposition of Mr.
James Matts saaith that, about fourteen years past, being att the
house of Mister Hugh Yeo, saaith that your depont being att supper
with Mr. Hugh Yeo and William Yeo, sitting by Mr. Yeo at supper
in company, yr depont saaith to Mr. Yeo that the young man,
William Yeo, would doe him some kindness in a short time being
he could write and cypher indifferently well etc." This was in
1679. See Accomac County Records, vol. 1678–82, p. 82.

CHAPTER V

The Old Field Schools

PERHAPS the greatest proportion of the children who, during the Seventeenth century, received an education, obtained it in what came to be known at a later date as the Old Field School. Such a school was established at some spot in convenient reach of every boy and girl in a whole neighborhood. In order to ensure this, it was customary to build the schoolhouse in some old field, long abandoned to pine and broom-straw, which occupied a central situation; and here during the hours when the school session was not in progress, the building remained locked, vacant, and silent; but during the hours of instruction was filled with the murmur of recitation, and the confused sound of whispering tongues and shuffling feet. From the adjacent forest, there came in summer the voices of birds singing among the branches, and in winter the roar of the wind in the bare tree-tops. The whole scene was marked by the spirit of extreme remoteness and seclusion; and only the presence of the shouting and dancing children in the hours of play, or the smoke curling up from the chimney in the hours of work, gave it any apparent connection with the world of human beings.

But not all the houses in which the sessions of the

so-called old field schools were held were situated in such lonely spots.[1] In many cases, the schoolhouse was really the teacher's residence, and was surrounded by the ordinary plantation outbuildings, whether the cabins of servants and slaves, or the stables and barns; and there was contiguous a more or less open area of country under cultivation. The majority of the persons keeping these neighborhood schools were, throughout the Seventeenth century, perhaps drawn from the circle of the clergymen, who thus endeavored to increase their incomes; and the schools they presided over were, in most cases, established in their parsonages, which almost always occupied a central situation. There could hardly, in those times, have been found outside of great seats of learning, a class more competent to teach than these early Virginian clergymen. All were men who had been educated in English schools offering the greatest advantages for acquiring knowledge then presented among the English-speaking people; and a very large number, as we have seen, had carried off the highest honors in the foremost English colleges. They belonged to the very class of persons, who, in England, devoted a large part of their lives to equipping young men for their entrance into the Universities; and it was only natural that their parishioners in Virginia should turn to them as, of all the residents of the community, the ones best fitted by scholarship and the time at their disposal to conduct

[1] As the land attached to the court-house was generally situated very conveniently for the people of the county, a schoolhouse was frequently built on that ground. In 1694, for instance, we find the county court of Essex granting permission to John Peatle to erect a schoolhouse "on some part of ye county's land purchased for the new court-house"; see Orders July 10, 1694. Robert Leightenhouse, in 1695, occupied a schoolhouse situated at Yorktown.

schools for the benefit of the great body of children belonging to their congregations. The case of Rev. Mr. Willson was not uncommon even as early as the middle of the century; in 1658, the planters of Elizabeth River parish employed him to teach their children; and in order to obtain for him a suitable schoolhouse, contracted to pay Mr. Thomas Edmunds annually one thousand pounds of tobacco for the use of his residence for that purpose. This fact shows the high value they attached to his services, for, in addition, they were at the expense of raising his salary.[1]

The readers who, from time to time, were appointed to fill the places of clergymen temporarily or permanently absent, very frequently performed the duties of teachers in the countryside schools. In the petition which Captain Hugh Campbell presented, in 1691, to the Governor and Council, after declaring that the people residing in certain districts of Isle of Wight, Nansemond, and Norfolk counties, lived at such a distance from a church that they were unable to attend public worship with regularity, he went on to recommend the appointment of persons, who, every Sunday, should read the prayers and a sermon at places convenient to the inhabitants of these districts. In order to add to the income to be derived from the large tracts of land which he proposed giving for the support of these persons, he urged that they should be licensed to teach school. The Governor and his advisers approved so heartily of the whole scheme that they instructed the justices of the three counties to promote it by every means in their power.[2]

[1] Lower Norfolk County Records, vol. 1656–66, pp. 180, 235; see also Lower Norfolk County Antiquary, vol. iii., p. 52.

[2] Norfolk County Records, vol. 1685–96, p. 173.

That the teachers in the schools of Virginia in these early times were not always persons who, failing in other pursuits, had taken advantage of the barest smattering of knowledge to earn a livelihood by giving lessons is shown by the precautions adopted at various periods to shut out all who were unable to furnish a satisfactory certificate of competency. One of the strictest of the requirements is to be found in the twenty-seventh clause of Howard's Instructions on his appointment: this clause provided that no teacher arriving from England should be allowed to follow his profession unless he could submit to the authorities a license granted him by the Bishop of London; and that, should he have come from some other quarter, then he must obtain the Governor's license before he would be permitted to open a school.[1] Nicholson received the like command on his appointment at the end of the century.[2] In 1686, Howard issued a general proclamation, in which all the schoolmasters residing in Virginia were warned that, should they fail to attend the General Court's next meeting at Jamestown in order to present testimonials of competency from their parishes' foremost citizens, then they were to be deprived of the right to give instruction. In addition to proof of learning and ability, they must show that they were upright and sober in their lives, and conformable in their religious opinions to the doctrines of the Church of England.[3] Many

---

[1] Colonial Entry Book, vol. 1685-90, pp. 34, 409.

[2] B. T. Va., vol. vii., p. 168.

[3] Howard, though instructed to summon the school-teachers to Jamestown, perhaps recognizing the difficulties in the way of their coming, deferred doing so until the Bishop of London offered a remonstrance. A copy of the Proclamation is recorded in several counties; see, for example, York County Records, vol. 1684-7,

of the teachers found it impossible to comply with this proclamation, owing to the distance to Jamestown and the smallness of their means. In a communication addressed to the Governor, the House of Burgesses informed him, with evident feeling, that, in consequence of these facts, "several knowing and skillful schoolmasters in their respective counties had left off their employments," and they, therefore, urged him to nominate in each county one or more fit persons to examine the qualifications possessed by the different teachers for the proper performance of their duties; and these persons should also be impowered to grant licenses to all schoolmasters whose competency was satisfactorily proven. The Governor seems to have readily assented to this suggestion.[1]

Nicholson, during his whole incumbency, evinced an extraordinary interest in whatever would increase the number and advance the usefulness of the schools. On several occasions, he offered assistance out of his private purse. When the new court-house erected at Jamestown to take the place of the old one destroyed at the time of the great Insurrection became so ruinous that the justices of James City were not willing to occupy it longer, he proposed to buy the building, and, after

p. 212, Va. St. Libr. There was, in 1693, a proposition before the Committee of Propositions to the following effect: "No one shall . . . undertake the education of youth but such as are the professed members of the Church of England and subscribe the canons." The House concurred in this proposition, although remarking that the laws already enacted to assure the same result were sufficient for the purpose; see entry for Oct. 13, 14, 1693, Minutes of House of Burgesses, Colonial Entry Book, vol. 1682-95; see also Minutes of Assembly Nov. 4, 1686, Colonial Entry Book, vol. 1682-95, p. 354.

[1] Minutes of Assembly Nov. 4, 1686, Colonial Entry Book, 1682-95, p. 354; see also Minutes of Assembly Nov. 8, 1686.

putting it again in a state of perfect repair, to convert it into a schoolhouse "for the advantage" of the inhabitants of that county and other parts of the Colony, who should send their children thither to receive an education. Since the Governor and Council, in their character as the General Court, acceded to the county justices' request that they should be permitted to hold their sittings in the General Court-house, it is quite probable that Nicholson's proposition was accepted, and the school established.[1] In 1691, in order to assure further the success of Captain Hugh Campbell's plan for the appointment of readers in the remoter parts of Isle of Wight, Nansemond, and Norfolk counties, who should, in addition to their other duties, teach the parishioners' children, Nicholson very generously offered to devote to their remuneration the whole of that share of the marriage and tavern fees derived from these counties, to which he was entitled by law.[2] Captain Campbell's proposition seems to have made such a favorable impression on the Governor's mind that he urged that it should be given a wider scope by each parish contributing to the payment of its clerk or reader, as a special inducement to him to set up a school within its limits. This suggestion was evidently intended to apply only to those parishes in which no such school had been established by the clergyman or a professional teacher. One of the strongest reasons prompting this zealous and enlightened official to throw his influence in favor of the Act of Assembly authorizing the laying off of towns at different eligible points in the Colony, was that each of these towns would afford an ample support to a schoolmaster competent to give

[1] Minutes of Council, Feb. 18, 20, 1690, B. T. Va., 1690, No. 14.
[2] Norfolk County Records, Orders January 27, 1691.

at least a course in reading and writing.[1] Nor did
Nicholson allow his absence from Virginia, even when
he had no expectation of returning, to cool his interest
in the education of its youth; in 1695, while he was
acting as the Governor of Maryland, he conveyed to the
justices of York county his lot in Yorktown for the use
of Robert Leightenhouse, who was at this time the
schoolmaster there; and should Leightenhouse cease
to teach, or remove his residence to some other community, then the lot was to pass into his successor's
occupation, should he be approved by the county
court.[2]

The justices' intervention in this instance was only
in conformity with the general supervision which they
and their fellows exercised over all the schoolmasters.
The county records show that the county court very
frequently recommended to the Governor particular
teachers whom they thought fully entitled to receive
the license required; for instance, in 1699, the justices
of Elizabeth City requested that officer to confer on
Stephen Lylly the right to teach; and the same year
they apparently made a similar request in Charles
Goring's behalf. The latter was declared to be competent to instruct youth in reading, writing, and
arithmetic; the former in writing and the English
tongue.[3] It would seem that at this time (and this
was also probably the case at earlier periods) the first
step on a pedagogue's part towards opening a school
was to petition the county court to obtain the necessary
license from the Governor; and in order to justify the
court in doing this, the applicant had to give proofs

[1] *Va. Maga. of Hist. and Biog.*, vol. vii., p. 157.

[2] *William and Mary College Quart.*, vol. ii., p. 17.

[3] Elizabeth City County Records, Orders Aug. 20, Sept. 18, 1699.

of his learning. The justices practically decided whether he should or should not be allowed to become a teacher, for if they found him incapable, they simply declined to recommend him to the Governor; and when they refused to recommend any one, it is not probable that that official bestowed the license in opposition to their decision. Indeed, the granting of licenses was a purely formal act on the Governor's part, as he, being called upon to make so many appointments of schoolmasters, was compelled to be guided by the recommendations of the county courts.

Every county court in Virginia was, about 1699, required to return to the Council Office at Jamestown a list of all the schools situated in its own jurisdiction; and also a statement as to whether the persons filling the position of teacher had obtained licenses or not. Should it be found that some were following this calling without having secured the necessary certificate, then they were to be granted such certificate without any charge, should an examination of their qualifications prove them to be fit and capable[1]; it was evidently the desire of the authorities from whom this order came that the advantage of retaining competent teachers, already busily occupied with their duties, should not be jeoparded by the imposition of any fee. Not infrequently, the county courts offered greater induce-

[1] Minutes of Council, June 21, 1699, B. T. Va., vol. liii. This order, which came from England, is preserved among the records of several counties; see Lancaster County Records, vol. 1696–1702, p. 84. In obedience to it, a report of a very interesting and valuable character must have been drawn up, but a diligent search among the records in Virginia and in the British State Paper Office has not so far enabled me to find it. The Virginia copies were probably destroyed in the burning of the General Court-house in Richmond at the evacuation in 1865.

ments still to draw schoolmasters within their respective jurisdictions; the action of the Henrico justices in 1686 was by no means exceptional; in the course of that year, they specially exempted Mr. Nathaniel Hall, who had recently removed from Gloucester county, from the payment of any taxes during a period of twelve months. This was always proof of an extraordinary solicitude to advance some purpose supposed to be unusually promotive of the community's welfare, as the relief of any one person from the levy simply increased the burden falling on the rest. The justices, in language worthy of the enlightened spirit animating them on this occasion, declared that they granted the privilege "for ye encouragement of learning and instruction of youth in this county by inviting able tutors here to reside."[1] It would appear, from the wording of this sentence, as if the policy followed in Mr. Hall's case was not confined to him, but was intended to apply to every schoolmaster who settled in the county with the view of pursuing his calling there.

The strong sentiment prevailing in the Colony in favor of giving extraordinary encouragements to schoolmasters in order to increase their number and assure their contentment, was revealed by the smallness of the fee which they were expected to disburse in obtaining a license. At first, they seem to have been required to pay only a few pounds of tobacco, simply to compensate the Governor's clerk for his trouble in writing out the certificate; but during Howard's administration a fee of twenty shillings was imposed.[2] This was one of the numerous exactions of that sordid

[1] Henrico County Minute Book, 1682–1701, p. 149.

[2] Minutes of Assembly Nov. 8, 1686, Colonial Entry Book, vol. 1682–95; Beverley's *History of Virginia*, p. 77.

and grasping official in his determined effort to make his position enrich him to the utmost in the shortest period possible. So serious a charge upon a class of men whom the people of the Colony were anxious to encourage does not, however, appear to have been continued for any great length of time.

In the record of the settlement of estates, there are frequent references to large sums due schoolmasters for the instruction of children. In the greater number of these cases, the creditor was a professional teacher who had set up a neighborhood school. Amongst the items of indebtedness of the Johnson property in York, in 1660, was one for the board and tuition of a member of the family amounting to one thousand and forty pounds of tobacco,[1] whilst the estate of Hugh Macmyal, of Henrico, in 1679, owed Mr. Everett two hundred pounds for a course of lessons given his son.[2] In 1686, the executors of Edward Tanner, of Surry, were called upon to pay seven hundred pounds of tobacco to Mr. John Harris for the education of the testator's children.[3] In all these cases, the teacher had agreed with the parents to impart instruction at a stipulated rate. Such also seems to have been the rule with John Higgs, the principal schoolmaster of Accomac. Having, about 1679, obtained a schoolhouse on Mr. Macklannie's plantation, he arranged with his scholars' fathers for each to contribute twenty pounds of tobacco towards the payment of the rent. Among his patrons was Mr. John Abbott, who gave a note for eight hundred pounds of tobacco in consideration that his children's instruction should last from June, 1679,

---

[1] York County Records, vol. for 1660, p. 94, Va. St. Libr.

[2] Henrico County Records, vol. 1677–92, orig. p. 87.

[3] Surry County Records, vol. 1684–6, p. 83, Va. St. Libr.

to April, 1680. Unfortunately, Higgs found it impossible to secure a sufficient number of patrons to meet the cost of the house leased from Mr. Macklannie, and, in consequence, he was compelled to find a cheaper house elsewhere, but as it was remote, Mr. Abbott withdrew his children from Higgs's care, and the court decided that he was under no obligation to pay more than four hundred pounds of the amount of his note.[1]

Valentine Evans, a leading schoolmaster of York at this time, seems to have charged for each pupil at the annual rate of twenty shillings, or twenty-five dollars in modern values, whilst Thomas Dalby, of Henrico, was allowed by the local court thirty shillings for the tuition of two youthful scholars during nine months.[2] In 1698, the executor of a schoolmaster who had resided in Isle of Wight county presented bills for the amounts which sixteen persons owed the deceased for their children's instruction; the fee apparently for each pupil had been fifty pounds of tobacco for every quarter, or seventeen pounds for a single month, whilst for five months the fee seems to have been about eighty-three pounds. The total amount due came to as much as twenty-one hundred and thirty-nine pounds of that commodity.[3] The General Assembly, in 1691,

[1] Accomac County Records, vol. 1678–82, pp. 143, 150.

[2] York County Records, vol. 1675–84, p. 598, Va. St. Libr.; Henrico County Minute Book, 1682–1701, p. 189, Va. St. Libr.

[3] The following is the list of the debts, which will be found in Isle of Wight County Records, vol. 1661–1719, p. 395:

Jno. Davis	dr for 3 months schooling	50 lbs.
Wm. Webb	dr " schooling	285 "
Widow Newman	dr " "	80 "
Richard Gray	dr " 5 months	83 "
Mr. Monger	dr " schooling	303 "
John Johnson	dr " 1 month	17 "
Wm. Balmer	dr " schooling	60 "

declined to adopt a proposition to the effect that the schoolmasters' remuneration should be determined by law. Each was left to make his own private contract.[1]

Numerous schoolmasters accumulated enough by their profession to purchase estates. In 1691, Daniel Pheters, of Rappahannock, conveyed to Samuel Coats, the principal schoolmaster of the county, a plantation of three hundred acres[2]; and there is no reason to think, in the light of the cheapness of land during this century, that such an acquisition by a man engaged in this pursuit was exceptional. The outstanding sums due the schoolmaster of Isle of Wight county, already referred to, were together large enough to have permitted him to buy a very considerable property.

Jno. Walton	dr for schooling		668 lbs.
Jas. Day	dr " { 4 months, daughter 1 month, son }		120 "
Wm. Webb, Jr.	dr " schooling		500 "
Edward Champion	" " "		95 "
Nicholas Miller	" " 3 months schooling		50 "
Wm. Brown	dr " schooling		361 "
Richard Lewis	dr " "		200 "
Jno. Harris	dr " "		100 "
Wm. Clarke	dr " 2 sons schooling		65 "
James Lafoe	dr " { Your son 50 daughter 100 }		150 "
Robert Kae	dr " schooling		100 "

[1] Colonial Entry Book, vol. 1682-95; see Minutes of Assembly for 1693.

[2] Rappahannock County Records, vol. 1682-92, p. 263, Orders Oct. 2, 1691.

CHAPTER VI

Free Schools: Those Projected in the Time of the Company

NOT all the schools in Virginia during the Seventeenth century were private, and only to be attended after the payment of a fee. As was to be expected when the population's English origin was recalled, there were also several free grammar schools established and endowed by citizens of the Colony in that spirit of benevolence which, in these early times, was far from uncommon among English-speaking people. Some of the most useful of the smaller institutions of learning in the Mother Country had been founded by the generosity of her noble-minded sons, and from generation to generation had, with little charge to English youth, furnished the means of acquiring at least a primary education. There were among the persons emigrating to Virginia men who were animated by the same feeling of practical philanthropy; and had the Colony's different communities been as thickly inhabited as the English, which would have assured the success of a free school with far more certainty than the prevailing sparsity of the population, there is reason to think that the number of endowed grammar foundations would, in proportion to the number of its people, and the length

of time the country had been settled, been as great in
Virginia as in England.

The earliest plan of a free school to be established in
Virginia was designed for the benefit of Indian youth.
In the month of February, 1619–20, some person, who
refused to reveal his name, placed in the hands of Sir
Edwin Sandys, the Treasurer of the London Company,
a box containing a bag of new gold, which, when
counted, was found to amount to five hundred and
fifty pounds sterling, a sum with a purchasing power of
nearly fourteen thousand dollars in our modern currency.
A letter preceding this gift had expressed the anony-
mous benefactor's wish that five hundred pounds sterling
should be used in instructing a "convenient number"
of young Indians in the art of reading, and also in
teaching them the principles of the Christian religion;
beginning when they were seven years of age, they were
to continue to be taught in the same manner up to
their twelfth birthday; and after that, until they were
twenty-one, they were to be carefully trained in some
branch of handicraft. The remaining fifty pounds
sterling of the sum presented was to be given to two
trustworthy persons as compensation for their making
a quarterly report to the Treasurer of the Company,
to contain a detailed account of the execution of the
purposes the benefactor had in view, as well as a full
list of the names of the children enjoying the benefits of
the gift.[1] In the following year, a complaint was heard
that, although the money had been delivered to the
patentees of Southampton Hundred, with directions
to carry out the generous donor's instructions, yet so
far the sum had been allowed to remain entirely

[1] Abstracts of Proceedings of Va. Co. [of London, vol. i., pp.
42, 44.

unemployed. The unknown philanthropist, when informed of this, expressed his willingness to increase his gift to one thousand pounds sterling, equal in value to twenty-five thousand dollars, provided that a certain number of male Indian children, having been sent for from Virginia, were entered among the scholars at Christ's Hospital. Should this proposition be thought by the Company to be impracticable, then he wished that the five hundred and fifty pounds sterling constituting his original gift should be expended in founding, within the boundaries of Southampton Hundred, a free school in which both English and Indian children might be educated. Sandys discouraged the employment of the money in either project. Indian boys, he said in substance, could not be easily brought to England; and should an effort be made to set up a free school in Virginia at that time, it would be impossible to obtain the, workmen necessary for the erection of the buildings, except at a very heavy expense, owing to their unwillingness to abandon the cultivation of tobacco, which they considered the only profitable occupation. Under these circumstances, the treasure designed to be devoted to the erection of the schoolhouse would be sufficient merely to raise a "small fabrick," instead of "accomplishing such a foundation as would satisfy men's expectations."

Martin's Hundred having declined to accept the gift, the patentees of Southampton Hundred finally decided to make use of it in a way that would indirectly promote the object the philanthropist originally had in view. Having increased the amount by adding to it a contribution from their own treasury, they determined to invest the entire sum in the erection of iron works, with the ulterior purpose of devoting the profits of the venture to the education of thirty Indian children. The managers of the Hundred, writing to Governor Yeardley, who occupied the post of its Captain, urged him to push the enterprise with great energy, as it was one "whereon the eyes of God, angels, and men were fixed." Yeardley, replying, declared that the Indian children whom it was proposed to instruct could only be obtained through a formal treaty with Opechancanough; and this he intended making the ensuing summer. Mr. Bluet, the foreman of the band of workmen sent out to the Colony to build the furnace, died, and the scheme, in consequence, received a severe setback. A new batch of mechanics having been dispatched, the work was resumed with such success that Sandys was able to express to the donor of the fund the hope that he would soon be fully satisfied by the "faithful account which the Company would be able at all times to give of the trust." But the great massacre of 1622 followed almost immediately, and falling with terrible suddenness on the little settlement around the new iron works (situated on Falling Creek, in the modern county of Chesterfield), destroyed the furnace, and utterly and finally dissipated the capital, which had, with such persistent benevolence, been sought to be used for the establishment of the first free school designed for the Indians' benefit.[1]

The first free foundation designed for the benefit of the Colony's white children exclusively seems to have been the one known as the East India School, which had its origin in a subscription taken up among the passengers and mariners on board the *Royal James* while returning from the Indies. At the Cape of Good Hope, that ship had met a number of vessels outward

[1] Abstracts of Proceedings of Va. Co. of London, vol. i., p. 163.

bound, and as they had given a good report of Virginia's prosperity, Rev. Mr. Copeland, the chaplain of the *Royal James*, induced the ship's company to contribute over seventy pounds sterling for the promotion of some benevolent work in the Colony. At first, it was undecided as to whether this should take the form of a church or a school, but it was in the end determined that a school should be established. Copeland, writing to numerous friends residing in India, urged them to make a liberal gift of money for the advancement of so excellent a scheme. In addition to the large sum subscribed by the passengers and mariners of the *Royal James*, there were specific presents of thirty pounds and twenty pounds sterling respectively from two benefactors, who refused to disclose their identity.[1] The London Company gave the name of "East India School" to the proposed institution as a mark of their appreciation of the zeal of the East India Company's officers in starting the project; and it was their design that this new school should become an adjunct to the college which they proposed erecting at Henrico.[2]

In the spring of 1622, Leonard Hudson, a skilled architect and carpenter, who was to build the schoolhouse, accompanied by his wife and five apprentices, left England in the *Abigail*, under Captain Barwick's command, and appears to have arrived safely in Virginia.[3] Steps had already been taken by the Company

[1] *Works of Captain John Smith*, p. 60, Richmond edition; Abstracts of Proceedings of Va. Co. of London, vol. i., pp. 146, 148; Randolph MS., vol. iii., p. 167.

[2] Abstracts of Proceedings of Va. Co. of London, vol. i., pp. 146-8; Campbell's *History of Virginia*, p. 158.

[3] *Works of Captain John Smith*, vol. ii., p. 65, Richmond edition; Randolph MS., vol. iii., p. 169.

to choose the persons upon whom should devolve
the immediate control and direction of the school's
affairs,—Rev. Mr. Copeland was appointed the rector,
and Mr. Dike, the usher or master. Mr. Dike had,
some time previous to February 1621–2, been warmly
recommended as a teacher well equipped to fill the
place; but the Company required him to obtain also a
certificate from the Governor of Virginia (to whom he
seems to have been known) that he was both competent and diligent in his calling. He was now in England,
and the Company informed him that, should he be able
to procure an expert writer to go out with him, who
would be able to give instruction in the rudiments of
arithmetic, they would bear the whole expense of his
transportation to the Colony. The term during which
Dike was to occupy the mastership of the East India
School was to continue for five years; and apparently
in addition to his salary, he was to receive at once a
patent to one hundred acres of land. As a further
encouragement, the Company promised to supply him
with all the books which he would require in following
his calling in Virginia; whatever ones the scholars in
his charge would need were also to be furnished by the
Company; but for these last, the children's parents were
expected to make payment.[1] It was probably to the
East India School that William Whitehead, of London,
in December, 1622, bequeathed twenty pounds sterling,
provided that an aunt, whom he named in his will,

[1] Abstracts of Proceedings of Va. Co. of London, vol. i., p. 167;
see entry for Febry. 27, 1621–2. At the end of his term of service,
Dike was to receive 500 acres of land in addition. Dike probably
never went over. Writing June 10, 1622, some months after the
massacre, the Company stated that "they did not send an usher
because they desire that the Colony may choose the schoolmaster
and usher, if any there"; see Randolph MS., vol. iii., p. 169.

died before him, and also that the school had been built within the first three years following his decease; should it not have been built within that time, the sum was to be spent in erecting a church on a site somewhere within the boundaries of Martin's Hundred.[1]

A site for the East India School was chosen in Charles City; but the great massacre of 1622 brought the whole scheme, which promised so much usefulness, to an abrupt end. A few years afterwards (1625), the Governor and Council, in a letter to the English Lords Commissioners, expressed a decided opinion that the school "would come to nothing."[2] There is no proof that the project was revived with energy after the terrible catastrophe of the massacre; and the prediction of these officers was, by the course of subsequent events, shown to be only too correct. The havoc worked by that catastrophe was, apart from the frightful loss of life accompanying it, in no respect a greater cause for sorrow than in the destruction it precipitated on this well-considered scheme for the establishment of an important free school in the heart of Virginia; such a school would not only, as time passed on, have conferred the inestimable blessing of free tuition on many thousands, but also have set an example of private benefaction, which, on account of the success attending its practical operation, would have been imitated by a great number of persons anxious to advance the cause of education in the Colony's various communities.

[1] See Will, Waters's *Gleanings*, vol. ii., p. 1028. It is possible that Whitehead's bequest was intended for the school which a previous unknown benefactor had proposed founding in Virginia by an expenditure of five hundred pounds sterling.

[2] Randolph MS., vol. iii., p. 192.

CHAPTER VII

Free Schools: The Symmes and Eaton

A S it was, the plan of the East India School very probably influenced Benjamin Symmes, about twelve years after the proposed institution had come to naught, to establish an endowed free school in Virginia. Symmes was born in 1590; and, in 1623, the year following the great massacre, so fatal to the East India and other benevolent schemes, he is found residing at Bass' Choice, situated in the modern county of Isle of Wight. As his will leaving valuable property for the support of the free school projected by the same document, bore the date of February 1634-5, his bequest precedes by several years the Rev. John Harvard's far more famous gift, which became the corner-stone of Harvard College. In reality, we are indebted to Benjamin Symmes for the earliest foundation for free education made in English America by a citizen of an English colony; and for that reason, his name is entitled to extraordinary honor in a land where the free school system has been carried to the highest state of usefulness perhaps to be observed on the globe. His school was established in the same thoughtful spirit and partook of the same lofty purposes as that noble group of endowed schools, which had, in the course of many centuries, been erected in the Mother Country by private generosity and benevolence,—the ever running fountain heads from which the members of generation after generation had drunk deeply of the enlightening and elevating waters of knowledge. There was not a single shire in England lacking one of these fine grammar schools; indeed, there was hardly an important town or a series of parishes unprovided with such an institution.[1] But for all those melancholy influences following upon the great economic, political, and social changes Virginia has passed through, the free school established by Symmes would be to-day equal in its record of usefulness, reaching back beyond the middle of the Seventeenth century, to those similar foundations in England which have been preserved in their original vigor by the happier conditions that have prevailed in that more stable land.

By the provisions of Symmes's will, the income from two hundred acres of land belonging to his estate, and the proceeds from the sale of the milk and of the increase of eight cows forming a part of his personality, were to be expended in affording a free education to the children residing in the parishes of Elizabeth City and Kikotan, from a point beginning at Mary's Mount and reaching as far as Poquoson River. This area of country was situated within the boundaries of Elizabeth City county. A schoolhouse was to be erected with the first money derived from the bequest; but all the profits accruing subsequently were to be devoted to the

---

[1] At the time of the Reformation, the English schools consisted of grammar, cathedral, college, monastery, hospital, guild, and independent schools. Most of these not only survived that great event, but also attained to an unexampled prosperity under its transmitted influence.

founder's general design. In March, 1642–3, about
eight years after the date of the will, the General
Assembly thought it necessary to pass a special Act
in order that this design might be carried out in the
strictest conformity with Symmes's directions; they
recognized his "godly disposition and good intent";
and expressed their determination to enforce his
wishes to the letter, as an encouragement to other
citizens to follow the noble example which he had set.
The whole phraseology of this memorable Act reveals
the high appreciation of education prevailing in
Virginia in these early times, and the gratitude felt
for every benefaction looking to its advancement.   By
the end of 1647, the school seems to have been resting
on a firm foundation, and was in active operation; the
schoolhouse was now finished; and the means of meeting
every expense was assured by the income obtained
from the land and a herd of forty milch cows.   The
institution was still in existence in 1694, in which year
Robert Crooke, the master, received two cows to
compensate him for his outlay in repairing the school
building.   In November, 1699, he gave notice that he
would resign his office at the "next fall of the leaf,"
and Samuel Snignell promptly petitioned the justices
of the county court to appoint him Crooke's successor;
and in doing so, declared his readiness to "undertake
ye education of ye children according to the design of
the donor."   The court seems to have thought favorably of his qualifications, for they chose him to fill the
position as soon as it was vacant; which, it would
appear, would not occur until the autumn of 1700.
It is to be inferred from the contents of the order
naming Snignell that the school's endowment had
suffered no diminution; the land had remained intact;

and the livestock had very probably steadily increased since 1647, at which date, the herd of cows was five times larger than it had been in 1635, when the bequest was first announced. The only limit to the increase in the size of this herd was fixed by the area of ground reservable for their pasturage. The management of the whole property seems to have devolved on the school-master, acting under the general supervision of the county court.[1]

The example set by Benjamin Symmes was, as anticipated by the General Assembly, soon followed by another citizen residing in the same county, who entertained the same enlarged views, and was animated by the same philanthropic spirit. This was Thomas Eaton, a physician, who, after living many years in Virginia, returned to England, where he seems to have died. As early as 1634, he had acquired a patent to about two hundred and fifty acres lying at the head of Back River, a stream entering the Chesapeake Bay a few miles below the mouth of the Poquoson.[2] The free school established by him was designed for the children of parents whose homes were situated within the boundaries of Elizabeth City county. Its original endowment greatly exceeded in value that of the Symmes Free School; this endowment consisted of an estate of five hundred acres of land in an improved agricultural condition and stocked with two negroes, twelve cows, two bulls, and twenty hogs. That there was a substantial residence on the plantation is shown

[1] For an account of Symmes's Free School, see Hening's *Statutes*, vol. i., p. 252; *William and Mary College Quart.*, vol. vi., p. 73; Elizabeth City County Records, Orders Nov. 20, 1693.

[2] *William and Mary College Quart.*, vol. vi., p. 72.

by the large quantity of household furniture included in the bequest.

The Eaton Free School was under the control of a board of trustees composed of the clergyman and churchwardens of the parish and the justices of the county court. This body was impowered to appoint a master, who, like the master of the Symmes Free School, doubtless served as the active manager.[1] The person in charge about 1691 was Ebenezer Taylor. As he enjoyed all the income and perquisites of the school, which were probably considerable, the county court, in 1692, required him to provide the necessary clothing for an old female slave forming a part of the endowment, whom he had so grossly neglected that the court described her as being almost naked. By the terms of the justices' order, he was to deliver to Mr. Henry Royall, one of the feoffees, for her use, one new cotton waistcoat, one petticoat, two yards of new canvas for a dress, one pair of new shoes and stockings, and three barrels of Indian corn. A few years later, this ancient negress was, by a second order of court, permitted to keep for her own support whatever corn and tobacco she should be able to produce by her own labor.[2] In addition to the money obtained from the sale of the different crops, and also of the increase of the herds of cows and hogs, there seems to have been some income derived from the sale of the fine timber growing on certain parts of the land; in 1694, Walter Bayley was authorized to cut down a portion of this

[1] *William and Mary College Quart.*, vol. xi., p. 20. The following item appears in the Elizabeth City county levy for Nov. 28, 1692: "To ye Secretary's office 3 patents of Eaton's land, 120 lbs. tobo."

[2] Elizabeth City County Records, vol. 1684–99, p. 118, Va. St. Libr.; see also Orders Dec. 19, 1692.

timber in order to use it in making a dam, and, no doubt, had to pay for the quantity which he thus employed.[1]   In 1699, a part of the tract was conveyed to William Williams[2]; and in the course of the following year, one of the negroes belonging to the estate was by Captain Henry Jenkins, probably a trustee of the school, sent out to Barbadoes, and there disposed of, perhaps because he was considered to be too vicious to be allowed to remain in Virginia.[3]

In 1697, George Eland, who seems to have been a physician by profession, was appointed by the trustees to the mastership of the school; and his term was to be renewed from year to year so long as they approved his management.   In return for teaching all the children residing within the boundaries of Elizabeth City county, he was to receive the several profits to be derived from the endowment[4]

The Symmes and Eaton Free Schools were beyond question the most useful institutions of that character situated in the Colony during the Seventeenth century. They both possessed the income they needed to furnish tuition without expense to a certain number of pupils; they were both subject to the supervision of the ablest, the most experienced, and the most responsible body of men in their several communities; and they each had a trained master in charge throughout the whole time of their existence.   What was the extent of the instruction which they gave?   We are informed that the master of the Eaton School was required to teach "English and grammar," which undoubtedly meant that

[1] Elizabeth City County Records, Orders Nov. 19, 1694.
[2] *Ibid.*, Orders June 19, 1699.
[3] *Ibid.*, Orders Aug. 20, 1699.
[4] *Ibid.*, Orders Nov. 18, 1697, Jany. 18, 1697–8.

the tuition was not confined to English studies, but that lessons in Latin, as in the private schools, were a part of the course. It would be inferred from the fact that "grammar" was taught that this course was carried beyond the mere rudiments of reading, writing, and arithmetic, and that an effort was made to impart an education equal to what is now to be obtained in the higher grades of the public schools. A similar tuition was, no doubt, given in the Symmes Free School. The endowment of neither institution seems to have been swelled, as time passed, by gifts from persons interested in the objects they were founded for; they were forced to rely on their original funds; and these evidently did not permit of their widening their field of usefulness by increasing the number of teachers and extending the course of study. Had the two schools been consolidated in the Seventeenth century, and had their common endowment been added to by the liberality of philanthropic citizens, they would have rendered unnecessary the establishment of William and Mary College at a later date, because, by the enlargement of their scope of instruction, which would have followed their union, they would have met the want in which that institution had its birth.[1]

[1] The two schools existed until 1805, when they were incorporated in one as the Hampton Academy. In 1852, the fund amounted to $10,000 and is still preserved apart from the state school fund. A portion was used in 1902, to erect in Hampton a handsome Academy building, which is known as the Symmes-Eaton Academy and is a part of the public school system.

CHAPTER VIII

Other Free Schools

THESE were not the only free schools in Virginia during the Seventeenth century; numerous others were projected, of which several at least were put in actual operation. As early as 1652, the county court of Northumberland gave their official approval to a petition offered by Hugh Lee, one of their number, which contained a well considered proposition looking to the establishment, at his own expense, of a free school in that county.[1] Only three years afterwards, John Moon, a citizen of Isle of Wight county, instructed his executors, in settling his estate, to reserve four female cattle, and to devote the income to be obtained from the sale of their male increase, as well as from the sale of the cows as they grew old, to meeting all the costs of providing a designated number of orphan children with an education, and "the like necessaries." It does not appear to have been the benefactor's purpose to set up a free school, but rather, in some free school already established, to furnish tuition to certain deserving pupils, who were too indigent to pay the ordinary fees.[2] In a similar spirit, Richard Russell, a zealous Quaker, whose home was situated in Lower Norfolk, bequeathed a portion of his estate

[1] Northumberland County Records, Orders Jany. 20, 1652.
[2] Isle of Wight County Deeds and Wills for 1655.

for the education of six children of impoverished parents residing near Elizabeth River; and if six more should present themselves, then a second portion of his estate was to be set apart for affording them the like tuition; and so on, so far as his property would go before being exhausted. In the case of this bequest, as of John Moon's, the testator's intention was apparently to supply the means of meeting the charge for instruction in a school already in existence.[1]

In 1668, Mr. King devised a tract of land, containing about one hundred acres, to the parish in which he resided, for the foundation and maintenance of a free school.[2] About seven years afterwards Henry Peasley left a large amount of property, consisting chiefly of a plantation covering six hundred acres, ten cows, and a breeding mare, for the endowment of a similar school projected by him for the benefit of Ware and Abingdon parishes in Gloucester county.[3] In the course of 1675, Francis Pritchard, of Lancaster, bequeathed a large amount for the like purpose provided that there was a failure of heirs to his estate in certain lines, which he designated in his will.[4] At the end of the next decade, William Gordon, of Middlesex, presented one hundred acres of valuable land as an endowment for a free school; and with the proceeds obtained from the sale of the crops of this plantation, a schoolhouse was soon erected, and a regular teacher employed, who, for some years, gave instruction, without expense, to the children in attendance.[5]

[1] Lower Norfolk County Records, vol. 1666–75, p. 28².

[2] *William and Mary College Quart.*, vol. v., p. 113.

[3] *Ibid.*, vol. vi., p. 82.

[4] Lancaster County Records, vol. 1674–89, pp. 67–9.

[5] *William and Mary College Quart.*, vol. vi., p. 8.

There is reason to think that there were other similar institutions in operation· in Virginia during the same period. It is only through the surviving county records that the fact of the existence of the minor free schools known to us has been preserved; unfortunately, the great bulk of these records, especially for many of the oldest counties, where such institutions were most likely to have been established, owing to their greater wealth and population, have been destroyed by the vicissitudes of various wars; and with them, all evidence that these counties once contained endowed schools of the character referred to, has been swept away. In his history, in which he described the Colony's condition in the century's closing years, Beverley informs us that there were

tracts of land, houses, and other things granted to free schools for the education of children in many parts of the country; and some of these are so large that of themselves they are a handsome maintenance to a master; but the additional allowance which gentlemen give with their sons render them a comfortable subsistence. These schools have been founded by the legacies of well inclined gentlemen. . . . In all other places, where such endowments have not been already made, the people join and build schools for their children, where they may learn on very easy terms.[1]

The author of these sentences, a man thoroughly familiar with every feature of Virginia at the time he was writing, would hardly have used so broad an expression as "in many parts of the country" had the number of free schools been limited to four or five. The scope of that expression would be fully intelligible to us, had all the records of all the counties

[1] Beverley's *History of Virginia*, p. 224.

survived to reveal to us what that number really was.

When Berkeley, in reply to the interrogatories of the English Commissioners in 1671, thanked "God that there were no free schools in Virginia,"[1] he made a statement which had no foundation in fact. The assertion seems especially preposterous as coming from a man who, at the moment he penned it, was in less than a day's journey of at least one county in which two free schools, the Symmes and the Eaton, were in active operation and assured of a permanent support by substantial and profitable endowment funds. Not only was Elizabeth City in possession of two free schools, but, as we have seen, at least two schoolmasters applied, in the course of a single year, for licenses to teach in private schools situated in that county. Berkeley's untruthful averment probably had its origin in a desire to impress at all costs the English authorities with his excessive loyalty to King and Church. "Learning," he continued, "had brought disobedience and heresy and sects into the world." The violence, which fell little short of the paroxysms of insanity, exhibited by him as soon as Bacon's followers had finally submitted, was foreshadowed in this foolish utterance, so often and so unjustly used to reflect upon the spirit animating the Virginian people during the Seventeenth century in their attitude towards education. These words, written only four years before Bacon took up arms in behalf of an oppressed people, must have made a singular impression on the minds of even the second Charles's advisers, who, with all their reactionary tendencies, looked upon the endowed schools of England as among the noblest foundations of their country. Charles himself in

[1] Hening's *Statutes*, vol. ii., p. 517.

reading them might well have anticipated the use of that strong expression which he applied to the monstrous old man when he heard of his wild course towards the unfortunate leaders of the rebellion.[1] They came with a particularly bad grace from Berkeley, who had enjoyed all the advantages of the highest education which that age afforded, and who, in early life, had won some notable triumphs as an English playwright; and they seem all the more remarkable when it is recalled that only eleven years before, he had shown extraordinary activity in his efforts to secure the establishment of a seat of learning in the Colony to partake of the joint character of a college and a free school. If he belittled the existing free schools so far as not to consider them schools at all because falling so much below the standards of similar institutions in England, then he evinced a spirit in this one matter evinced by him in no other relating to the favorable reputation of Virginia. Having occupied his office for a longer period than any one of his predecessors, he had become identified with the country to a degree not observed in any of the previous Governors; and his ordinary disposition was to exaggerate and not to underrate whatever would redound to its advantage, because he regarded it with all the affection and interest of a permanent resident. Only some perverted view closely approaching the inconsequence of dotage could have made him believe that the Colony's credit required him thus to ignore the existence of at least two free schools, which were important enough to have engaged at different times the General Assembly's attention.

[1] "The old fool has killed more people in that naked country than I have done for the murder of my father."

CHAPTER IX

Higher Institutions: The Indian College

WHAT attempt was made during the Seventeenth century to establish in Virginia seats of learning where a higher grade of instruction might be given than that received in the private and in the free schools? It was not many years after the first settlement of the Colony that active steps were taken to found a college; this was primarily designed for the education of Indian youth in the Christian faith; but it was also intended to furnish the planters' children with an opportunity to obtain advanced tuition.[1] The funds with which this institution was to be erected, and afterwards supported, were in part collected by means of the letters-patent ordered by James I, in 1617, to be issued throughout the Kingdom for the purpose of securing individual contributions. At a meeting of the General Court of the Company, held in May, 1619, it was announced that fifteen hundred pounds sterling, equal to thirty-five thousand dollars in purchasing power, had been received; and of this sum eight hundred pounds was in the form of actual money, and the remainder in the form of the Company's stock, purchased or transferred, it would appear, to pro-

[1] Stith's *History of Virginia*, p. 163, London edition.

mote so laudable an object. It was reported at the
same meeting that there was a very fair prospect that
a large addition would be made to this fund, for at
least one among the bishops, whose aid had been
solicited, had sent word that, just as soon as the royal
warrant should be placed in his hands, he would exert
himself to induce the people residing within the boundaries of his diocese to contribute liberally to it.

The Treasurer of the Company, on the same occasion,
expressed the opinion that it would be unwise to use
in building the College the sum already collected,
but rather that it should be safely invested, and the
interest accruing therefrom, as soon as it had sufficiently
accumulated, alone employed for that purpose. In
the same spirit of prudence, he also urged that a
large area of fertile land situated at Henrico should
be reserved for the institution's advancement; and
in order to make this land productive as soon as possible,
he recommended that fifty tenants should be dispatched
thither to bring it into a state of profitable tillage.
One half of the income thus acquired should be permitted to remain in the hands of the tenants themselves as compensation for their care and labor,
while the other half should be reserved as a fund for
pushing forward the College's general work, and maintaining the tutors and scholars.[1]

So much at heart did the Company have the foundation of the College that, in the fundamental orders
and constitutions adopted in 1619 and 1620, there

[1] Abstracts of Proceedings of Va. Co. of London, vol. i., p. 6.
Smith states that the site of the College was twenty miles from
Henrico; it lay about five miles from Pierce's plantation on the
Appomattox River; *Works of Captain John Smith*, vol. ii., p.
75, Richmond edition.

was inserted a clause requiring the annual appointment of a carefully selected commission, composed of five or seven persons, who were expected to take under their charge all the business relating to the establishment of the institution. This commission was instructed to adopt measures for the early collection of the different sums subscribed for carrying out this great work; and also to consult together as to the plans it would be wisest to follow in pushing that work to a finish. The Treasurer was ordered to keep separate accounts of the college funds, and from time to time to make special reports respecting them to the auditors, and through the auditors, to the General Court of the Company. These various provisions show, not only the extraordinary interest which this body took in the proposed seat of learning, but also the practical manner in which they endeavored to ensure its early and successful inauguration.[1]

The noble purposes to be subserved by the projected college induced several benevolent persons in England to contribute to its endowment by gifts either of money or of sacred objects. Nicholas Ferrer bequeathed to it three hundred pounds sterling, to be paid just as soon as ten Indian children had begun to receive tuition under its care.[2] In the course of the same year,

[1] Orders and Constitutions, 1619, 1620, p. 24, Force's *Hist. Tracts*, vol. iii.

[2] Broadside, 1619, Doct. 46, British Colonial Papers, vol. i. Until the College was in a position to give such instruction, twenty-four pounds sterling, by Ferrer's directions, were to be annually distributed among "three discreet and godly young men in the Colony to bring up three wild young Indians in some good course of life"; see *Works of Captain John Smith*, vol. ii., p. 40, Richmond edition. Twenty years afterwards, in order to secure the benefit of this clause of Ferrer's will, Mr. George Menifie presented to the General Court "an Indian boy of the county of Rappahannock"

some person, who refused to disclose his name, presented "fair plate and other rich ornaments" for a communion table designed for the college chapel[1]; and in the following year, a second person, who also concealed his identity, bestowed "many excellent religious books," and also a very curious and rare map of that part of America lying along the Atlantic coast. The example of these benefactors was followed by Rev. Thomas Bargrave, who, from having held a living in the Colony, was so much interested in the College's advancement, that, when he died, he bequeathed it a collection of volumes valued at one hundred marks.[2] Among the works forming a part of its library were one of St. Augustine's treatises translated into English, and the writings of Dr. Perkins, a distinguished clergyman of that day, of strong Calvinistic principles.[3]

The income to support the institution after the buildings had been finished was to be derived from four sources: first, the proceeds of the labor of the tenants to be assigned to the College lands; secondly, the amounts to be paid for the support of the pupils

who had been baptized, and for ten years had been educated among the English colonists by Captain William Parry and Mr. Menifie. The boy was examined and found to be well informed as to the doctrines of the Christian religion, and he had also been taught how to read and write. "For his better supportation in the education of the said Indian boy," Menifie petitioned the court for a certificate testifying to the preceding facts. The Governor and Council, "approving and commending the care that had been used towards this youth," readily recommended Menifie's "suit for the £8 per annum part of the £24 towards the maintenance of said youth"; General Court Orders for 1640, Robinson Transcripts, p. 31.

[1] Broadside, 1619, Doct. 46, British Colonial Papers, vol. i.

[2] *Works of Captain John Smith*, vol. ii., p. 60, Richmond edition.

[3] Abstracts of Proceedings of Va. Co. of London, vol. i., p. 94.

capturing the endowed scholarships and fellowships offered by the East India School[1]; thirdly, the interest from the College fund when invested by the Treasurer of the Company; and, finally, the tuition fees of such of the planters' children as would, in the course of each year, attend. By 1620, the money already collected by popular subscription had, no doubt, been put into a shape that would annually bring in a large sum; and by this time also, the College lands, spreading over ten thousand acres, had been carefully laid off, and one hundred tenants sent out to till them.[2] This ground, which was probably as fertile as any in Virginia, seems to have been, in some part at least, situated on the south side of the James River; but the far greater part lay on the north side of that stream, beginning at Henrico and running thence towards the Falls.[3] In more recent times, many estates widely celebrated for their productiveness have been carved out of this noble domain, and it has always formed one of the most valuable areas of its extent in that division of country. At the date when reserved by the Company for the use of a seat of learning, it was still in its primæval condition, but as the Colony's population increased, every acre of its surface was sure to come

---

[1] *William and Mary College Quart.*, vol. vi., p. 71.

[2] Abstracts of Proceedings of Va. Co. of London, vol. i., p. 66.

[3] *Va. Maga. of Hist. and Biog.*, vol. ii., p. 159; Brown's *First Republic*, p. 322; Randolph MS., vol. iii., p. 180. In the "Patentees of Land in Virginia" it is stated that the University was assigned 10,000 acres on the northern side of the River (see MacDonald Papers, vol. i., pp. 295, 307). It also speaks of "other lands belonging to the College." As we shall see later on, the "College Plantation" was situated in the Surry county of that day, and this was no doubt a part of the "other lands" referred to. Besides, Coxendale seems to have been embraced in the grant; see Brown's *First Republic*, p. 322.

under cultivation, to the extraordinary profit of whoever should be entitled to the proceeds. A large proportion of the soil lay in the immediate valley of the river, and thus possessed, not only the extreme fertility of bottom lands, but also all those facilities for the transportation of crops furnished by the proximity of deep water. By itself alone, this great tract made up a vast endowment worthy of the memorable scheme it was designed to advance,—an endowment not exposed to those different vicissitudes which are so often destructive of mere personality. Time could not obliterate that form of property; it would only add to its value. Whatever fertility cultivation would take away, the muddy waters of the stream, in the periodic freshets, would quickly restore.

As if to give an additional assurance of success to a scheme offering such excellent prospects of a permanent income, the Company, in 1620, dispatched to Virginia George Thorpe, a member of the King's Privy Chamber, and a man distinguished for zealous piety and fine scholarship, with a commission to take charge of the affairs of the projected institution. In order to afford him and those who should follow him a support, without any need of paying them regular salaries, an area of land covering three hundred acres, with ten tenants to cultivate it, was assigned in perpetuity to the office of manager.[1] In 1619, the General Assembly had urged the Company to send out the mechanics of various kinds who would be required to erect the buildings[2]; it was probably

[1] Abstracts of Proceedings of Va. Co. of London, vol. i., pp. 12, 54, 63.

[2] Colonial Records of Virginia, State Senate Doct., Extra, 1874, p. 16. The College had no burgess in the Assembly of 1619, but ten years later, the "plantation at the College" was represented

the men dispatched in response to this earnest appeal who, some time previous to 1622, contracted with Thorpe to supply the bricks for the main structure.[1] But whatever steps had been taken towards the actual construction of the college were brought to a sudden and terrible halt by the bloody catastrophe occurring in the March of that year; seventeen persons residing on the College lands perished in that frightful episode[2]; and among them was Thorpe himself, whose extraordinary efforts for the Indians' conversion did not save him from the fatal stroke of the tomahawk. His death was a severe blow to the great scheme which he was so deeply interested in; for not only had the undertaking lost a most capable and indefatigable head, but the whole immediate community in which that undertaking was to be pressed to a complete consummation was thoroughly disorganized, although not dispersed, by the success of the Indian plot.

The Company refused to yield to a feeling of discouragement. In May, 1623, thirteen months after the massacre took place, there were still attached to the College lands numerous persons who had survived the Indian assault.[3] The Company now gave strict instructions as to what these remaining tenants should do for their holdings' improvement, and also as to the amount of rent which each should pay; for instance, they were required to erect substantial dwelling houses, to plant orchards, and to lay off gardens; and in return for the use of the soil, were expected,

by Lieut. Thomas Osborne and Matthew Edlowe; see Hening's *Statutes*, vol. i., p. 138.

[1] Neill's *Virginia Company of London*, p. 330.

[2] *Works of Captain John Smith*, vol. ii., p. 75, Richmond edition.

[3] Abstracts of Proceedings of Va. Co. of London, vol. ii., p. 189.

in addition to working six days for the public benefit,
to deliver to the public store annually one pound
of silk, twenty bushels of corn, and sixty pounds
of tobacco.[1] Above all, the Company ordered the
Governor and Council to see that the bricklayers
engaged by Thorpe to construct the College building
should be compelled to go on and carry out their
contract.[2] "The work, by the assistance of God,
shall again proceed," the Company proudly declared
when unjustly reflected upon by the faction led by
Alderman Johnson and others[3]; and the energetic
steps taken by this body almost immediately after
the massacre show that these words were not spoken
in idleness. But an event far more blighting to the
College's prospects than that great catastrophe was
now impending; this was the revocation of the Company's charter, which was finally consummated only
a year after their noble resolve was pronounced.
But for that revocation, the Company would, without
doubt, have pressed the scheme to the completion
so carefully and prudently provided for. The massacre had not diminished the College's endowment;
the fertile lands still remained untouched, and only
needed a new supply of laborers to afford the entire
amount of income justly expected of them; the large
fund collected by individual subscriptions, the additional sums bequeathed by benevolent testators, all
were still intact. The devoted manager, Thorpe,
had fallen, it is true, but it was not impossible to fill
his place by the appointment of some one equally

---

[1] Randolph MS., vol. iii., p. 170.

[2] Neill's *Va. Co. of London*, p. 330.

[3] These words appear in the Company's reply to the petition
of Alderman Johnson.

pious, equally zealous, and equally efficient. Had
the Company's letters-patent not been recalled, the
College, before the end of a decade, under the influence
of that body's direct and energetic supervision, would
have been placed on a lasting foundation. The
original plan of making the education of the Indians
its primary object would have been rejected altogether
in consequence of the massacre, and the institution
would have stood forth as the earliest of all the seats
of learning established on the American Continent
for the benefit of the transplanted English. It would,
in all probability, have survived to the present day
in sufficient vigor to acquire a new growth of prosperity under the influence of the more fortunate conditions now beginning to prevail,—conditions certain
to expand to an even more extraordinary degree in
the future. Virginia, in such an institution, would
have possessed a foundation that would have been
clothed with the deeply romantic interest thrown around
the colleges of the Old World by the beautifying
touch of time, and by the glorious achievements of
their sons on every stage of action through a succession
of centuries.

Three years after the charter was recalled, the
scheme of the College was so entirely in abeyance,—
it was, indeed, so wholly lacking in a direct representative in the Colony,—that when Governor Yeardley's
widow wished to deliver up the valuable articles given
to the institution by English benefactors, and long
retained in her husband's custody in anticipation of
its early foundation, there was no one, except the
Governor and Council, who appeared to have the slightest authority to receive them. It was in these officials'
possession that she was compelled to place the silver

gilt cup, the two chalices in their cloth-of-gold cover, the crimson velvet carpet with its gold and silver fringe, the white damask communion cloth, and the four embossed books on Divinity, which pious and philanthropic friends had fondly hoped would adorn the chapel and library of the projected seat of learning beyond the Atlantic.[1] The College itself soon became a mere name, which crops up here and there in the records of subsequent years only in connection with the conveyance of the lands assigned by the Company for the institution's support. As late as 1666, nearly half a century after the scheme was first broached, one of the tracts belonging to the College was still known as the "College Plantation."[2] In that year, there were standing on the estate three tobacco barns, each sixty feet in length, a farmhouse fifty feet, and three dwelling houses ranging from thirty to fifteen feet. It was estimated at this time that there was derivable from the property an annual income of six pounds sterling. During the following year, the memorable storm always designated as the "Great Gust," the most frightful recorded in the Colony's annals, occurred, and all the buildings and the larger proportion of the timber of the place were hurled by the tempest to the ground. At the end of 1670, the estate had declined in value so much that the proceeds from it were not supposed to exceed four pounds sterling, a falling off in amount of one third. A new tobacco barn sixty feet in length had been erected, and presumably several cabins and a large dwelling house. An order was issued by the Governor

[1] Robinson Transcripts, p. 72.

[2] This plantation was composed of lands lying in the Surry county of that day.

and Council that the whole property should be appraised, an indication that the title had not even yet passed to private parties, although it would appear that the lands had been rented on long leases.[1]

A remarkable scheme for the establishment of a university in the Colony was outlined in the will of Edward Palmer, who died about 1624, in London. Palmer owned a large amount of property in both New England and Virginia. He provided that, in case there was a failing of heirs in certain lines of descent from him, his estate in America was to be used in founding and maintaining a great seat of learning on the James River; and with this were to be connected subordinate schools to be known by the name of Academia Virginiensis and Oxoniensis. The most advantageous site which the Colony afforded was to be chosen for these combined institutions; and preparatory to building, the utmost care was to be taken in bisecting the plat with a series of streets or alleys not less than twenty feet in breadth. Whoever could prove that he was sprung in the male branch from John Palmer, of Leamington, the benefactor's grandfather, was to be admitted to all the classes, both in the Academies and the University, without first having to pay a fee after the manner of the scholars; and as a spur to diligence in the hours ordinarily devoted to recreation, the pupils, it would appear, were to receive without cost lessons from two painters, one set of which was to be given in water-colors, and

[1] The barn was built by the "attorney of Mr. Stanford" who, in 1666, had obtained an order from the General Court against "the 3 parte of Francis Newton called the College." Newton was probably the lessee. "From the College to Smith's Fort" is an expression used in a list of tithables in the Surry Records for 1668: see vol. 1645–72, p. 341; see also p. 387, Va. St. Libr.

the other in oil.[1] As the anticipated failure in the line of descent did not occur, this scheme for the establishment of a great college in Virginia was never put to the test of actual experiment.   It seems, from some points of view, to have been as visionary as the Grand Model drawn up at a later date by the philosopher Locke for the social and political division of the people of the Carolinas.

[1] This part of the will is rather obscure, and its meaning only arrived at by inference; see Waters's *Gleanings*, p. 982.

CHAPTER X

Higher Institutions: Projected College of 1660–1

A N anxiety to advance the cause of education by the establishment of a college was, throughout the Seventeenth century, constantly present in the minds of the persons residing in Virginia who had the interests of learning most at heart. It did not require many years to pass after the Company's fall to convince such persons that, if the Colony was ever to possess a seat of advanced instruction, it must be founded chiefly, if not entirely, by the generous contributions of the inhabitants themselves, for there was now no single body in England resembling the Company which would use a direct and powerful influence to induce the English people to give money in support of such a scheme, or would expend large sums on its own account to assure success. A project of this kind must be started in Virginia; and it was only possible to arouse the interest of Englishmen in it by the solicitation of capable agents sent to the Mother Country, who would first have to enlist the English authorities' approval and sympathy. Before the close of the third quarter of the century, there had been at least one memorable scheme set on foot in the earnest hope that the Colony, chiefly by its own exertions, would be able to carry it to a happy completion; this occurred in 1660, a very short time after the Protectorate had come to an end; the communities of Virginia at this time did not perhaps contain more than twenty-five thousand people, for, in 1649, eleven years before the date of this educational scheme, the size of the population had been estimated at fifteen thousand; and in 1675, fifteen years after that date, it was estimated at fifty thousand. Not only was the number of inhabitants in 1660 still comparatively small, but the amount of wealth, represented by lands, crops, and live stock alone, had not yet reached large proportions. Nevertheless, so eager was the desire among the leading citizens that the Colony should possess an important seat of learning that they unhesitatingly deemed the country rich and populous enough to justify the erection of such an institution; and felt confident that, were it once built, it could be easily supported by the contributions of the Virginians themselves.

During the session of the General Assembly held in the winter of 1660–1, at least three Acts were passed with a view of founding in Virginia an institution that would partake of the character both of a college and a free school. By the terms of the first Act,—and the second followed the first very closely in tenor,— this institution's design was declared to be, in a general way, to advance the interests of learning and to spread abroad the spirit of piety; and, in a special way, to afford to the young opportunities of instruction in the higher branches of knowledge, and to train candidates for the ministry. By the terms of the third statute, the projected institution was described as "a college of students of the liberal arts"; and its main objects were stated to be to encourage learning, nourish religion, and provide, from year to year, a sufficient number of graduates in theology to fill the vacant pulpits of the Colony.

How was to be raised the fund to meet the cost of purchasing a site and erecting the necessary buildings? This was to be done by personal subscription. The list of contributors led off with the names of the Governor and members of the Council, who bound themselves in considerable sums expressed in both money and tobacco. The justices of the county courts, who formed the wealthiest body of men in Virginia as representing its largest landowners, were urged to follow their example; and they were also directed to swell the roll by securing the names of all persons willing to give pecuniary aid to the scheme. Nor was the probability that assistance of this kind might be obtained in England overlooked; a petition was to be presented to the King with the view of getting his consent to issue letters-patent addressed to persons throughout the Kingdom requesting contributions towards the building of the proposed institution. The General Assembly were so confident that the necessary money would be collected from all these different sources, that, in one of the three Acts which they passed respecting the College, they gave orders that a site should be purchased, and the structures required erected with "all convenient speed." Not until these two steps had been taken were the subscribers to the fund to be called upon to make payment of the different sums they had agreed to contribute.[1]

Why did the scheme of establishing a college in Virginia during the sixth decade of the century prove

[1] The Acts and Orders relating to the proposed college will be found in Hening's *Statutes*, vol. ii., pp. 25, 30, 37. See also Revised Laws, 1662, Colonial Entry Book, vol. lxxxix., p. 7.

so unsuccessful? There is some reason to think that, at this time, the people of the Colony were not in possession of sufficient means to justify them in subscribing the amount really required to found so costly an institution; and the room for the doubt appears all the wider if no aid was to be obtained from persons in England in carrying the project through. There is no evidence that such assistance was sought in an active way. If there was any step taken in that direction, it probably ended in disappointment, and the promoters of the scheme were left with no other resource but to secure contributions in Virginia alone, —a resource that perhaps soon revealed itself to be not altogether adequate. But it may well have been that the chief reason for the scheme's failure lay in the character of the General Assembly itself. Probably, the most selfish legislative body that ever convened in Virginia was the one which, by its prorogation from session to session, came to be known as the Long Assembly. This Assembly remained, by this subterfuge of Berkeley, in existence for fourteen years without a single dissolution to make an election of a new House of Burgesses legally necessary. It was this Assembly, so openly defiant of public sentiment, which was expected to provide an endowment for the proposed college. Under the influence of Berkeley, the boisterous representative in the Colony of the reactionary and shameless spirit then prevailing in the different branches of the restored royal government in England, the members of this Assembly did not hesitate to lay new burdens on the people, and to show in every way in their power that they declined to recognise any responsibility for their own wrong doing. No scheme like the one looking to the

establishment of a superior seat of learning, or to the
advancement of any form of public good, was likely to
have the support of men who openly regarded their
office as a means of enriching themselves personally,
or of consolidating and prolonging their individual
power indefinitely.

However restricted may have been the fortunes of
the Virginian people at large at this period, there was
no reason why a great tract of fertile land belonging
to the public domain should not have been reserved,
after the example set during the Company's existence,
to form an endowment for the proposed college. Such
a tract would have brought in no income immediately,
but as the Colony's population spread, it would have
been easy to divide that whole area among numerous
tenants under an obligation to pay a profitable rent.
Had the members of the Long Assembly appropriated
for the benefit of the projected seat of learning one
half of the amount which they voted as an annual
addition to their own salaries, that sum would, in
a few years, have become the nucleus of a large college
fund, which, by accretions from the rental of the
college tract, would, before the close of the century,
have enabled the authorities to establish the proposed
institution on a sound and permanent footing. As
year followed year, and the Long Assembly, refusing
to dissolve, grew more and more callous and self-
seeking, the last hope of building such an institution
faded away; men, under the influence of the arbitrary
acts which that body committed, or which its baneful
example encouraged others of inferior authority,
like the vestries, for instance, to commit, became
apprehensive lest they should be deprived even of
their fundamental and inalienable privileges as English

subjects. Popular suffrage was abolished; the right to be represented in the House of Burgesses was threatened by the Assembly's attempt to make itself a perpetual body[1]; and property was practically confiscated by excessive taxation. It is no ground for surprise that the scheme of the College sank out of view under the weight of such crying reasons for popular discontent, a discontent which was to find its last expression in a great insurrection.

[1] The only elections which occurred during the existence of the Long Assembly were those held to fill vacancies in the House occasioned by the deaths of members.

CHAPTER XI

Higher Institutions: William and Mary College

THE disorder and poverty succeeding the uprising of
1676, diverted men's minds for many years from
the plans of establishing a college in Virginia, but
the mere hope that some day such an institution would
be founded was probably never absent. There were
two powerful influences to keep this feeling constantly
nourished:—first, as the century drew on, the number
of prominent citizens who had been born in England
and educated in its most conspicuous schools, steadily
increased, and naturally they did much to create a
public sentiment highly favorable to advanced instruction; secondly, the remoteness of the Mother Country,
and the extraordinary dangers of the voyage thither,
made even the wealthiest parents, however eager
to give their children every advantage of the most
extended tuition, hesitate to send them so far from
home. It was in this combination of feelings that
the College of William and Mary had its real origin;
but it became a practical possibility by the force of
several other influences:—first, the growth of the
Colony's wealth and population towards the end of
the century; second, the destruction of the reactionary
Stuart dynasty; and third, the sagacity, public spirit,

and energy of Governor Nicholson and Commissary Blair.[1]

The active interest shown by Nicholson in the scheme to establish the College is one of the most honorable features of his administration, an administration which, in spite of his foibles, was marked by so much that was useful, far-sighted, and generous. In July, 1690, at a time when, in Howard's absence, he filled the office of Lieut.-Governor, he proposed at a Council meeting to revive the "design of a free school and college," already projected, as he himself stated, by "some pious men"; and he earnestly recommended that a number of persons should be appointed to take the subscriptions of all who were willing to contribute towards the foundation of so beneficent an institution. The Council seems to have agreed at once to the suggestion; several persons were named; and the Governor was requested to confer on them the power to act.[2] In a proclamation issued by Nicholson in the course of the same year, he called upon the justices of the several county courts to send to Jamestown a report containing a full list of the citizens residing within their respective jurisdictions, who were inclined to assist in advancing the scheme of the College.[3]

On May 7, 1691, a resolution was offered in the House of Burgesses declaring that the most advantageous site for the proposed institution would be the land of Ralph Green, the younger, situated on the north side of York River, in Gloucester county, and

---

[1] In an address by the House of Burgesses dated May 11, 1699, that body declared that, after the King, Nicholson was the chief promoter and supporter of the College; see Minutes of Assembly, May 11, 1699, B. T. Va., vol. lii.

[2] Colonial Entry Book, 1680–95, p. 372.

[3] B. T. Va., 1690, No. 3, Unassorted Papers.

at this time occupied by Thomas Baytop.[1] Accompanying this resolution was a list of the persons' names who, by their wealth, ability, and social rank, were considered to be worthy of the honor of being appointed members of the Board of Trustees.[2] On the following day, the debate was resumed, and after a more careful discussion of the advantages and disadvantages of the site suggested, it was decided that William Buckner's land lying on the south side of the river, would be a more convenient locality in which to build the College; perhaps as being nearer to the centre of the Colony's population. Mr. Christopher Robinson was, on the 15th, impowered by the Burgesses to announce to the Council the conclusion which they had reached; and also to request that body to choose four from among their own number, as well as four from among the clergy, who, joined to ten persons selected by the Burgesses, should be authorized to receive the royal charter. The Council gave their approval to the latter plan, and at once proceeded to appoint William Cole, Ralph Wormeley, William Byrd, and John Lear to represent their own body, and Rev. James Blair and Rev. John Banister, and whichever two other clergymen these two should name, to represent the Church; but they demurred to the site selected for the institution, and suggested instead that it should be chosen near a town. To this proposed

[1] B. T. Va. 1691, No. 28, Unassorted Papers.

[2] Trustees or the feoffees who were named on this occasion were "Secretary Cole, Ralph Wormeley, Esq., Cols. Edward Hill, John Page, Nathaniel Bacon, Thomas Milner, Lawrence Smith, William Fitzhugh, Miles Cary, Mr. Christopher Robinson, Mr. Henry Hartwell, Mr. James Blair, Mr. Robert Carter, Mr. Benjamin Harrison, Major Charles Scarborough, and Captain John Smith"; see Minutes of Assembly, May 8, 1691, Colonial Entry Book, 1682-95.

change the House finally consented; and after an exhaustive debate, they decided it would be best to build the College on land which had belonged to the late Colonel Robert Townsend, but was now in John Smith's possession. This land, which lay on the south side of York River, was situated near the place chosen as the site for York Fort. It was considered by the Burgesses to be advisable that the number of trustees should not exceed twenty, four of whom were to be chosen from among the members of the Council, and four from among the members of the clergy, whilst the remainder were to be nominated by the House. The Burgesses finally concluded to restrict their representatives on the board to nine; and in order that their choice might fully reflect the majority's wishes, each member of that body was directed to prepare a list of the nine persons whom he considered most worthy of being selected. This list he was required to place on the table in the Assembly hall; and when all the lists had been handed in, a committee, composed of Henry Hartwell and two others, was appointed to examine them, and to report the nine names receiving the largest number of votes. A count disclosed the fact that the persons chosen were Nathaniel Bacon, John Page, Thomas Milner, Christopher Robinson, Charles Scarborough, Benjamin Harrison, Miles Cary, Henry Hartwell, and Captain John Smith. Later, the Burgesses selected, as the associates of Rev. James Blair and Rev. John Banister, chosen by the Council as the clergy's representatives, Rev. John Farnefold and Rev. Stephen Fouace; and they gave directions that the names of all these gentlemen, along with the names of the four Councillors previously selected by that body, should be inserted in the document containing the instructions already drawn up for the guidance of Rev. James Blair as the agent appointed to visit England for the purpose of obtaining the charter.[1]

On May 20th, five days after the Board of Trustees had been nominated, the General Assembly prepared an address to the King and Queen, in which they declared that they were deeply moved by the pressing necessity imposed on the Colony to supply its youth with an opportunity of obtaining the most advanced and liberal education; and also to afford its vacant parishes the means of securing promptly pious and learned clergymen to fill their pulpits in order to assure "comfort and instruction" to their congregations. In its present condition, the Colony, so they stated, could offer neither. The remedy, the General Assembly earnestly averred, would be the establishment of a free school and college in Virginia, which would also be an unmistakable expression of its people's hearty concurrence in supporting the Protestant Religion and the Church of England. Having mentioned that they had appointed Commissary Blair to present their petition for a charter, they prayed that the projected college might receive the name, *The College of King William and Queen Mary*, in honor of their Majesties.[2]

[1] For the preceding details, see Minutes of House of Burgesses, Oct. 15, 1691, in B. T. Va., 1691, No. 28; see also Minutes of the House, May 15, 1691, Colonial Entry Book, 1682–95.

[2] Minutes of Assembly, May 20, 21, 1691, B. T. Va., 1691, No. 28. President Lyon G. Tyler has justly remarked that "this college was the first in America to be recognized by the royal will, and the first to take rank in theory at least with Oxford and Cambridge as their Majesties' royal college"; *William and Mary College Quart.*, vol. vi., p. 84.

The Assembly granted two hundred pounds sterling to Blair as a fund to cover all the expenses which he was expected to incur during his visit to England.[1] Two days later, on May 22d, he was impowered while in the Mother Country to borrow whatever sums he should have occasion to disburse in an effort to secure a favorable reply to the petition for the charter, provided that the total amount did not exceed that allowed for his private outlay.[2] In the elaborate series of instructions drawn up by the General Assembly, he was required to leave for England by the first ship setting sail, and on his arrival there to be governed by the advice of the Bishop of London, in whose diocese Virginia was embraced. The great object to be accomplished by him was declared to be to procure a charter for a free school and college, in which Latin, Greek, Philosophy, Mathematics, and Divinity should be taught. He was to obtain permission that this institution should he established on the land formerly held by Colonel Edward Townsend at a point situated on the south side of York River, and near the spot chosen for the erection of York Fort; that it should be designated as "William and Mary College"; that it should be founded in the names of the trustees already selected by the General Assembly; that this Board should have the management of all the property belonging to the College, and control

[1] Minutes of Assembly, May 20, 21, 1691, B. T. Va., 1691, No. 28.
[2] Minutes of Assembly, May 22, 1691, Colonial Entry Book, 1682–95. On April 28, 1692, the House of Burgesses adopted a resolution allowing Blair one hundred pounds sterling for disbursements as occasion arose "in managing ye affairs of ye Free School." This money was deposited in the hands of Gawen Corbyn, a merchant of London.

over its revenues and the like; that they should be required to take the usual oaths of office, and subscribe the Test against Popery; that they should perform the duties of their position without remuneration, should possess a common seal, should enjoy the power to choose in the beginning the teachers of the institution, and to fill any vacancies which might occur; that they should be authorized to adopt all orders and ordinances found to be necessary, provided that no order or ordinance adopted was repugnant to the laws of England or Virginia, or the canons of the Anglican Church; that they should have the right to appoint new members of the Board when the old either died or removed from the Colony; and also to elect a chancellor, who should preside over the practical working of the College, and act as its spokesman and representative on every public occasion.[1]

Blair was further ordered to engage a competent schoolmaster, usher, and writing master to fill the corresponding positions in the proposed free school; he was also directed to obtain the royal permission to collect benevolences throughout the Kingdom towards meeting the cost of establishing the College; and also to solicit personal gifts and subscriptions for the same purpose. Although, after his arrival in England, every facility was offered him, he seems to have found some difficulty in engaging for the various chairs to be filled, persons of satisfactory acquirements.[2] But this was a matter of secondary importance in comparison with the question of procuring funds for the support of the institution.

[1] B. T. Va., 1691, No. 23, Unassorted Papers.
[2] Letters of Blair to Nicholson on Dec. 3, 1691, *Va. Maga. of Hist. and Biog.*, vol. vii., p. 160.

In a memorial to the English Government adopted by the General Assembly, December 11, 1691, they stated that two thousand pounds sterling, equal in purchasing power to at least thirty thousand dollars, a very large sum for the people at that period to raise, had already been subscribed in Virginia; and they declared that, whatever deficiency might exist after the King had added his contribution, would be made up by their own body. One means of doing this proposed was to lay a tax on all liquors imported into the Colony; and other measures of a like character were to be adopted should it turn out to be necessary :— for instance, they suggested that a tax of one penny a pound should be placed on all tobacco exported to some point within the American Colonies, and that ten thousand acres situated on the southern bank of the Blackwater River, and one hundred thousand situated in Pamunkey Neck, should be appropriated for the College's support. As an additional means of raising revenue, the Surveyor-Generalship of Virginia might be bestowed on the institution. Since the incumbent of this office appointed the county surveyors and shared in their profits, it alone would afford an income that would fall little short of one hundred pounds sterling each year. The revenue to be derived by the College from the possession of this office was expected to be increased by the fact that the students in the school of mathematics would be fully competent to make the surveys.

The General Assembly further recommended that all escheated lands not otherwise disposed of by law should become the College's property; and they apparently also recommended that, in imitation of the great English Universities, the institution should have the power to appoint clergymen to livings. Nor did they think that the Virginians' generosity had been exhausted by the subscriptions already made; on the contrary, they believed that additional sums, in the form of gifts and benevolences, would be contributed if earnestly solicited. The General Assembly also urged that the two thousand pounds sterling then in bank to the credit of the royal quit-rent account, and unappropriated for any special purpose, should be devoted to meeting the expense of establishing and supporting the projected College.[1]

This weighty memorial received the careful consideration of the English authorities. Not many months passed before they presented their conclusions in the form of a report, in which it was stated that the following revenues, so far as they were not appropriated for other purposes, might be made available for the College's use:—first, a sum amounting to about nineteen hundred and eighty-six pounds sterling lying in the hands of Mr. Blaithwayt, the Auditor-General; secondly, the quit-rents of Virginia, which were estimated at one thousand pounds sterling per annum; thirdly, an equivalent, in the form of tobacco sold in England, for the tax of one penny a pound imposed on all shipments of that commodity from Virginia to any of the Colonies; fourthly, ten thousand acres situated on the Blackwater River and in Pamunkey Neck respectively, a total of twenty thousand; and, finally, all escheated lands of which no other disposition had been made.[2]

---

[1] B. T. Va., Dec. 11, 1691, No. 71.

[2] *Ibid.*, 1692, No. 116. The question as to how the clergy in Virginia were to be better supported was also considered in this report.

It will be seen from the preceding that the English authorities had adopted substantially all the General Assembly's recommendations. There seems to have been some opposition expressed to the application of the surplus in Mr. Blaithwayt's hands towards the College's erection and support, on the ground that as this sum "was the only ready cash in all the plantations," it should be carefully preserved for use in case of a great emergency, such as an invasion by the French or a descent of the Indians, which it was said, men had recently begun to fear very vehemently. Possibly with the view of shaking the English Government's resolution by dwelling on the strong probability that the fund would be needed for this purpose, it was declared that all the military magazines and fortifications in Virginia had been lately reported to be in a very bad condition; how were these defenses to be repaired, should this fund be expended in founding the projected institution? [1]

[1] B. T. Va., 1692, No. 116.

CHAPTER XII

Higher Institutions: William and Mary College (*Continued*)

IT was not until the first of September, 1693, that
Blair was able in person to place in the hands of the
Governor sitting in Council a copy of the charter
for the establishment of the College. It bore the
date of February 8, 1692–3, and its acquisition had
been made possible only by the indefatigable energy,
zeal, and sagacity shown by him throughout the whole
of his noble and beneficent mission. In the vigorous
prosecution of that mission, he had been especially
strenuous in laying emphasis on the great impulse
which such an institution would give to the prosperity
of religion in America.[1] It had always been a satisfaction to the English ecclesiastical authorities to
think that such a nursery of piety would be established in the New World; that it would be begun "in
an Episcopal way"; and that it would be conducted
by unswerving conformists[2]; and this feeling on their
part, Blair had succeeded in so confirming that they
had responded to his appeal by affording him the most

---

[1] He did not always find sympathetic hearers, as is proven by
the well-known anecdote of his conversation with Seymour. Seymour was not disposed to encourage the project. "But my Lord,"
remonstrated Blair, "the Colonists have souls to save." "Souls!
Damn their souls!" was the brusque reply, "make tobacco."

[2] Beverley's *History of Virginia*, p. 80.

active and powerful assistance. In the King also he had found, from the first hour of his arrival, an earnest and sympathetic supporter. It must have caused him extraordinary pride and happiness to return to Virginia with the invaluable document in his custody; and the moment at which he placed it in the possession of the Governor and Council was, no doubt, the most deeply satisfactory one of his life.[1]

The charter was first formally read; it was then entered in the minutes of the Council; and afterwards, as the final step, transmitted to the Secretary's office with a view to its being recorded. One warrant for eleven hundred and thirty-five pounds and fourteen shillings addressed to the then Auditor, the elder William Byrd, and another for eight hundred and fifty pounds, addressed to the executors of the elder Nathaniel Bacon, the late Auditor, were promptly drawn under the authority of the royal order granting the surplus in the control of Mr. Blaithwayt for the College's use. These two warrants were made payable to Francis Nicholson and the gentlemen named in the charter as the Board of Trustees.[2] This seems to have been the first fund appropriated to begin the construction of the College.

About three weeks (Sept. 20) after this memorable scene occurred, the full Board of Trustees formally visited the House of Burgesses, where, after they had been received in state, Blair gave a graphic and detailed description of his successful endeavor to secure the charter; and his speech having been concluded, the

---

[1] To show their appreciation of the value of Blair's services, the Assembly voted him £250; see Minutes of Assembly, Nov. 14, 1693, Colonial Entry Book, 1682–95.

[2] Minutes of Council, Sept. 1, 1693, Colonial Entry Book, 1680–95.

Board withdrew from the hall. The document was then read, and the twenty-fifth of October assigned as the day on which a site for the College should be selected, as this question had been expressly left open by the charter's provisions. An interval of a month was allowed before the final choice should be made, in order that the Trustees might have a full opportunity to visit the different sites suggested, and to compare their advantages. When the twenty-fifth of October arrived, the House adopted a resolution requiring all the Trustees happening at that time to be in Jamestown to appear at the bar on the following day. On this occasion, Blair, who seems to have always acted as the Board's spokesman, contented himself with reading a paper in which he had set forth the respective conveniences and inconveniences of the Middle Plantation, Yorktown, York Old Fields, and the Green plantation in Gloucester county. Immediately on the Trustees' withdrawal, the House rejected a proposition designating the Townsend plantation as the College site; and the same fate seems to have overtaken a proposition to build it on the tract in Pamunkey Neck assigned to the institution. Finally, it was decided that the Middle Plantation offered more advantages and fewer inconveniences than any other spot mentioned as appropriate for the purpose, and it was, therefore, definitely adopted as the one on which the College should be built.[1] This place presented two aspects of superiority over the others discussed:— first, it was very central in relation to the then inhabited parts of the Colony; and secondly, it had been always remarkable for its salubrious air. These two

[1] Minutes of Assembly, Oct. 20, 25, 26, 1693, Colonial Entry Book, 1682–95

important considerations turned the balance in its favor.

It was provided by an Act of Assembly that the College should be erected as near the Church at Middle Plantation as convenience would permit. One of the earliest of the additional measures now adopted for the institution's support was the imposition of a graduated tax on the different kinds of hides annually exported from the Colony, such as deer-skins, the skins of beaver, otter, wild cat, mink, fox, raccoon, musk-rat, and elk. The sums obtained from this source were to be paid to the Board of Trustees by the collectors.[1] A few days after the passage of this Act, however, the Assembly declined to exempt from the levies the masters and scholars of the College, or the artizans and working men who might be employed about it.[2]

The College's foundation stone does not seem to have been laid until the eighth of August, 1695, on which occasion, the Governor and Council were formally invited by the rector, Captain Miles Cary, to be present, an honor immediately accepted.[3] The ceremony took place on the land bought of Captain Thomas Ballard for the sum of one hundred and seventy pounds sterling. This land covered an area of over three hundred acres.[4] By the middle of October, the building

[1] Hening's *Statutes*, vol. iii., pp. 122, 123.

[2] Minutes of Assembly, Oct. 31, 1693, Colonial Entry Book, 1682–95.

[3] "His Excellency was pleased to acquaint the Council that Capt. Miles Cary, Rector of William and Mary College, did inform him that the Committee had appointed Thursday August 8 next for ye laying ye foundation of ye said College"; Minutes of Council, July 25, 1695, B. T. Va., vol. liii.

[4] These details and those following will be found in the state-

operations were well under way; eighteen months afterwards, two sides of the square (which had been adopted
as the architectural design for the structure), had been
carried up to the point of the roof; and the roof itself,
the Trustees reported, would soon be put on and
shingled.[1]   Two years later, the College had so far been
completed that the work of the grammar school had
begun.   Brick, stone, and wood alike entered into the
building's construction.   The earliest purchase of brick
seems to have been made of Col. Daniel Parke, who
no doubt had manufactured this material on his own
plantation, whilst the stone was perhaps obtained from
a quarry in the vicinity.   Some of the bricklayers
appear to have been sent for from England.   All the
stores were bought of Perry and Lane, the great
mercantile firm of London, which, for many years, had
enjoyed a large trade with the Colony.

A statement of the accounts down to February 27,
1696–97, shows that, previous to that date, the expen-
ditures for every reason, including the cost of the land
and building material, the fees of lawyers and surveyors,
the wages of clerks and artizans, and the like, amounted
to the round sum of thirty-eight hundred and thirty-
four pounds sterling.   What were the funds with which
these heavy charges were paid?   Roughly speaking,
they consisted of the following: first, the sum of nineteen hundred and eighty-five pounds and fourteen
shillings granted, as we have seen, by the King and
Queen out of the balance of the quit-rents in bank;
secondly, donations held by the Treasurer, equal in
value to five hundred and nine pounds; and thirdly,

---

ment of Debits and Credits recorded in B. T. Va., 1697, vol. vi.,
p. 88; see also Report of Trustees, p. 83.

[1] B. T. Va., 1697, vol. vi., p. 83.

three hundred pounds obtained by the "privateers."
To these sums must be added special gifts from Perry
and Lane, Col. Ludwell, and Rev. Mr. Fouace. The
whole was estimated to be about thirty-one hundred
and eighty pounds sterling. The sum which had
accrued from the various import and export duties
assigned to the College, amounted by October, 1695,
to four hundred and forty-one pounds sterling. In
spite of all these large sums combined, the deficit, when
the first balance was struck, came to about one hundred
and seventy pounds sterling; but this was promptly
made good by the trustees' advances.[1]

By the following April, the funds in hand had begun
to run so low that the Trustees complained to Governor
Andros that the work of building and furnishing the
College had been brought almost to a stop; and as one
means of obtaining the money so urgently required,
they reported that they had requested Blair, the
President of the institution, to undertake a second
mission to England.[2] It does not appear that the
Trustees applied to the General Assembly for assistance
at this time, probably because in October of the previous
year, that body, when Andros had recommended that
they should make an appropriation for the College's
encouragement, had replied that the country was
"in no capacity to do this."[3] The depression in the
value of the Colony's main commodity, tobacco, seems
to have caused so much delay on the part of many who
had subscribed towards the institution's establishment,
that, in 1699, the Trustees found themselves obliged
to bring suit against the delinquents. In one county

[1] B. T. Va., 1697, vol. vi., p. 83.
[2] *Ibid.*
[3] Minutes of House of Burgesses, Oct. 3, 1696, B. T. Va., vol. lii.

alone, that year, eleven such judgments were entered ranging from one to five pounds sterling.[1] The proposition to impose a general tax for the College's assistance at this time must have been broached in the House of Burgesses, for we find among the grievances recorded in the minutes for 1699, one from Isle of Wight county containing a strong protest against such a charge, on the ground that the people were so much impoverished.[2] The lands granted to the College in Pamunkey Neck, and on the south side of the Blackwater River, must now have assured a certain amount of income, for, three years before, the effort to lease them had proved successful.[3]

The institution had reached such a secure footing before the end of the century that bequests from two persons of distinction, who died previous to that date, were used for its benefit. Henry Hartwell left it fifty pounds sterling outright, and also one hundred pounds for the establishment of scholarships; dependent, however, upon the contingency of his nephew's life.[4] The gift of Robert Boyle was far more important in amount, but perhaps not quite so practical in character; in his will he gave directions that Brafferton Manor, in Yorkshire, valued at fifty-four hundred pounds sterling, should be purchased, and the income, estimated to be about two hundred and fifty pounds sterling annually, expended in spreading Christianity among the Indians of North America. The whole of this income, with the exception of one fifth reserved for use among the tribes residing in New England, was, through Macajah Perry, the agent of Virginia in London, delivered to the

---

[1] Henrico County Records, Orders March 1, 1699.

[2] Minutes of Assembly, May 10, 1699, B. T. Va. vol. lii.

[3] B. T. Va., 1697, vol. vi., p. 83.

[4] Hartwell's will in Waters's *Gleanings*, pp. 313, 314.

Trustees of William and Mary College, with the understanding that they were to procure clothes, lodging, and
tuition for nine or ten young Indians, who were to be
trained according to rules laid down by Lord Burlington
and the Bishop of London. They were to be taught
how to read and write, and also instructed in all those
arts and sciences which the Englishmen of that day
had to learn; but first of all they were to acquire a
thorough knowledge of the principles of the Christian
religion. This bequest seems to have become available
as early as 1700, for, in the course of that year, Governor
Nicholson wrote to Robert Hicks and John Evans, two
well known Indian traders, through whom the Indian
youths were to be obtained, that room in the College
would be ready for these youths by "the next summer";
that the age of each should not exceed eight years;
and that they should be accompanied by a woman of
their own race in order that they might not forget their
native tongue by disuse.[1]

The original plan adopted for the division of the course
of instruction designed for the white scholars entered
in the College, was that there should be a grammar
school in which Latin and Greek should be taught; a
school of Philosophy and Mathematics; and one of
Divinity and Oriental Languages. The expectation in
the beginning was that each of these schools would
require at least two able masters and professors.[2]
The Charter itself made provision for the establishment
of five chairs; one was to be dedicated to Latin and

[1] See Letter of Nicholson among the unbound Va. MS. at Fulham
Palace; see also MS. at Lambeth Palace for full account of Brafferton Manor. Some of these papers have been published in *William
and Mary College Quarterly*.

[2] See Memorial concerning the College, Dec. 11, 1691, B. T.
Va. No. 71.

Greek, one to Mathematics, one to Moral Philosophy, and two to Divinity.[1] Writing in April, 1697, the Trustees stated that they had been able to open the grammar school under the care of an excellent schoolmaster and writing master. The first accounts of the institution show the entry on the pay-roll of the names of only Mr. Mongo Inglis, the schoolmaster, Mr. Mullikin, the usher, and Rev. James Blair, the President. The salaries of these officers were respectively twenty-five, thirty, and one hundred and fifty pounds sterling per annum.[2] In 1699, Mr. Inglis was designated as the "Humanity Professor," whilst John Hodges succeeded Mr. Mullikin as the usher of the school.[3] Ten years after the College was founded, Inglis himself complained that it still remained a mere grammar school without those professorships of Philosophy, Physics, Mathematics, and Divinity, which had been originally intended.[4] But this fact did not prevent the institution's possibilities from being fully understood even at this early period; the mere fact that it had been established at all, after so many difficulties had been overcome, was one which to all thoughtful minds augured well for its future greatness.

Although the College did not rise above the importance of a grammar school at this time, it nevertheless possessed after the manner of Oxford and Cambridge Universities, the right to return a member to the Assembly.

[1] See Campbell's *History of Virginia*, p. 347.

[2] B. T. Va., 1694, vol. vi., p. 88. Inglis at a later date seems to have been paid an annual salary of eighty pounds sterling.

[3] Minutes of Assembly, May 17, 1699, B. T. Va., vol. lii. Inglis's hours for giving instruction were from 7 o'clock to 11 o'clock in the morning and from 2 to 6 o'clock in the afternoon; see *Va. Maga. of Hist. and Biog.*, vol. iv., p. 254.

[4] Present State of ye College, 1703, *Va. Maga. of Hist. and Biog.*, vol. ix., p. 251.

As its board of electors was restricted to the President, Masters, and Professors of the institution, it constituted a borough of a unique character for Virginia, though not for England. In 1696, when these officers were formally summoned to meet in the Court-house at Jamestown to choose a Burgess, no one appeared, and the College went, that year at least, without a representative.[1] At this date, the privilege of casting a vote was perhaps in the enjoyment of two men only, the President and the schoolmaster, although the usher and writing master may each also have had a voice.

The extraordinary interest taken in the institution's success by the most influential persons of the Colony was reflected in the final adjournment of the House of Burgesses in April, 1699, in order to attend the College exercises on May Day. When that body again assembled, Governor Nicholson congratulated them on having so readily and heartily joined with him in solemnizing so memorable an event. "The most proper place for you on that occasion," he exclaimed, "I concluded to be at his Majesty's College of William and Mary, where you might not only be eye witnesses of one of his royall Majesty's bounties and royal favors to Virginia, but also judges of the improvement of your youth in learning and education; and I hope in God you are satisfied as to both." That the Burgesses were pleased is shown by their felicitations to Nicholson a few days later; they dwelt upon the great happiness afforded them by their having had an opportunity in person to observe "the improvement of their youth in knowledge and literature"; and they declared that they considered it "an unspeakable blessing to have their children

---

[1] Minutes of House of Burgesses, Sept. 25, 1696, B. T. Va., vol. lii.

brought up in so fair a way of being rescued from barbarous ignorance." [1]

The commencement held at the College in the following year was an event of so much distinction that the memory of it long survived. A great multitude of people were in attendance, and it was noted at the time, with justifiable pride, that the spectators were not drawn entirely from Virginia, but that very many hailed from Colonies situated as far away as New York and Pennsylvania. The planters, with their families, from all the surrounding counties had come in their coaches or on horseback, whilst the strangers from a distance had sailed down the coast in their sloops. [2] It was a scene full of animation and novelty, and one of the first to foreshadow the great part which the institution was soon to play, not only in the educational affairs, but also in the social life, of the Colony. With both the College and the Assembly centred in Williamsburg, [3] that little town was destined, in a few years, to assume the aspect of a small capital, from which was to radiate throughout Virginia the influences of a larger culture, both social and literary. Tried by the standards of modern institutions of the like nature, the little seat of learning founded in this remote plantation community seems but a small establishment after all; but if we look on it, as we should, as the earliest beacon to cast the beam of advanced scholarship far and wide through the first of the Southern Colonies, it assumes a beneficent significance far out of

[1] Minutes of Council, May 2, 12, 1699, B. T. Va., vol. lii.

[2] Campbell's *History of Virginia*, p. 361.

[3] In urging the removal of the capital to Williamsburg in 1699, Nicholson declared "that it would be a greater kindness to the College than if you had given £2000 for the use of it." See Minutes of Council, May 18, 1699, B. T. Va., vol. lii.

proportion to its course of studies or the number of its students. Above all, if we gauge the value of its work by the great men whom it nourished even before the Revolution, this college becomes at once clothed with all the dignity of an institution which has made a profound impression on the destinies of a powerful nation. Jefferson, the author of the Great Declaration, and the Founder of American Democracy; Marshall, the Interpreter of the Constitution; Monroe, the proclaimer of the Doctrine which has resounded throughout the world,—such were three of the sons, to name only the most eminent, who, when their minds were most sensitive to impressions, sat at the feet of this Alma Mater, and who, by the achievements of their after lives, reflected extraordinary distinction on her teachings.[1] In spite of two great social and political revolutions, which scattered broadcast the seeds of destruction as they occurred, the College still survives, a venerable monument of a glorious past, still full of promise of a long and useful career in the future.[2]

[1] John Tyler was also an alumnus of this institution.

[2] In recent years, William and Mary College, through the work especially of its President, Lyon G. Tyler, has become closely identified with historical investigations which have thrown much new light on the past of Virginia, whether as a Colony or as a State.

CHAPTER XIII

Libraries: Value Attached to Books

IF Berkeley, in his memorable reply, in 1671, to the inquiries of the English Commissioners, had been satisfied to return thanks to God because there was no printing press to be found in the Colony at that time, he would have been much nearer the truth than in foolishly congratulating himself on the imaginary absence of free schools.[1] It was always easy for those in authority to destroy such an instrument for enlightenment, should one exist. Previous to 1680, there does not seem to have been a single printing press in Virginia. When it was then considered desirable to put the laws in type, a copy in handwriting had to be sent to England; such was the course pursued by the General Assembly at its session in the winter of 1661–2.[2] In 1680, John Buckner, a merchant residing in Gloucester county, imported a printing press, and it would appear also a trained printer, William Nuthead by name, to manipulate it. That he had the General Assembly's countenance and support in 1680 at least was shown by his receiving an order from this body to print the Acts passed in the course of that year. Accused at a

---

[1] "Learning had brought disobedience and heresy and sects into the world, and printing had divulged them, and libels against the best government"; Hening's *Statutes*, vol. ii., p. 517.

[2] Hening's *Statutes*, vol. ii., p. 147–8.

later date of working without a license, and summoned before the Governor and Council to answer the charge, he was required to give bond to refrain from using his press until the royal pleasure as to whether it should be permanently stopped or not, was ascertained.   In reply to an inquiry, a command came from England that no one residing in the Colony should, on any occasion whatsoever, be allowed to operate such a press[1]; but this prohibition was slightly modified by the instructions drawn up for Howard's guidance a few years afterwards: that Governor was enjoined to forbid the use of the printing press within his jurisdiction unless a special license had been first obtained from him.[2]   Howard, as well as his immediate successors, must have been indisposed to grant such a privilege, for apparently no such press was introduced at any time during the remaining years of the century; as late as 1698, Andros, in transmitting to England copies of recently enacted laws, was forced to apologize for the rude form in which they were presented, on the ground that "all conveniences for putting them up handsomer were lacking in Virginia."   There seems to have been good reason why excuses should be offered, for, about this time, the English authorities grew so impatient with the rough appearance of the documents received by them from the Colony, that they sent over a great quantity of ruled paper, with directions that thereafter such paper alone was to be used in all communications with the English Government.[3]

[1] Minutes of Council, Feb. 25, 1682–3, Colonial Entry Book, 1680–95; *Va. Maga. of Hist. and Biog.*, vol. i., p. 406; *William and Mary College Quart.*, vol. vii., pp. 9, 10; Hening's *Statutes*, vol. ii., p. 518.

[2] Colonial Entry Book, 1685–90, p. 59.

[3] Letter of Andros to Secry. of State, June, 1698, B. T. Va., vol. vi., p. 361.

From the preceding facts, it may be safely concluded
that the large number of books to be found in Virginia
during the Seventeenth century had, perhaps, without
a single exception, been printed outside of the Colony's
boundaries. The far greater proportion of these
volumes had been printed in England; the remainder
were from the presses of Holland and France. The
collections of English books indicate that the planters,
under the influence of the education acquired by them
in the schools of the Mother Country or of the Colony
itself, looked upon reading as not the least important
form of amusement in which they could seek recreation.
We learn from the records of Lower Norfolk that, in
1647, Jacob Bradshaw, of that county, "received his
death at the hands of God by lightning and thunder of
Heaven, as he was lyinge on a chest and readinge in a
Booke." It is possible that some bigoted enemy of
learning, under whose observation this incident may
have fallen, held up Bradshaw's fate as a judgment
from the Almighty, but, from the testimony of the few
surviving county records, there is room for thinking
that such an occupation of the time was not unknown
even among the members of the class furnishing most of
the manual laborers.[1] Many instances are found of
books being owned by such mechanics as blacksmiths,

---

[1] Lower Norfolk County Records, vol. 1646–51, p. 51. Capping verses seems to have been a not infrequent amusement.
"Depn. of Richard Cox saith that yor. Depont. being at the House
of Lieut. Col. John Tilney in company with Alexander Gibson
and Thomas Johnson, yr. Depont. heard ye sd. Col. Tilney and
ye sd. Gibson capping verses, upon wch. ye sd. Col. Tilney fell
out, and ye sd. Tilney bade Gibson begone out of his house, and
yr. Depont. did then and there see ye sd. Col. Tilney strike ye sd.
Gibson a great blow on the back with a tobacco stick or some such
like." See Accomac County Records, vol. 1676–78, p. 106. Another case is recorded in vol. 1673–76, p. 337.

carpenters, and the like; though the volumes in their possession were few in number, it is not improbable that, for this reason, if for no other, these volumes had been the more carefully and frequently read.

One of the most remarkable proofs of the interest felt in the Colony at this time in books is brought to light in the special bequests so often made of them by will. A few instances may be given. In 1652, Thomas Gibson, of York, left his entire collection of volumes to his son; and three years later, Richard Stanwell, of Lower Norfolk, followed his example.[1] The wife of Rev. Robert Dunster, of Isle of Wight county, was, in 1656, the beneficiary of a similar bequest from her husband[2]; and Captain Robert Ellison, of York, from his friend, Henry Waldron.[3] In 1667, Richard Russell, of Lower Norfolk, a zealous member of the Quaker sect, instructed his executors to divide his collection of books (twenty-five in number of titles, though perhaps as many as fifty or sixty volumes in all) among seven friends belonging to the same faith as himself. These volumes were, no doubt, of a religious character.[4] By the terms of Laurence Washington's will, drawn about 1675, all his books were to be delivered to his son John as soon as he came of age.[5] Three years later, John Michael, of Northampton, bequeathed to his "dear and pious brother" all the works in his collection written in the Dutch language.[6]

---

[1] York County Records, vol. 1633-94, p. 38. Va. St. Libr.; Lower Norfolk County Records, vol. 1651-56, p. 179.

[2] Isle of Wight County Deeds and Wills for 1656.

[3] York County Records, vol. 1657-62, p. 19, Va. St. Libr.

[4] Lower Norfolk County Records, vol. 1666-75, pp. 28[2], 33[2]. See also Lower Norfolk County Antiquary, vol. i., p. 105.

[5] Rappahannock County Records, vol. 1664-73, p. 101, Va. St. Libr.

[6] Northampton County Records, vol. 1674-79, p. 340.

James Love, apparently at one time a ship-surgeon,
who died in Rappahannock county about 1681, left
by will "a large cedar chest full of books" to Captain
John More, of the sea going vessel *Alexander*, a citizen
of Bristol, in England.[1] Nathaniel Walker, of Northampton, followed the example of George Mortimer, of
the same county, in bequeathing all his volumes to a
friend.[2] By the provisions of the will, dated 1684, of
Francis Pigott, also of Northampton, his collection of
books, with the exception of the Latin and Greek, was
to be divided among his three sons as soon as the youngest reached the age of twenty-one. All the works
printed in the two ancient languages were to pass
immediately to the eldest, in whose care the whole set
was to remain until the hour for division should arrive.
The younger sons were to be allowed in the interval to
take away any special book which they desired to read,
on condition that they left with their brother a note
expressing their willingness to return the volume
whenever he had occasion to use it.[3] It would appear
that this library was one of importance both in the
number and variety of its works; and that it was highly
valued by its owner is shown by the minuteness of his
directions for its disposition.

A few years after Mr. Pigott's death, Mrs. Ann
Bevill, of Henrico, by deed of gift during her lifetime,
divided her collection of books equally between her two
sons.[4] Henry Kent, a citizen of the same county,

[1] Rappahannock County Records, vol. 1677–82, p. 90, Va.
St. Libr.

[2] Northampton County Records, vol. 1679–83, p. 49, vol. 1683–
89, p. 25.

[3] *Ibid.*, vol. 1683–89, p. 123.

[4] Henrico County Records, vol. 1677–92, see Wills for 1686.
This gift was entered of record, an evidence that the collection of
books was a large and valuable one.

whose personal estate was appraised at twelve thousand
and six hundred pounds of tobacco, bequeathed forty-
five books, amounting perhaps to one hundred volumes
or more, to his heirs.[1] In 1690, Col. John Carter left
by will to Robert Carter all those works in his library
written in the Latin tongue, or relating to the subject
of law.[2] In the course of the same year, Edward
Foliott, of York, instructed his executors to divide his
collection of English works into two equal shares, and
to deliver one share to each of his "two sons-in-law,"
Henry and Charles Hansford.[3] Col. Arthur Smith, of
Isle of Wight county, in 1693 bequeathed "all his
bookes" to his son[4]; and his example was imitated
about the same time by John Wallop, of Accomac; who,
however, reserved by name a few, with directions that
they should become his daughter's property.[5] This
was also done in 1695, by Henry Awbrey, of Essex, the
exception in his case being for the benefit of his wife[6];
and a similar exception was, in 1697, made by William
Catlett, also of Essex, who left the remainder of his
library to his brother.[7] Conquest Browne, of Westmoreland, in 1698, bequeathed all his books outright to
his son; William Fitzhugh, on the other hand, who died
a few years later, divided his collection between two
sons, William and Henry.[8]

It very frequently happened that a particular book
was held in such extraordinary esteem by its owner that,

[1] Henrico County Records, vol. 1677–92, orig. p. 388.
[2] Lancaster County Records, original vol. 1690–1709, p. 4.
[3] York County Records, vol. 1687–91, p. 490, Va. St. Libr.
[4] Isle of Wight County Records, vol. 1661–1719, p. 331.
[5] Accomac County Records, Wills for 1693.
[6] Essex County Records, vol. 1692–95, p. 352, Va. St. Libr.
[7] Essex County Records, Orders April 11, 1697.
[8] Westmoreland County Records, vol. 1690–99, p. 143; *Va. Maga. of Hist. and Biog.*, vol. ii., p. 277.

in drawing up his will, he was moved to bequeath it by name to some one whom he regarded with feelings of the strongest affection or gratitude; for instance, in 1643, after leaving to Col. John Tilney all his chirurgical treatises, Dr. John Holloway ordered his executors to deliver his Greek Testament in folio to Rev. John Rosier; his catechism to Mr. Philip Taylor; and a volume entitled *The Humiliation for Sinne* to Mr. John Fullard.[1] In a like spirit, Francis Slaughter, of Rappahannock, in 1657, left Hooker's *Ecclesiastical Polity* to Mr. Moore Fauntleroy, his brother-in-law.[2] William Burdas, of Lower Norfolk, about the same time bequeathed to different friends copies of works entitled the *English Physician*, the *Practice of Physick*, the *Dispenser* and *Thoughts on Surgery*, all of which were, no doubt, highly acceptable from their usefulness in cases of sickness.[3] Arthur Hoppin, of the same county, followed his example by presenting by will two books, one of which was Heyland's well known cosmography.[4] To one friend, John Kirby, of Northumberland, bequeathed, in 1667, the *Practice of Piety;* to another his *Reveries;* and to another still, a third favorite volume.[5] John Sampson, of Rappahannock, several years later, instructed his executors to deliver to Mrs. Sarah Suggett his small Bible adorned with silver clasps, his *Herne* in folio, his *Heaven Opened*, and the *Life and Death of Mr. John Janway;* whilst Mr. John Taverner was to be presented with his copy of the *Religio Medici*, and the publications of the French Academy.[6] John Wallop

[1] Northampton County Records, Orders Aug. 31, 1643.

[2] Rappahannock County Records, vol. 1656–64, orig. p. 83.

[3] Lower Norfolk County Records, vol. 1666–75, p. 25 ².

[4] *Ibid.*, vol. 1666–73, p. 34.

[5] Northumberland County Records, Wills, vol. 1666–72.

[6] Rappahannock County Records, vol. 1677–82, orig. p. 61.

in 1693, left to his daughter, not only the family Bible, but also two works known by the titles of the *Woman's Counsillor*, and the *Countess of Kent's Choyce Manualls*.[1]   Christopher Branch, of Henrico, valued a Latin book in his possession so highly that he bequeathed it to one of his friends as an evidence of his affection.[2]

Such are a few of the very numerous instances preserved in the surviving county records of the Seventeenth century which might be given to show the esteem in which many testators held particular books belonging to their collections.

[1] Accomac County Records, Wills for 1693.
[2] Henrico County Records, vol. 1677–92, orig. p. 209.

CHAPTER XIV

Libraries: Size of Collections

THE inventories of the personal property appraised during the Seventeenth century throw a light more remarkable than even that of the wills on the extent to which books formed a part of the planters' estates in these early times. Two facts should be borne in mind in estimating their number and value by the entries found in these inventories: first, the number of books is based on the number of titles, and not on the number of volumes; it would be within the bounds of strict accuracy to calculate that, on the average, there were at least two volumes to each title, for some of the titles, we know, represented as many as five or six volumes; secondly, in the appraisement, only the book's physical condition was considered, which, either from age or constant reading, was generally highly dilapidated; under these circumstances, the pecuniary value was always rated extremely low, and forms, therefore, no real criterion of the book's intrinsic merit from a literary point of view. Copies belonging to the same edition of the same work, might, in the same appraisement, be entered at figures ranging very widely apart from each other.

To give in these pages either the full number, or the complete list, of the titles of the books owned in Virginia during the Seventeenth century would be manifestly impracticable, even if the records of all the counties had survived to the present day. In one county alone, Lower Norfolk, there are still preserved the names of more than one hundred owners of books for a single interval not exceeding fifty years.[1] Some of the collections contained hardly a dozen volumes; others, on the other hand, contained such a number and variety of titles that they would be justly considered, even in our own times, to constitute libraries of importance. I shall select from each of the counties whose records have come down to us, at least in part, the names of the owners of the principal collections of books, and as far as possible state the size and value of these collections,—a matter of difficulty even when the number of titles is mentioned, as the number of volumes remains a matter of speculation to be approximated only by striking the probable average.

First, as to the collections of books owned in Lower Norfolk county. Here, as elsewhere, the character of the works is often largely religious. Of the five in George Lock's possession, in 1641, one was a Bible and another, the *Practice of Piety*, a proportion frequently observed.[2] A part of the personal estate of Philip Felgate, designated as "gentleman," consisted, in 1647, of a "parcell of bookes," valued at eighty pounds of tobacco,[3] whilst the collection belonging to John Yates's estate was supposed to be worth about two hundred and twenty pounds of the same commodity.[4] In both of these cases, the volumes' physical condition

[1] The interval between 1640 and 1690. See the various issues of the Lower Norfolk County Antiquary.

[2] Lower Norfolk County Records, Orders Sept. 6, 1641.

[3] *Ibid.*, vol. 1646–51, p. 47.

[4] *Ibid.*, p. 94.

was alone considered, and as that condition was probably bad, their number is likely to have been much larger than their appraisement would appear to show. The estate of John Kemp included seven works treating of chirurgery; and, in addition, there were others of a more general character; such, for instance, as Aristotle's *Problems*.[1] Among the items of Edward Hodges's personal estate, an estate appraised at eleven hundred and thirty-three pounds of tobacco, were two works which alone were valued at fifty pounds.[2] Of those included in the inventory of John Pigott's collection, one was Hakluyt's *Travels*.[3] The works forming a part of the personal estate of John Gilham, who died about 1651, numbered eight titles, equal perhaps to sixteen volumes.[4] Captain John Sibsey's collection was kept in the hall of his residence, an apartment which, in those times, frequently served as a family sitting-room, where books could be most conveniently arranged for use.[5] George Clayne, whose estate was appraised in 1654, owned a considerable number of volumes written in the Dutch language; among them a large Bible.[6] Of the six books belonging to Cornelius Lloyd's estate, three were of the same religious character.[7] The number embraced in the Yeardley inventory did not exceed nine titles, which would represent a collection perhaps of about twenty volumes.[8] The books belonging to the estate of Roger Fountain were entered at four hundred pounds of tobacco, an amount signifying,

[1] Lower Norfolk County Records, vol. 1646–51, p. 96.
[2] *Ibid.*, p. 126.
[3] *Ibid.*, p. 175.
[4] *Ibid.*, vol. 1651–56, p. 8.
[5] *Ibid.*, p. 54.
[6] *Ibid.*, p. 93.
[7] *Ibid.*, p. 168.
[8] *Ibid.*, p. 203.

at the rate of two pennies a pound, a valuation of fifty dollars.[1]

The collection of Col. William Moseley, also of Lower Norfolk, whose home was adorned with beautiful portraits, and whose family was in possession of much costly jewelry, was so large that, after his death, it was appraised at three thousand pounds of tobacco; this would represent in modern figures between three and four hundred dollars,—a valuation, however, which fails to give a perfectly accurate idea as to this collection's importance, whether the size or the character of its contents be considered, owing to the fact that very many of the books may have been in bad condition from age or use. Their extraordinary variety is indicated by the fact that they represented four languages, namely, English, Dutch, French, and Latin. Col. Moseley, although an Englishman in blood, had emigrated to Virginia from Holland, where he had acquired a thorough knowledge of the Dutch and French tongues; and, no doubt, he was made familiar with Latin by his early education.[2]

The number and the variety of the books often entered in an inventory at a comparatively small valuation, is strikingly illustrated in the case of the collection belonging to Mrs. Sarah Willoughby, a resident of Lower Norfolk, who died about 1673. Although appraised at only five pounds sterling, this collection contained fifty-five titles, which would indicate between one hundred and one hundred and ten volumes. Among the books of a religious character belonging to it were one Bible in folio and two in quarto, a

---

[1] Lower Norfolk County Records, Inventories for 1666. When new, these books were probably valued at three times this amount.

[2] Lower Norfolk County Antiquary, vol. i., p. 122.

Bible printed in the Latin language, two testaments, Eusebius's *Ecclesiastical History*, *Ye Soul's Progress to ye Celestial Canaan*, *Preservation against Sin*, a volume of sermons, an exposition of the Commandments, and also of the Lord's Prayer, a treatise on the Divine Essence and Attributes, *Cases of Conscience*, *Ye Safe Way*, *Ye Destruction of Babylon*, and *Wisdom in Three Books*. The fields of History and Biography were represented by the annals of Turkey, and the Lives of Louis the Thirteenth and Charles the Second. There were among the works of a more miscellaneous nature, Sandys's *Travels*, *Essays of Lord Montague*, *The Seaman's Practice*, *The Seaman's Calendar*, *The Birth of Mankind*, a volume on midwifery, *A Discourse for Englishmen*, a *Grammar and Dictionary*, a treatise on Trigonometry, Heyland's *Cosmography*, *Virginia or ye South Part of It*, *Propositions of War and Peace*, *Ye History of Animals*, *Directions for Planting Mulberry Trees*, and Æsop's *Fables*. Mrs. Willoughby also possessed a considerable number of books written in the Latin tongue, such as the *Metamorphoses* of Ovid, and other works by that author, the *Poems of Virgil*, and the *Orations of Cicero;* in addition, there were three small Latin books, and a book of Latin verses.[1]

The collection belonging to Thomas Reynolds, also a citizen of Lower Norfolk, who died about 1673, was almost entirely of a religious character; it included such standard works of that class as the *Practice of Piety*, and *The Whole Duty of Man*, volumes hardly less popular in the households of those times than the *Pilgrim's Progress* at a later day.[2] Among the books owned by William Green, of the same county, were

[1] Lower Norfolk County Records, vol. 1666–75, p. 169.
[2] *Ibid.*, p. 156[2].

Ye Civil Wars in England, *Advice to a Son*, and the *Seaman's Practice*.[1]   Edward Bragge, whose will was offered for probate about the same time, seems to have possessed only a few books.[2]   On the other hand, the collection of Samuel Ball was quite large; it included nineteen works printed in English and bound in quarto or octavo, one in large quarto, perfectly new and very thick, and two in folio.   There were also thirty small letter books, some bound in folio and some in quarto; in addition, there were four works in folio, and twenty-nine in quarto unbound; and finally, thirty-two English books, some bound in quarto and some in octavo. This collection consisted of one hundred and seventeen titles; if we omit the letter books from consideration, it is probable that it contained at least one hundred and fifty volumes.   Its scholarly character is shown by the fact that thirty of the works were the productions of Latin authors.[3]   The collection belonging to William Archer, who resided in Norfolk county, where he died about 1695, numbered as many as one hundred titles, which would probably represent a library equal at the least to one hundred and fifty volumes.[4]

[1] Lower Norfolk County Records, vol. 1666–75, p. 188.

[2] *Ibid.*, vol. 1675–86, p. 55².

[3] *Ibid.*, vol. 1686–95, p. 155²; see also Lower Norfolk County Antiquary, vol. ii., p. 36.

[4] Norfolk County Records, vol. 1695–1703, p. 9.   Among the other owners of books who resided in Lower Norfolk county were Thomas Casson or Causon (1651), Christopher Burroughs (1653), Henry Watson, Thomas Wilkes, Charles Edgerton, Thomas Hardinge, John Boote, John Lawrence (1666–70), Robert Porter (1666), Evan Williams (1673), William Simpson (1675), William Hanbrom (1678), Robert Spring, Geo. Fowler, James Wishart (1675–86), Tristram Mayo, William West (1684–5), William Daynes, Richard Wright, Francis Lake (1687–8), Walter Bartin, Richard Jones (1691), John Sanford, Thomas Jackson, Francis Land, Henry Southern, Richard Stairling (1691–1700).

Perhaps, the largest number of books belonging to a citizen of Princess Anne county, a county formed by the division of Lower Norfolk about 1691, was the property of Thomas Cocke. It will be of interest to mention some of the titles of the works included in this collection, as they are fairly representative of many of the collections existing at this time:—among them were the *History of Great Britain, History of all the Kings of England, Defense of the Reformation, Observation of the Turk's Government, Voyages and Adventures of Sir Francis Drake, Travels of Ulysses, Jure Maritimo, Office of a Complete Attorney,* and *Complete Laws of Virginia, The Young Clerk's Guide, The Complete Justice, The Seaman's Calendar, The Nonconformist's Plea for Peace, Explanations of Proverbs,* Greenhill's *Sermons, Voice of the Rod,* Fox's *Time and the End of Time, Plain Man's Way of Worship, Divine Meditations, Schooling of the Untaught Bridegroom,* a large church Bible and three small testaments, a Book of Common Prayer, *Poorman's Family Book, Discourse concerning Comets,* and the *History of a Coy Lady.*[1]

The books belonging to Martha Williamson, also a resident of Princess Anne county, were, at the time the inventory of her personal estate was taken, valued at seven pounds and thirteen shillings, an amount which would indicate that her collection was about as large as Thomas Cocke's, already enumerated in part.[2]

The inventories recorded in Isle of Wight county in the interval between 1668 and 1679 contain entries which show that the principal citizens of that division of the Colony possessed respectively a considerable

[1] Princess Anne County Records, vol. 1691–1708, p. 162.
[2] *Ibid.,* p. 227.

number of books.[1]   Sometimes, their collections are designated simply as "parcells,"—an indefinite term often signifying many volumes, as we learn from other sources of information.   Such was the general description given to the collections of John Watson, John Long, and Francis Ayres, each doubtlessly varying in size greatly from the other two.   The books owned by Robert Bracewell, who died about 1668, were valued at five hundred pounds of tobacco, an amount that, at two pennies a pound, would represent an appraisement of about one hundred dollars in modern values, indicating a large number of volumes, especially if they were in a damaged condition, as was the case so generally.   Edward Yalden, who died in the following year, possessed seventeen books, and also two almanacs,—a collection perhaps of about thirty volumes.   In the interval between 1679 and 1690, the principal owners of books residing in this county were John Bromfield, Thomas Pitts, Thomas Cullen, and John Jenning, whose joint collections were appraised at a figure exceeding eighteen hundred pounds of tobacco.   The books belonging to Col. Joseph Bridger, perhaps the principal citizen of Isle of Wight county, were entered in the inventory of his personal estate at four pounds sterling; but this low valuation is explained by the fact that the volumes were for the most part in a dilapidated state.   On the other hand, the collections of Captain John Goodrich and James Fullogh were appraised at seven hundred and four hundred pounds of tobacco respectively.[2]

Among the planters of Surry county owning a small

[1] For the names that immediately follow, see Isle of Wight County Records for the years of the Seventeenth century succeeding 1669.

[2] For Bridger, see Isle of Wight County Records, vol. 1661–1719, p. 255; for Fullogh and Goodrich see Records for 1698 and 1699.

number of books were Andrew Robinson, George **Wat-kins**, and Peter Dale; their joint possessions in this respect came to forty titles, which would perhaps indicate collections amounting in all to seventy or eighty volumes. One of the works belonging to Andrew Robinson's son was Quarles's *Poems*, a proof of some taste for belles-lettres. Robert Spencer, like Captain John Sibsey, of Lower Norfolk, already mentioned, arranged his books on shelves in the hall of his residence, probably his family's ordinary sitting-room. The number of titles amounted to seventeen, which would perhaps signify a collection of about thirty volumes.[1]

Among the different articles carried off from the residence of Captain Chamberlaine, of Henrico, by Nathaniel Bacon's troops were several books,—a proof that, among the insurgents, there were some persons who possessed literary taste, whether disposed or not to recognise the rights of property.[2] Of the volumes belonging to the personal estate of Francis Eppes, one of the wealthiest planters of the same county, two were English dramas, while a third was the Bible in quarto containing the Apocrypha.[3] William Farrar, whose personal estate was valued at thirty-one thousand one hundred and five pounds of tobacco, owned a considerable collection of works; among them Dr. Sanderson's *Sermons*, Josephus's *History*, *The Commonwealth*, and *Legal Precedents*. The entire number were valued at only two hundred pounds of

---

[1] See Surry County Records:—Robinson, vol. 1645-72, p. 350, vol. 1671-84, p. 200; Watkins, vol. 1671-84 p. 72; Dale, *Ibid.*, p. 177, Spencer, *Ibid.*, p. 450, Va. St. Libr. Other owners of books in this county were John Twyford (1678), Edmund Howell, George Proctor, William Scarborough (1671-84).

[2] Henrico County Records, vol. 1677-92, orig. p. 30.

[3] *Ibid.*, p. 97, Va. St. Libr.

tobacco, but on the specific ground that they had fallen into a dilapidated condition from age and long use.[1] Among Farrar's other contemporaries residing in Henrico who possessed books were Captain James Crews,—a conspicuous figure in the troubles of 1676, —Richard Kennon, John Howard, Charles Clay, Thomas Bottomley, and Thomas Batte.[2] Thomas Shippey, whose personal estate was appraised in 1684 at nineteen thousand seven hundred and twenty-seven pounds of tobacco, possessed a collection amounting to twelve titles, or to about twenty-four volumes.[3] Nathaniel Hill, probably a physician by profession, left at his death, in 1690, among other books, ten bearing on the subject of medicine, two arithmetics, and a volume known as *The Clerk's Guide*. There were also in this collection two works printed in Latin.[4] The collection of Henry Randolph, long a prominent citizen of the county, contained twenty-nine titles in folio, eight in quarto, and more than fifty in octavo and duodecimo. The number of books belonging to him probably amounted to as many as two hundred volumes.[5] John Foisin, a merchant of French nativity, possessed at his death, in 1693, among other works, a collection of thirty-four printed in the French language; and his Bible was also printed in the same tongue.[6] The inventories of numerous citizens of the county at this time disclose the damaged condition of many volumes after passing through so many hands during a

[1] Henrico County Minute Book, 1682–1701, p. 10, Va. St. Libr.
[2] Henrico County Records, vol. 1677–92, orig. pp. 155, 226, 297, 379; vol. 1688–97, pp. 111, 235, Va. St. Libr.
[3] Henrico County Records, vol. 1677–92, orig. p. 282.
[4] *Ibid.*, vol. 1688–97, p. 182, Va. St. Libr.
[5] *Ibid.*, p. 428, Va. St. Libr.
[6] *Ibid.*, p. 463, Va. St. Libr.

long course of years; for instance, it was stated of Charles Blanchvile's collection that it consisted of a "parcell of very old books without beginning or ending," [1] whilst those belonging to Francis Redford's estate were described as "old and imperfect." [2]

[1] Henrico County Records, vol. 1688–97, orig. p. 501.
[2] *Ibid.*, p. 492, Va. St. Libr.

CHAPTER XV

Libraries: Size of Collections (*Continued*)

NUMEROUS owners of books were found in all the counties situated in the Northern Neck from the first years following their settlement. In the interval between 1648 and 1653, there were included among such owners residing in Northumberland planters as well known as James Claughton, William Nicholls, John Dennis, and John Cocks.[1] The collection of Jane Porge, of the same county, who died about 1651, contained, in addition to three Bibles and a *Practice of Piety*, nine works printed in the Latin tongue.[2] The books belonging to Col. John Mottram, also of Northumberland, whose personality was appraised in 1655, related to a considerable variety of subjects,— among them were a *History of France*, a *History of Rome* written in the Latin language, a treatise on Wills and Testaments, the *Sergeant at Law*, *Statutes of Elizabeth*, Parry's *Chirurgery*, *Treatise on ye Law of God*, *Godly Observations*, *Parliament of Christ*, and *Differences between Religions*. In addition to these works, his collection contained thirty-nine titles representing volumes of a smaller size.[3] Among the owners of

[1] Northumberland County Records for 1648–53.

[2] *Ibid.*, Orders May 20, 1651.

[3] *Ibid.*, Orders July 4, 1655.

books residing in the same county whose collections are entered simply as "parcells," signifying a considerable or an inconsiderable number of works, were William Nash and Thomas Shaw.[1]

The collection of Richard Sturman, of Westmoreland, who died about 1671, seems to have contained about nineteen titles, which would perhaps indicate about forty volumes.[2] Among the books owned by John Annis, of the same county, whose estate was appraised the same year, were Norwood's *Epitome*, the publications of the French Academy translated, a *Description of the World*, Blunt's *Voyage into the Levant*, *Ye Glory of ye Church*, Clowes's *Care of Gunshot Wounds*, Cooke's *Anatomy*, French's *Art of Distillation*, *Vade Mecum*, *An Act for Subsidies*, and Wing's *Art of Surveying*.[3] In 1674, Robert Jadwin's collection consisted of eighteen works, but they were described in the inventory of his personal estate as old and dilapidated.[4] The collections of William Snowdall and Samuel Vaughan were entered in their inventories simply as "parcells of books."[5]

William Fitzhugh, who had enjoyed a superior education, was in the possession of the largest collection in the hands of any one citizen residing in Stafford county. That it contained an unusual number of volumes is shown by the term applied to it in the text of his will,—he there refers to it as a "Study of Books," which would seem to indicate that a special apartment was required to supply space for its accommodation.

[1] Northumberland County Records for July, 1657, also for 1671.

[2] Westmoreland County Records, Orders June 1, 1671.

[3] *Ibid.*, Orders April 17, 1671.

[4] *Ibid.*, vol. 1665–77, folio p. 189.

[5] *Ibid.*, Orders June 30, 1675, July 19, 1677.

Some light is thrown on the character of this "Study" by the various orders given by him in his correspondence with his London agents with a view to the purchase of such volumes as he desired; for instance, in 1698, he directed one of them to send him a copy of all the statutes passed since the twenty-second year of Charles the Second's reign, the second and third parts of Rushworth's *Historical Collections*, Dr. Thomas Burnett's *Theory of the Earth*, the complete works of the author of the *Whole Duty of Man*, Lord Bacon's *Remains*, Collins's *Abridgement of the Records of the Tower*, Buchanan's *De Jure*, Boyle's *Letter to a Friend concerning Specific Physic*, *Secret History of Charles the Second and James the Second*, *Secret History of Whitehall until the Abdication*, and the *Memorable Actions of King William the Third*. This brief list, which represents only a single order, reveals a certain breadth of literary interest very frequently reflected in the small libraries of that day, as the owners were entirely dependent upon their own collections whenever they had occasion to investigate any special subject strongly appealing to them. History, Law, Medicine, Physics, Morals,— there were works of high reputation. in those times relating to each of these departments of thought in this comparatively small number of volumes dispatched on a single vessel to this planter and lawyer in Virginia.[1]

During the forty-six years between 1654 and 1700, the appraisement of personal estates in Lancaster shows the presence in that county of numerous collections of books; the term "parcells" occurs in at least twenty-five instances, and in some, if not in all, signified several dozen volumes at the lowest. William Brocas, who died about 1655, possessed an assortment made up,

[1] Letters of William Fitzhugh, July 21, 1698.

for the greater part, of works written in the Spanish, Italian and Latin tongues.[1] Robert Beckingham, a merchant of wealth and prominence, owned, in addition to other books, eight in folio, valued at a figure as high as three hundred and twenty pounds of tobacco, and one at eighty pounds. These volumes were probably adorned with costly illustrations.[2] Among the owners of small libraries who were Beckingham's contemporaries were Elias Edmonds, William Tignor, Thomas Hackett, David Miles, Walter Heard, Richard Taylor, and Thomas Wilks. An attachment issued against the personal estate of Dr. John Harris in 1683 included, as part of the property to be seized, fifteen "great and small books."[3] Col. John Pinkard, whose personal estate was valued at four hundred and seventy-six pounds sterling, seems to have possessed only four; and they were worth but a few shillings.[4] On the other hand, Colonel John Carter's collection contained a set of volumes remarkable, not only for their number, but also for the variety of the subjects to which they related; Religion, History, Law, Medicine, Physics, and Belles-lettres,—there were works in this little library touching upon some phase of each of these fundamental topics.

The names of some of Colonel Carter's books may be given in order to show the general character of one of the largest collections owned by any single planter of Lancaster county during the last quarter of the century. The department of History was represented by Rushworth's great work in its several parts, Plutarch's

[1] Lancaster County Records, vol. 1652–56, p. 203.
[2] *Ibid.*, Inventories for 1676.
[3] *Ibid.*, Orders April 11, 1683.
[4] *Ibid.*, Orders Jany. 8, 1690.

Lives and Josephus's *History of the Jews;* Science by Bacon's *Natural History*, Markham's *Country Farm*, Blith's *English Husbandry*, Booth's *Architecture*, Briggs's *Arithmetic*, Spencer's *Logic;* Medicine and Surgery by two works relating to chirurgery, by one relating to scurvy and dropsy, and one to the practice of physic, and also by Salmon's *Dispensatory* and the *Poorman's Family Book;* Religion by Diodati's and Haynes's *Annotations on the Bible at large*, Byfield's *Annotations on the Epistles of St. Peter*, Baxter's *Saints' Everlasting Rest* and *Life of Christ*, and also by his *Christian Directory* and *On Infidelity*, Newman's *Concordance*, Browning's *Sermons*, *Practice of Piety*, several Bibles, Testaments, and Common Prayer books. Among the dictionaries possessed by Colonel Carter were two English, one English-French, one English-Greek, and one English-Spanish. The department of general literature was represented in part by the Countess of Montgomery's *Urania*, Homer's *Iliad*, Ovid's *Epistles* translated into English verse, Ogilby's *Virgil*, also translated, *Cleopatra, a Romance, Cassandra, a Romance, Eikon Basilisk*, Markham's *Masterpiece*, and *Spanish and French Dialogues*. The entire collection was composed of fifty-five titles, which would indicate its numbering about one hundred volumes.[1]

The library of Ralph Wormeley, Secretary of the Colony, who resided at Rosegill, situated in Middlesex county, contained a collection of books amounting to as many as three hundred and seventy-five titles, which would probably signify that the number of volumes fell little short of six or seven hundred. An analysis of the titles shows that, in this collection, there were thirteen works relating to Grammar and the history of

[1] Lancaster County Records, Orders January 27, 1690-91.

words; thirty-three to Law and Politics; thirteen to
Geography, and the description of places; eighty-six to
History and Biography; twenty-two to Medicine; one
hundred and twenty-three to Religion and Morals;
four to Travels; five to Commerce; and twenty-three
to various arts.   On general subjects, there were
fifty-five works, some printed in English and some in
Latin; among the latter were copies of Virgil, Horace,
Cicero, and other Roman authors equally celebrated.
The English classics, including numerous comedies and
tragedies, were also well represented.   There were
eighteen works printed in the French language. Among
the other books which the library contained were
thirteen standard dictionaries in the English, French,
Spanish, and Latin tongues.[1]

    The collection of books owned by William Colston,
of Richmond county, amounted to one hundred titles;
it contained perhaps as many as two hundred volumes;
and it required for its accommodation the entire space
of an alcove situated next to the chimney piece in the
hall of his residence.   This was known in the household as the "closet."[2]   The collection belonging to
Arthur Spicer, the foremost lawyer in the Northern
Neck, who was also a resident of the same county,
exceeded the Colston collection by two titles only.
Naturally, the number of works relating to his profession predominated among the two hundred or more
volumes which perhaps made up this library; at least
fifty-two titles treated of the various sides of juris-
prudence; and in addition there were six works devoted
to History, and one to Biography.   Thirty-five bore

    [1] A complete list of the books forming the Wormeley Library
will be found in *William and Mary College Quart.*, vol. ii., pp. 170–4.
    [2] Richmond County Records for 1701; see also *William and Mary
College Quart.*, vol. iii., p. 132.

upon religious and moral subjects, whilst among the remainder were copies of many celebrated Latin classics as well as copies of English.[1]

One of the earliest owners of books residing in Rappahannock county was James Williamson, whose personal estate was appraised in 1657, the year of his death; his collection at that time, which was described simply as a "parcell," was in a very dilapidated condition resulting from age and long use.[2]   The collection of Dr. Henry Willoughby, a resident of this county about 1679, was so large that it would be regarded as a very respectable library even at the present time; the number of titles it contained amounted to at least two hundred; and it would probably not be an exaggeration to say that there were in it four hundred volumes in all.   As works on Law predominated in Arthur Spicer's library, so in Dr. Willoughby's, works on Medicine occupied the first place; the number of titles relating to this subject alone came to forty-four; and of this number, one half at least were printed in folio and quarto.   This collection of medical works represented the foremost treatises devoted to that science which had appeared up to this date; and in excellence was very probably quite equal to any collection owned by the English physicians of those times.   It presents in a very favorable light the qualifications of the principal medical practitioners of Virginia in that age.   This library, like Arthur Spicer's, also contained a very large number of books bearing upon the subject of Religion and Morals, a feature characteristic of every important collection found in

[1] Richmond County Records for 1701; see also *William and Mary College Quart.* vol. iii. p. 132.

[2] Rappahannock County Records, vol. 1656–64, orig. p. 77.

the Colony during this century. Of this section of Dr. Willoughby's collection, two works were printed in folio, twenty in quarto, twenty-seven in octavo, and twenty-five in duodecimo. Nor was his library lacking in works relating to the different branches of Law; on the contrary, there were thirty-eight separate titles devoted to this general topic in its various aspects; and of these, two were printed in folio, four in quarto, nine in octavo, and twenty-three in duodecimo. In the department of History, there were six works printed in folio, and twelve in quarto. Twenty-eight of the titles related to subjects of general interest; and these included copies of many classical authors.[1]

Among other owners of books residing in Rappahannock county during the interval between 1677 and 1685, were Thomas George and Thomas Perkins; the volumes owned by the latter, who is entered in the records as "clerk," signifying that he was a clergyman, were appraised at nearly twelve hundred pounds of tobacco. Additional owners were Major Henry Smith (whose books were kept in his bedroom), Evan Morgan, Thomas Harper, John Gilson, William Fauntleroy, John Palmer, James Andrews, and George Jones.[2] John Sampson, a merchant, who died about 1680, possessed, among other works of value, Browne's *Religio Medici*, a very popular volume in the Colony among men of literary taste. Quarles's *Fons Lacrymarum*, and *Heaven Opened*, a religious book appearing in nearly all the libraries of those times. Powell's *Concordance*, which was also owned by Sampson, was equally as well known. His collection also included such other works of a moral tone as *Heart Kept from Desponding, Of Friendship and*

---

[1] Rappahannock County Records, vol. 1677–82, orig. p. 25.
[2] *Ibid.*, pp. 19–83.

of a Friend, Of the Proverbs, and *Divine Fancies*.
Among its contents too was a French grammar, and
also numerous copies of the laws of Virginia. And
like most of the colonial libraries of that day, it
contained *The Seaman's Calendar* and the *Poorman's
Family Book*.[1]

The collection belonging to the Debers estate, of
Rappahannock, included, along with other works,
eight written in the Latin tongue, apparently copies of
celebrated Roman authors. There were also three
volumes of sermons printed in quarto, besides numerous
small volumes relating to subjects of general interest.[2]
Among the other owners of books residing in Rappahannock, or in Essex, a county formed from Rappahannock
towards the end of the century, were Thomas Roberts,
William Sergeant, Christopher Blackburne, Anthony
and John Smith, Martin Johnson, and Robert Jackson.[3]

[1] Rappahannock County Records, vol. 1677–82, orig. p. 61.

[2] *Ibid.*, p. 50.

[3] *Ibid.*, pp. 6, 7, Va. St. Libr.; Essex County Records, vol.
1692–95, pp. 315, 373, 401, Va. St. Libr. See also Records for
1696, orig. p. 47; also Orders Sept. 22, 1698.

CHAPTER XVI

Libraries: Size of Collections (*Continued*)

PASSING from these communities, which for the most part had been occupied by English settlers barely fifty years, to such counties as Accomac, Northampton, and York, first seated not long after the Colony's foundation, we discover even more remarkable evidences of the fact that, during the Seventeenth century, many Virginians were in possession of a large number of well selected volumes.   Let us examine first the inventories of Northampton and Accomac, the two counties forming what has always been designated as the Eastern Shore.   As early as 1641, the appraisement of the Cugley estate showed among its items of property a "parcell of old books," a term which, as already pointed out, often indicated a collection of some importance.[1]   Dr. John Holloway possessed, in addition to thirteen works relating to the subject of chirurgery, written in either Latin or English, twenty bearing upon a great variety of topics of general interest; among them a Greek Testament in folio, bequeathed by him, as we have seen, to his friend Rev. John Rosier.[2] John Severne's collection, like the Cugley, was entered

---

[1] Accomac County Records, vol. 1640–45, pp. 59, 65, Va. St. Libr.

[2] Northampton County Records, Orders Aug. 31, 1643; Feb. 10, 1643–44.

in the inventory of his personal estate simply as a "parcell of books," but probably amounted to a considerable number of volumes. The collection of Philip Chapman, on the other hand, was in such a torn and dilapidated state that it was declared to be in part mere "pieces of books"; in addition, however, he owned eleven works in a very fair condition.[1] Among other owners of collections living previous to 1650 were Martin Rennett and William Berryman. Henry Pedinton, whose estate was appraised about 1647, was in possession of a large number of religious books. The collection of Mrs. Jane Lemman did not exceed twenty titles; and George Clarke's, twenty-six. Both of these persons died about the same time as Pedinton.[2] The collection belonging to William Penley included a *History of Turkey*, Stowe's *History or Chronicle*, and the *King's Meditation*.[3] One of the apartments in Peter Wilkins's residence was designated as the "Study," and here his books, consisting chiefly of works on Divinity and History, were carefully arranged on shelves.[4]

Owing to the presence on the Eastern Shore of numerous citizens born in Holland, it is no cause for surprise to find that, among the works forming the libraries in that part of the Colony, there were very many written in the Dutch language. Lawrence Jacobson, who died in 1666, owned about thirteen books of different sizes, bearing on different subjects, printed in this

[1] Northampton County Records, Orders, January 7, March 1, 1644–45.

[2] *Ibid.*, Pedinton, Orders April 5, 1647; Lemman, Orders March, 1649; Clarke, Orders April 16, 1650; Rennett, Orders May 12, 1648; Berryman, Orders June 28, 1648.

[3] Northampton County Records, 1651–54, p. 9.

[4] *Ibid.*, vol. 1654–55 p. 110.

tongue.[1]   The collection of Dr. George Nicholas Hack, a leading physician of Accomac county, but a native of Cologne, consisted for the most part of works written in either the low or high German dialect.   Eight of these were printed in folio, two in quarto, and twelve in octavo.   At least fifty-four of the books belonging to this library were written in the Latin tongue.   Seventeen of these volumes were printed in quarto and large octavo, whilst the remainder were printed in smaller sizes.   A considerable proportion of the collection was written in English.[2]   Among the books making up Colonel Southey Littleton's collection were Æsop's *Fables*, two works in the Latin language, Dr. Sanderson's *Sermons*, *Ye Difference of Sacraments*, *Body of the Common Law*, *Laws of Virginia*, *History of the New England War*, *Doctrine of Triangles*, and the *London Dispensary*.[3]

The collection of Charles Parkes, a resident of the same county, contained a large number of volumes: it included, among other works, fifteen relating to Theology alone, the majority of which were printed in octavo; and there were besides, eleven titles confined to historical subjects.   The number of volumes bearing upon different phases of the two great topics, Divinity and History, probably came to as many as fifty, or even more.   Two of the most interesting works

---

[1] Northampton County Records, vol. 1664–74, folio p. 34.

[2] *Ibid.*, Orders April 17, 1665; Accomac County Records, vol. 1664–71, p. 29.   Deposition of John Nelson: "I being in his ye sd Capt. George Nicholas Hack's house in a room where there was a bedstead and a table in the sd room, there was two or three London Gazettes lay on the sd table, and this deponent took one of them into his hand"; see Accomac County Records, vol. 1682–97, p. 172.

[3] Accomac County Records, vol. 1676–90, p. 295.

belonging to this collection were Speed's *Chronicle*, and the *Travels of Sir Francis Drake*. Parkes followed the gunsmith's calling, but must have been a man with a strong taste for literature.[1] Among the personal property of Edward Bibbe, also of Northampton county, appraised after his death, was a collection of sixteen books; and of Captain William Kendall, thirty-one, besides a volume relating to Law. The collection of George Dewey was entered in his inventory simply as a "parcell of books," which gives no distinct indication as to the number of volumes.[2]

The county of York, as one of the wealthiest in the Colony, included among its inhabitants numerous owners of books. As early as 1645, Richard Watson, a citizen of this county, was in the possession of a collection amounting to thirty titles in folio, and fifty in quarto, with perhaps copies of other works published in smaller sizes. This library probably contained as many as two hundred volumes.[3] Among the contemporaries of Watson owning collections were Richard Winne, Geo. Hopkins, William Kellaway, and Thomas Deacon.[4] John Eaton, who died about 1646, leaving a personal estate valued at twenty-seven hundred and two pounds of tobacco, transmitted to his heir "a Bible and other books."[5] The collection of Giles Mode, whose personal property was appraised about ten years later, was entirely composed of works

[1] Northampton County Records, vol. 1692–1707, p. 131.

[2] *Ibid.*, Inventories for 1696, 1697; see also vol. 1689–98, p. 499.

[3] *William and Mary College Quart.*, vol. iii., p. 181.

[4] York County Records, vol. 1638–48, p. 276, Va. St. Libr.; see also Records for the years 1645 and 1648.

[5] York County Records, vol. 1638–48, p. 137, Va. St. Libr.

written in the Dutch language.[1]   One of the entries
in the inventory of Hugh Stanford, whose death
occurred about the same time, was an item of "twelve
or thirteen small books."[2]   John Brodnax's collection
contained about the same number; and this was also
true of the collection of Charles Kiggin.[3]   Among
other owners of books residing in York county about
1658, were John Gosling, Roger Lewis, Stephen Page,
Philip Stevens, and John Heyward.[4]   That such owners
were often generous in lending to their neighbors
volumes of unusual interest was shown by an order of
court of this date requiring the guardians of Edward
Johnson to return to Mr. Thomas Loving the copy of
St. Augustine's works which Johnson's father had
borrowed.[5]   The collection of Thomas Ludlow, who
died about 1660, was, in the inventory of his estate,
appraised at two hundred and fifty pounds of tobacco.[6]
A somewhat higher valuation was placed on Robert
Clarke's, as it contained, among other volumes, two
copies of works published in a very large shape.[7]
Among the principal owners of books residing in the
county between 1665 and 1667, were Jeremiah Fisher,
John Thomas, George Morris, Thomas Whitehead,
and William Hughes.   One of the titles belonging to
Hughes's collection was *Dr. Tailor's Book*, which was
probably the sermons of the famous clergyman of that
name.[8]

[1] York County Records, vol. 1657–62, p. 60, Va. St. Libr.

[2] *Ibid.*, p. 61, Va. St. Libr.

[3] *Ibid.*, p. 80, Va. St. Libr.

[4] *Ibid.*, pp. 60, 94, 116, 247, 348, Va. St. Libr.

[5] *Ibid.*, p. 90, Va. St. Libr.

[6] *Ibid.*, p. 275, Va. St. Libr.   [7] *Ibid.*, p. 153, Va. St. Libr.

[8] York County Records, vol. 1664–72, pp. 24, 77; Records, vol. 1671–94, p. 25; vol. 1657–62, pp. 212, 398, Va. St. Libr.

One of the largest collections of books in York county during the latter half of the Seventeenth century was owned by Matthew Hubbard, whose personal estate was appraised at his death in 1667; it contained numerous works relating to various departments of thought—among them, for instance, in Belles-Lettres, Ben Jonson's *Remains* in folio, *Astrea, a French Romance*, Donne's *Poems* and Æsop's *Fables;* in Travels, the works of Captain John Smith and Purchas's *Pilgrimage* in folio; in Religion and Morals, a Latin Bible in quarto, Prynne's *Against the Prelacy*, *Exposition of the Commandments*, Young's *Antidote against Grief*, *Divine Fancies*, *Advice to a Sonne*, *God a Good Master*, *Practice of Piety*, *Boanerges and Barnabas*, *Christ Set Forth*, *Latin Common Prayer*, and *Miscellany of Prayers;* in Medicine, Riverius's *Book of Physic*, *Physician's Library* in folio, Culpeper's *Dispensatory* and *Anatomy* in folio, and the *Institution of Physick*. Among the works relating to subjects of a more general character were Reder's *Dictionary*, *French Accidence*, *Swedish Intelligencer*, and *Tutor to Astronomy*.[1]

Although this collection, according to the inventory, contained "thirty-one titles with other old books," probably as many as seventy or a hundred volumes in all, a large proportion of which, as will be seen by the enumeration, were works of literary value, nevertheless the whole was appraised at a figure so low as two pounds and ten shillings, a proof of the correctness of our previous statement that a valuation of this kind was based wholly on the books' physical condition, and was, therefore, in itself no real indication either of their number or their literary importance. The inference is irresistible that where a collection's valuation only is

[1] York County Records, vol. 1664–72, p. 464, Va. St. Libr.

recorded, the collection itself was generally much larger and more choice intrinsically than the appraisement would lead one to suppose.

Among the owners of books residing in York about 1670 were William Grimes, Adam Miles, Joseph Croshaw, Nicholas Bond, and James Moore.[1] The collection of Paul Johnson numbered seventeen titles. John Baskerville possessed works in English valued at three pounds sterling, and in Latin at one pound; this would represent an appraisement of one hundred dollars in modern figures, which would indicate a collection of some importance.[2] In the collection of Richard Stock, who died about 1671, there were two volumes relating to the life of Cleopatra.[3] Among the items appearing in the inventory of Jonathan Newell's personal estate were "sixty-three books of several sorts," which would point to a library of about one hundred and twenty volumes.[4] The collection owned by Captain Francis Matthews, who died in 1674, amounted to thirty-two titles, or probably to sixty volumes in all.[5] Richard Croshaw, whose death occurred a few years later, possessed a collection of fifteen titles in a well preserved condition, whilst the remainder, valued at two pounds sterling, were described in his estate's appraisement as being merely a "parcell of old books." If we follow the analogy of the Hubbard collection, the number of titles belonging to Mr. Croshaw fell little short

[1] York County Records, vol. 1664–72, p. 277; vol. 1662–74, pp. 290, 401, 445, 448, 543, Va. St. Libr.

[2] *William and Mary College Quart.*, vol. iii., p. 181.

[3] York County Records, vol. 1664–72, p. 532 Va. St. Libr.

[4] *Ibid.*, vol. 1675–84, orig. p. 140. Newell also left at his death a "parcel of pictures of several sorts and sizes and six oyle pictures."

[5] York County Records for 1674, see vol. 1671–94, p. 186, Va. St. Libr.

of fifty-five, an indication that his library amounted
to about one hundred volumes.[1] Dr. Francis Haddon,
Croshaw's contemporary, left at his death two "parcells
of books," one of which was cómposed of works printed
in English, and one of works printed in Latin.[2]   Other
owners of books residing in the county at this time were
Nicholas Toop, Elizabeth Bushrod, and William Allen.[3]
The collection belonging to James Vaulx, who died in
1678, was valued at one pound and ten shillings, whilst
that of Robert Spring, who died five years later, was
valued at one pound and twelve shillings.   Each of
these collections was in a torn and decayed state;
both probably contained one half as many volumes
as the Hubbard library, if an inference can be drawn
from the total amount of their respective appraise-
ments.   This would represent about twenty-five titles,
or fifty volumes.[4]

The number of books forming a part of the personal
estate of Capt. John Underhill, a prominent citizen
of York county, was appraised, in 1682, at fifteen
pounds sterling; which represented a collection at
least seven times more valuable than the Hubbard;
and, following the analogy of the latter, amounted to
about two hundred, or even to two hundred and fifty,
titles, making up a library that fell little short of four
hundred volumes.   In purchasing value, fifteen pounds
sterling was the equivalent of at least three hundred
dollars; a library containing a large proportion of old
and hand-worn books must have been of an unusual
size to have been set down at so high a figure.[5]   **The**

[1] York County Records, Inventories for 1677.

[2] *Ibid.*, vol. 1671–94, p. 99, Va. St. Libr.

[3] *Ibid.*, Inventories for 1678, 1679, 1681.

[4] *Ibid.*, Inventories for 1678, 1683.

[5] *Ibid.*, Inventories for 1682.

collection of James Goodwyn, who died in 1678, was valued at one pound, five shillings; Mrs. Elizabeth Digges's, independently of her great Bible, at four pounds sterling; Henry Power's at five pounds; and James Whaley's at three pounds and seven shillings. These four persons were in possession of books appraised as a whole at fifteen pounds sterling, a sum which would seem to indicate that their joint collections contained at least two hundred titles or four hundred volumes.[1] The library belonging to Robert Booth was appraised at nearly the same figure.[2]

How many books were contained in a collection entered in an inventory as worth fourteen pounds is shown by the number belonging to Henry Sandford, which were appraised at only five pounds and eleven shillings; according to the description of his personal estate, there were "in one trunk, twenty-five English books valued at one pound and fifteen shillings; twenty-three Latin and Greek books, and a parcel of unbound books, valued at one pound and ten shillings; a Greek New Testament and five Hebrew books, valued at one pound and four shillings." Here were fifty-four titles, representing probably a hundred volumes, and many of them, no doubt, the works of the great Latin and Greek authors, which, owing to the books' physical condition, were appraised at only four pounds and nine shillings, a sum not exceeding one hundred dollars in purchasing power. In addition, there was a "parcell of old books" appraised at twelve shillings, and also a volume printed in quarto. A volume bearing the name: *An Essay towards the Amendment of ye last English Translation*

[1] *William and Mary College Quart.*, vol. iii., p. 246.
[2] York County Records, vol. 1687–91, p. 380, Va. St. Libr.

of Ye Bible, completed the number.[1] Following the analogy of this collection, Robert Booth's library, valued at fourteen pounds sterling, contained not less than three hundred volumes. Among his contemporaries residing in York who were in possession of numerous books were John Keene, Capt. Charles Hansford, Nicholas Sebrell, Susannah Perkins, James Archer, Robert Dobbs, John Wooding, and Andrew Geddes.[2]

The surviving records of Elizabeth City county cover only the last few years of the Seventeenth century and yet their entries show the presence, in that century, during this short period, of numerous owners of books. A part of the collection belonging to William Marshall consisted of "ye Map of the World and four lesser Maps," whilst Isaac Malyn's collection included several volumes in the Dutch language.[3] Simon Hollier possessed a set of the Virginia Laws, and also fifteen "printed books." The collection of Edmund Swaney was described simply as a "parcell of books old and new." Other owners of small libraries who resided in this county at this time were John Powers, Thomas Holland, and Thomas Allamby.[4]

Such is a brief account of some of the most important collections of books belonging to citizens of the Colony during the Seventeenth century. The list is far from being a complete one even for those counties the records of which were not destroyed during the storms of War and Revolution that have so often swept over Virginia.

[1] *William and Mary College Quart.*, vol. iv., p. 15.

[2] York County Records, vol. 1690–94, pp. 359, 407, 409, Va. St. Libr.   See also Inventories for 1697 and 1698.

[3] Elizabeth City County Records, vol. 1684–99, pp. 299, 317, Va. St. Libr.

[4] *Ibid.*, pp. 302, 310, 314, Va. St. Libr.

Only about one hundred and thirty volumes of these records remain intact where originally there were probably not less than five hundred or even one thousand volumes. With the exception of Henrico and Elizabeth City (and possibly also of Warwick and Charles City), whose records have been only partially preserved, not a single county contiguous to the east bank of James River below Richmond, the first division to be seated, can show a page of legal papers belonging to this century.[1] All the colonial records of Nansemond, New Kent, and Gloucester counties have perished; and so with those of a wide area of country along the upper tributaries of the York River which played a great part in the early history of the Colony. Therefore, even if a full list of all the owners of books in Virginia during that period, whose names and the size of whose collections could be obtained from the surviving records of the century, were given, it would not represent perhaps one fifth of the persons then in possession of such collections. I have gleaned from the records which have come down to the present times sufficient evidence at least to show that there were many owners of books in each county; and that the whole number of books to be found in the Colony amounted to many thousand volumes. It would, I think, be strictly within the bounds of accuracy to say, as a reasonable inference from facts already brought forward, that the number of collections, large or small, existing in the last quarter of the century fell little short of a thousand; and estimating such collections at

---

[1] If any records of the century survive in Warwick or Charles City County, they are contained in a single stray volume, which perhaps has been returned after having been carried off to the North in the great War of 1861–65.

an average of twenty volumes, a figure too low rather than too high, it would probably be no exaggeration to assert that the number of volumes composing these collections, as a whole, exceeded twenty thousand. It should, however, be borne in mind that copies of certain popular books appeared in every collection of importance, which would serve to diminish the number of separate titles.

CHAPTER XVII

General Culture

THERE are several unmistakable indications that a high degree of culture prevailed among the members of at least a section of the upper planting class.[1] As we have seen, a very considerable proportion of the books composing the libraries of the Seventeenth century were written in the Latin and Greek languages, and were copies of the most celebrated of the ancient classics. There is no reason to think that these works were preserved simply for ornament or ostentation; rather every probability points to the fact that they were read and studied. It should be remembered that a very large number of the citizens

[1] Writing of England in the Seventeenth century, Macaulay states that "few knights of the shire had libraries so good as may now be perpetually found in a servants' hall or in the back parlour of a shop-keeper. An Esquire passed among his neighbours for a great scholar if Hudibras or Baker's Chronicle, Tarlton's Jests and the Seven Champions of Christendom lay in his hall window among the fishing rods and fowling pieces"; *History*, Chapt. iii. Again he writes: "Many Lords of Manors had received an education differing little from that of their manual servants. The heir of an estate often passed his boyhood and youth at the seat of his family with no other tutors than grooms and gamekeepers and scarce afterward learning enough to sign a mittimus. If he went to school or college, he generally returned before he was twenty to the seclusion of the old Hall, and there, unless his mind was very happily constituted by nature, soon forgot his academical pursuits in rural business and pleasures." See *History*, Chapt. iii.

of Virginia during this century were men like Richard
Lee, the elder Nathaniel Bacon, John Page, William
Randolph, the elder Robert Beverley, William Fitzhugh, and hundreds of others of almost equal prominence, who not only had been born in England, but had
acquired in the institutions there the learning that
would enable them to read the works of the great Latin
and Greek authors with facility. These authors were
perhaps more familiar to the Virginians of these early
times than they are to the Virginians of the present
day, in spite of the wider range of modern culture.
At that period, when the collections of books were
comparatively small, each volume was perused with
more frequency, and its contents were more thoroughly
mastered; it is this fact which largely accounts for the
dilapidated condition distinguishing so many of these
collections at the time of their appraisement. Read
and reread, the classical works of Greece and Rome
became a part of the daily lives of those whose learning
enabled them to enjoy the unequaled beauties of these
ancient writers. Nor did the character of the collections of books in this century, when regarded from
other points of view, show any inferiority of literary
taste; not only were the volumes relating to History
and Biography, and Belles-lettres proper, very numerous in every important library, but there was also an
extraordinary number of volumes bearing upon moral
subjects in general, one of the very highest departments of thought which can engage the attention of
the human mind.

Apart from the presence of so many well chosen books,
the surviving letters of the foremost Virginians of the
Seventeenth century prove that they possessed no
small degree of culture. The letter books of two alone,

William Fitzhugh and the elder William Byrd, have come down to us in their original shape. Although they are but copies, and were thrown off hurriedly, or at least without any view to their permanent preservation as casting a vivid light on that remote past, nevertheless, they form admirable examples of the kind of correspondence,—the purely business,—to which they belong. There are found scattered through the county records a number of casual letters written by citizens of the Colony, showing their authors to have been men who had enjoyed the fairest opportunities for education which that age afforded. There is, for instance, entered in the records of Accomac, for the year 1636, a letter from Samuel Mathews's pen which is vigorous and direct in thought and clear and strong in style.[1] A letter from Susan Moseley to Capt. Francis Yeardley, now preserved among the records of Lower Norfolk, is admirably expressed for the time[2]; and so are all the letters addressed to his relatives in England by Hugh Yeo, who resided on the Eastern Shore.[3]

Among the records preserved in the British Public Record Office in London, there are numerous communications (some of which are in the form of ordinary letters) written by Virginians of the Seventeenth century. Two of these may be specially mentioned as fair examples of the others. One, a letter from Charles Scarborough dated June 16, 1682, and penned in Accomac, is not only correctly spelt, so far as any fixed standard existed at that time, but also clearly and even

[1] Accomac County Records, vol. 1632–40, p. 50, Va. St. Libr.

[2] Lower Norfolk County Records, Orders Nov. 10, 1652; Lower Norfolk Antiquary, vol. ii., p. 122.

[3] Accomac County Records, vol. 1678–82 p. 124 et seq.

gracefully expressed.[1] Far more remarkable, however, was the letter which Benjamin Harrison wrote, in 1698, to the English authorities touching the supposed inefficiency and fraudulency of the collectors of customs in performing the duties of their office. Harrison himself had been accused by Col. Daniel Parke of conveying a cargo of tobacco to Scotland without first securing the necessary clearance papers. Smarting under this charge, he expressed himself, in his recrimination, with a clearness, directness, and trenchancy, not equalled in many documents of the same kind belonging to that age. The significance of this letter seems the more striking from a purely literary point of view when it is recalled that Harrison was a native of Virginia, and that he had received his entire education in the schools of the Colony. The choiceness and copiousness of his language, the artfulness he showed in arranging his matter, and the strength and eloquence he imparted to his denunciations,—all bear the most impressive testimony to the superior literary training which he had obtained without finding it necessary to seek an education in the institutions of the Old World.[2]

The second Robert Beverley was also a native of Virginia, and so far as the records show, received his early education in its schools. His *History* is one of the most admirable specimens of historical writing produced in any of the English Colonies, whether we consider it from the point of view of its literary expression, arrangement, or power of thought. Its atmosphere is pervaded by the freshness to be expected of an author describing a community still close to all

[1] British Colonial Papers, vol. xlviii., No. 106.
[2] B. T. Va. 1698, vol. vi., p. 303.

the primeval forms of Nature; and the book also breathes a spirit of quiet and lurking humor that gives a glow to its driest statement of facts.[1]   William Fitzhugh, who was fully competent to carry out such a purpose, designed at one time to write an account of Virginia,—its people, climate, soil, history, and the like, but his intention, probably owing to the interference of his numerous interests, remained unrealized.[2]   If a similar ambition ever arose in the breasts of other Virginians, it passed with the same lack of practical results.

There is no evidence that any work of imagination was produced in the Colony during the Seventeenth century; the nearest approach to such a work were the felicitous translations of Ovid's *Metamorphoses*, and the First Book of the *Æneid*, made by George Sandys on the banks of the James about the time the frightful massacre of 1622 occurred.   There is a touch of pathos in the fact that the accomplished Treasurer found consolation for all the horrors of that event, and some relief perhaps for his longing as a scholar, in turning these great Latin writers into verse in the shade of the primeval oaks and within the sound of the whispering waters of that beautiful wilderness.   As he dropped for a moment his poetical task, his mind may well have speculated as to the fountains from which the great stream flowing at his feet had sprung, and the mysterious forests, haunted by red men, wild beasts, and birds alone, through which it had glided down for immemorial ages.   The world of Ovid and Virgil was another world, not simply in time but in place.

[1] Beverley is not known to have been the author of any other work.

[2] Letters of William Fitzhugh, May 13, 1687.

The situation and the surroundings of their translator, they, with all their power of divination, could not have conceived of; and it was well that, with the savage's cry still echoing in his ear, he had so noble a work to absorb his energies and divert his thoughts.

The public Declarations of Parliament in the most stirring years of the Seventeenth century were not finer, either in spirit or expression, than some of the Declarations issued by the Virginian House of Burgesses during the course of the same period. For elevation, eloquence, and keen argumentative force, few public papers of that period equal or surpass the Declaration of 1651, in which the General Assembly protested against the Act of Parliament prohibiting all commercial intercourse between the Colony and other countries. Many of the reports made by the Governors and Councils in the form of letters to the English authorities are among the most admirable public documents of that time; nor was such excellence confined to those emanating from the Colony's highest officials; in the long series of grievances presented, at the request of the English Commissioners, after the suppression of the rebellion of 1676, by the greater number of the counties, we have a collection of public papers penned by local committees, which in force and clearness of expression, in weightiness and propriety of statement, and dignity and earnestness of spirit, bear witness in the most unmistakable manner to the character, ability, and acquirements of the writers, who were drawn apparently indiscriminately from the great body of the population.

There is practically no evidence whatever of illiteracy among the men who, from decade to decade, during the Seventeenth century, directed the political affairs of

Virginia. A careful personal examination of the hundreds,—it might be even said,—the thousands of original communications to the English Government from the authorities of the Colony, now preserved in the British Public Record Office in London, has failed to disclose to me a single case of an official, who, being unable to attach his name in full, was compelled to make his mark; and this is as true of the communications signed by the House of Burgesses as of those signed by the Governor and Council. A remarkable corroboration of this statement will be found in letters to the English authorities resembling the one despatched in 1624; thirty-one signatures, including that of every member of the General Assembly, were appended to this document; each name was not only signed in full, but also written down in an easily legible hand.[1]

Among the great number of justices occupying seats on the county court bench, I have noted in the surviving records of these courts only four who were in the habit of signing legal papers by making their marks. These men were Thomas Curtis, of Gloucester county, Thomas Batte of Henrico, Arthur Allan, of Surry, and a member of the Keeling family of Lower Norfolk.[2] It is not certain, however, that they made their marks merely because they were ignorant of how to write; it is not improbable that they were prevented from signing their names by some physical infirmity rendering their hands useless. Batte was not only a man in possession of a good estate, but also, as the son or grandson of a graduate of Oxford University, had,

[1] British Colonial Papers, vol. iii., 1624–25, No. 4.

[2] Curtis, *William and Mary College Quart.*, vol. ii., p. 163; Batte, Henrico County Records, vol. 1677–79, orig. p. 275; Allan, Surry County Records, vol. 1645–72, p. 207, Va. St. Libr.

from his youth, been accustomed to hold education in high esteem. This was shown by the fact that his own son was able to write, as we learn from the county records. Allan was, for many years, the most prominent citizen of Surry county, and among the wealthiest planters residing there. He, like Batte, belonged to a family that had enjoyed every social and intellectual advantage. Justice Keeling was not the first or last of his family to play a leading part in the public service of Lower Norfolk; and if he had been permitted to grow up without acquiring the art of writing, it was due to no lack of wealth, or fine social and intellectual traditions in the circle of his home. If these men of gentle descent, in the enjoyment of large estates, and occupying positions of great influence in their counties, were really unable to write, not because of physical infirmity, but from naked ignorance, then they constituted remarkable exceptions to the great body of persons performing the same judicial functions.

CHAPTER XVIII

Degree of Illiteracy

I T is no fair test of the degree of illiteracy prevailing in the Colony to compare the number of wills signed with the full name with the number signed with a mark alone. An examination of the county records will show that an extraordinary proportion of the wills were entered in the books very soon after they were drawn. The shortness of this interval in so many cases is an indication that the testators were, as a rule, in such an advanced state of illness at the time the documents were written that their deaths followed very quickly; mere physical weakness must, therefore, in the course of a century have prevented many hundreds from doing more than attaching their marks to their last testaments; and they were perhaps only capable of performing even this simple act with the assistance of those standing by their bedsides. In the light of these probabilities, I have not considered it safe to base an extended estimate of the literacy and illiteracy of the Virginian people, during the Seventeenth century, on the number of wills found in the county records signed with the full name as compared with the number signed with a simple mark only. I have confined my calculations to the relative number of signatures and marks attached to deeds of conveyance, depositions, and jury inquests alone. The information obtained by means of the inquests and depositions is perhaps more valuable even than that obtained from the conveyances. The conveyances indicate the degree of literacy or illiteracy prevailing in the circle of property owners only, among whom, owing to their possession of means to meet the cost of an education, the degree of illiteracy is apt to have been smaller than among any other section of the community. The landholders were the class most favored by fortune; and their condition, in any one respect, could not be taken as shared by persons less happily situated in the matter of estate. On the other hand, the witnesses in courts whose depositions are recorded, were drawn from every class, except the slaves, forming the social and political body of the Colony. The foremost men in the community as well as the humblest and most obscure, the richest and poorest alike, appeared in this character in court; and an estimate of the number of such signing the depositions in full, or with a mark, would reflect very fairly the degree of literacy and illiteracy prevailing among the people at large, irrespective of their possessions. This is also true of an estimate based on the signatures in full and marks attached to the jury inquests; except that here we would have to exclude from the calculation the agricultural servants as well as the slaves. Every grade of freemen, however, were represented on these juries. The juries whose verdicts (with the signatures in full or marks of the jurymen appended) were most frequently placed on record, were those which had decided some dispute respecting title to land, or had met at the coroner's call to inquire into the particular circumstances attending a murder, suicide, or a death by accident. The members were always described as "men of the neighborhood," and, from every point of view, were a popular body.

The four tables I am about to present in order to show the degree of illiteracy prevailing among the men and women considered separately, or among the whole population irrespective of sex, are the results of a comparison of nearly eighteen thousand names which I was at pains to copy *literatim* from the county records. The names thus copied were those attached to deeds of conveyance, depositions, and inquests of juries alone; and they constitute practically the whole number of those to be found in the records so attached. The name of a large property holder or prominent citizen, appeared many times appended to such legal documents, but, as far as possible, no single name, however often it might occur in the records, was counted by me more than once. The conclusions reached will be found to be substantially, if not precisely, correct.

TABLE I. EXTENT OF THE ILLITERACY PREVAILING AMONG THE MEN AS SHOWN BY JURY ENTRIES.

	Number of Juries.	Number of Persons Signing Their Names.	Number Making Their Marks.
Westmoreland County......	4	28	20
Accomac County..........	13	92	64
Northampton County.......	14	89	79
York County..............	21	137	115
Essex County.............	8	50	46
Isle of Wight County.......	8	43	53
Rappahannock County......	4	37	11
Henrico County............	33	239	157
Surry County..............	75	451	449
Total.................	180	1166	994

The preceding table contains the summary of one hundred and eighty juries impanneled in nine counties in the course, for the most part, of the last half of the Seventeenth century. An examination of the figures will show that, in a total number of twenty-one hundred and sixty persons serving on these juries, eleven hundred and sixty-six were able to sign their names in full; in other words, slightly over fifty percent of the male population represented by these persons had been educated sufficiently to acquire the art of writing, and its corollary, the art of reading also. Let us now inquire as to the relative proportion among the men,—on the one hand, of the persons able to write their names; and, on the other, of the persons compelled by ignorance to make their marks in signing the conveyances and depositions appearing in the county records.

TABLE II. EXTENT OF THE ILLITERACY PREVAILING AMONG THE MEN AS SHOWN BY DEEDS AND DEPOSITIONS.

	Period.	Number Signing in Full.	Number Making Their Marks.
Lower Norfolk County......	1646–98	1156	783
Isle of Wight County.......	1643–1700	359	260
Surry County..............	1652–84	519	381
Henrico County............	1677–97	307	337
Elizabeth City County......	1693–99	142	48
York County...............	1657–1700	967	662
Middlesex County..........	1673–1700	143	55
Essex County..............	1692–99	192	126
Lancaster County..........	1652–94	723	260
Rappahannock County......	1654–99	943	584
Northumberland County....	1652–77	277	204
Westmoreland County......	1653–77	369	210
Northampton County.......	1647–98	791	522
Accomac County...........	1641–97	551	574
Total.................	1641–1700	7439	5006

In a total number of twelve thousand, four hundred and forty-five names of men attached to depositions and deeds of conveyance, seventy-four hundred and thirty-nine were signed in full, and five thousand and six were signed with a cross mark alone. The explanation of the higher proportion of the male literates as shown by Table II as compared with Table I, lies in the fact that the signatures to the deeds of conveyance embraced those of all the landowners residing in the counties named, during the periods represented, and it was among the members of this section of the community, owing to their possession of property, that education had been carried the furthest.

There are numerous evidences that illiteracy prevailed to a greater extent among the women than among persons of the opposite sex. The same condition was observed in England during the whole of this century. The proportion of literates among the female emigrants to Virginia was, in consequence of this fact, much smaller than among the male; and the disproportion in the Colony itself was not lessened by any superior advantages which women possessed there for acquiring an education. The Old Field Schools, where the majority of the children received instruction, were, no doubt, attended by a larger number of boys than of girls owing to the former's greater ability to overcome daily the distance intervening between their homes and the school houses. It is, however, a cause for surprise to find so frequently in Virginia at this time women belonging to families of great prominence among the landowners who, by their ignorance of the art of writing, were compelled to make their marks. Nor were these women restricted to the natives of the Colony: Mary, the wife of John

Utie, one of the wealthiest and most conspicuous
citizens of Virginia about 1639, was unable to sign
her name in full[1]; and this was also true of Elizabeth, the wife of Stephen Charlton, of Accomac,[2]
a citizen equally wealthy and prominent, who was,
however, careful to obtain for his daughter the
best facilities for education the country afforded.
It was also true of the wife of Col. John Upton,
of Isle of Wight County; of Mary, the wife of Col.
George Mason; of Grace, the wife of Col. John
Ashton; and of Elizabeth, the wife of Col. Raleigh
Travers.[3] The wives of William Farrar and John
Cocke, of Henrico, were unable to write; so also
were Mary, the wife of John Washington, of Westmoreland; Sarah, the wife of John Thoroughgood, of
Lower Norfolk; and also Sarah, the wife of Argall
Yeardley of the same county.[4] These were among
the wealthiest and most distinguished citizens of
the Colony.

In 1667, Eleanor, Barbara, and Anne Calthorpe, of
York, the three daughters of the head one of the most
conspicuous families residing in that part of the Colony,
petitioned the local court to make a division of their
inherited estate; neither of the three apparently was
able to write, although two of the sisters were nearly

[1] York County Records, vol. 1633–94, p. 17, Va. St. Libr.

[2] Accomac County Records, vol. 1640–45, p. 221, Va. St.
Libr.

[3] Isle of Wight County Deeds and Wills for 1651; Westmoreland
County Records for 1655; Lancaster County Records, fol. 1666–82,
p. 91; Rappahannock County Records, vol. 1656–64, p. 202, Va. St.
Libr.

[4] Henrico County Records, vol. 1677–92, orig. pp. 233, 390;
see also Lower Norfolk County Records; for Mrs. Washington, see
York County Records, vol. 1633–94, p. 254, Va. St. Libr.

twenty years of age, and one, sixteen.[1] A case of this kind seems the more remarkable when it is recalled that at least one of the parents, the father, if not both the father and mother, had received an education. The wives of numerous clergymen of distinction were unable to write: such was the case with the wife of Rev. William Thompson, of Surry; of Rev. Thomas Teakle, of Accomac; and of Rev. Samuel Eborne, of Bruton parish. It was also the case with the wife of John Fawsett, the King's Attorney on the Eastern Shore.[2]

There are in the surviving county records the names of about three thousand women attached to depositions and deeds of conveyance. An estimate of the degree of illiteracy prevailing among the members of that sex, based on this list, would embrace representatives of every class, from the owner of landed property in her own right, to the wife of the poorest agricultural servant.

[1] York County Records, vol. 1664–72, orig. p. 166.

[2] This was also true of the wife of Rev. Robert Parke of Surry; see Surry County Records, vol. 1671–84, pp. 24, 393, Va. St. Libr.; Northampton County Records for 1674; York County Records, vol. 1691–1701, orig. pp. 53, 116; Accomac County Records, vol. 1673–76, p. 182. Writing of the literacy of the English women of position during the same period, Macaulay states in his *History* (Chapt. iii.) that the library of the Lady of the Manor and her daughters "consisted of a prayer book and a receipt book . . . even in the highest ranks, and in those situations which afforded the greatest facilities for mental improvement, the English women of that generation were decidedly worse educated than they have been at any other time since the revival of learning . . . during the latter part of the Seventeenth Century, the culture of the female mind seems to have been almost entirely neglected . . . ladies highly born, highly bred, and naturally quick-witted were unable to write a line in their mother tongue without solecisms and faults of spelling such as a charity girl would now be ashamed to admit."

TABLE III. EXTENT OF ILLITERACY PREVAILING AMONG THE
WOMEN, AS SHOWN BY DEEDS AND DEPOSITIONS.

	Period.	Number Able to Sign Their Names.	Number Making Their Marks.
Lower Norfolk County......	1646–98	101	414
Isle of Wight County.......	1643–1700	20	169
Surry County..............	1652–84	32	156
Henrico County............	1677–97	25	51
Elizabeth City County......	1693–99	16	29
York County...............	1657–1700	86	260
Middlesex County..........	1673–1700	14	28
Essex County..............	1692–99	10	53
Lancaster County..........	1652–97	107	138
Rappahannock County......	1654–99	132	463
Northumberland County.....	1652–77	15	73
Westmoreland County......	1653–77	34	70
Northampton County.......	1647–98	89	196
Accomac County...........	1641–97	75	210
Total.................	1641–1700	756	2310

The preceding table reveals the fact that, among
the entire female population of the Colony, without embracing the slaves, only one woman of
every three was able to sign her name in full, as
compared with at least three of every five persons of the opposite sex, as shown by our second
table.

Let us now consider the whole body of the male and
female inhabitants independently of the slaves. The
following table, based upon fifteen thousand names
attached to depositions and deeds of conveyance,
shows the degree of illiteracy prevailing among members of both sexes, and of all classes of the white
population.

TABLE IV. EXTENT OF ILLITERACY AMONG THE WHITE
POPULATION AS A WHOLE.

	Period.	Number of persons signing deposi-tions in full.	Number of persons making marks to deposi-tions.	Number of persons signing deeds in full.	Number of persons making marks to deeds.
Lower Norfolk Co....	1646–98	107	115	1150	1082
Isle of Wight "	1643–1700	35	29	344	400
Surry "	1652–84	14	24	537	513
Henrico "	1677–97	66	114	266	274
Elizabeth City "	1693–99	1	2	157	75
York "	1657–1700	67	117	986	805
Middlesex "	1673–1700	...	...	157	83
Essex "	1692–99	6	7	196	172
Lancaster "	1652–94	18	11	812	387
Rappahannock "	1654–99	...	...	1075	1047
Northumberland"	1652–77	59	65	233	212
Westmoreland "	1653–77	30	65	373	215
Northampton "	1647–98	331	378	549	340
Accomac "	1641–97	274	441	352	343
Total..........	1641–1700	1008	1368	7187	5948

As the signatures in full attached to deeds of conveyance represented the property holders, it is no ground for surprise to find that the number of persons of both sexes who, under these circumstances, were able to write their names was very considerably larger than the number unable to write. On the other hand, it was only to be expected that the number of persons who would be able to sign the depositions in full would be smaller than the number unable to sign except with a mark, because the witnesses were drawn as much from the class lacking in the means to obtain an education as from the class possessing the means. We discover from the preceding table that there were eight thousand one hundred and ninety-five persons residing in the Colony, during a certain period, who had acquired the ability to write, as compared with seven thousand three hundred and sixteen who had failed to acquire that ability. <u>In other words, the extent of the general illiteracy was limited to less than one half of the white population.</u>[1]

---

[1] In a petition for pardon made in 1676 by forty followers of Bacon, eighteen, or nearly one half, were able to sign their names in full. These men belonged for the most part to the most obscure section of the class of freemen; see Surry County Records, vol. 1671–84, pp. 226–7, Va. St. Libr. Of the four hundred and thirty-eight persons whose names were attached to the "Grievances" of Isle of Wight, Nansemond, James City, and New Kent Counties, a series of papers presented to the English Commissioners in 1676, one hundred and eighty-five signed their names in full. This lacked about thirty-five of being one half of the whole number; see Winder Papers, Va. St. Libr.

4
45
$8
3 60
45
4.10
8.10
16.00

Essays in
Col. American
Hist Goodman